My name is Amélie!
Today, the lady who cares for me
took me all over for an energetic
walk. Then I bit the dirty old dude
who never leaves the house! Now,
then! Bring me some Kentucky
Fried Chicken! And make haste!!

—*Yūki Tabata('s Dog)*, 2015

YŪKI TABATA
was born in Fukuoka Prefecture
and got his big break in the 2011
Shonen Jump Golden Future Cup
with his winning entry, *Hungry
Joker*. He started the magical fantasy
series *Black Clover* in 2015.

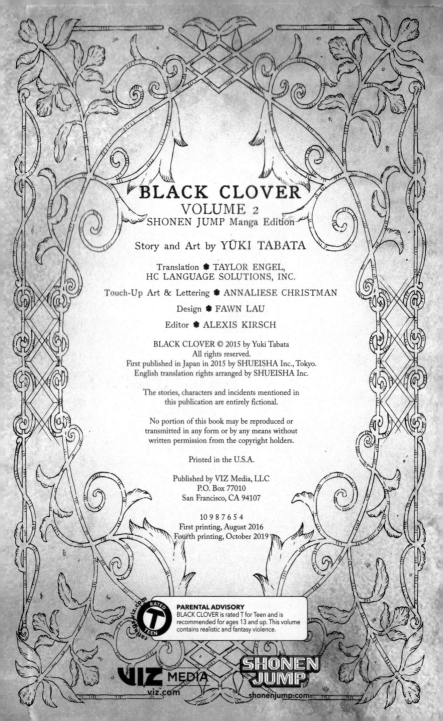

BLACK CLOVER
VOLUME 2
SHONEN JUMP Manga Edition

Story and Art by YŪKI TABATA

Translation ❀ TAYLOR ENGEL,
HC LANGUAGE SOLUTIONS, INC.

Touch-Up Art & Lettering ❀ ANNALIESE CHRISTMAN

Design ❀ FAWN LAU

Editor ❀ ALEXIS KIRSCH

BLACK CLOVER © 2015 by Yuki Tabata
All rights reserved.
First published in Japan in 2015 by SHUEISHA Inc., Tokyo.
English translation rights arranged by SHUEISHA Inc.

The stories, characters and incidents mentioned in
this publication are entirely fictional.

Printed in the U.S.A.

Published by VIZ Media, LLC
P.O. Box 77010
San Francisco, CA 94107

10 9 8 7 6 5 4
First printing, August 2016
Fourth printing, October 2019

VIZ MEDIA
viz.com

SHONEN JUMP
shonenjump.com

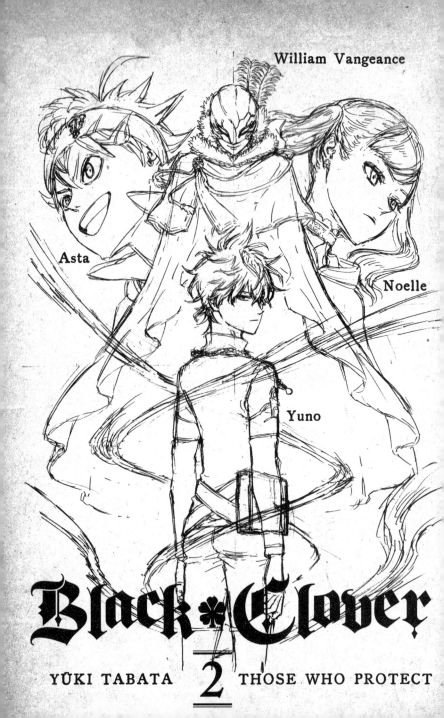

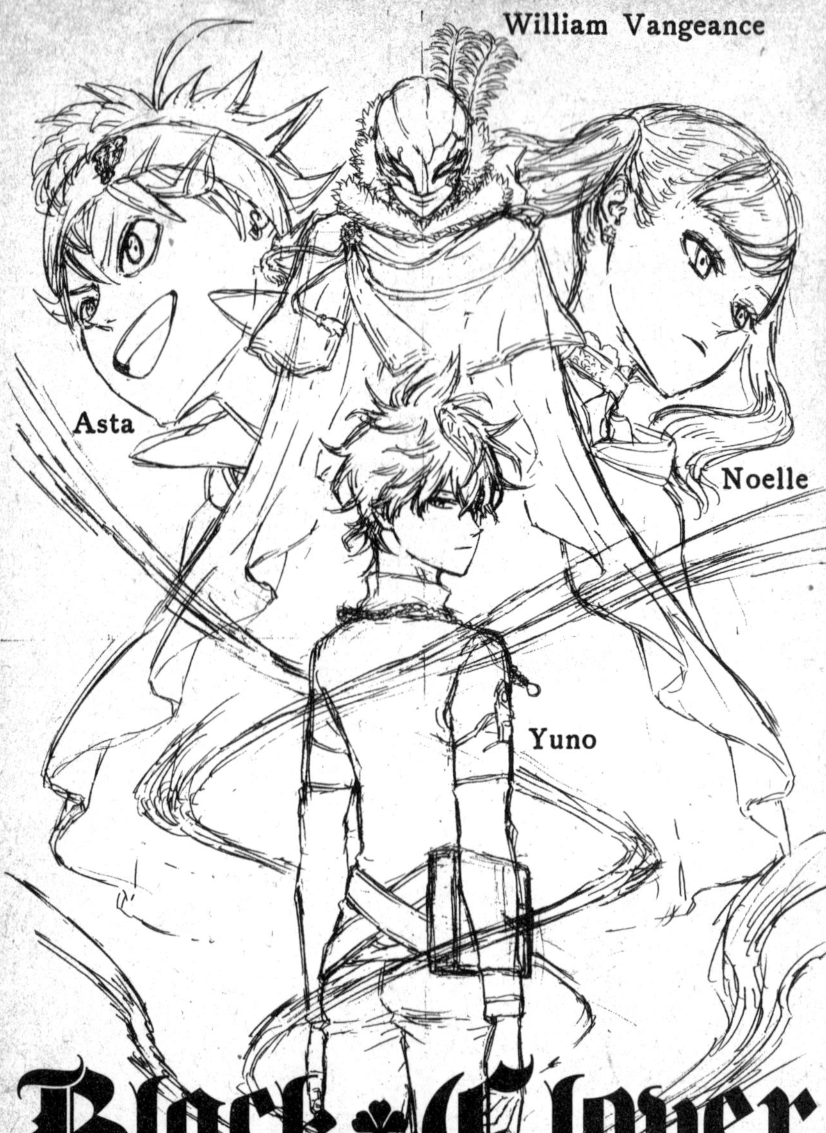
William Vangeance
Asta
Noelle
Yuno

Black Clover

YŪKI TABATA 2 THOSE WHO PROTECT

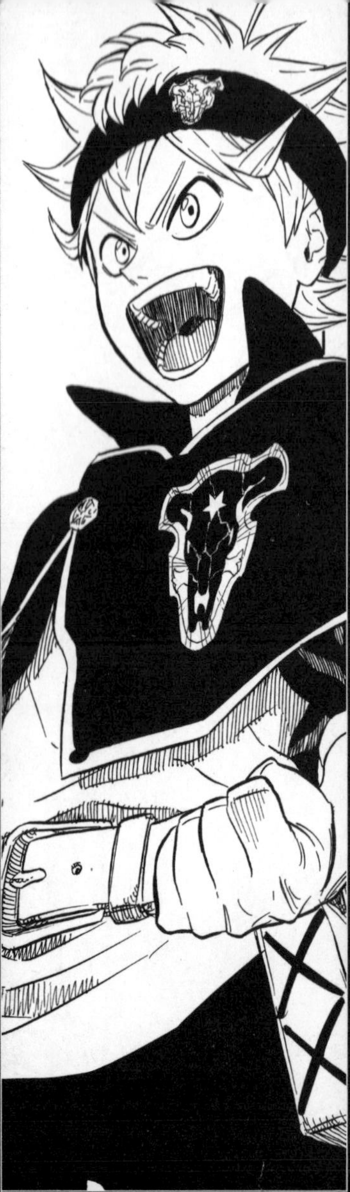

Asta

Member of the Black Bulls. Although he has absolutely no magic, this enthusiastic boy is working to become the Wizard King through sheer guts and a tough, well-trained body. He has an anti-magic grimoire that negates and repels his opponents' magic.

Yuno

Iember of the Golden Dawn. He is Asta's best riend and rival and has been training alongside him ince they were little to become the Wizard King. He s the bearer of the four-leaf clover grimoire, which s said to be granted only to chosen ones. A user of vind magic.

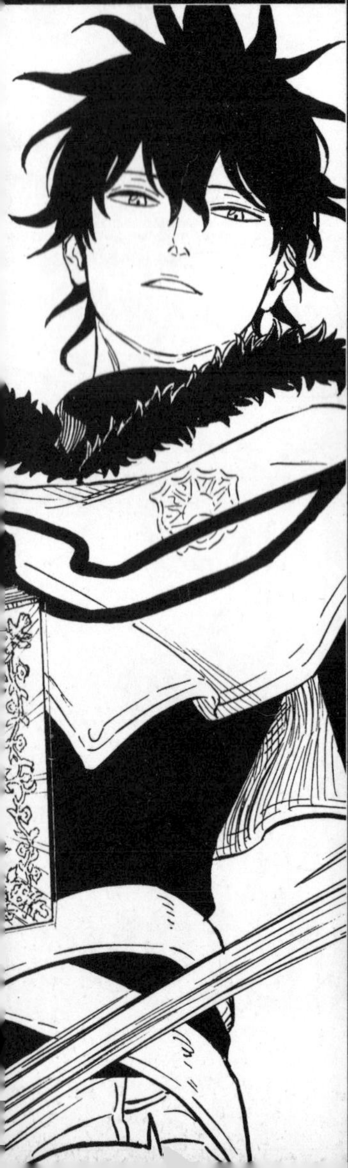

Magna Swing

A member of the Black Bulls. He has a delinquent's temperament, but he can also be gallant. A user of flame magic.

Yami Sukehiro

Captain of the Black Bulls. He looks fierce and has a hot temper, but he's very popular with his group.

Luck Voltia

A member of the Black Bulls. He's a battle maniac who smiles constantly and has a problematic personality.

Noelle Silva

A member of the Black Bulls. She's the daughter of royalty and as impudent as can be. A user of water magic.

Heath Grice

A user of ice magic who attacked the village of Saussy. He appears to be looking for something...

Vanessa Enoteca

A member of the Black Bulls. She's a mage who was exiled from a distinguished family and has an unparalleled love of liquor.

S T O R Y

In a world where magic is everything, Asta and Yuno are both found abandoned on the same day at a church in the remote village of Hage. Both dream of becoming the Wizard King, the highest of all mages, and they spend their days working toward that dream.

The year they turn 15, both receive grimoires, magic books that amplify their bearers' magic. They take the entrance exam for the Magic Knights, nine groups of mages under the direct control of the Wizard King. Yuno, whose magic is strong, joins an elite group known as the Golden Dawn. Asta, however, has no magic at all and thus joins the Black Bulls, a group of misfits. The two have finally taken their first steps toward becoming the Wizard King...

Having become a full-fledged member of the Black Bulls, Asta's first mission is to hunt a boar in the impoverished village of Saussy. However, when he arrives there, he finds the villagers under attack by a mysterious man with powerful magic. In an attempt to save them, Asta launches himself right into a fierce battle...

BLACK ✱ CLOVER

CONTENTS

BLACK ❈ CLOVER

2

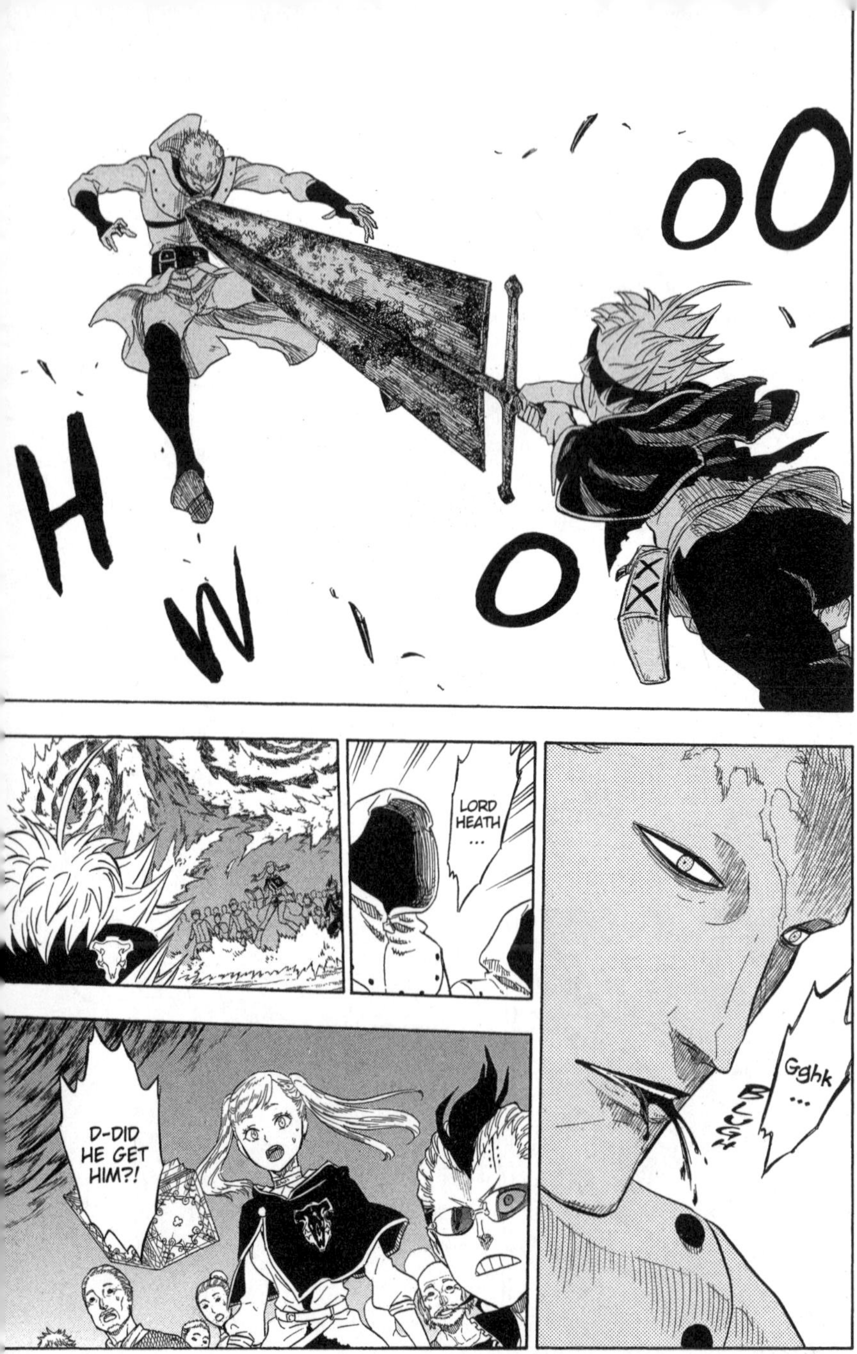
HWOOO
Gghk...
BLUGH
LORD HEATH...
D-DID HE GET HIM?!

Page 8: Those Who Protect

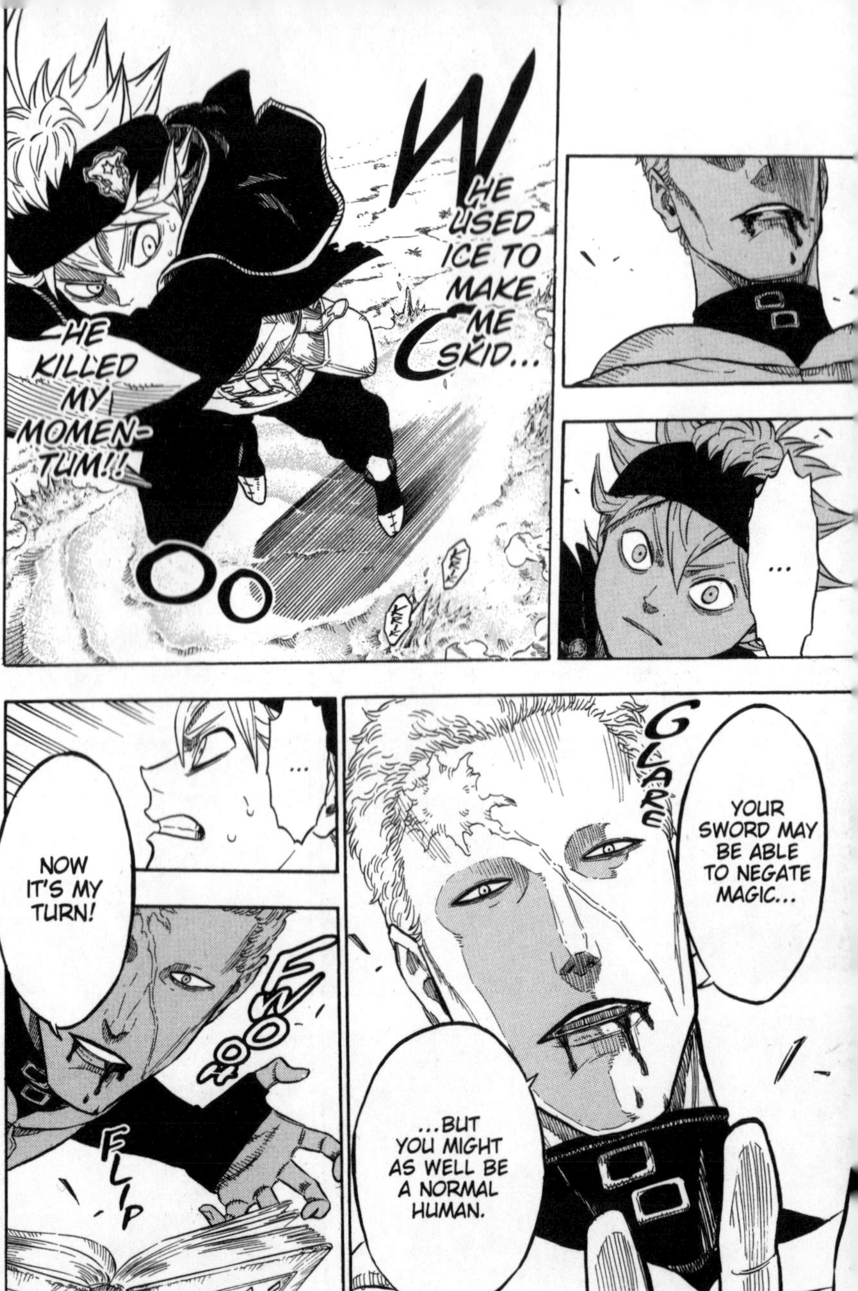
...
HE USED ICE TO MAKE ME SKID...
HE KILLED MY MOMEN-TUM!!
KRIK
KRIK
GLARE
YOUR SWORD MAY BE ABLE TO NEGATE MAGIC...
...BUT YOU MIGHT AS WELL BE A NORMAL HUMAN.
...
NOW IT'S MY TURN!
FWOOSH
FLIP

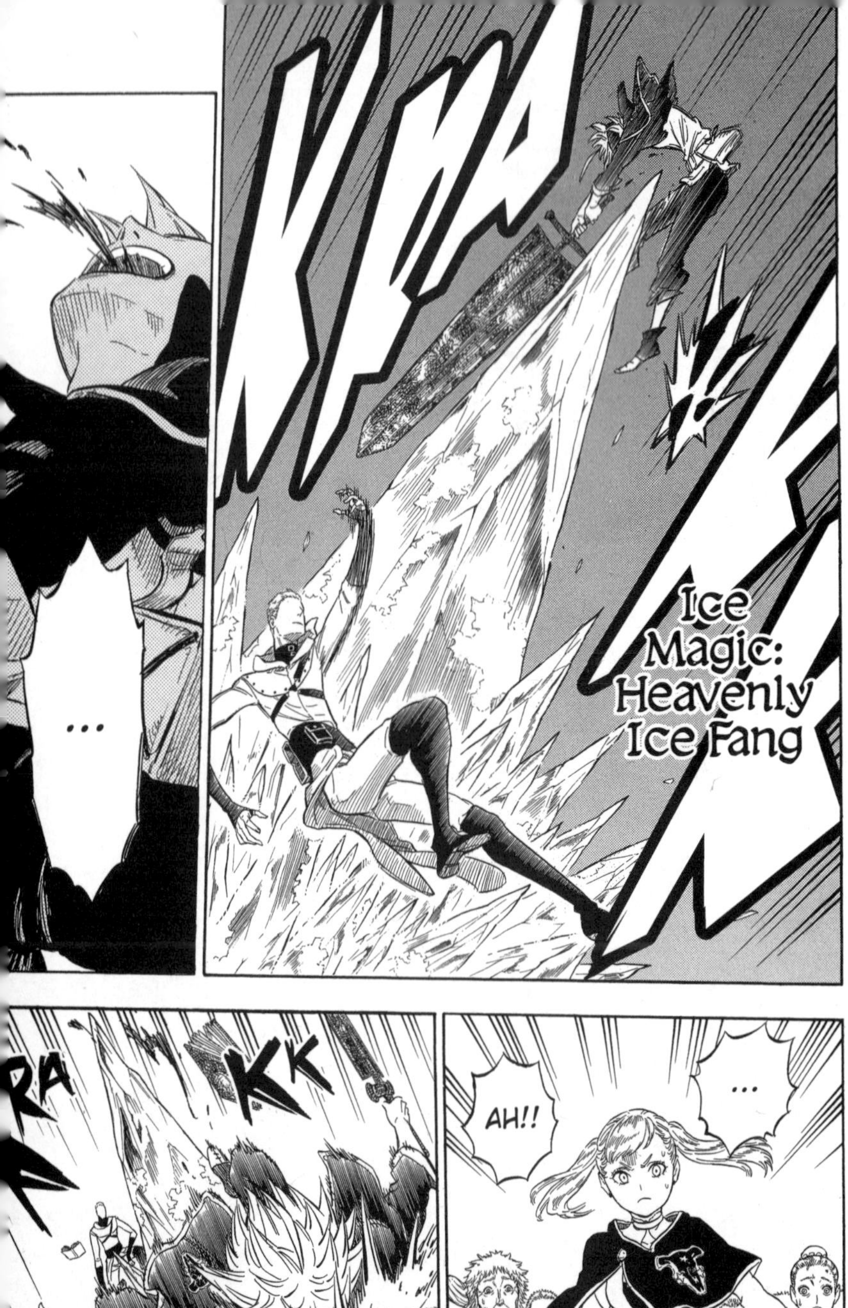
Ice Magic: Heavenly Ice Fang
...
...
AH!!
KK
RA

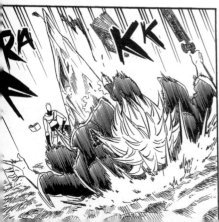

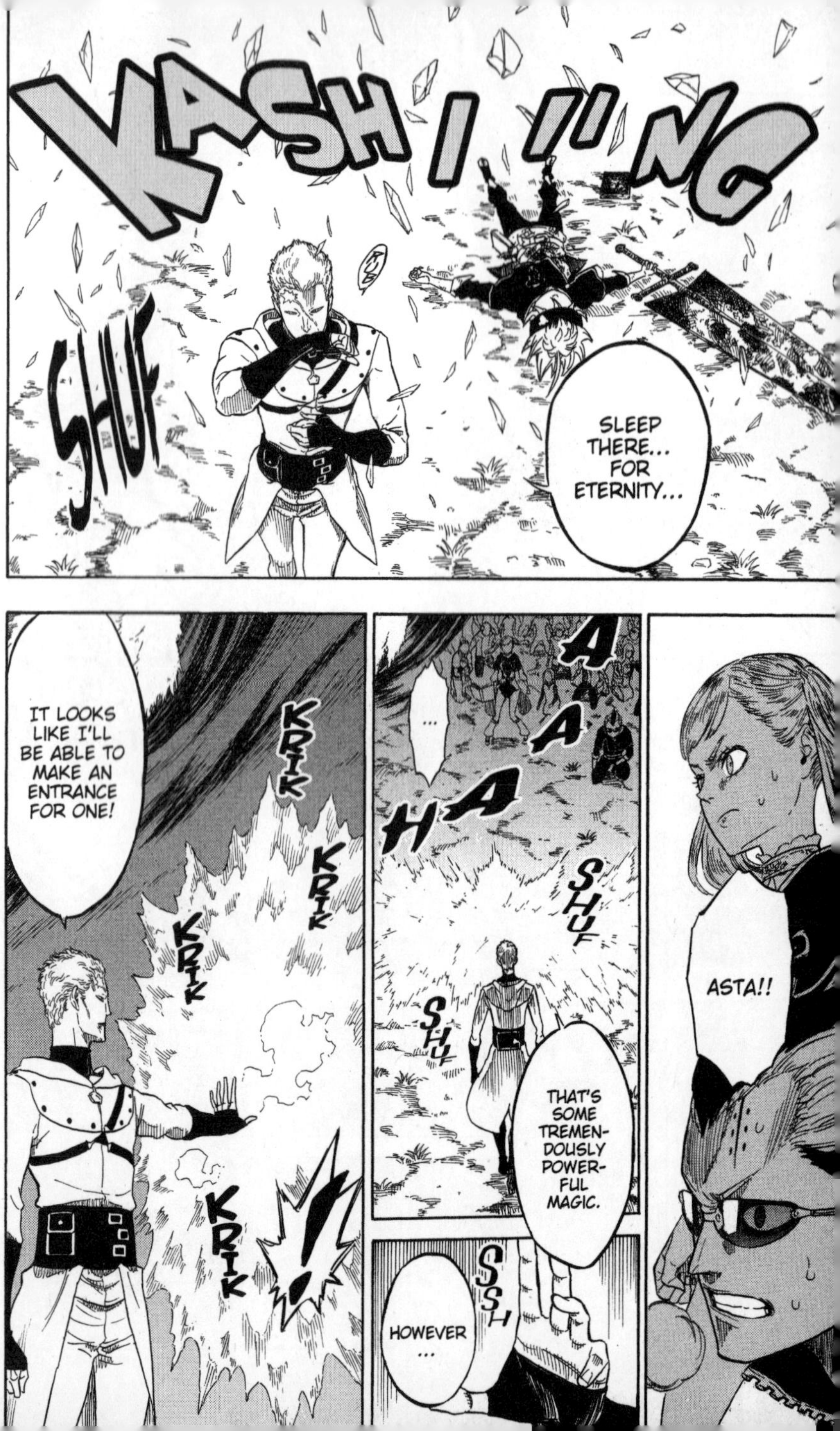
KASHIN'NG
SHUF
SLEEP THERE... FOR ETERNITY...
ASTA!!
HAAAA
...
SHUF
SHUF
THAT'S SOME TREMENDOUSLY POWERFUL MAGIC.
SSH
HOWEVER ...
IT LOOKS LIKE I'LL BE ABLE TO MAKE AN ENTRANCE FOR ONE!
KRIK
KRIK
KRIK
KRIK

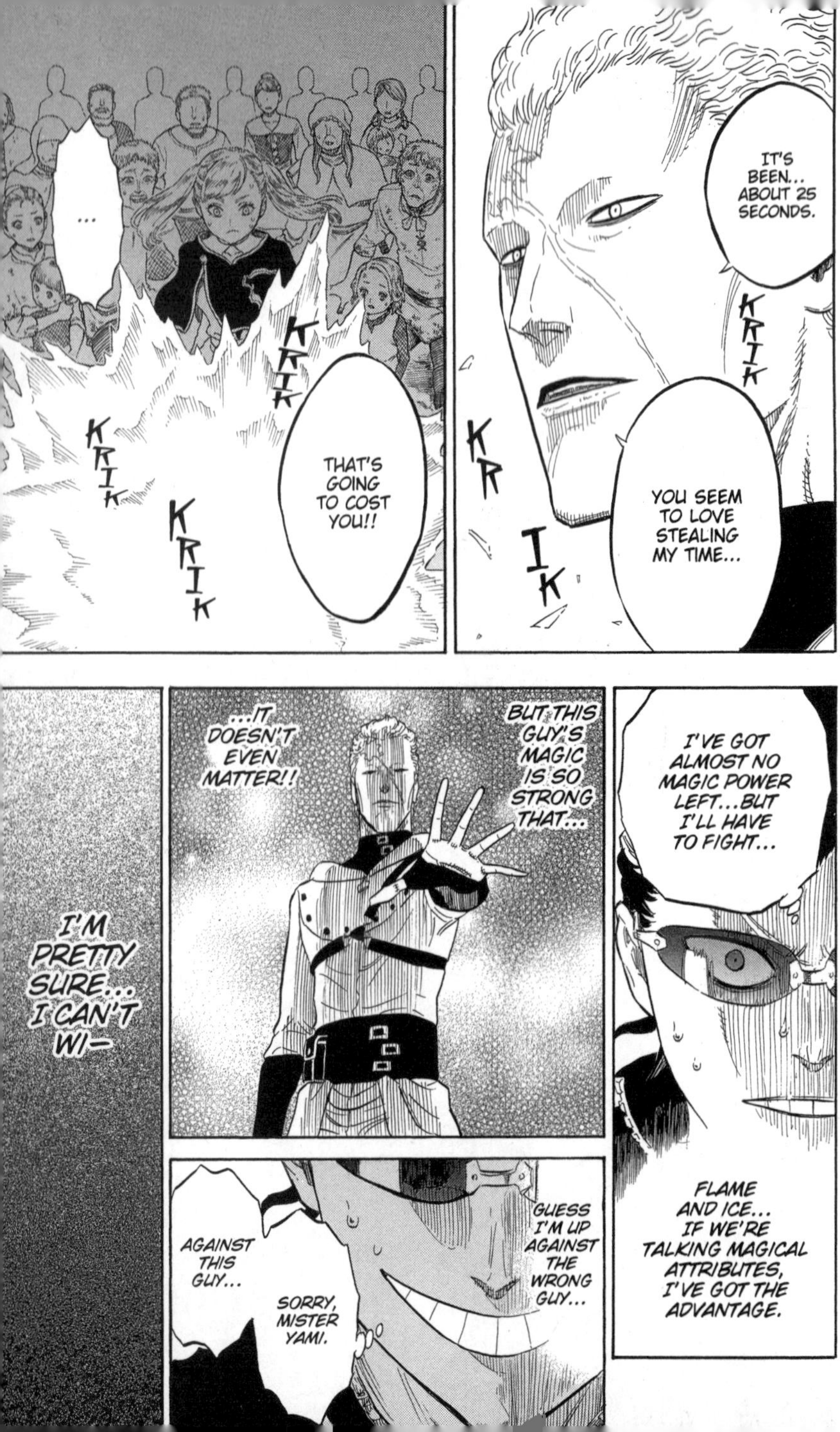
IT'S BEEN... ABOUT 25 SECONDS.
KRIK
YOU SEEM TO LOVE STEALING MY TIME...
KRIK
THAT'S GOING TO COST YOU!!
KRIK
KRIK
KRIK
...
I'VE GOT ALMOST NO MAGIC POWER LEFT...BUT I'LL HAVE TO FIGHT...
FLAME AND ICE... IF WE'RE TALKING MAGICAL ATTRIBUTES, I'VE GOT THE ADVANTAGE.
BUT THIS GUY'S MAGIC IS SO STRONG THAT...
...IT DOESN'T EVEN MATTER!!
GUESS I'M UP AGAINST THE WRONG GUY...
AGAINST THIS GUY...
SORRY, MISTER YAMI.
I'M PRETTY SURE... I CAN'T WI–

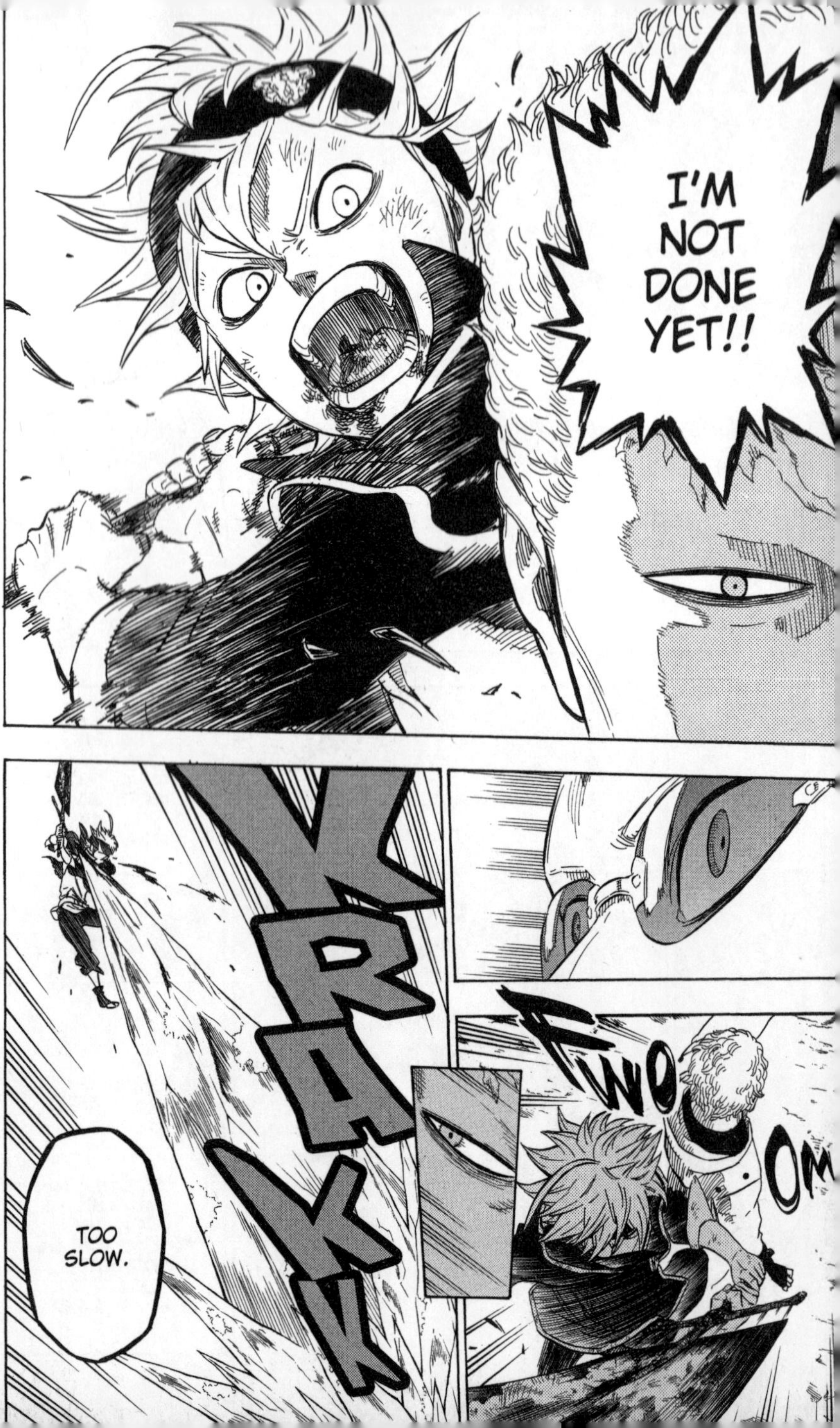
I'M NOT DONE YET!!
FWOOOM
KRAK
TOO SLOW.

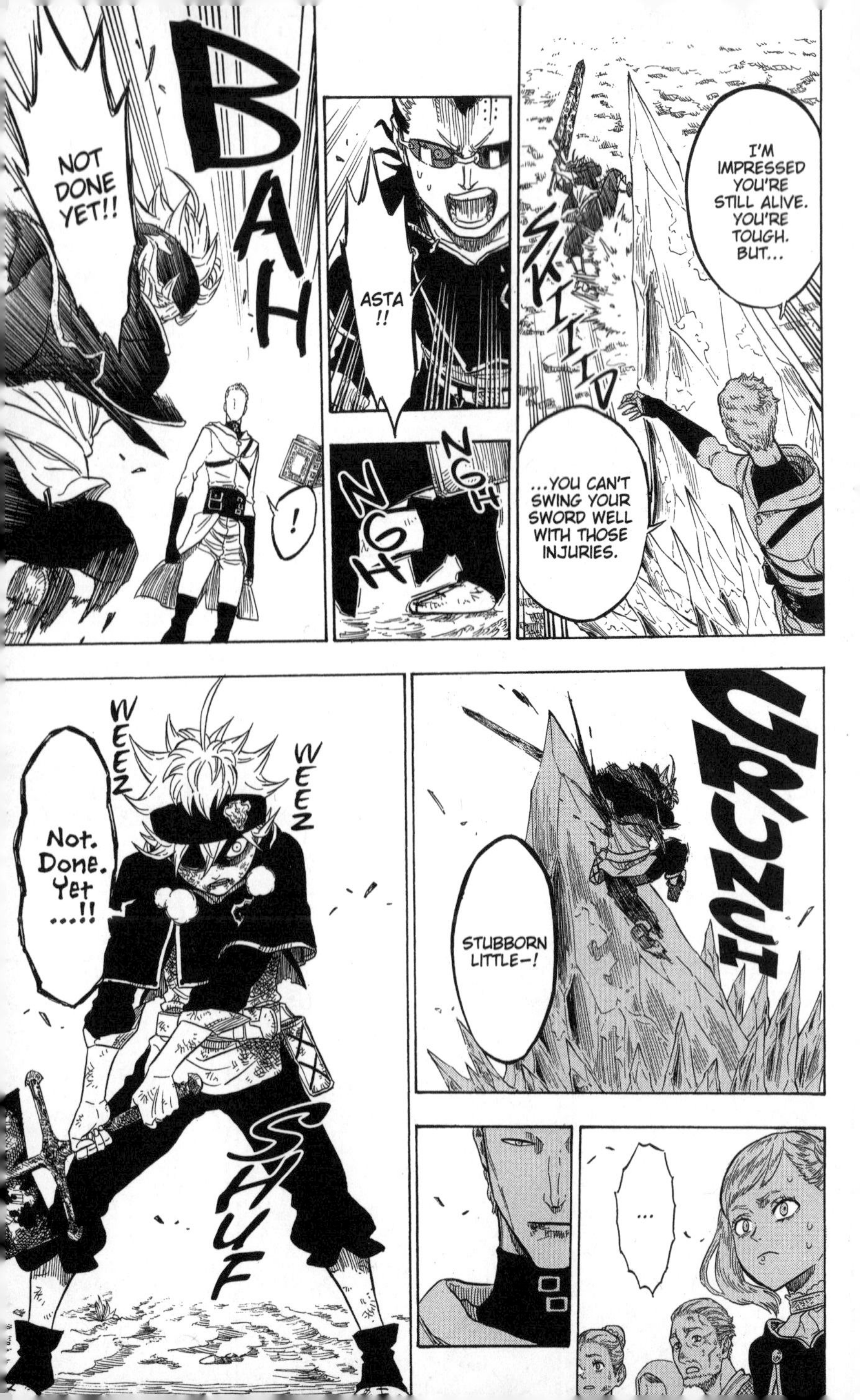
I'M IMPRESSED YOU'RE STILL ALIVE. YOU'RE TOUGH. BUT...
SKIIID
...YOU CAN'T SWING YOUR SWORD WELL WITH THOSE INJURIES.
ASTA!!
NGH
NGH
BAH
NOT DONE YET!!
!
STUBBORN LITTLE—!
...
WEEZ
WEEZ
Not. Done. Yet ...!!
SHUF

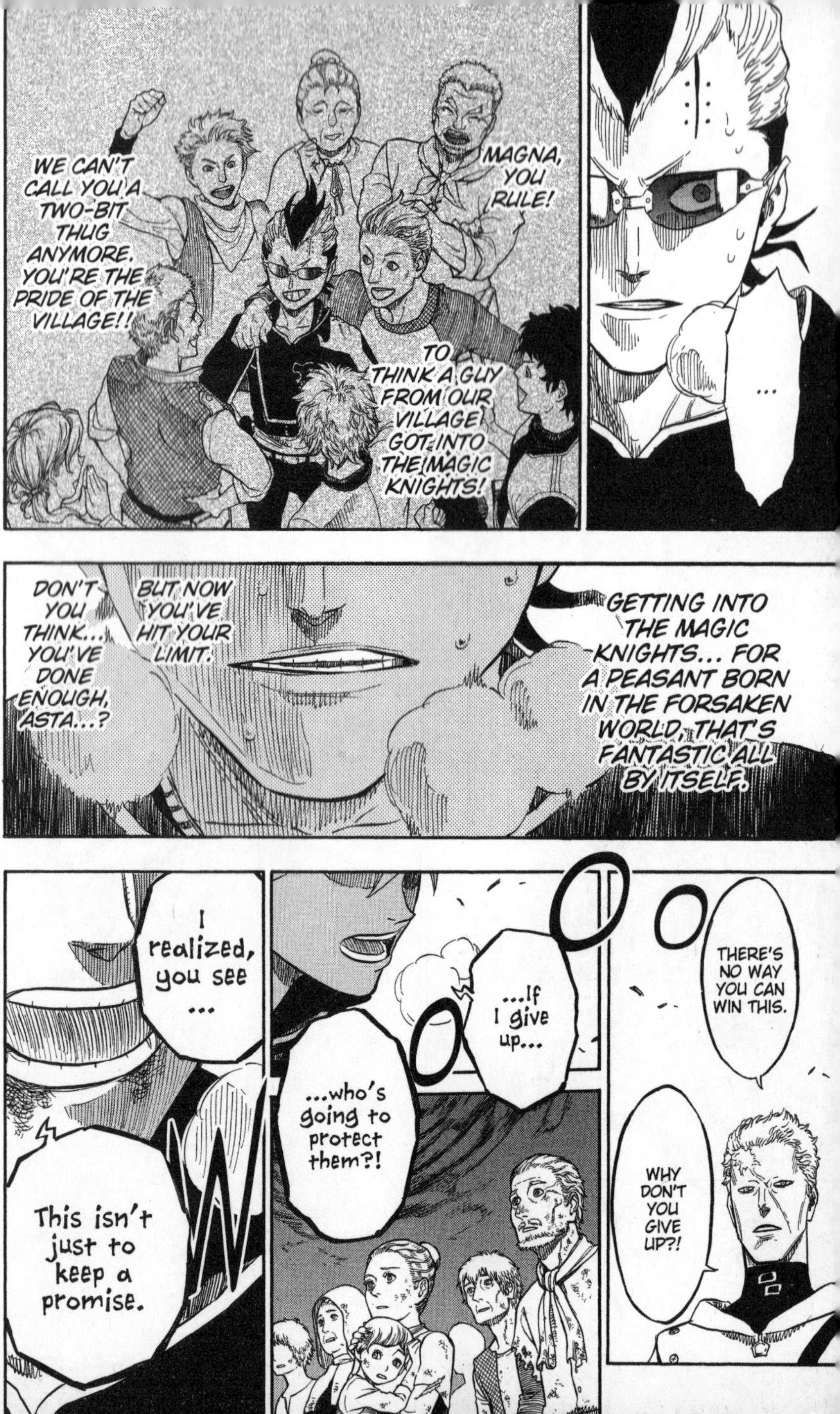
...
MAGNA, YOU RULE!
WE CAN'T CALL YOU A TWO-BIT THUG ANYMORE. YOU'RE THE PRIDE OF THE VILLAGE!!
TO THINK A GUY FROM OUR VILLAGE GOT INTO THE MAGIC KNIGHTS!
GETTING INTO THE MAGIC KNIGHTS... FOR A PEASANT BORN IN THE FORSAKEN WORLD, THAT'S FANTASTIC ALL BY ITSELF.
BUT NOW YOU'VE HIT YOUR LIMIT.
DON'T YOU THINK... YOU'VE DONE ENOUGH, ASTA...?
THERE'S NO WAY YOU CAN WIN THIS.
WHY DON'T YOU GIVE UP?!
...If I give up...
...who's going to protect them?!
I realized, you see...
This isn't just to keep a promise.

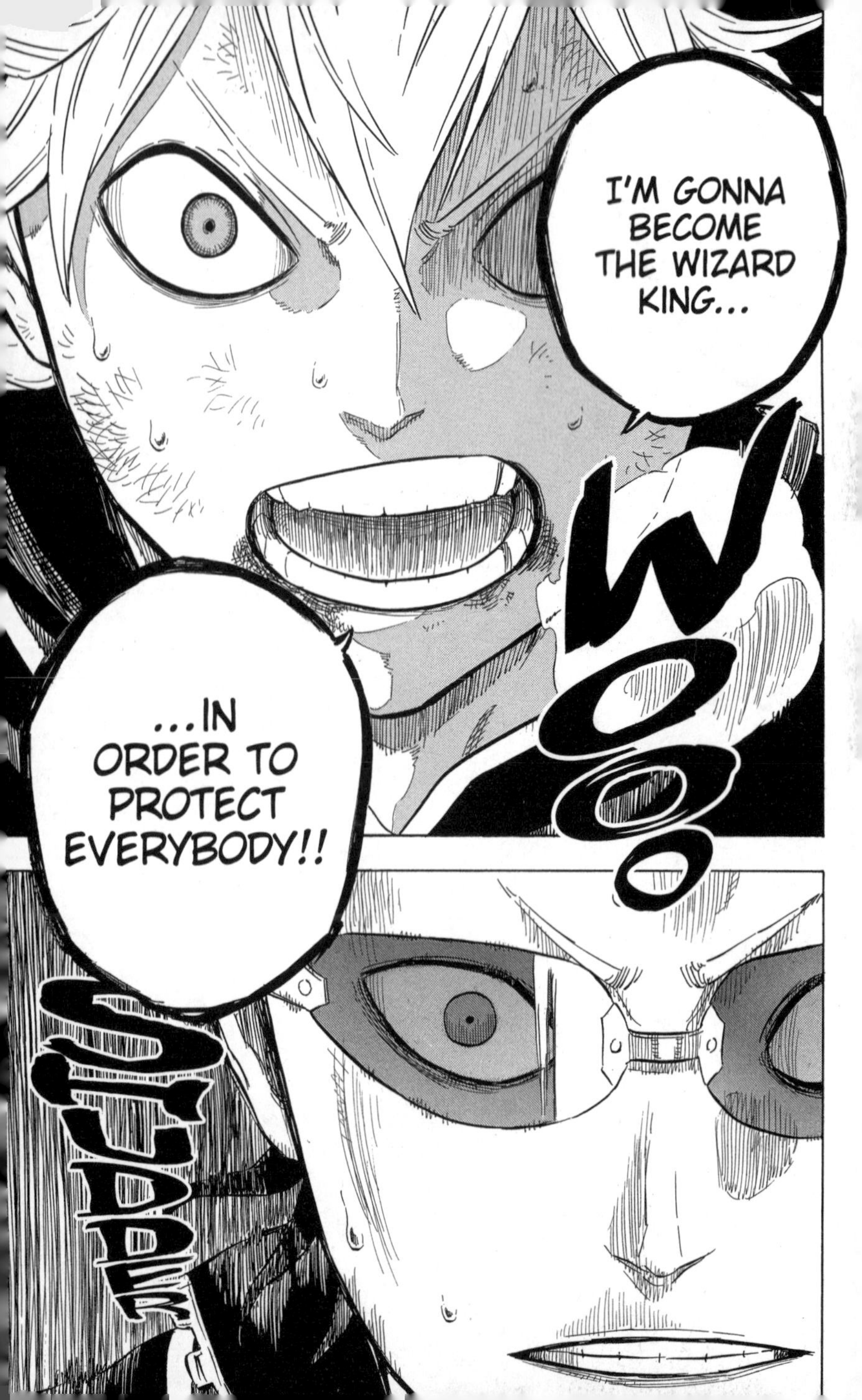
I'M GONNA BECOME THE WIZARD KING...
WOOOO
...IN ORDER TO PROTECT EVERYBODY!!

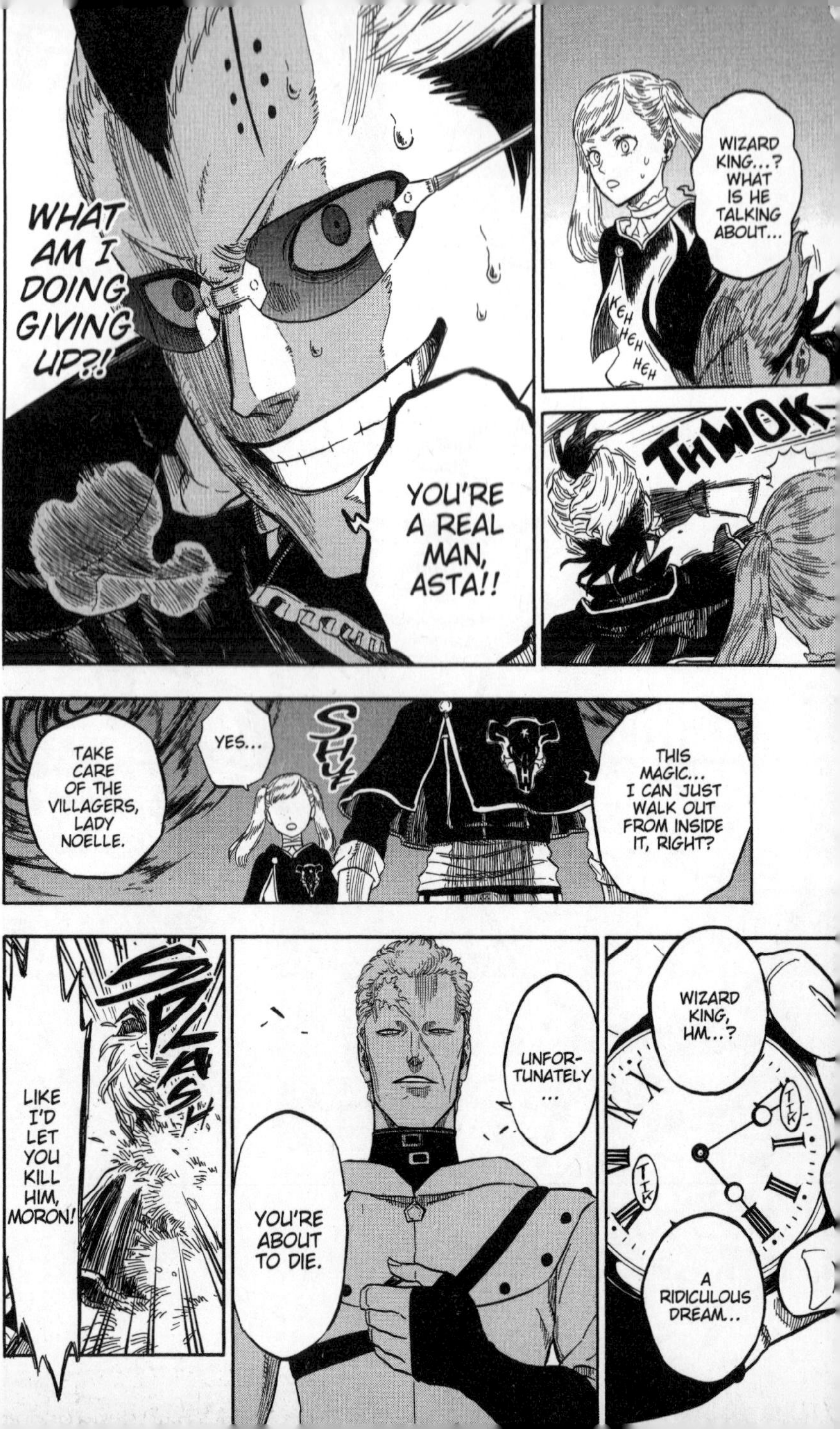
WIZARD KING...? WHAT IS HE TALKING ABOUT...
KEH HEH HEH HEH
THWOK
YOU'RE A REAL MAN, ASTA!!
WHAT AM I DOING GIVING UP?!
THIS MAGIC... I CAN JUST WALK OUT FROM INSIDE IT, RIGHT?
YES...
TAKE CARE OF THE VILLAGERS, LADY NOELLE.
WIZARD KING, HM...?
TIK
TIK
A RIDICULOUS DREAM...
UNFORTUNATELY...
YOU'RE ABOUT TO DIE.
LIKE I'D LET YOU KILL HIM, MORON!

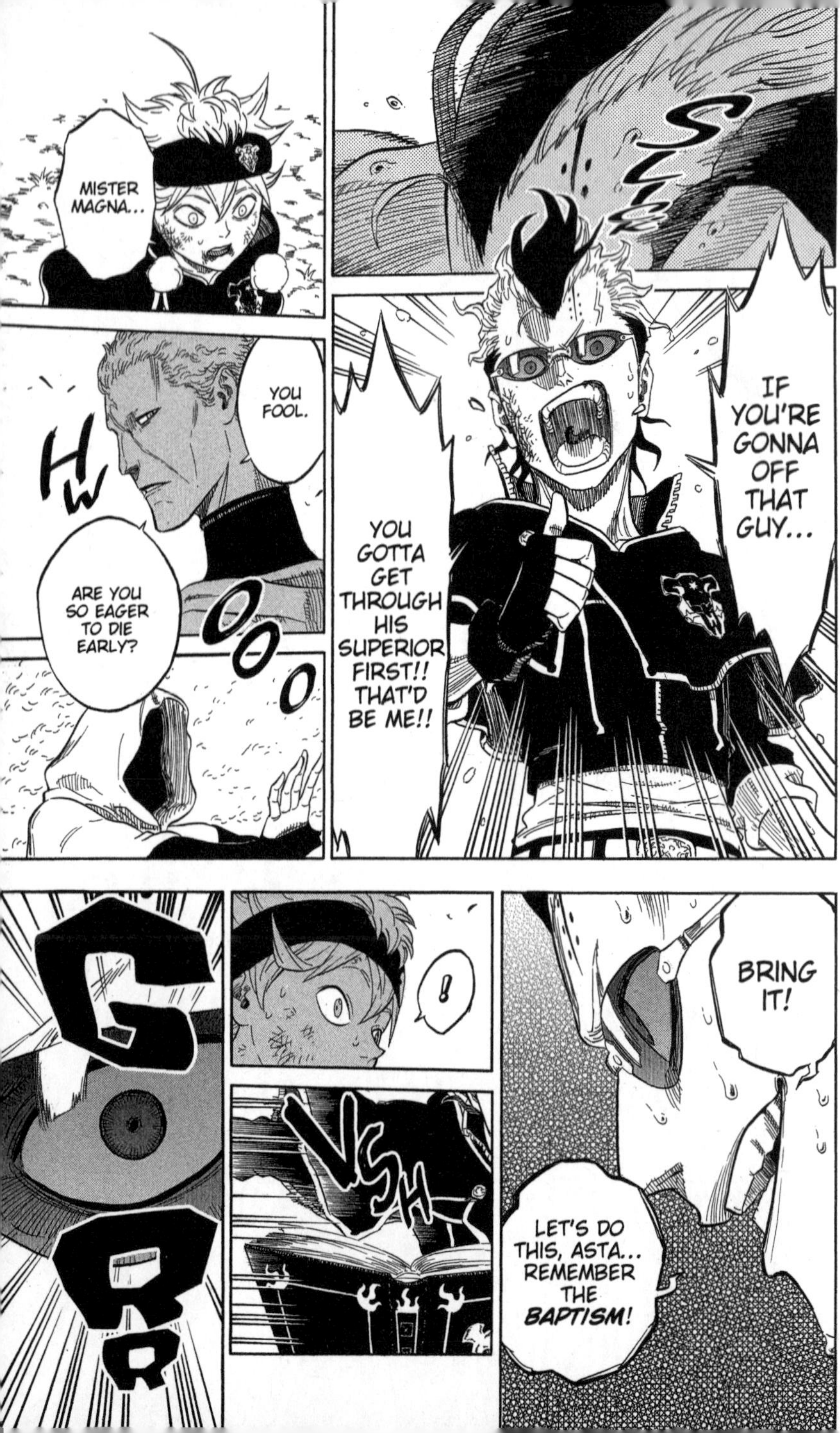
IF YOU'RE GONNA OFF THAT GUY...
YOU GOTTA GET THROUGH HIS SUPERIOR FIRST!! THAT'D BE ME!!
MISTER MAGNA...
YOU FOOL.
HWOOO
ARE YOU SO EAGER TO DIE EARLY?
BRING IT!
LET'S DO THIS, ASTA... REMEMBER THE *BAPTISM*!
!
VSH
GRR

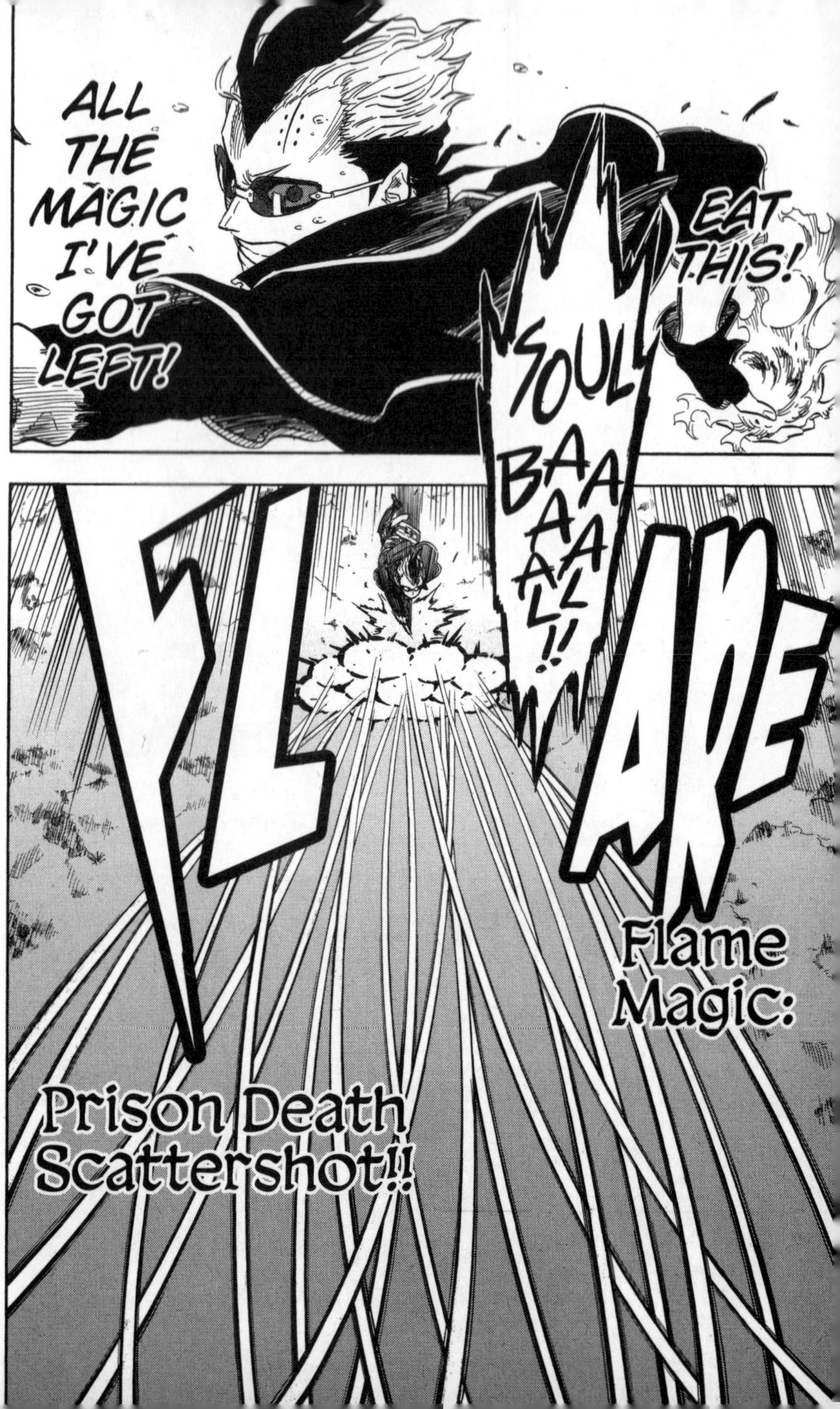
EAT THIS!
ALL THE MAGIC I'VE GOT LEFT!
SOUL BAAAAALL!!
FLARE
Flame Magic:
Prison Death Scattershot!!

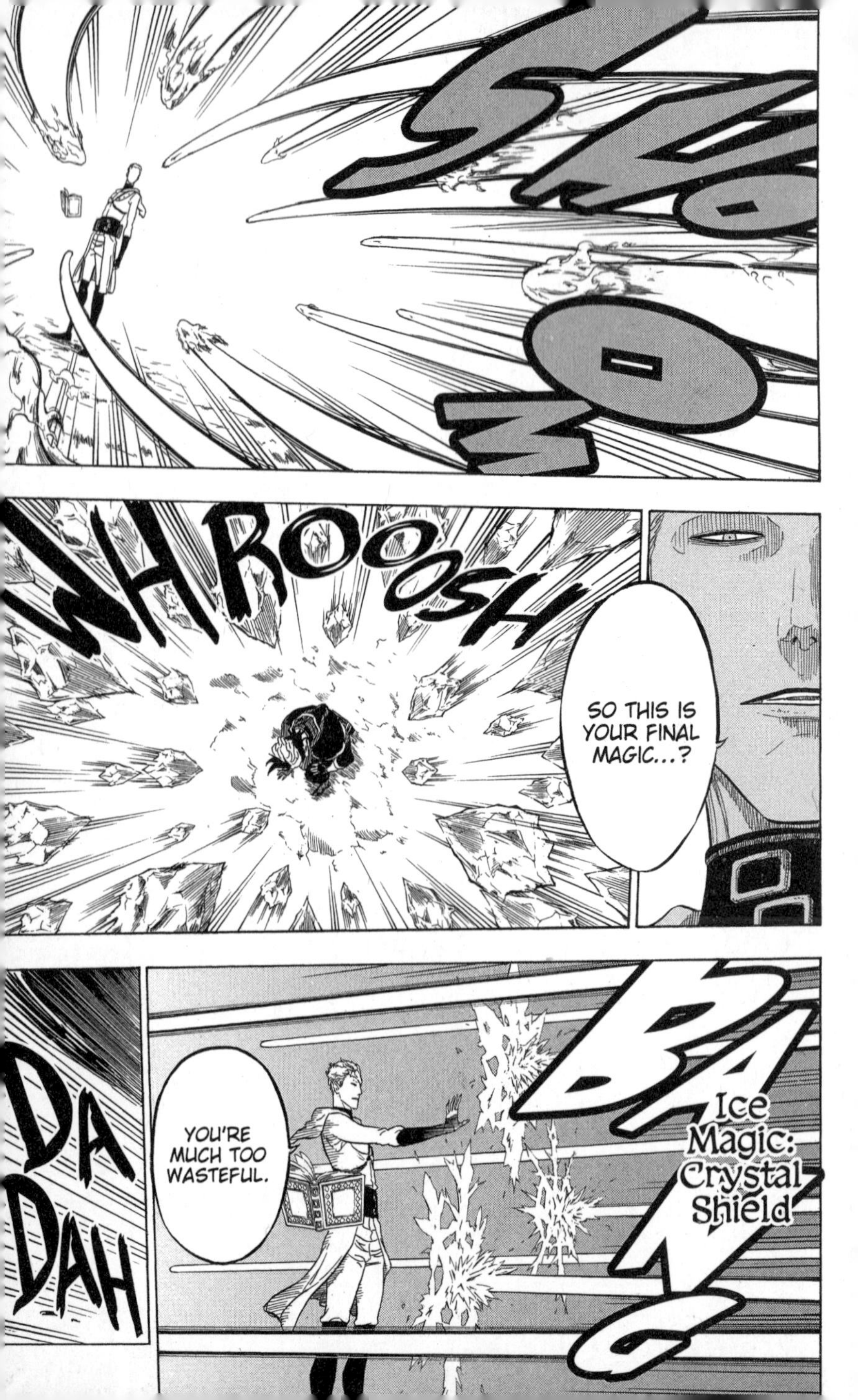
SHOOM
WHROOOSH
SO THIS IS YOUR FINAL MAGIC...?
BANG
Ice Magic: Crystal Shield
YOU'RE MUCH TOO WASTEFUL.
DA DAH

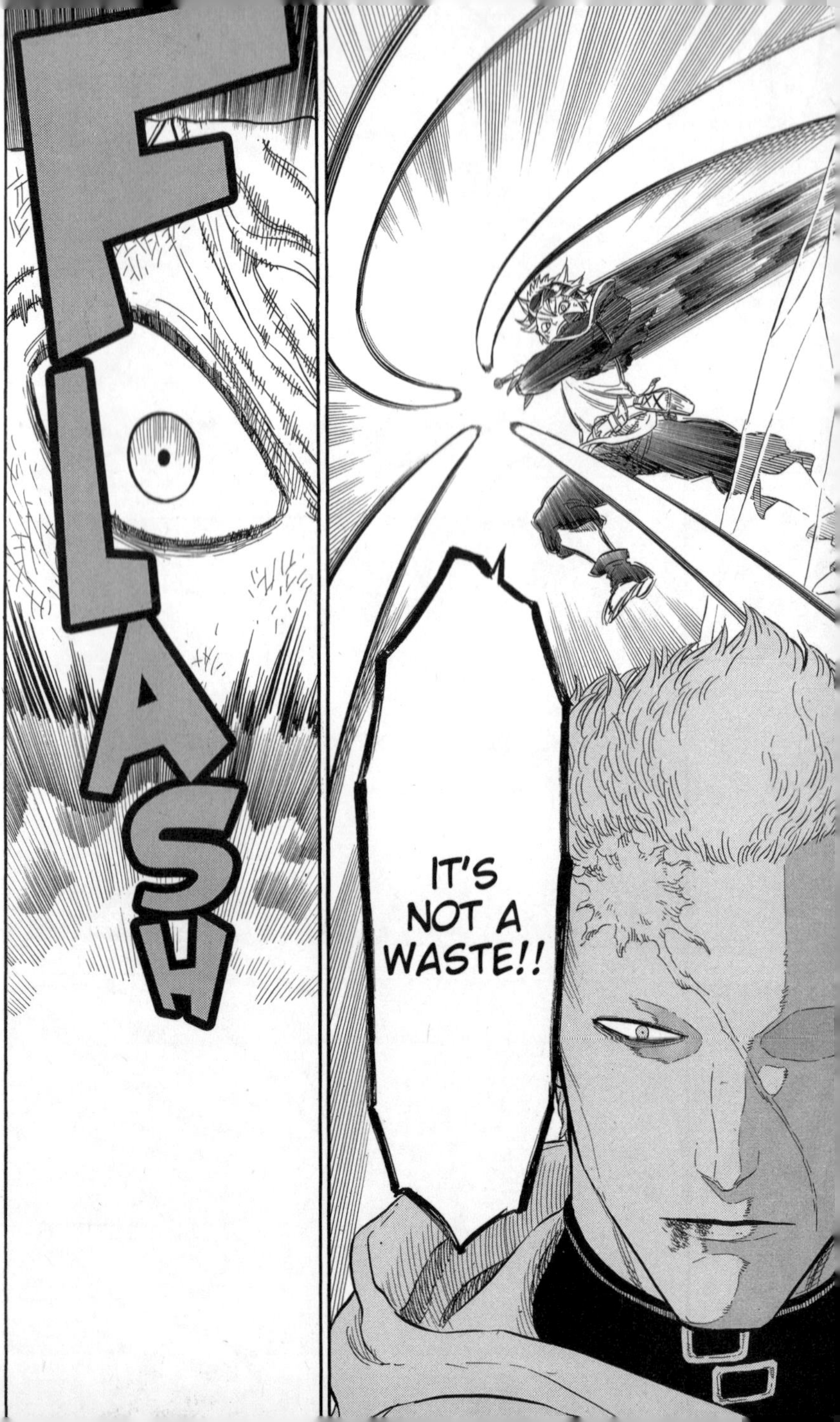
IT'S NOT A WASTE!!
FLASH

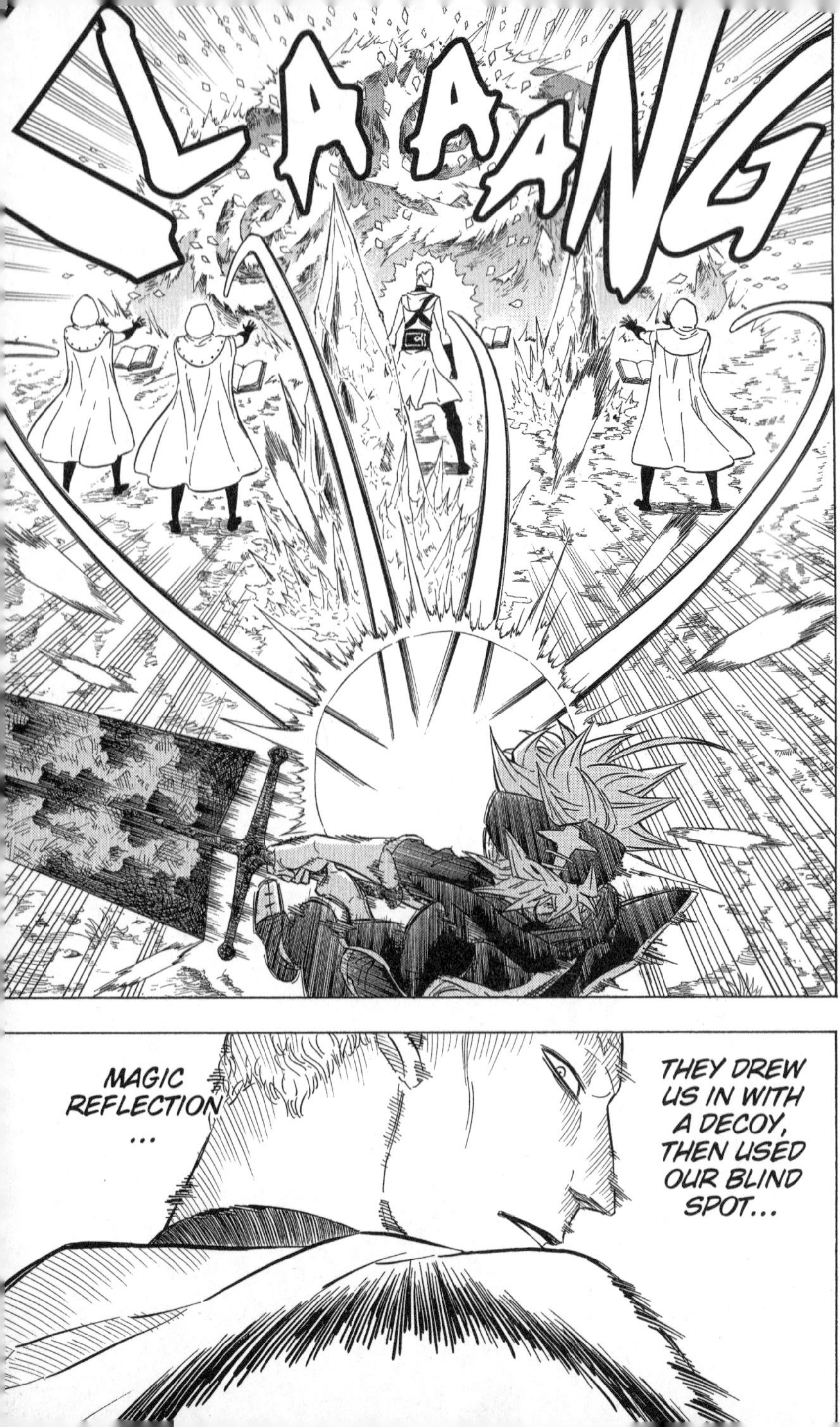
LAAANG
THEY DREW US IN WITH A DECOY, THEN USED OUR BLIND SPOT...
MAGIC REFLECTION...

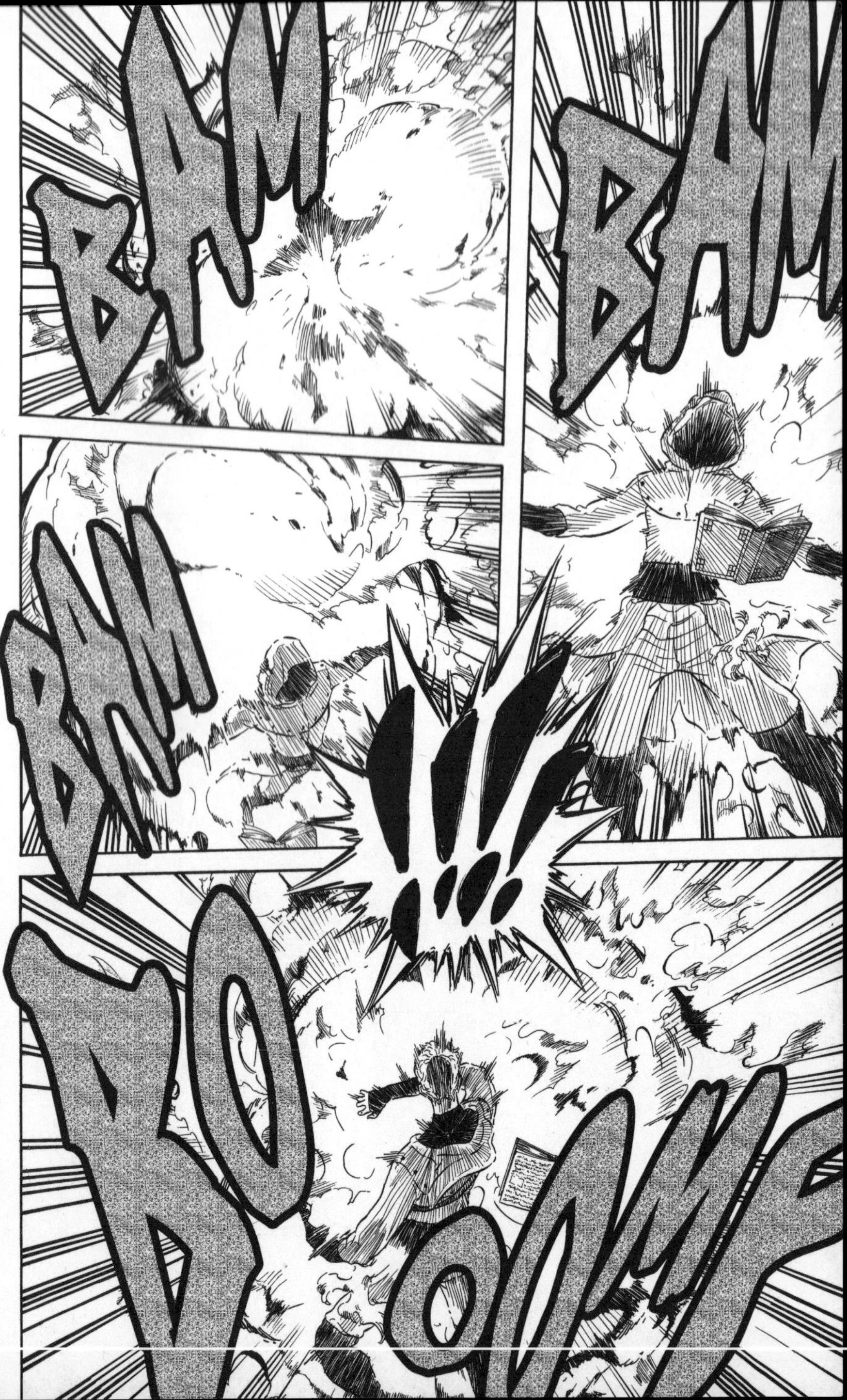
BAM
BAM
BAM
!!!
BOOM

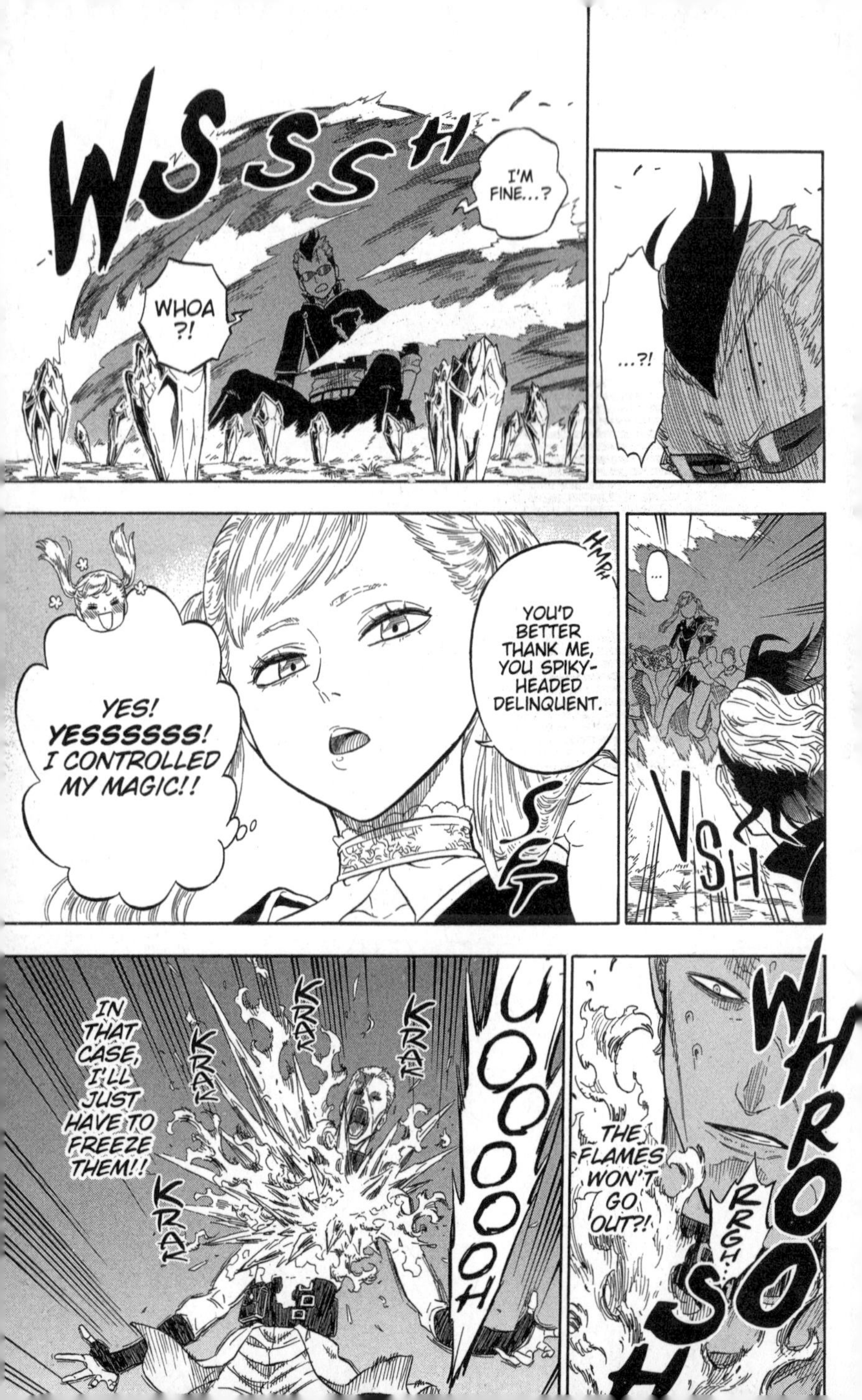
...?!
I'M FINE...?
WSSSH
WHOA ?!
...
VSH
HMPH
YOU'D BETTER THANK ME, YOU SPIKY-HEADED DELINQUENT.
SFT
YES! YESSSSSS! I CONTROLLED MY MAGIC!!
WHROOSH
RRGH...
THE FLAMES WON'T GO OUT?!
UOOOOOOH
KRAK
KRAK
KRAK
KRAK
IN THAT CASE, I'LL JUST HAVE TO FREEZE THEM!!

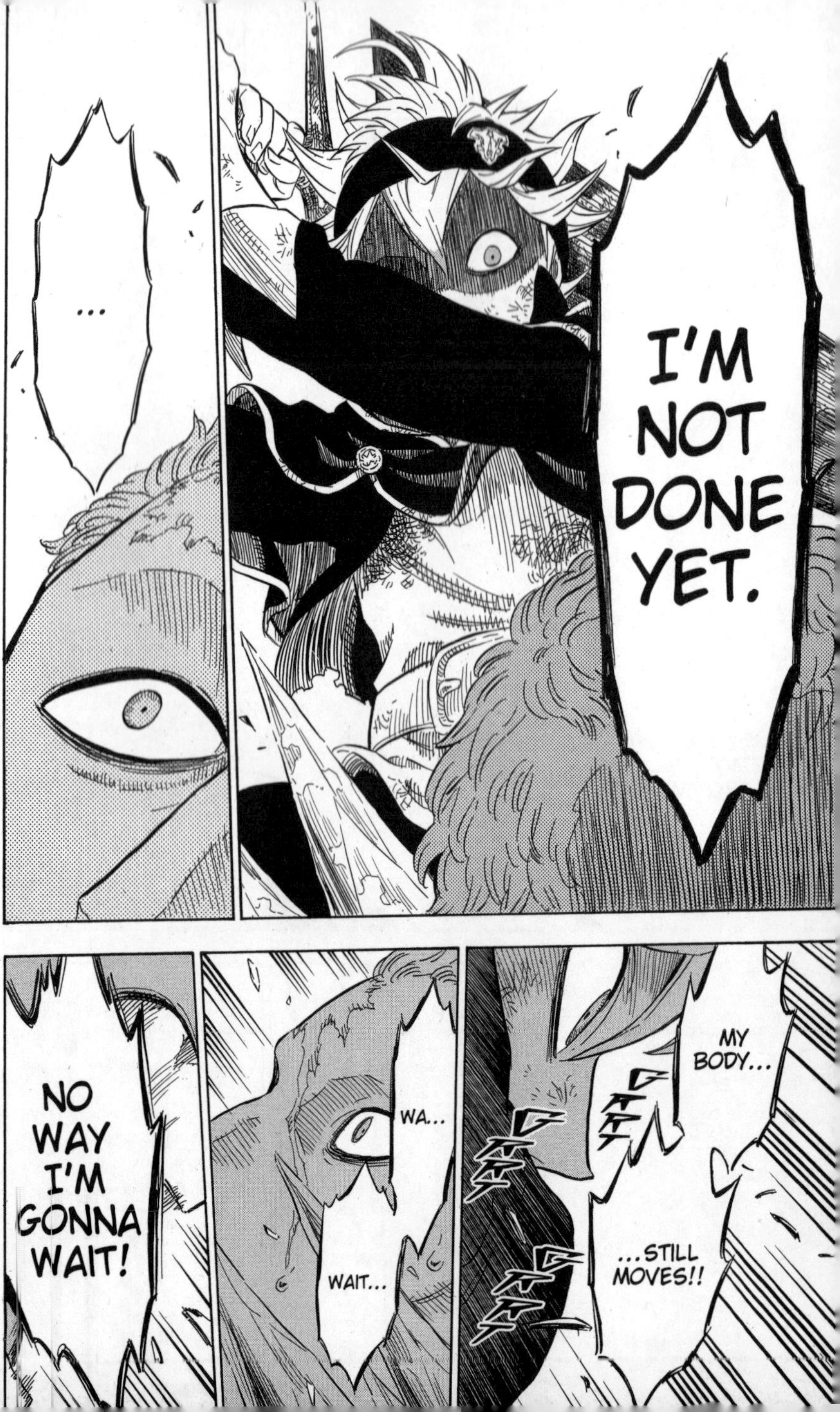
I'M NOT DONE YET.
...
MY BODY...
...STILL MOVES!!
WA...
WAIT...
NO WAY I'M GONNA WAIT!

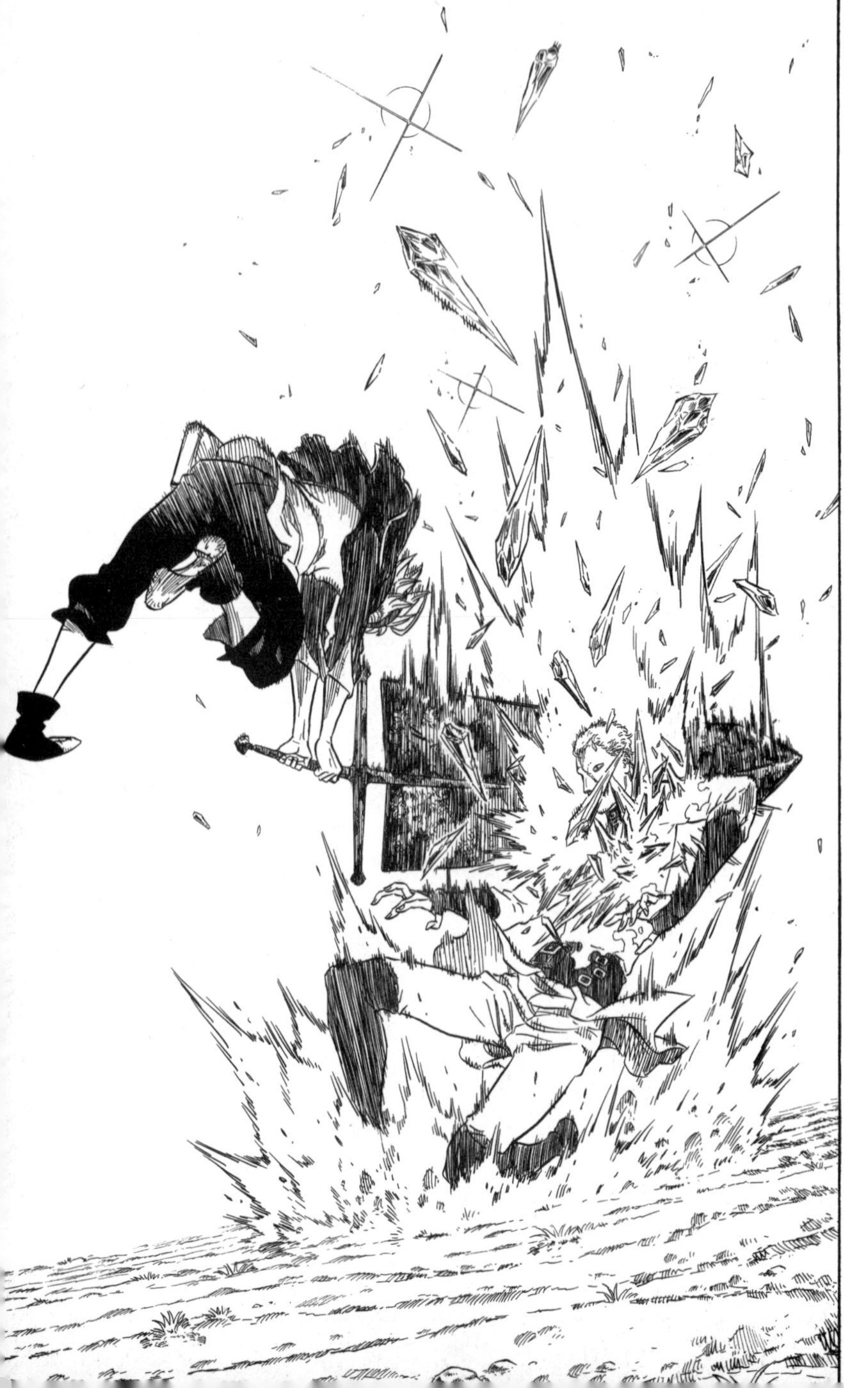

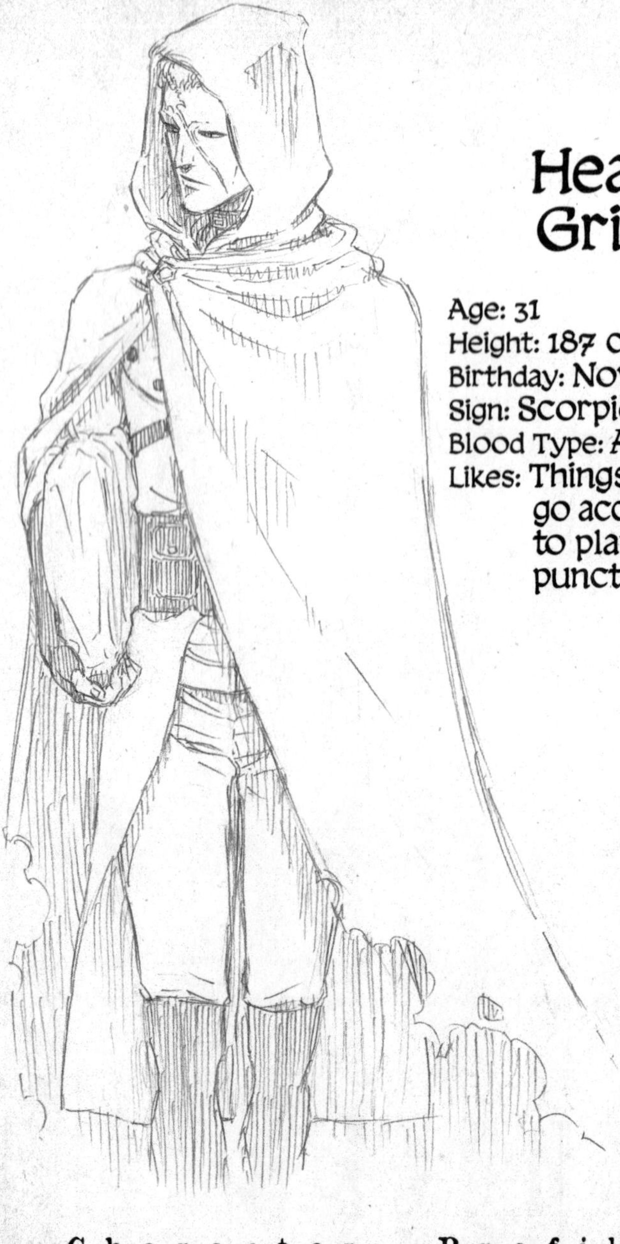

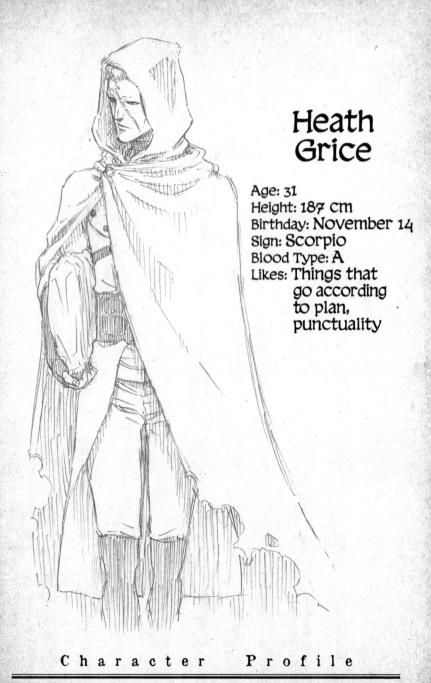

Heath Grice

Age: 31
Height: 187 cm
Birthday: November 14
Sign: Scorpio
Blood Type: A
Likes: Things that go according to plan, punctuality

Character Profile

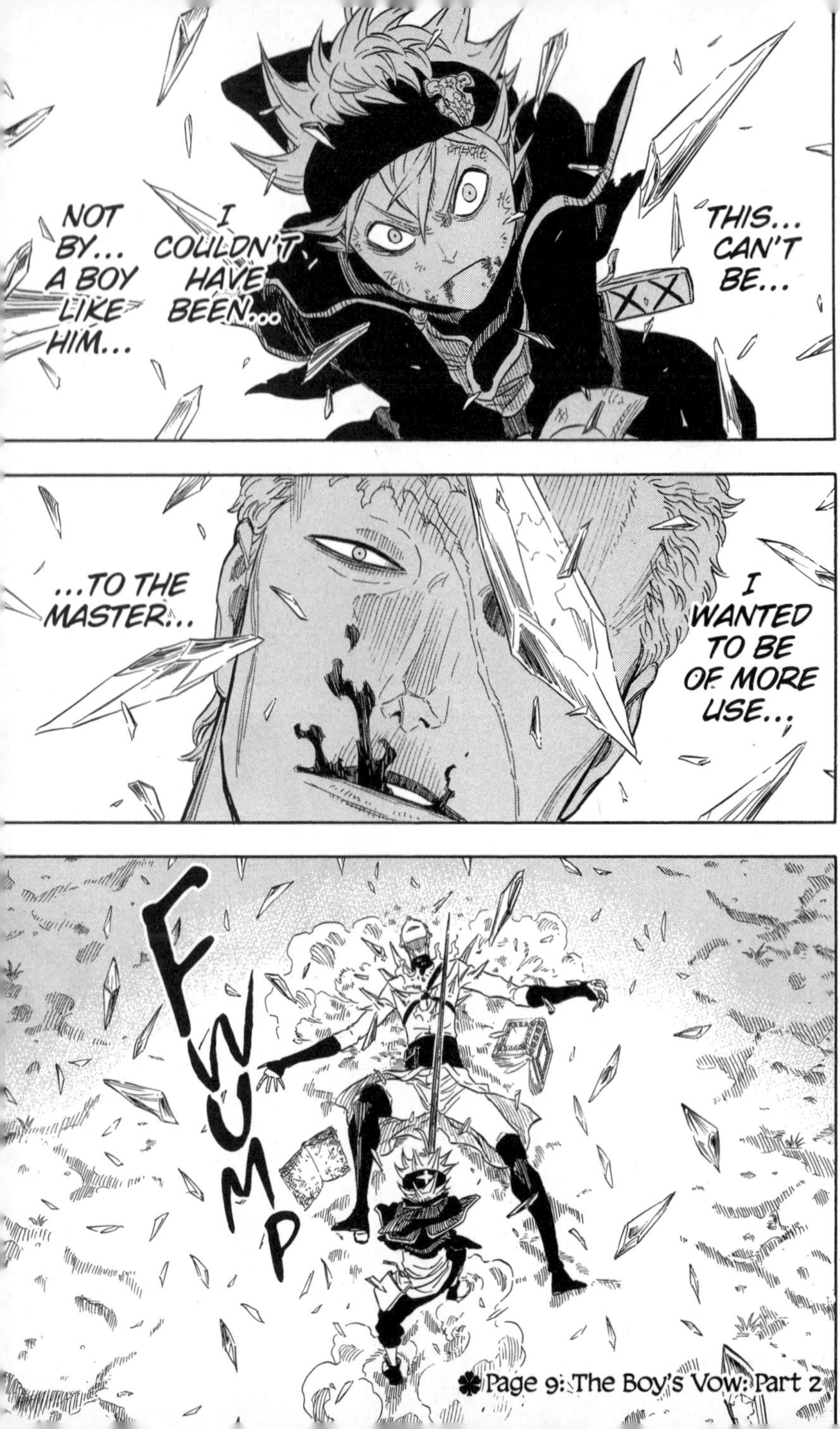
THIS... CAN'T BE...
I COULDN'T HAVE BEEN...
NOT BY... A BOY LIKE HIM...
I WANTED TO BE OF MORE USE...
...TO THE MASTER...
FWUMP

Page 9: The Boy's Vow: Part 2

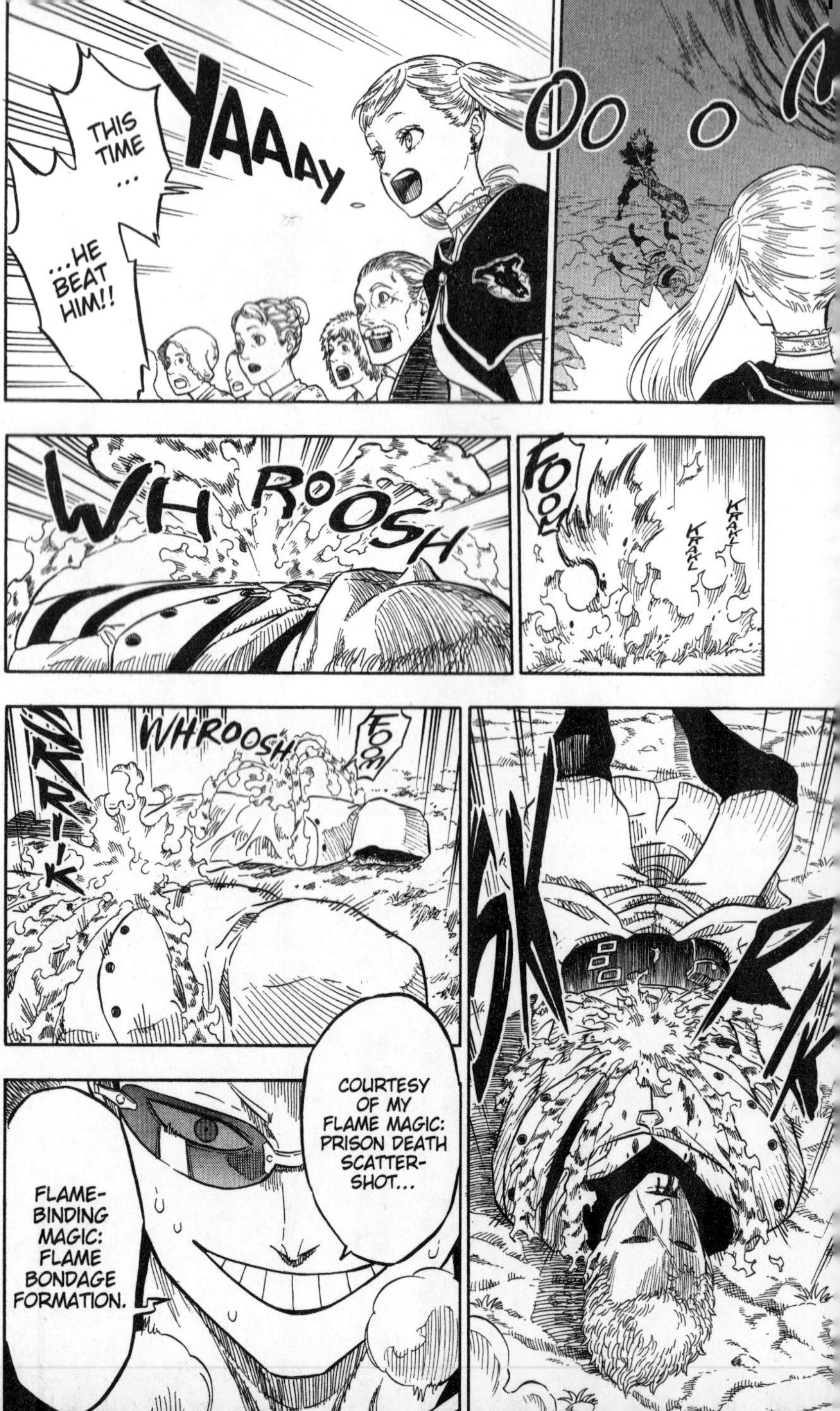
OOO O
YAAAAY
THIS TIME...
...HE BEAT HIM!!
FOOM
KRAK KRAK
WHROOSH
SKRRK
SKRRIK
WHROOSH
FOOM
COURTESY OF MY FLAME MAGIC: PRISON DEATH SCATTER-SHOT...
FLAME-BINDING MAGIC: FLAME BONDAGE FORMATION.

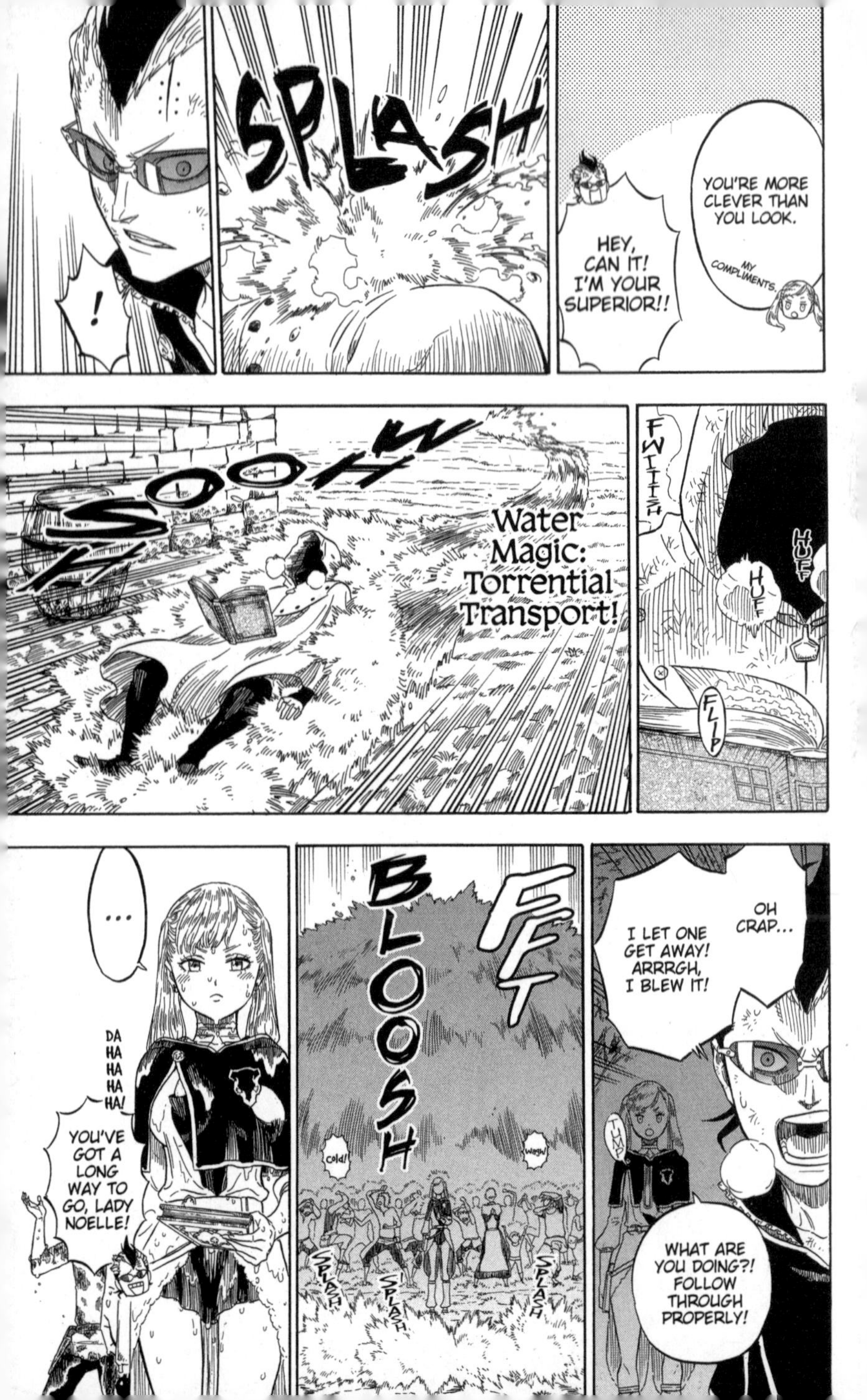
YOU'RE MORE CLEVER THAN YOU LOOK.
MY COMPLIMENTS.
HEY, CAN IT! I'M YOUR SUPERIOR!!
SPLASH
!
FWIIISH
HUFF HUFF
FLIP
WHOOSH
Water Magic: Torrential Transport!
OH CRAP...
I LET ONE GET AWAY! ARRRGH, I BLEW IT!
TUMP
WHAT ARE YOU DOING?! FOLLOW THROUGH PROPERLY!
FFT
BLOOSH
Wagh!
Cold!
SPLASH
SPLASH
SPLASH
...
DA HA HA HA HA!
YOU'VE GOT A LONG WAY TO GO, LADY NOELLE!

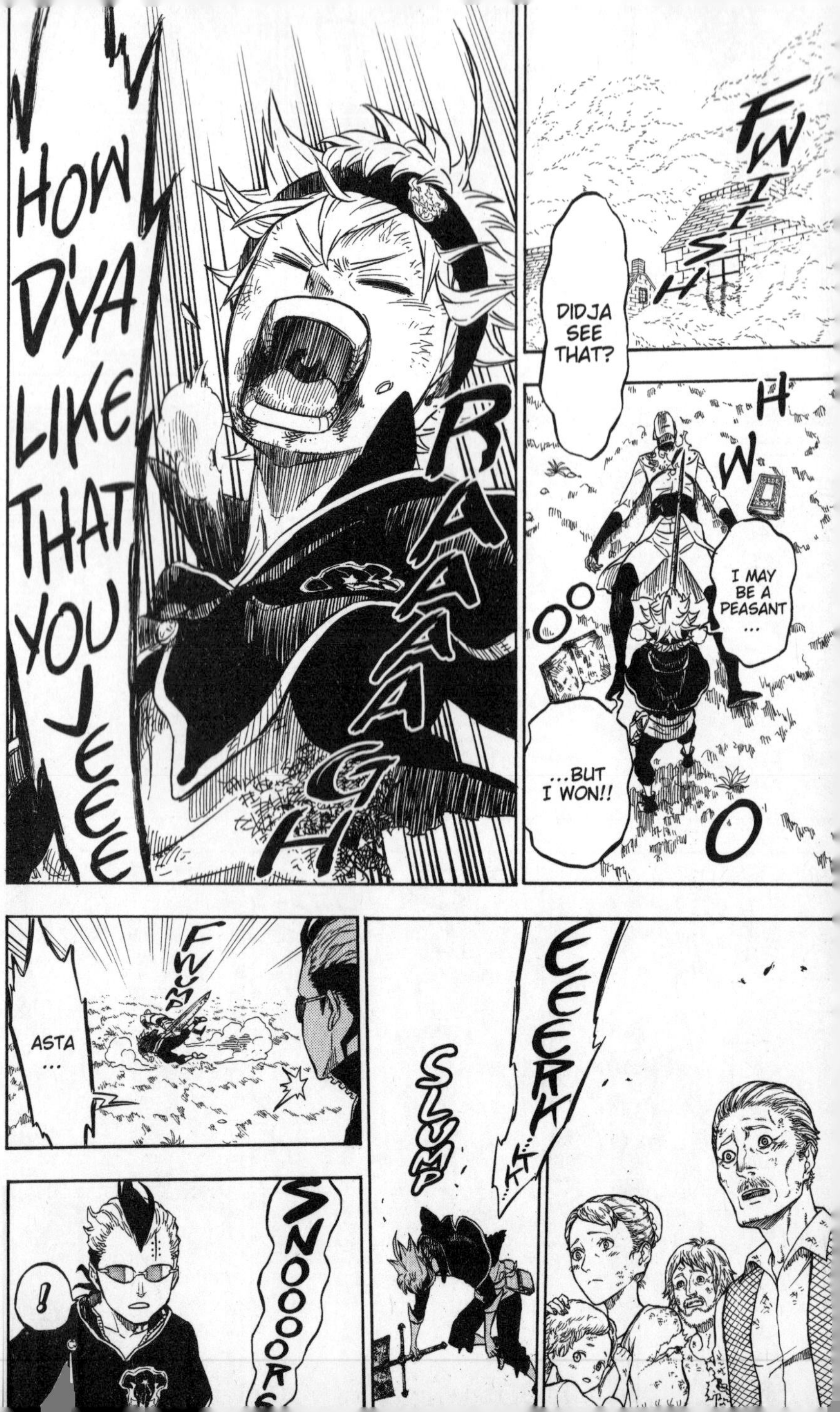
FWISH
DIDJA SEE THAT?
WHOOO
I MAY BE A PEASANT...
...BUT I WON!!
HOW D'YA LIKE THAT YOU JEEEE
RAAAAAGH!
EEEERK...KT
SLUMP
SNOOOORG
FWUMP
ASTA...
!

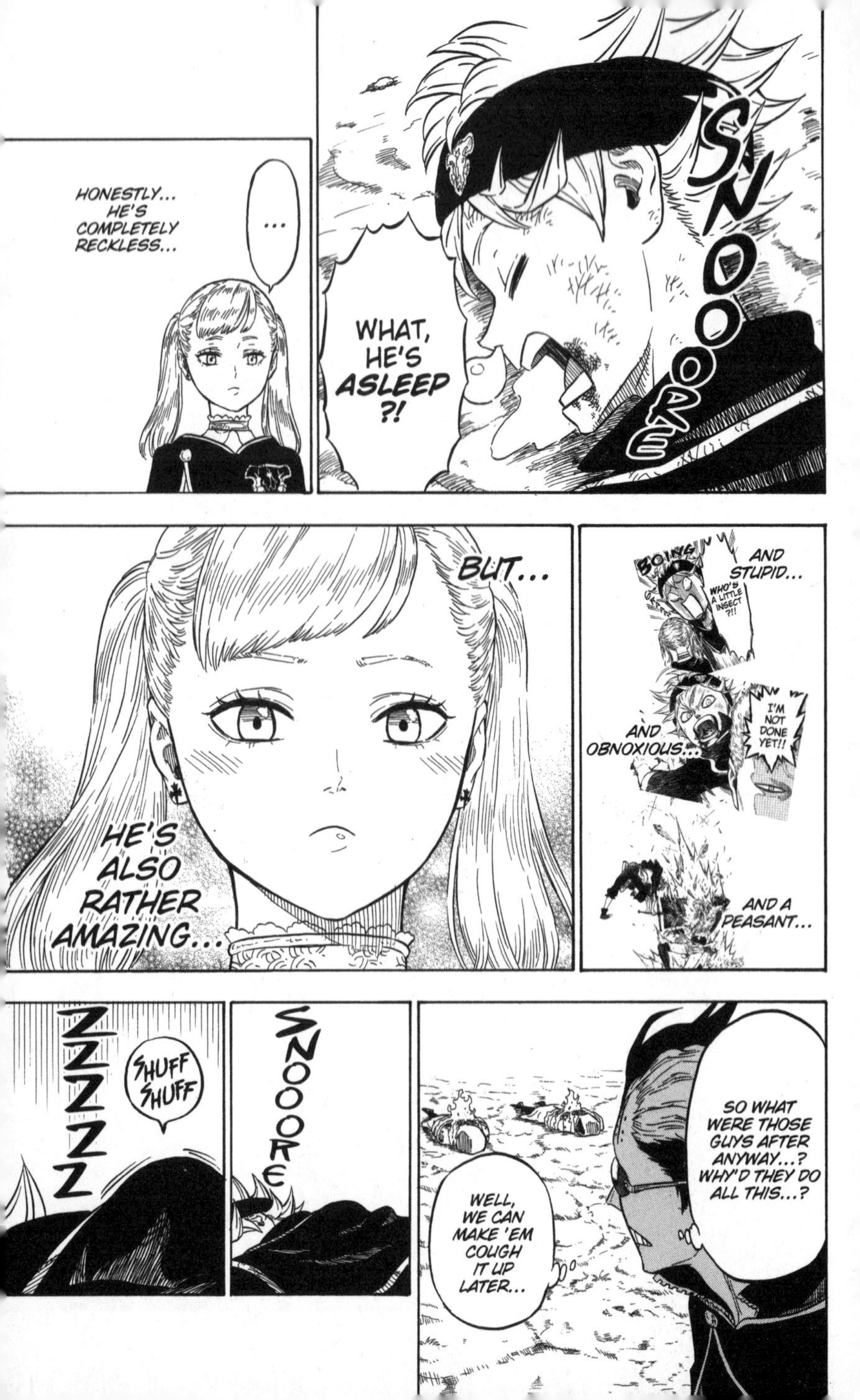
SNOOOORE
WHAT, HE'S ASLEEP?!
...
HONESTLY... HE'S COMPLETELY RECKLESS...
AND STUPID...
BOING
WHO'S A LITTLE INSECT?!!
I'M NOT DONE YET!!
AND OBNOXIOUS...
AND A PEASANT...
BUT...
HE'S ALSO RATHER AMAZING...
SO WHAT WERE THOSE GUYS AFTER ANYWAY...? WHY'D THEY DO ALL THIS...?
WELL, WE CAN MAKE 'EM COUGH IT UP LATER...
SNOOOORE
ZZZZZ
SHUFF SHUFF

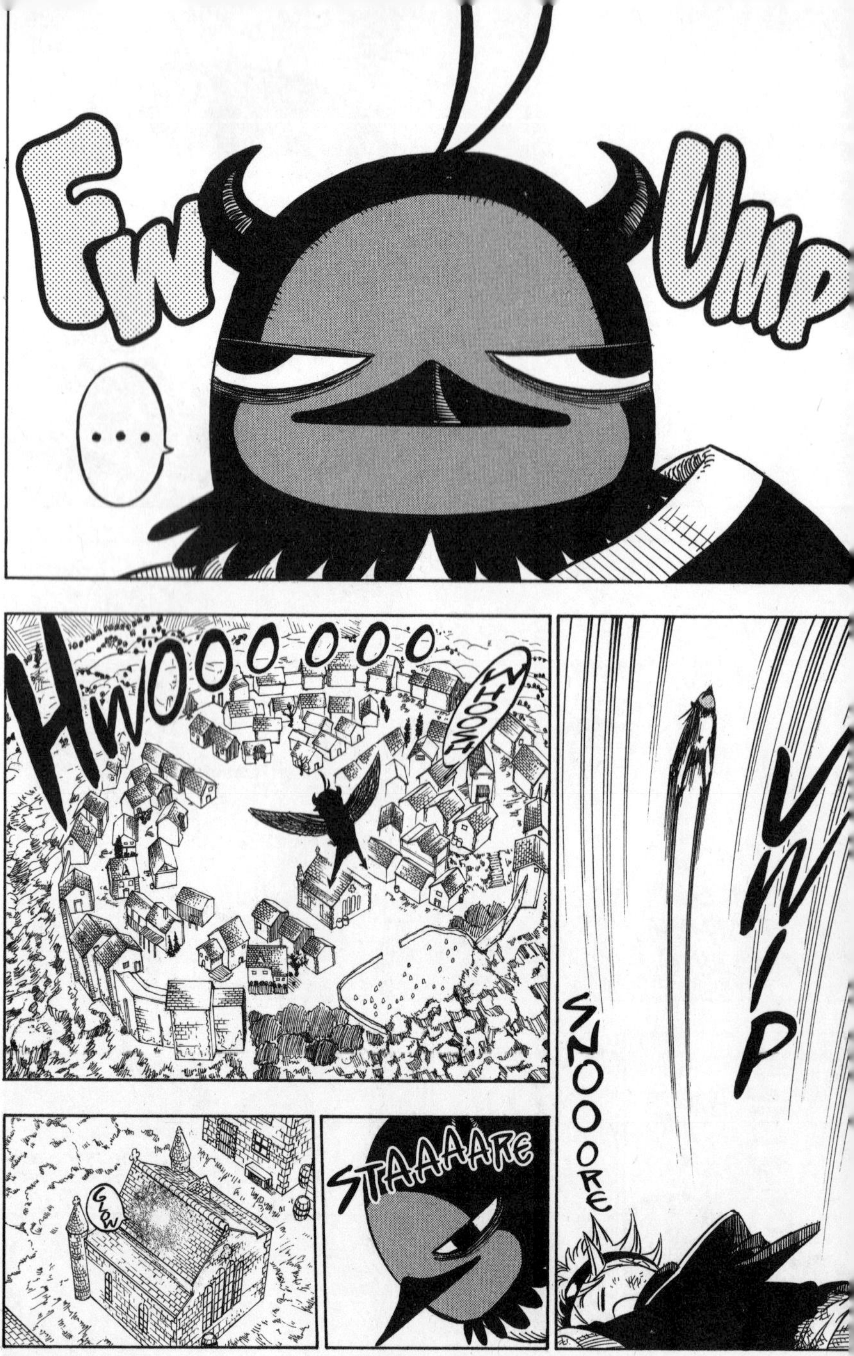
FWUMP
...
WHIP
SNOOOORE
HWOOOOOO
WHOOSH
STAAAARE
GLOW

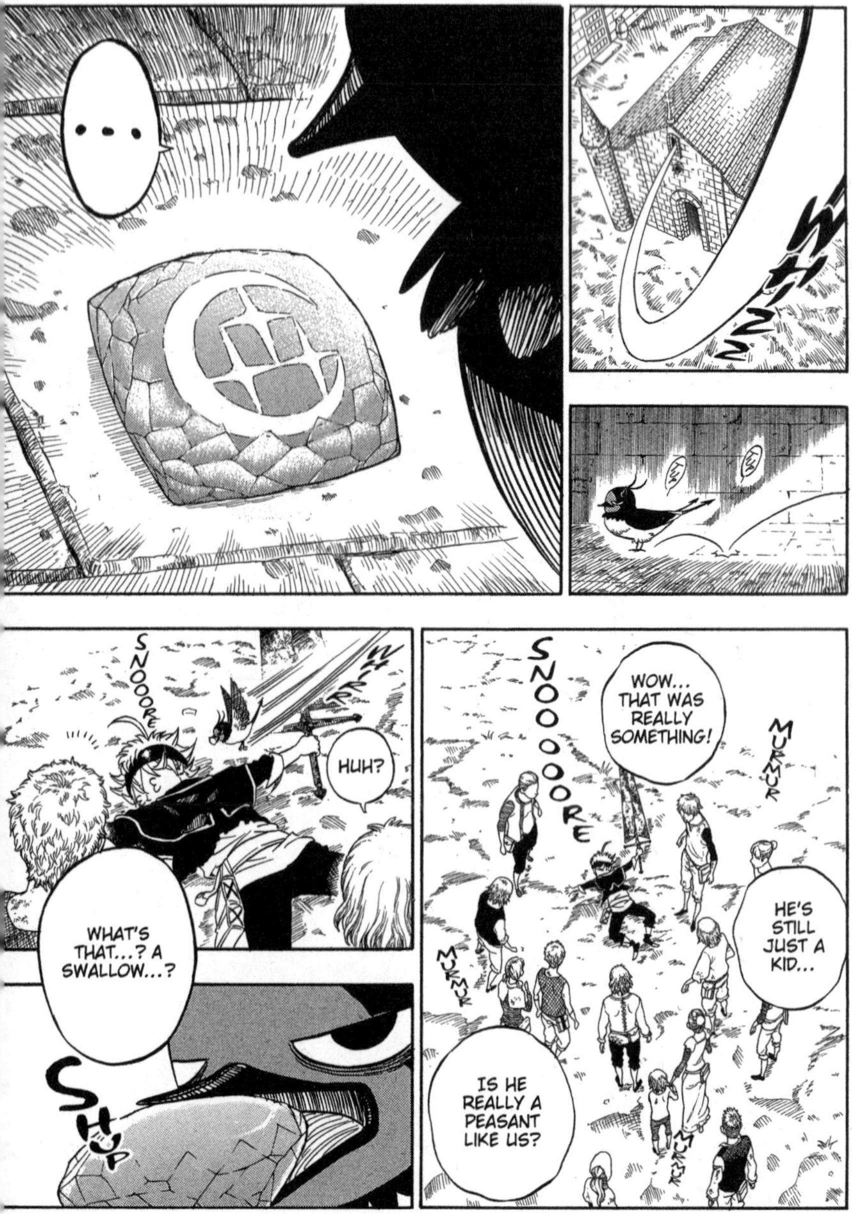
WHIZZ
...
SNOOOOOORE
WOW... THAT WAS REALLY SOMETHING!
MURMUR
HE'S STILL JUST A KID...
MURMUR
IS HE REALLY A PEASANT LIKE US?
MURMUR
SNOOORE
WHIRR
HUH?
WHAT'S THAT...? A SWALLOW...?
SHUP

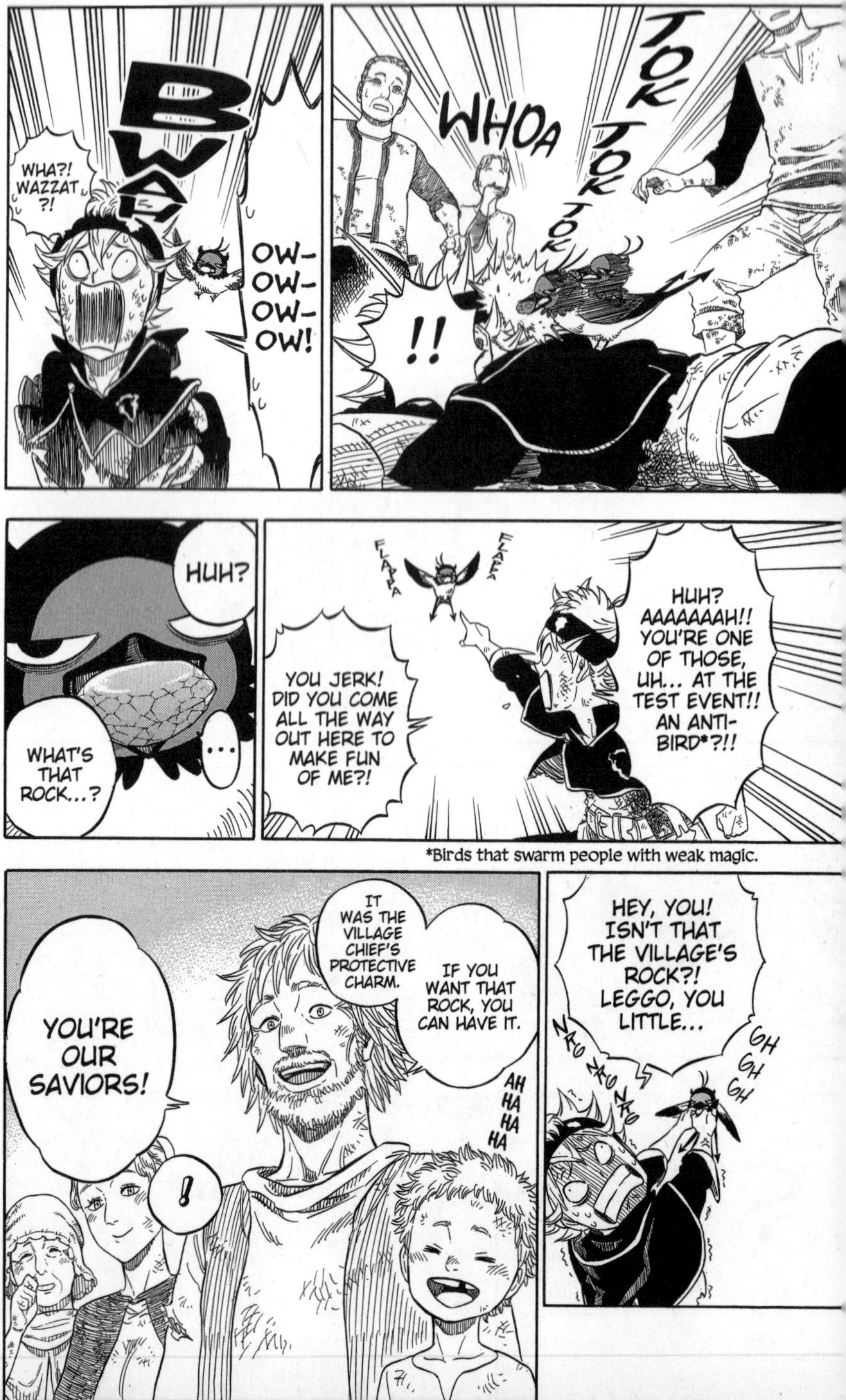
TOK TOK TOK
WHOA
!!
BWAH
OW-OW-OW-OW!
WHA?! WAZZAT?!
FLAPPA
FLAPPA
HUH? AAAAAAAH!! YOU'RE ONE OF THOSE, UH... AT THE TEST EVENT!! AN ANTI-BIRD*?!!
YOU JERK! DID YOU COME ALL THE WAY OUT HERE TO MAKE FUN OF ME?!
HUH?
...
WHAT'S THAT ROCK...?
HEY, YOU! ISN'T THAT THE VILLAGE'S ROCK?! LEGGO, YOU LITTLE...
GH GH GH
IT WAS THE VILLAGE CHIEF'S PROTECTIVE CHARM.
IF YOU WANT THAT ROCK, YOU CAN HAVE IT.
AH HA HA HA
YOU'RE OUR SAVIORS!
!

*Birds that swarm people with weak magic.

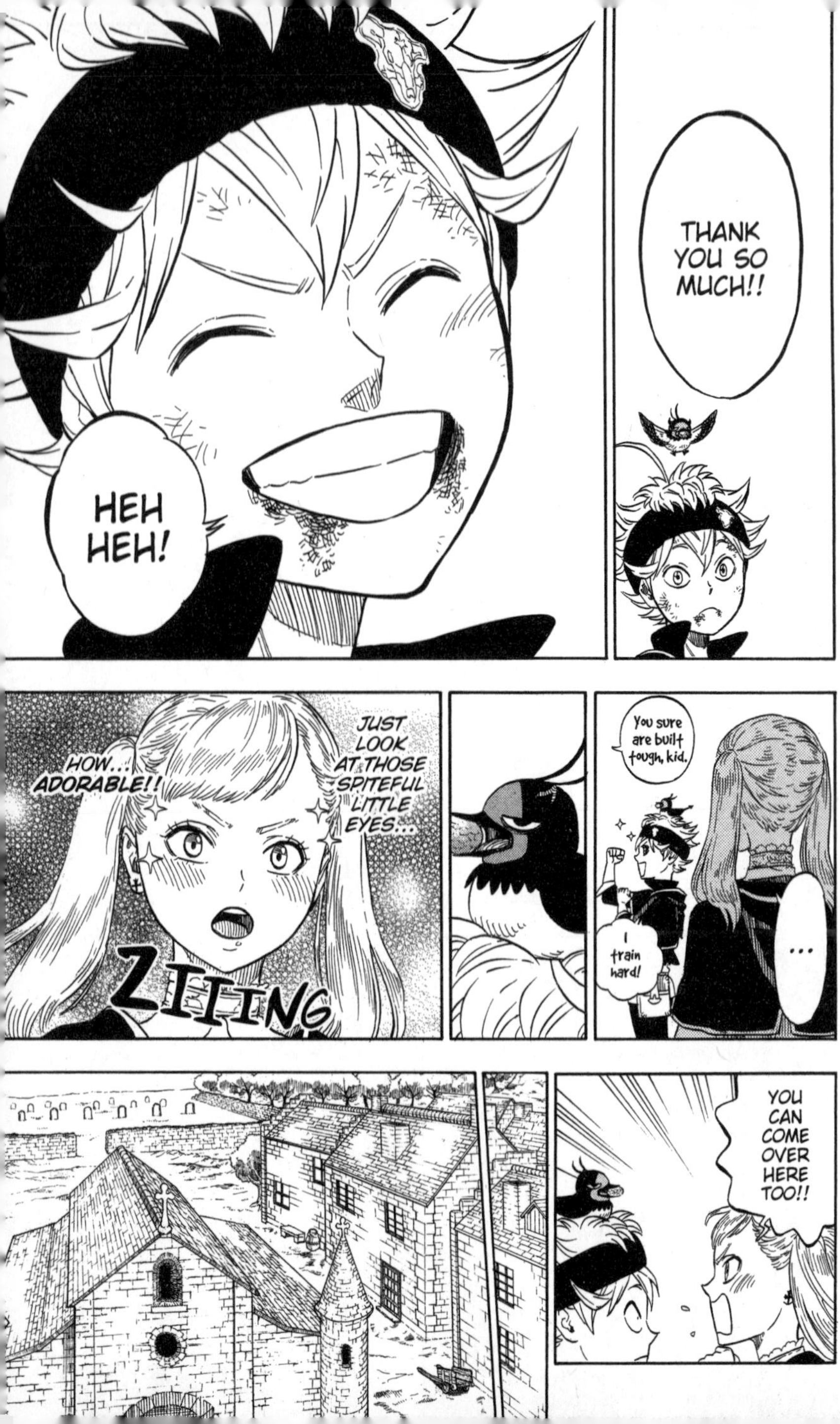
THANK YOU SO MUCH!!
HEH HEH!
You sure are built tough, kid.
I train hard!
...
JUST LOOK AT THOSE SPITEFUL LITTLE EYES...
HOW... ADORABLE!!
ZIIING
YOU CAN COME OVER HERE TOO!!

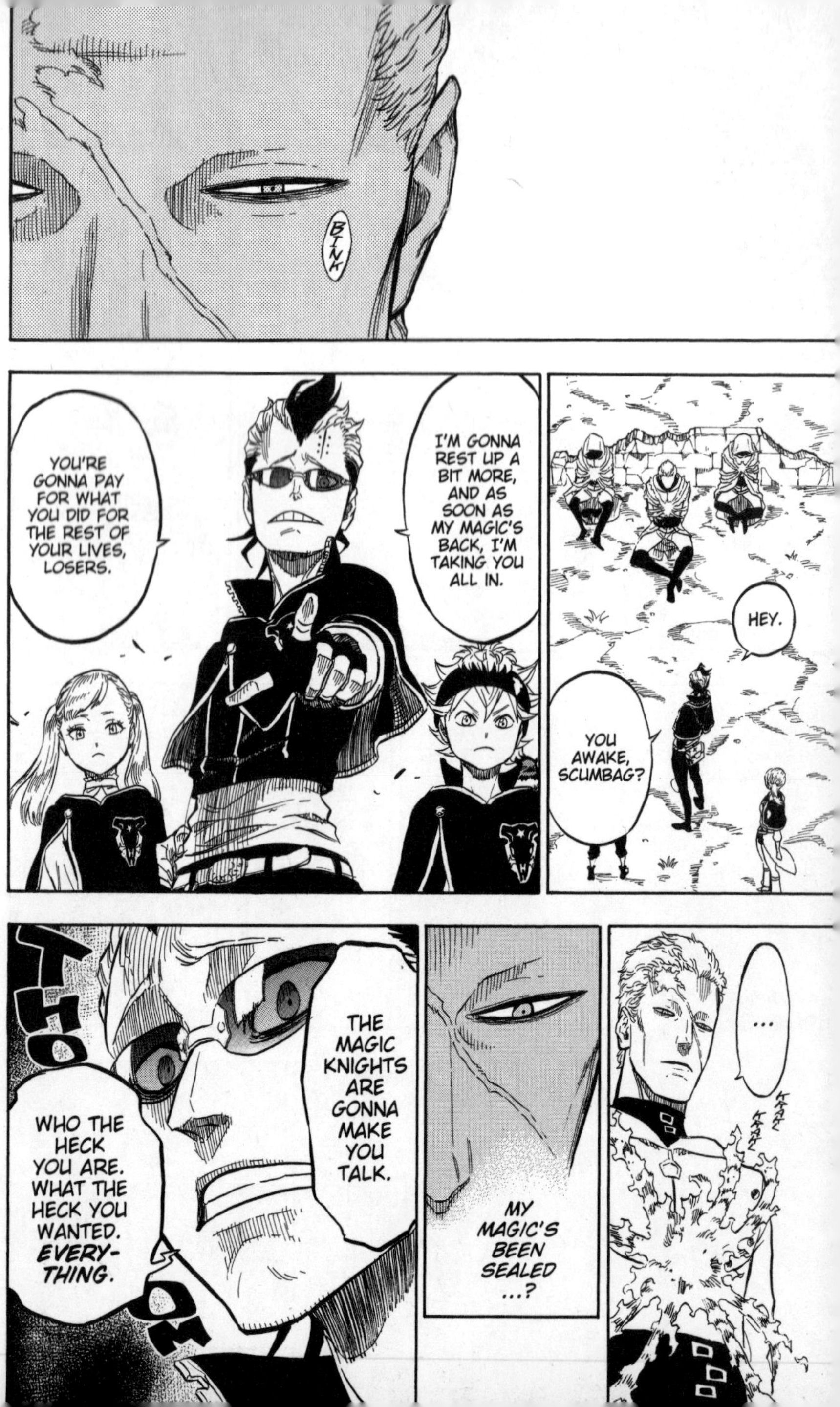
BINK
HEY.
YOU AWAKE, SCUMBAG?
I'M GONNA REST UP A BIT MORE, AND AS SOON AS MY MAGIC'S BACK, I'M TAKING YOU ALL IN.
YOU'RE GONNA PAY FOR WHAT YOU DID FOR THE REST OF YOUR LIVES, LOSERS.
...
KRAKL
KRAKL
MY MAGIC'S BEEN SEALED ...?
THE MAGIC KNIGHTS ARE GONNA MAKE YOU TALK.
WHO THE HECK YOU ARE. WHAT THE HECK YOU WANTED. *EVERYTHING*.
THOOM

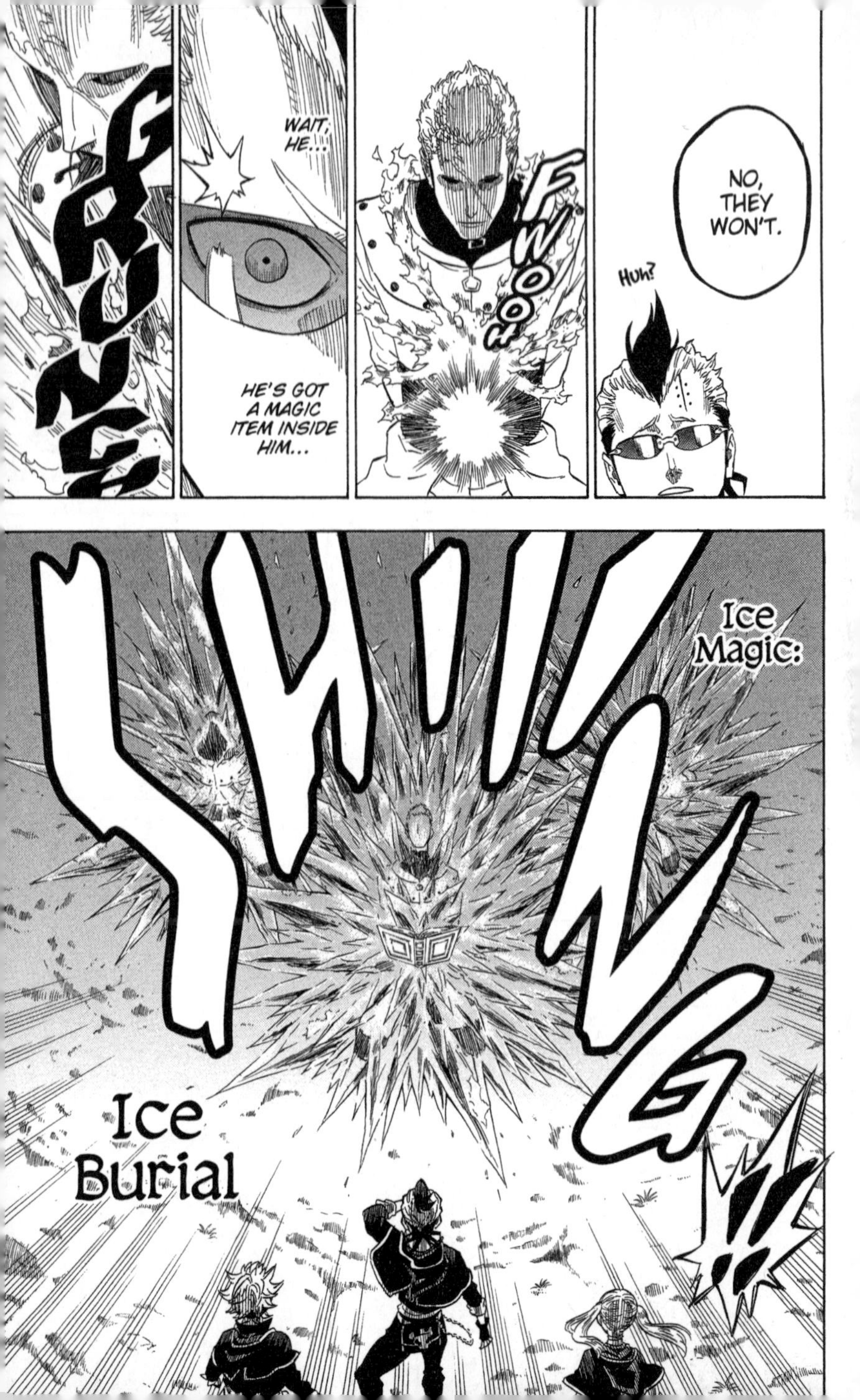
NO, THEY WON'T.
Huh?
FWOOOH
WAIT, HE...
HE'S GOT A MAGIC ITEM INSIDE HIM...
Ice Magic:
Ice Burial

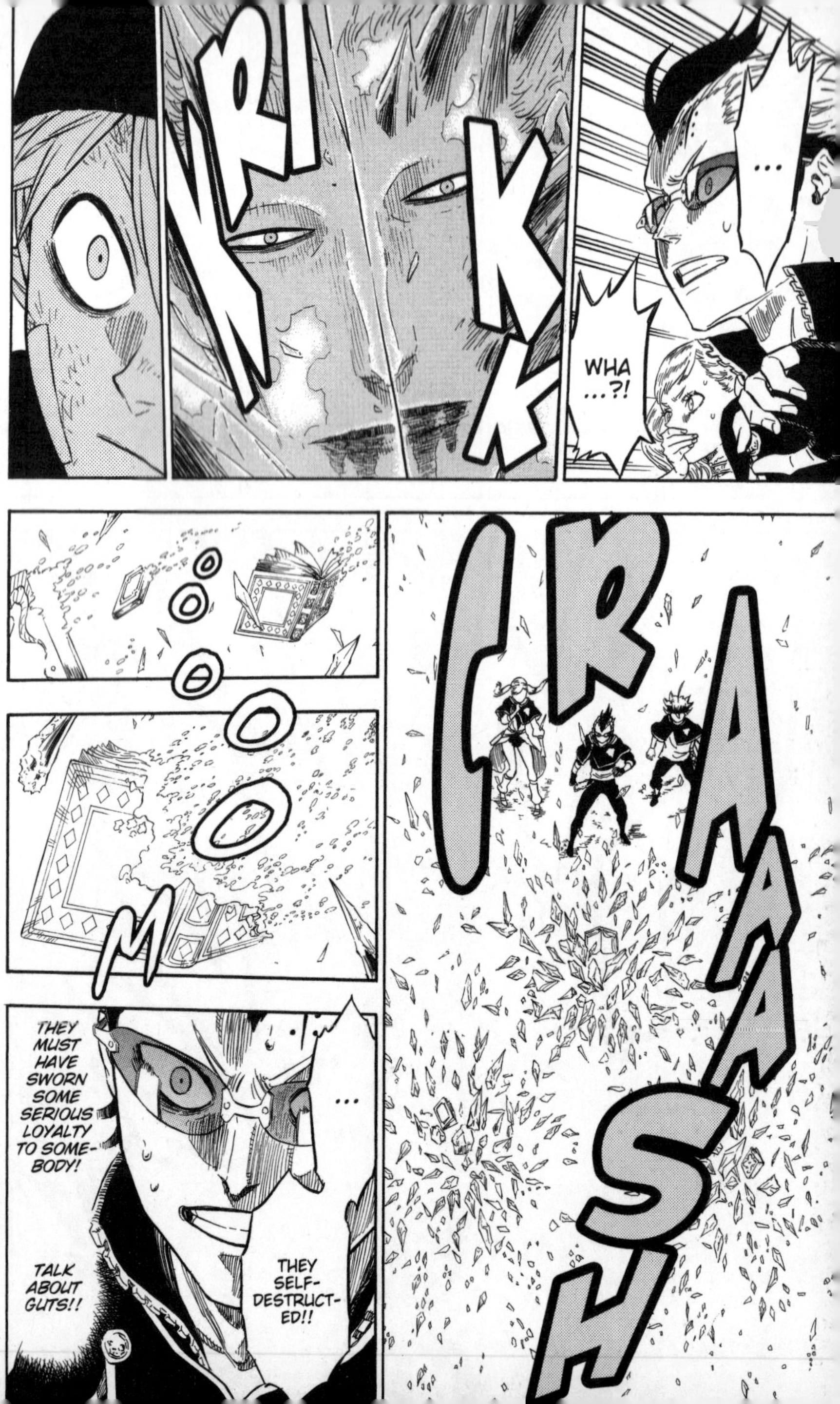
...
WHA ...?!
KRIKKK
CRAAAASH
OOOOOM
...
THEY SELF-DESTRUCTED!!
THEY MUST HAVE SWORN SOME SERIOUS LOYALTY TO SOMEBODY!
TALK ABOUT GUTS!!

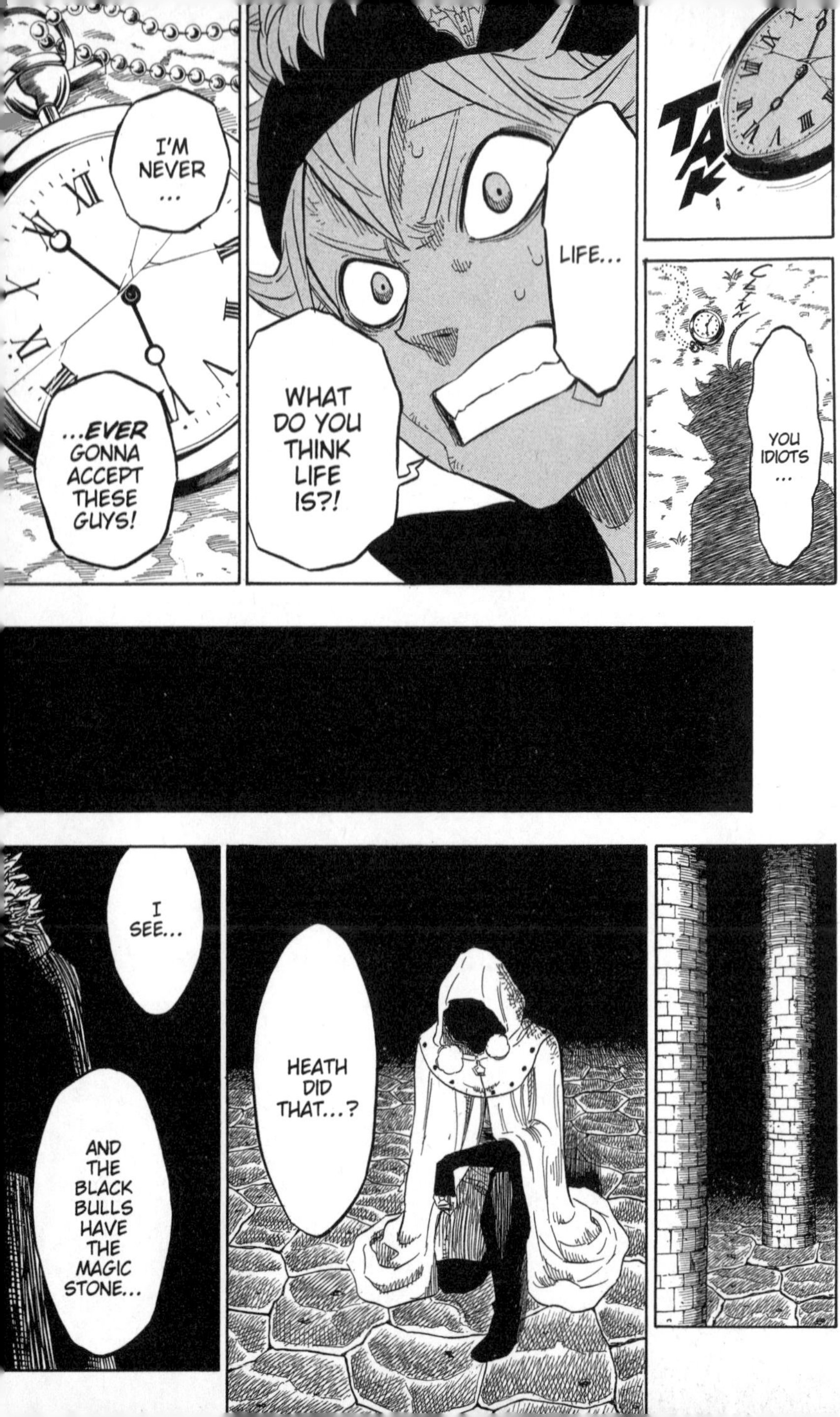
TAK
YOU IDIOTS...
LIFE...
WHAT DO YOU THINK LIFE IS?!
I'M NEVER...
...EVER GONNA ACCEPT THESE GUYS!
HEATH DID THAT...?
I SEE...
AND THE BLACK BULLS HAVE THE MAGIC STONE...

STILL, THE BLACK BULLS ARE NOTHING. WE CAN DO WHATEVER WE LIKE WITH THEM, WHENEVER WE CHOOSE.

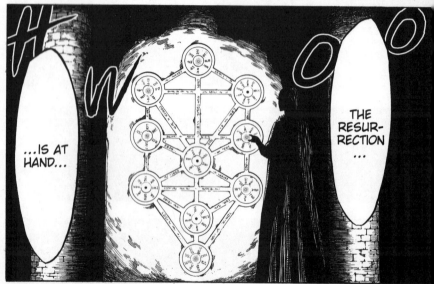

...IS AT HAND...

THE RESUR- RECTION...

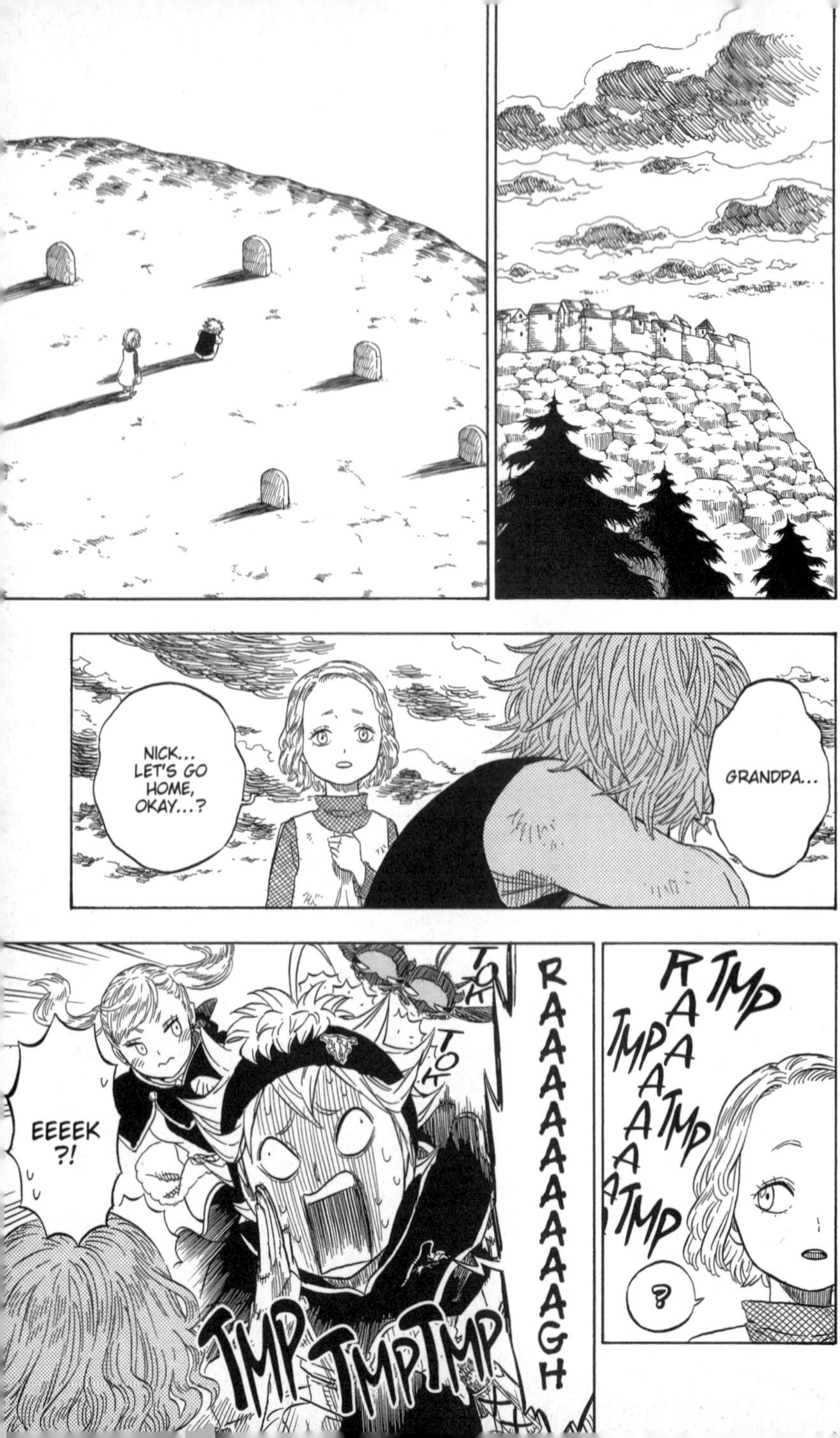
GRANDPA...
NICK... LET'S GO HOME, OKAY...?
TMP
RAAAAAA
TMPTMPTMP
?
RAAAAAAAAAAAAAGH
TOK TOK
EEEEK ?!
TMP TMPTMP

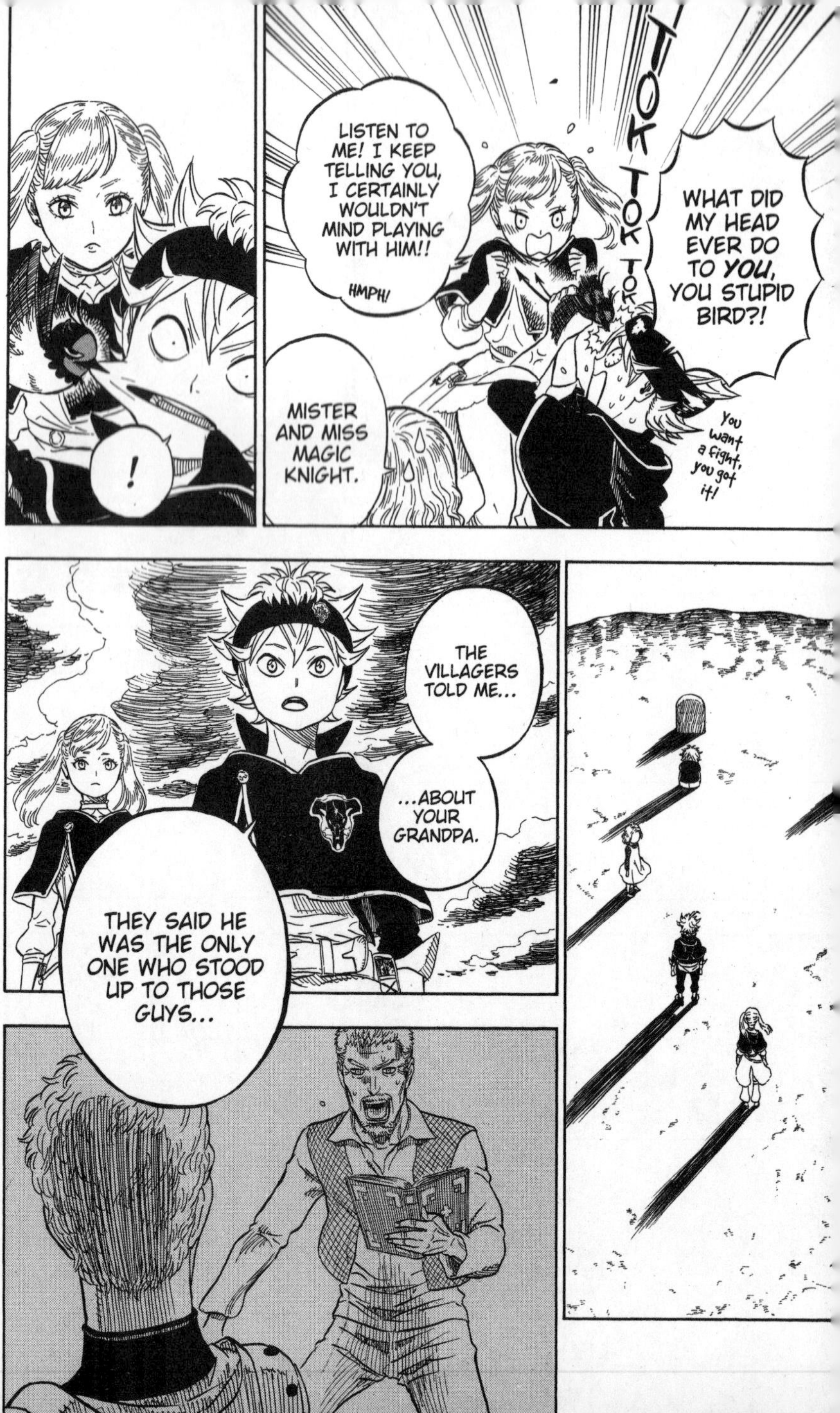
TOK TOK TOK
WHAT DID MY HEAD EVER DO TO *YOU*, YOU STUPID BIRD?!
You want a fight, you got it!
LISTEN TO ME! I KEEP TELLING YOU, I CERTAINLY WOULDN'T MIND PLAYING WITH HIM!!
HMPH!
MISTER AND MISS MAGIC KNIGHT.
!
THE VILLAGERS TOLD ME...
...ABOUT YOUR GRANDPA.
THEY SAID HE WAS THE ONLY ONE WHO STOOD UP TO THOSE GUYS...

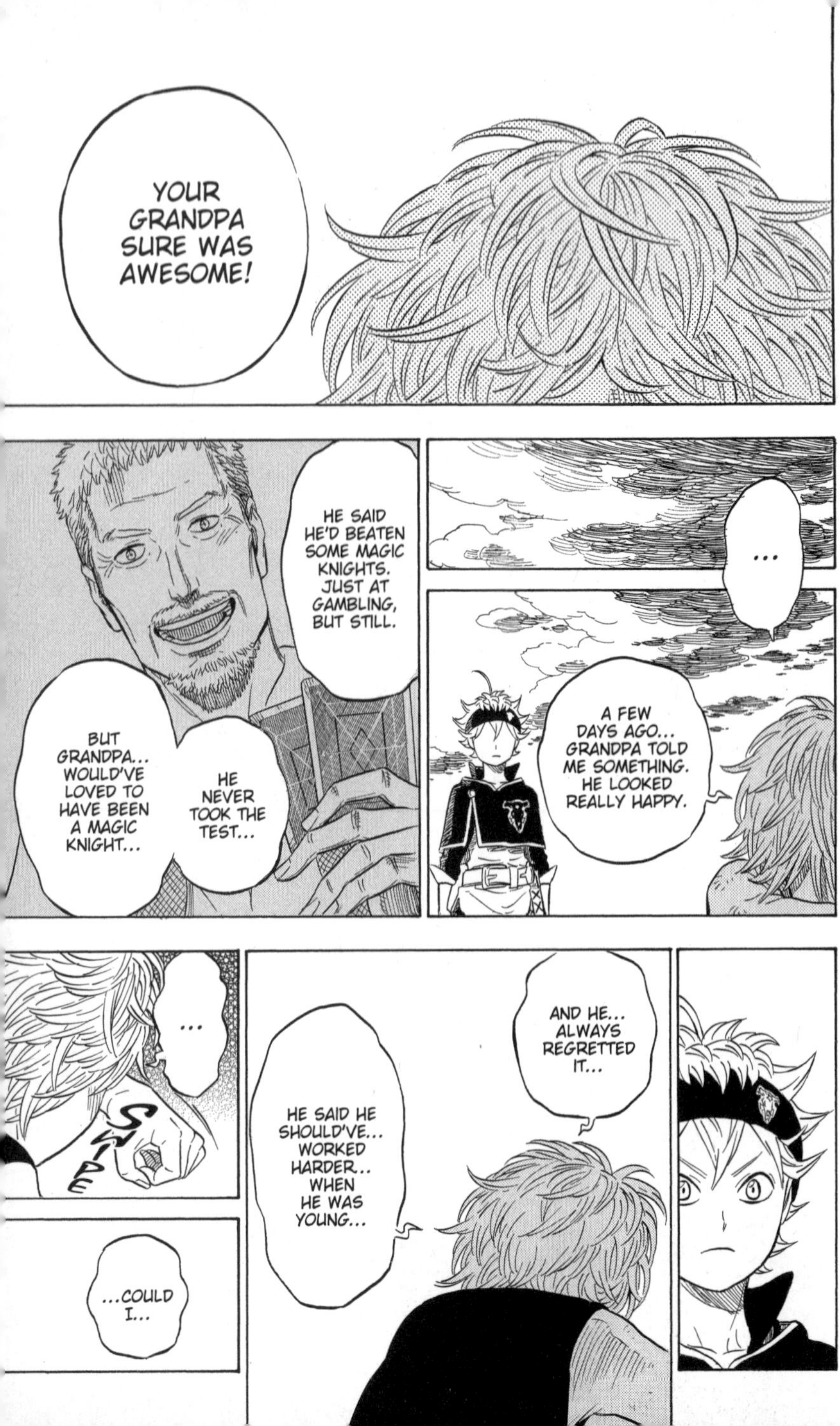
YOUR GRANDPA SURE WAS AWESOME!
...
A FEW DAYS AGO... GRANDPA TOLD ME SOMETHING. HE LOOKED REALLY HAPPY.
HE SAID HE'D BEATEN SOME MAGIC KNIGHTS. JUST AT GAMBLING, BUT STILL.
HE NEVER TOOK THE TEST...
BUT GRANDPA... WOULD'VE LOVED TO HAVE BEEN A MAGIC KNIGHT...
AND HE... ALWAYS REGRETTED IT...
HE SAID HE SHOULD'VE... WORKED HARDER.. WHEN HE WAS YOUNG...
...
SWIPE
...COULD I...

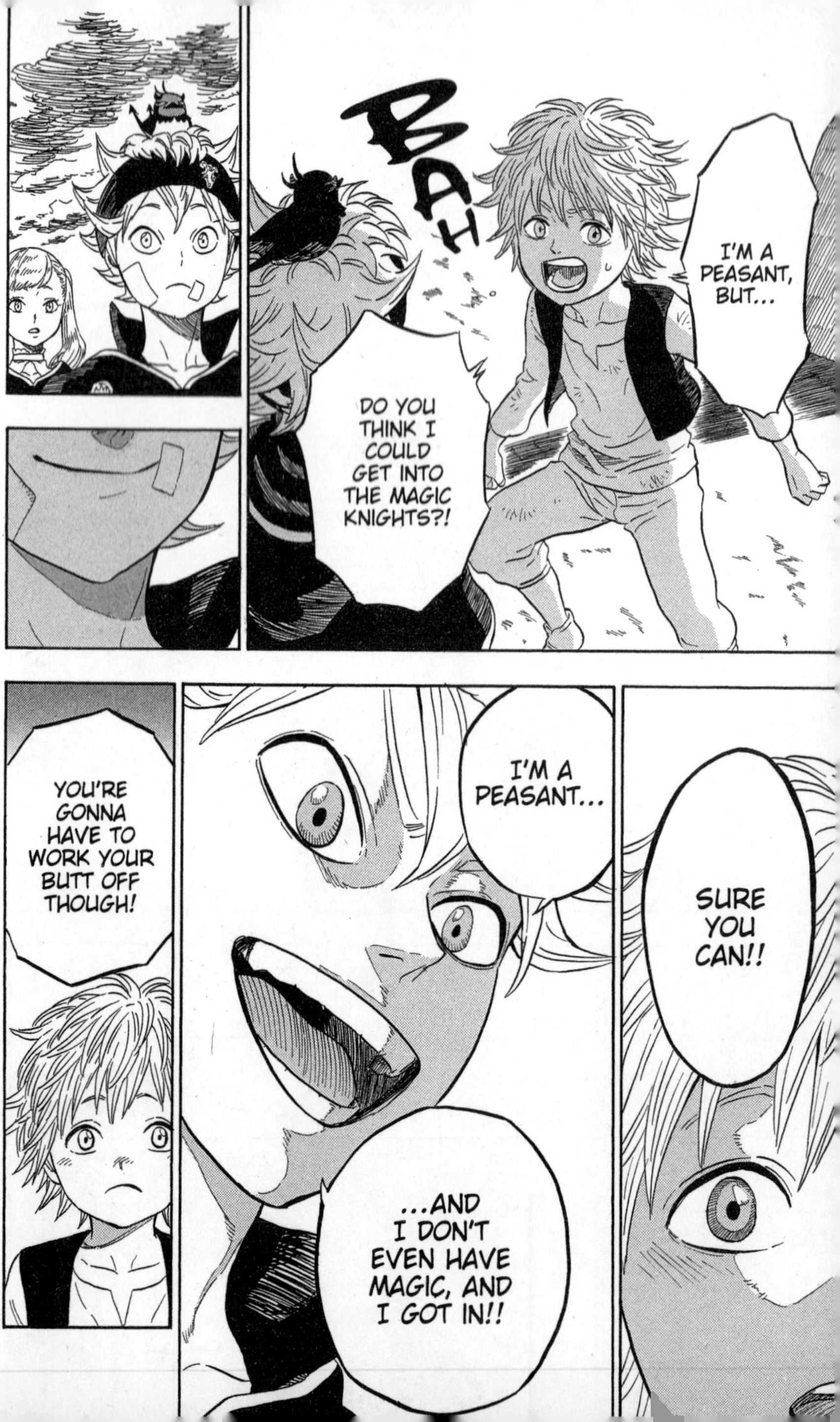
I'M A PEASANT, BUT...
BAH
DO YOU THINK I COULD GET INTO THE MAGIC KNIGHTS?!
SURE YOU CAN!!
I'M A PEASANT...
...AND I DON'T EVEN HAVE MAGIC, AND I GOT IN!!
YOU'RE GONNA HAVE TO WORK YOUR BUTT OFF THOUGH!

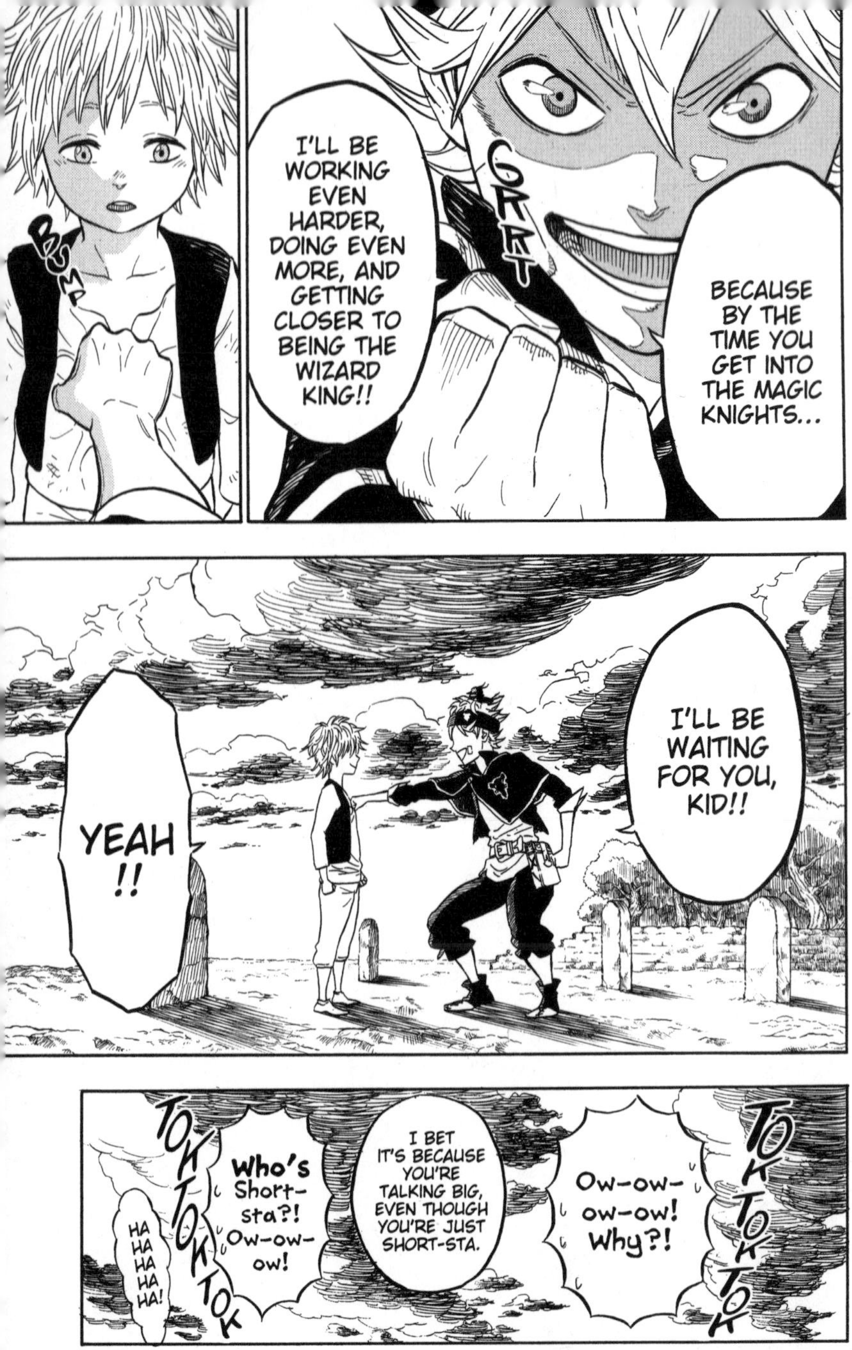
BECAUSE BY THE TIME YOU GET INTO THE MAGIC KNIGHTS...
GRRT
I'LL BE WORKING EVEN HARDER, DOING EVEN MORE, AND GETTING CLOSER TO BEING THE WIZARD KING!!
BUMP
I'LL BE WAITING FOR YOU, KID!!
YEAH!!
TOKTOKTOK
Ow-ow-ow-ow! Why?!
I BET IT'S BECAUSE YOU'RE TALKING BIG, EVEN THOUGH YOU'RE JUST SHORT-STA.
Who's Short-sta?! Ow-ow-ow!
HA HA HA HA HA!
TOKTOKTOK

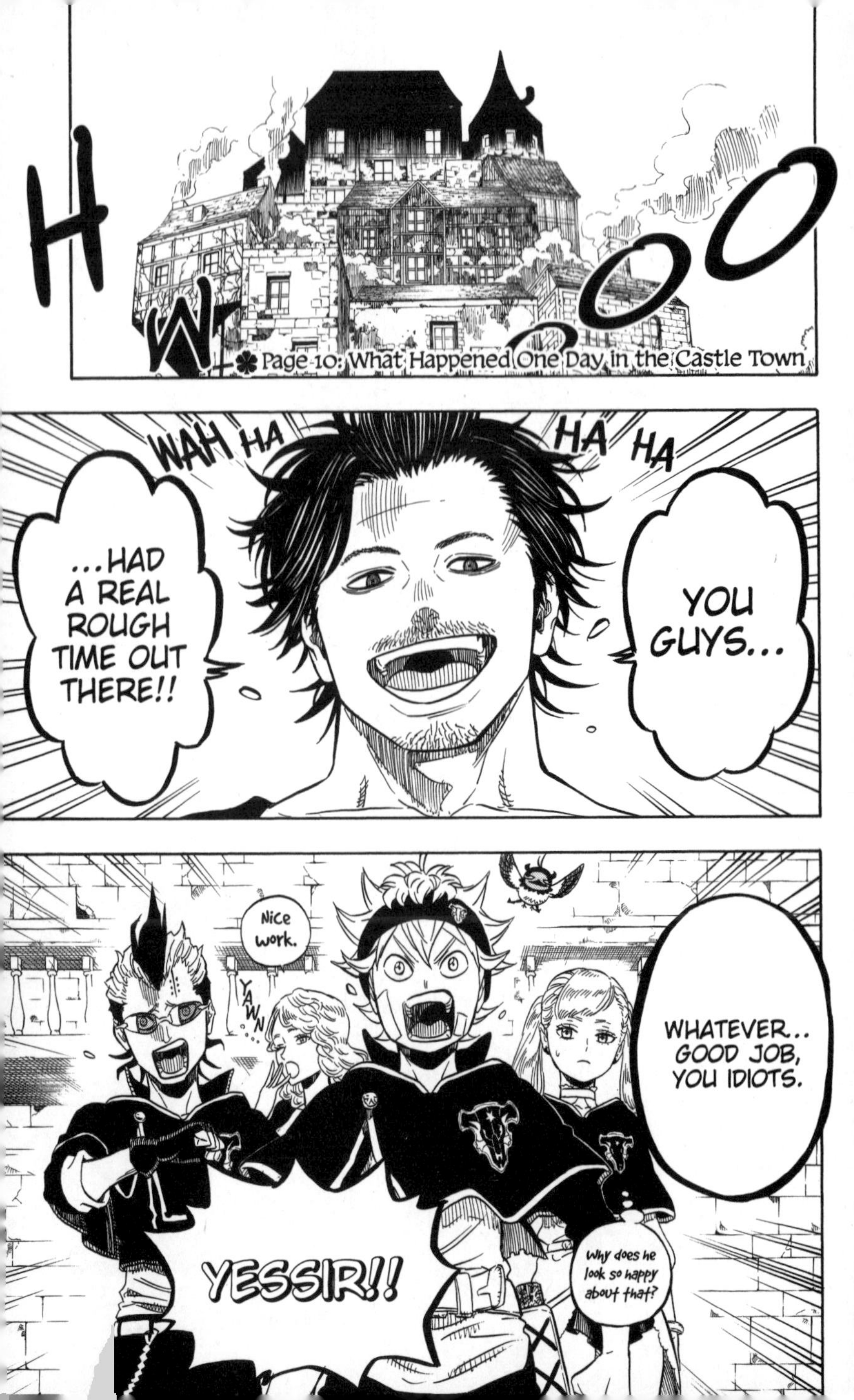
HOWOO
Page 10: What Happened One Day in the Castle Town
WAH HA HA HA
YOU GUYS...
...HAD A REAL ROUGH TIME OUT THERE!!
WHATEVER.. GOOD JOB, YOU IDIOTS.
Nice work.
YAWN
YESSIR!!
Why does he look so happy about that?

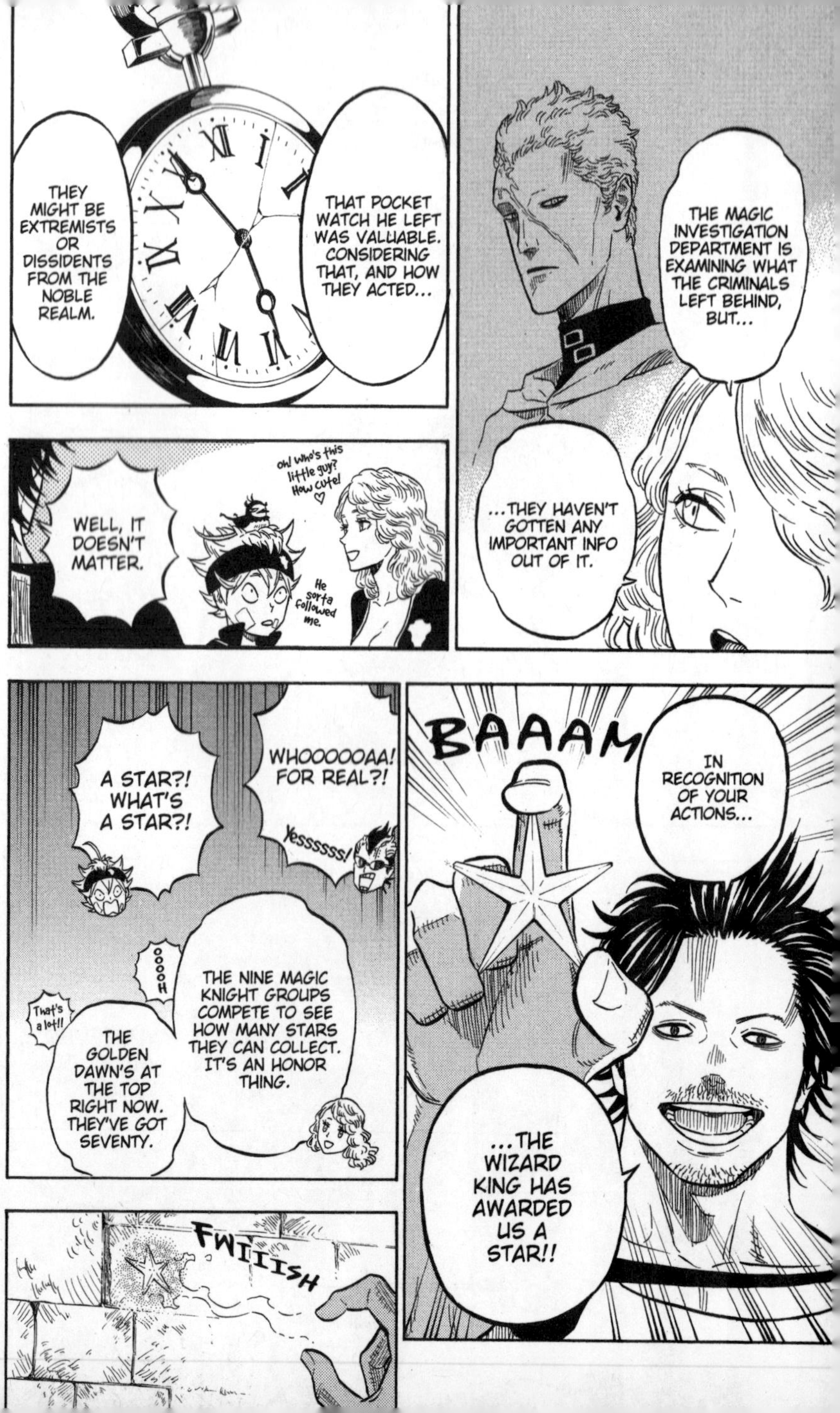
THE MAGIC INVESTIGATION DEPARTMENT IS EXAMINING WHAT THE CRIMINALS LEFT BEHIND, BUT...
...THEY HAVEN'T GOTTEN ANY IMPORTANT INFO OUT OF IT.
THAT POCKET WATCH HE LEFT WAS VALUABLE. CONSIDERING THAT, AND HOW THEY ACTED...
THEY MIGHT BE EXTREMISTS OR DISSIDENTS FROM THE NOBLE REALM.
Oh! Who's this little guy? How cute! ♡
He sorta followed me.
WELL, IT DOESN'T MATTER.
BAAAM
IN RECOGNITION OF YOUR ACTIONS...
...THE WIZARD KING HAS AWARDED US A STAR!!
WHOOOOOAA! FOR REAL?!
Yesssssss!
A STAR?! WHAT'S A STAR?!
THE NINE MAGIC KNIGHT GROUPS COMPETE TO SEE HOW MANY STARS THEY CAN COLLECT. IT'S AN HONOR THING.
OOOOH
That's a lot!!
THE GOLDEN DAWN'S AT THE TOP RIGHT NOW. THEY'VE GOT SEVENTY.
FWIIIISH

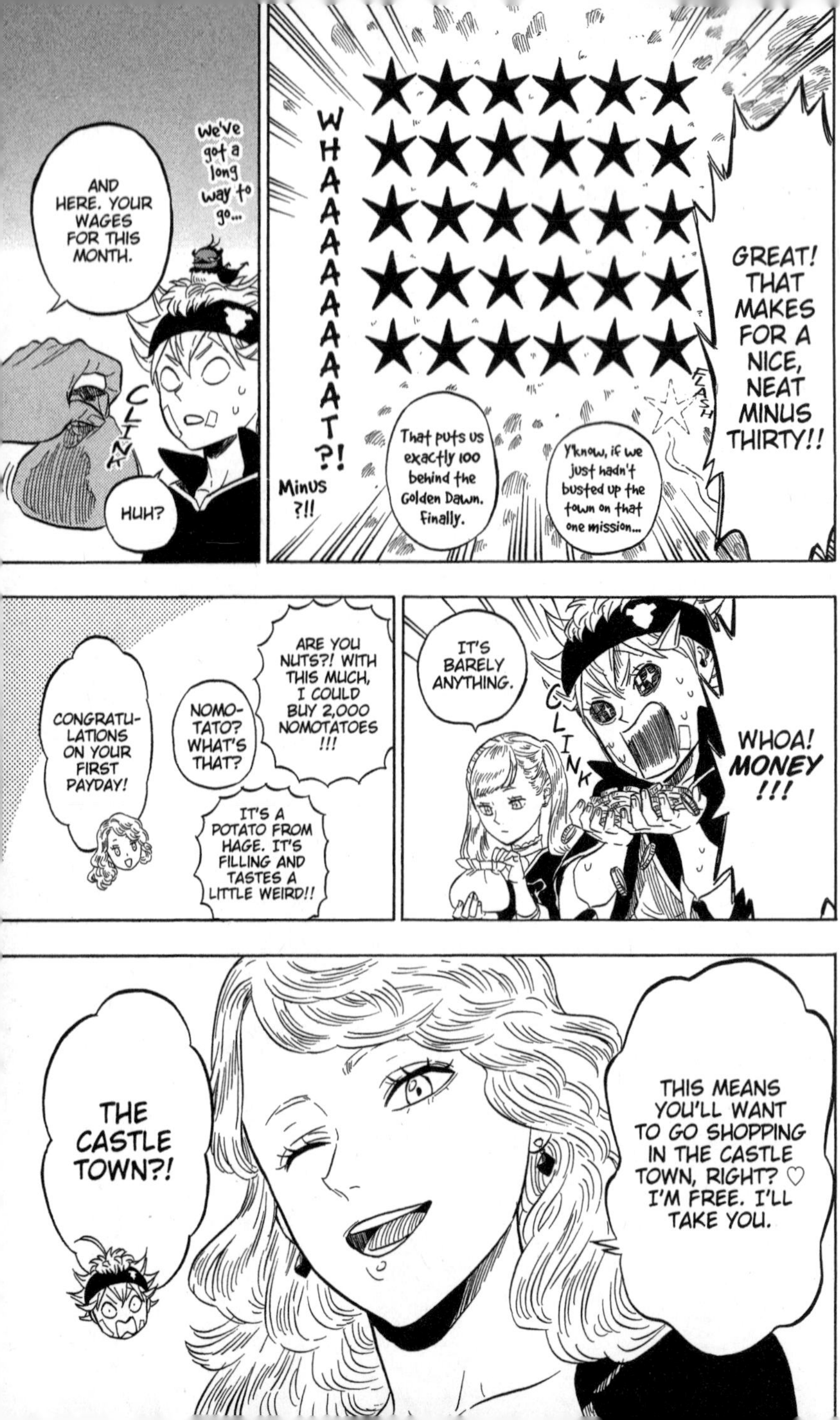

GREAT! THAT MAKES FOR A NICE, NEAT MINUS THIRTY!!
FLASH
Y'know, if we just hadn't busted up the town on that one mission...
That puts us exactly 100 behind the Golden Dawn. Finally.
WHAAAAAAAAAAT?!
Minus ?!!
we've got a long way to go...
AND HERE. YOUR WAGES FOR THIS MONTH.
CLINK
HUH?
WHOA! MONEY!!!
CLINK
IT'S BARELY ANYTHING.
ARE YOU NUTS?! WITH THIS MUCH, I COULD BUY 2,000 NOMOTATOES!!!
NOMO-TATO? WHAT'S THAT?
IT'S A POTATO FROM HAGE. IT'S FILLING AND TASTES A LITTLE WEIRD!!
CONGRATULATIONS ON YOUR FIRST PAYDAY!
THIS MEANS YOU'LL WANT TO GO SHOPPING IN THE CASTLE TOWN, RIGHT? ♡ I'M FREE. I'LL TAKE YOU.
THE CASTLE TOWN?!

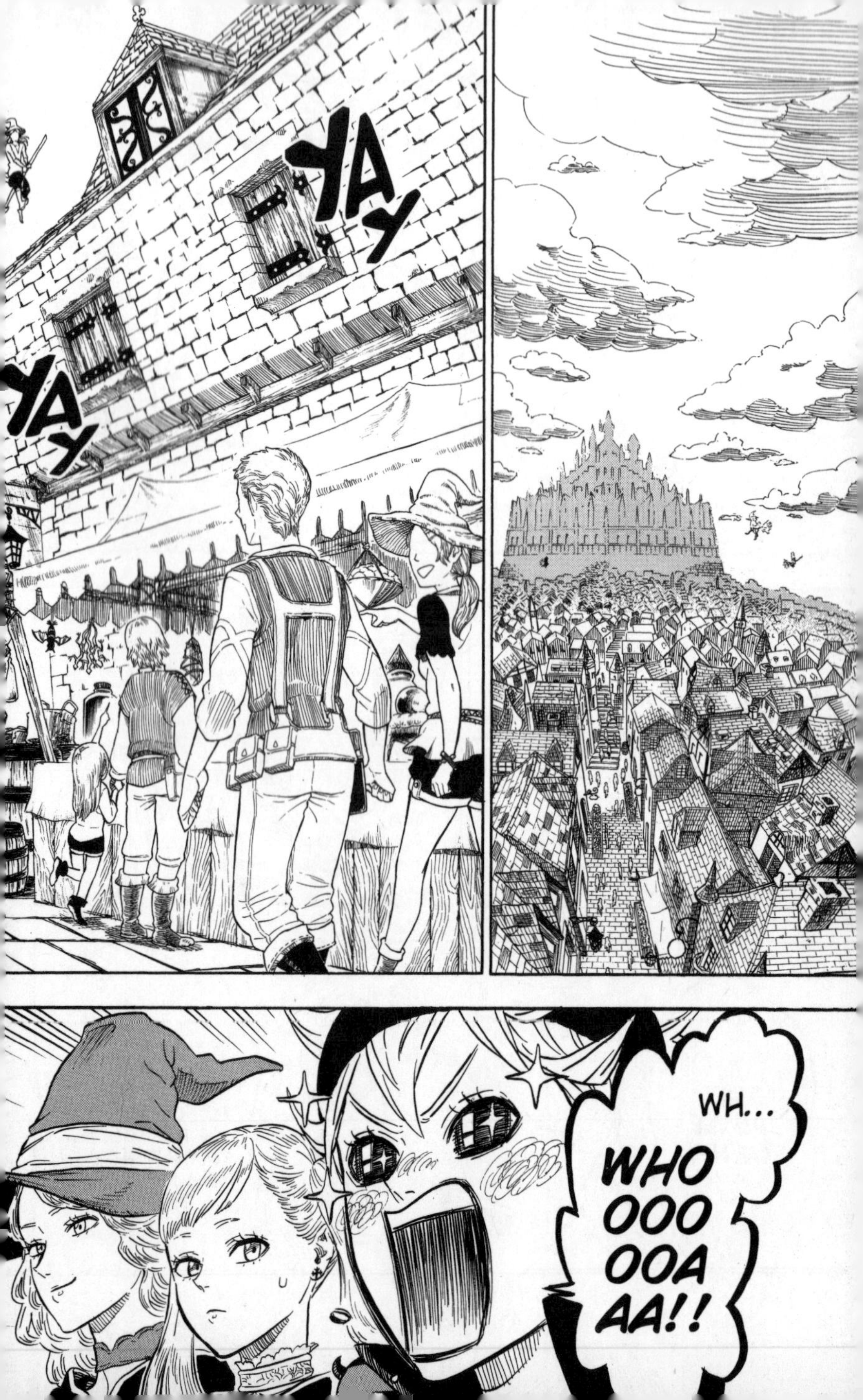
YAY
YAY
WH...
WHOOOOOOAAA!!

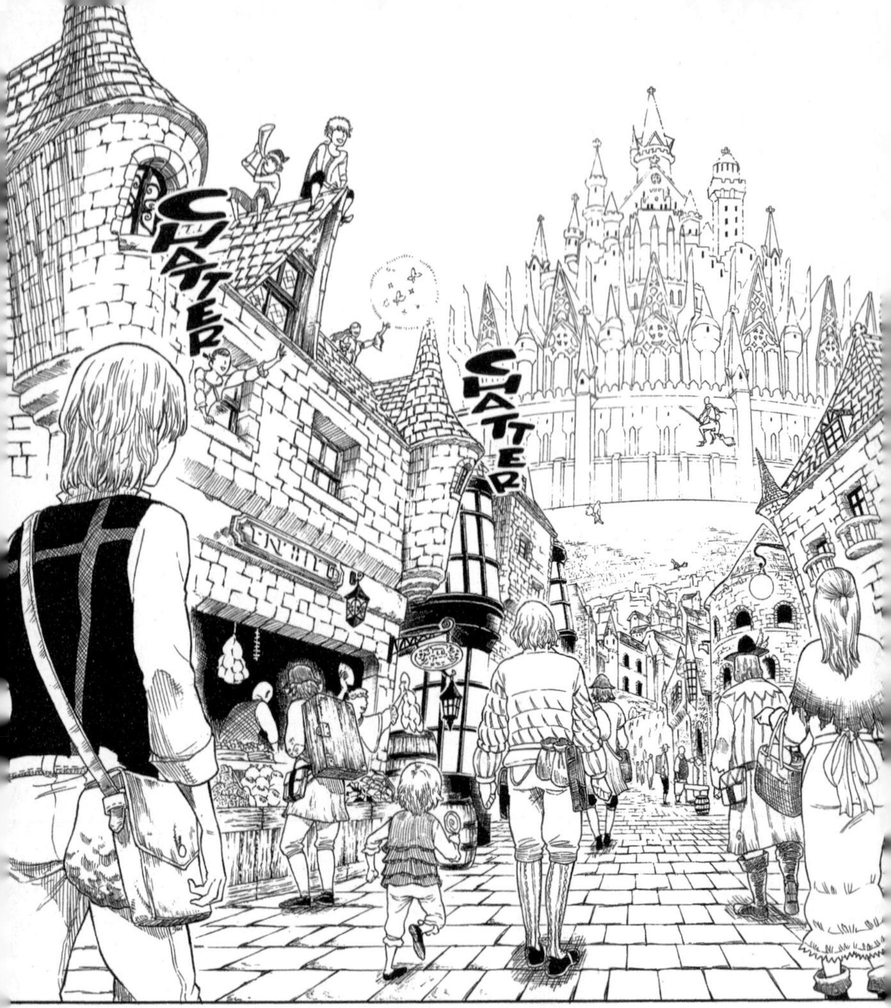
CHATTER
CHATTER

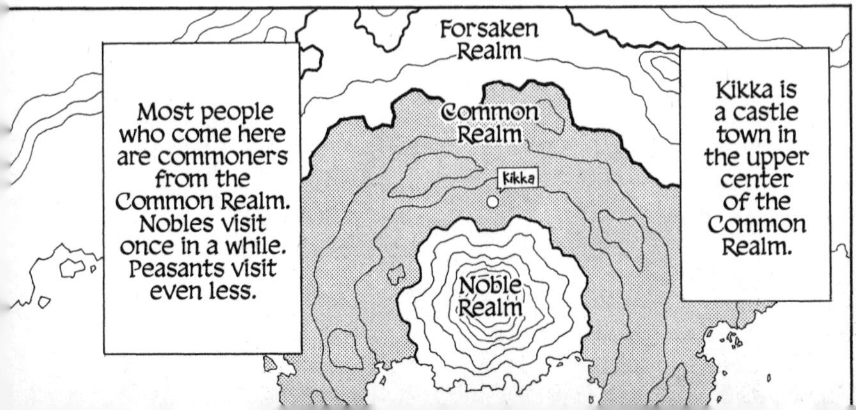
Kikka is a castle town in the upper center of the Common Realm.
Forsaken Realm
Common Realm
Kikka
Noble Realm
Most people who come here are commoners from the Common Realm. Nobles visit once in a while. Peasants visit even less.

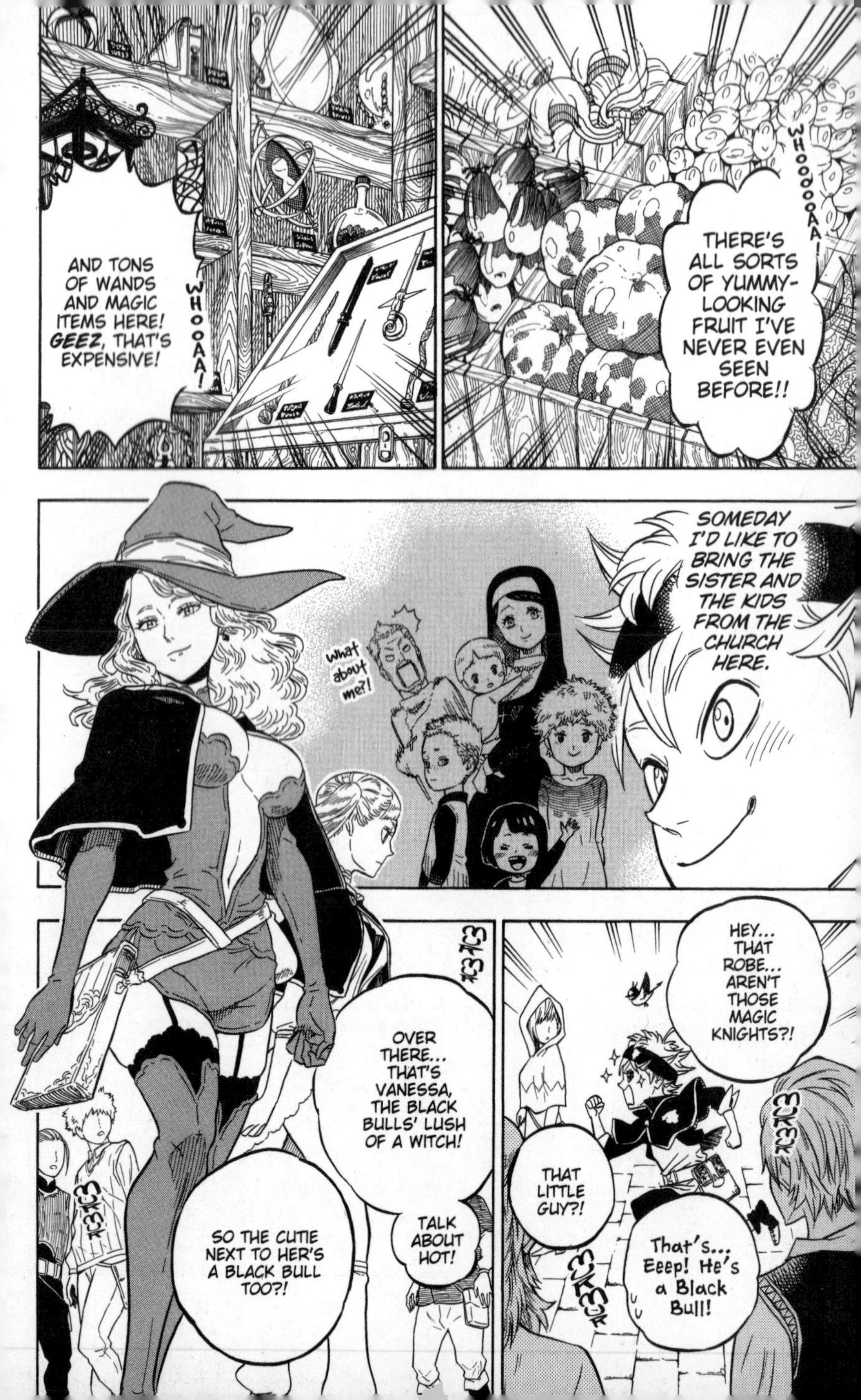
WHOOOOAA!
THERE'S ALL SORTS OF YUMMY-LOOKING FRUIT I'VE NEVER EVEN SEEN BEFORE!!
WHOOAA!
AND TONS OF WANDS AND MAGIC ITEMS HERE! GEEZ, THAT'S EXPENSIVE!
SOMEDAY I'D LIKE TO BRING THE SISTER AND THE KIDS FROM THE CHURCH HERE.
what about me?!
HEY... THAT ROBE... AREN'T THOSE MAGIC KNIGHTS?!
THAT LITTLE GUY?!
That's... Eeep! He's a Black Bull!
OVER THERE... THAT'S VANESSA, THE BLACK BULLS' LUSH OF A WITCH!
TALK ABOUT HOT!
SO THE CUTIE NEXT TO HER'S A BLACK BULL TOO?!

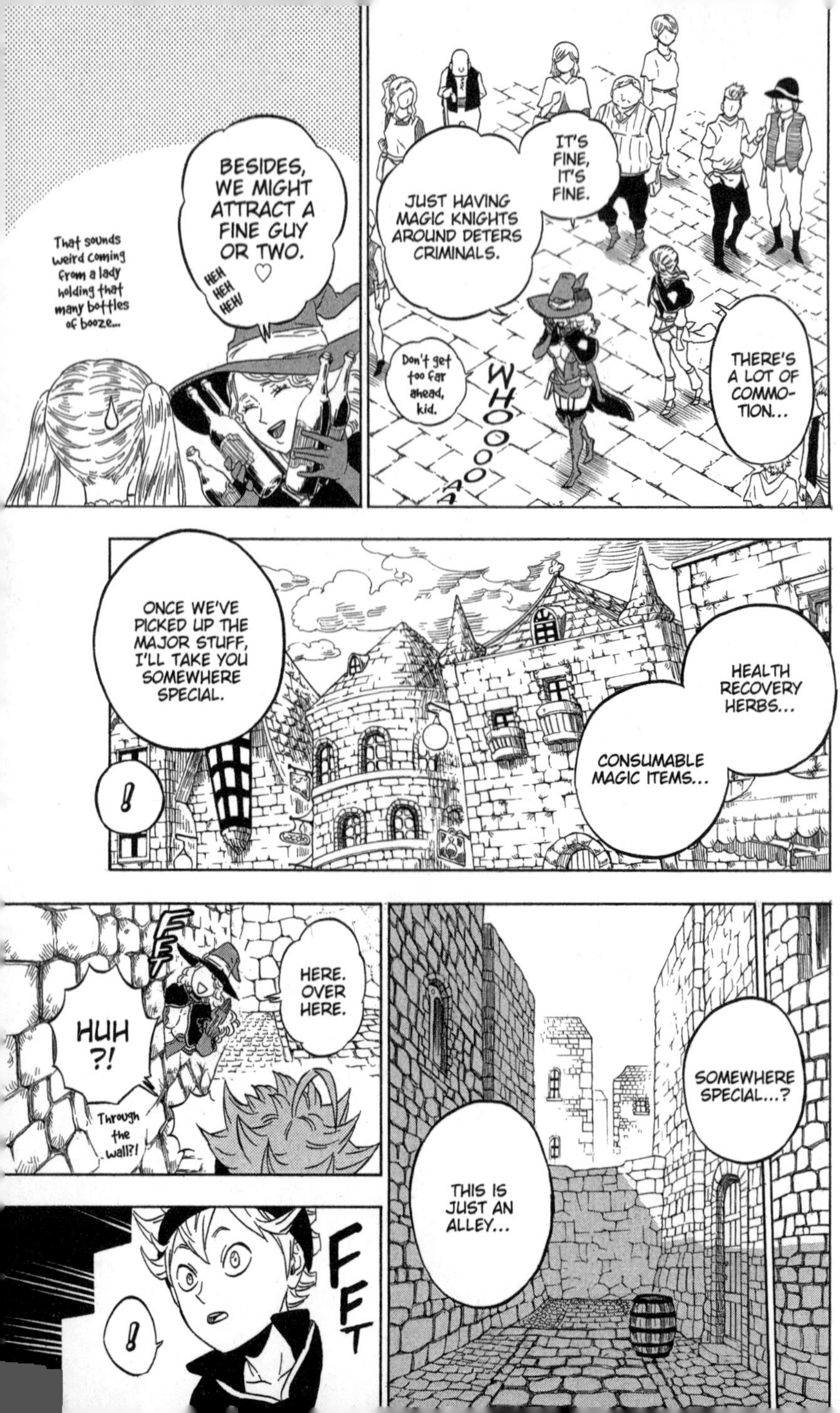
IT'S FINE, IT'S FINE.
JUST HAVING MAGIC KNIGHTS AROUND DETERS CRIMINALS.
THERE'S A LOT OF COMMOTION...
Don't get too far ahead, kid.
WHOOOOOA
BESIDES, WE MIGHT ATTRACT A FINE GUY OR TWO. ♡
HEH HEH HEH!
That sounds weird coming from a lady holding that many bottles of booze...
HEALTH RECOVERY HERBS...
CONSUMABLE MAGIC ITEMS...
ONCE WE'VE PICKED UP THE MAJOR STUFF, I'LL TAKE YOU SOMEWHERE SPECIAL.
!
SOMEWHERE SPECIAL...?
THIS IS JUST AN ALLEY...
HERE. OVER HERE.
FFT
HUH ?!
Through the wall?!
FFT
!

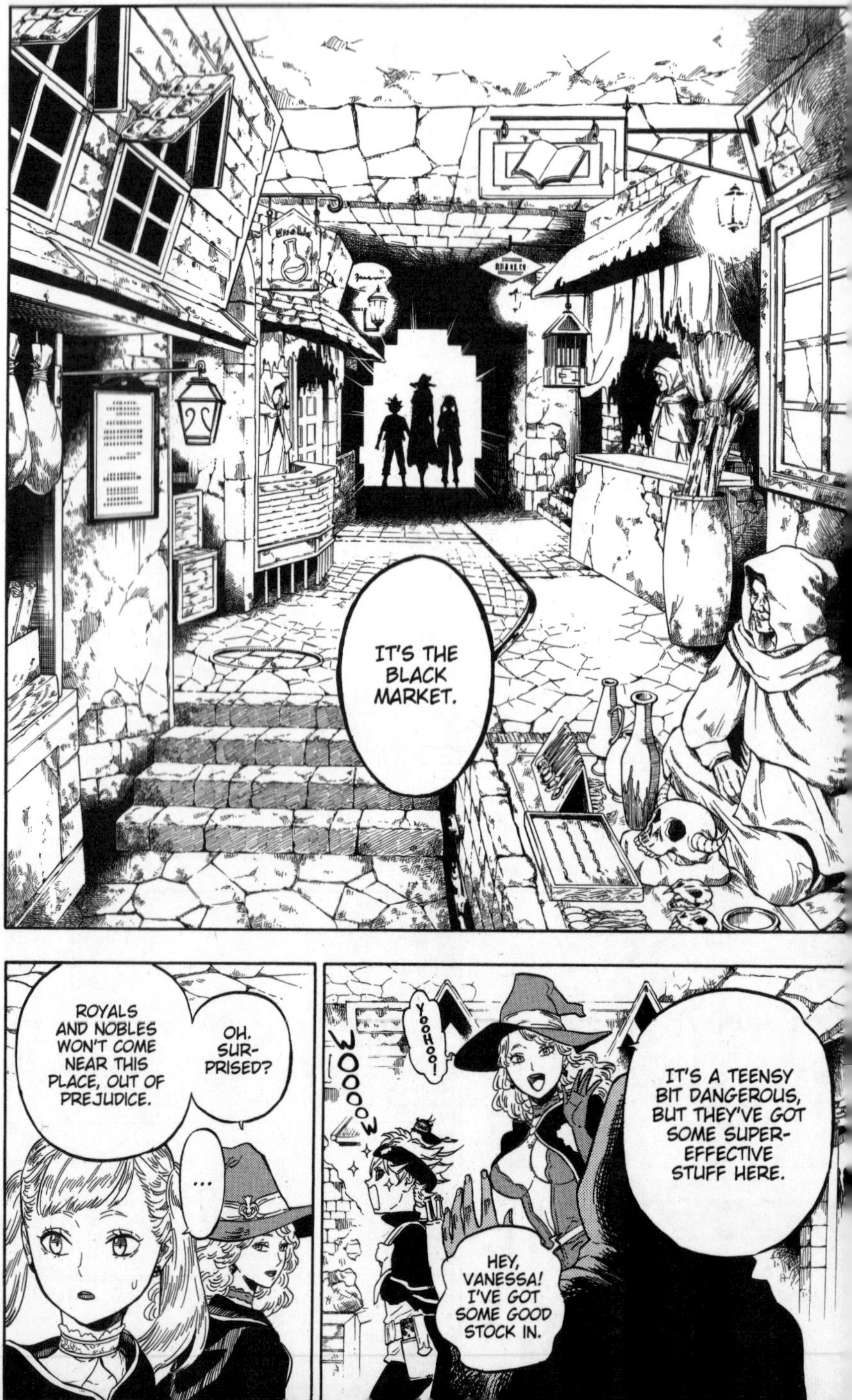
IT'S THE BLACK MARKET.
IT'S A TEENSY BIT DANGEROUS, BUT THEY'VE GOT SOME SUPER-EFFECTIVE STUFF HERE.
YOOHOO!
WOOOOOW
HEY, VANESSA! I'VE GOT SOME GOOD STOCK IN.
OH. SUR-PRISED?
ROYALS AND NOBLES WON'T COME NEAR THIS PLACE, OUT OF PREJUDICE.
...

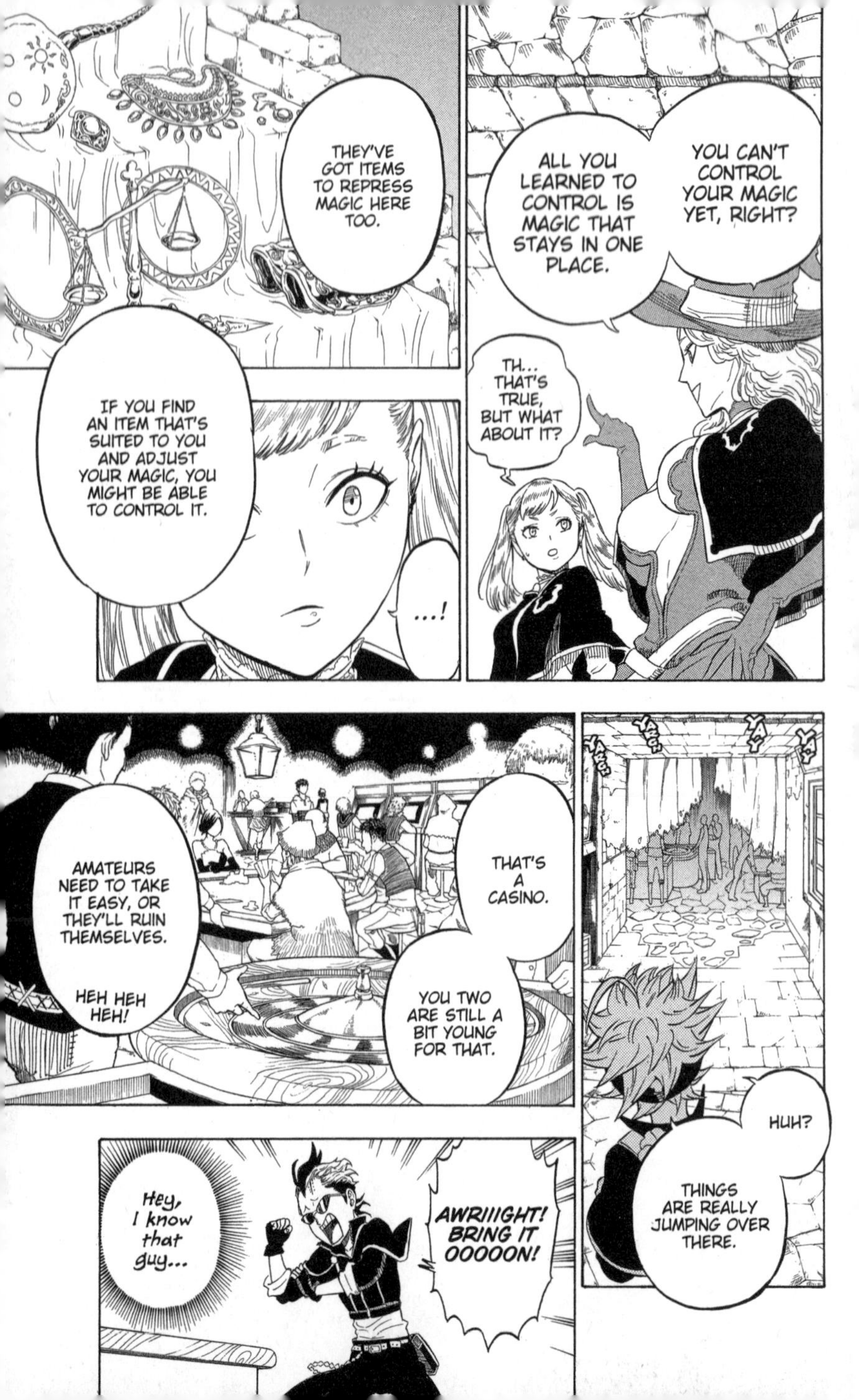
YOU CAN'T CONTROL YOUR MAGIC YET, RIGHT?
ALL YOU LEARNED TO CONTROL IS MAGIC THAT STAYS IN ONE PLACE.
TH... THAT'S TRUE, BUT WHAT ABOUT IT?
THEY'VE GOT ITEMS TO REPRESS MAGIC HERE TOO.
IF YOU FIND AN ITEM THAT'S SUITED TO YOU AND ADJUST YOUR MAGIC, YOU MIGHT BE ABLE TO CONTROL IT.
...!
YAY
YAY
YARGH
YARGH
HUH?
THINGS ARE REALLY JUMPING OVER THERE.
THAT'S A CASINO.
YOU TWO ARE STILL A BIT YOUNG FOR THAT.
AMATEURS NEED TO TAKE IT EASY, OR THEY'LL RUIN THEMSELVES.
HEH HEH HEH!
AWRIIIGHT! BRING IT OOOOON!
Hey, I know that guy...

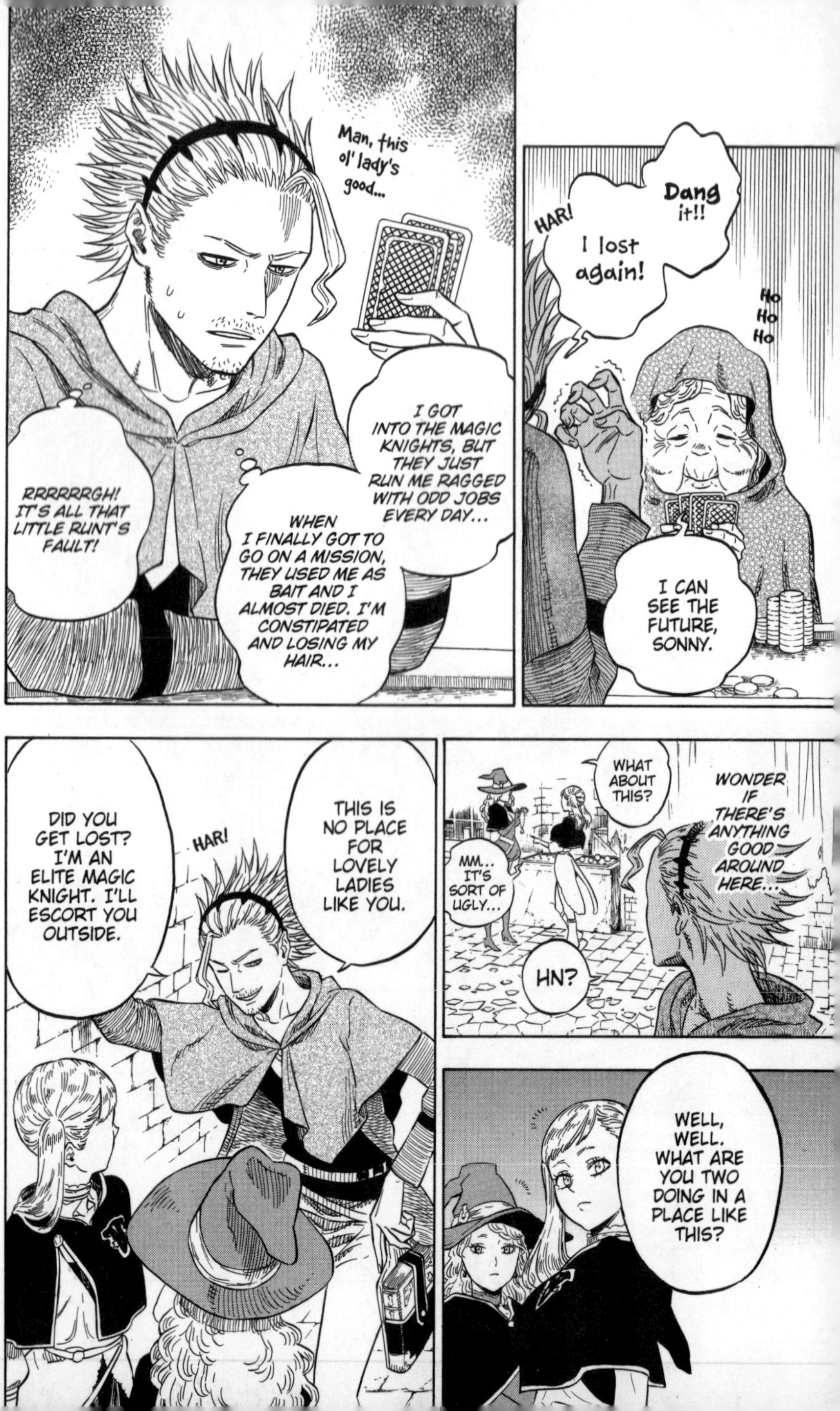
Dang it!! I lost again!
HAR!
Ho Ho Ho
I CAN SEE THE FUTURE, SONNY.
Man, this ol' lady's good...
I GOT INTO THE MAGIC KNIGHTS, BUT THEY JUST RUN ME RAGGED WITH ODD JOBS EVERY DAY...
WHEN I FINALLY GOT TO GO ON A MISSION, THEY USED ME AS BAIT AND I ALMOST DIED. I'M CONSTIPATED AND LOSING MY HAIR...
RRRRRRGH! IT'S ALL THAT LITTLE RUNT'S FAULT!
WONDER IF THERE'S ANYTHING GOOD AROUND HERE...
WHAT ABOUT THIS?
MM.. IT'S SORT OF UGLY...
HN?
WELL, WELL. WHAT ARE YOU TWO DOING IN A PLACE LIKE THIS?
THIS IS NO PLACE FOR LOVELY LADIES LIKE YOU.
HAR!
DID YOU GET LOST? I'M AN ELITE MAGIC KNIGHT. I'LL ESCORT YOU OUTSIDE.

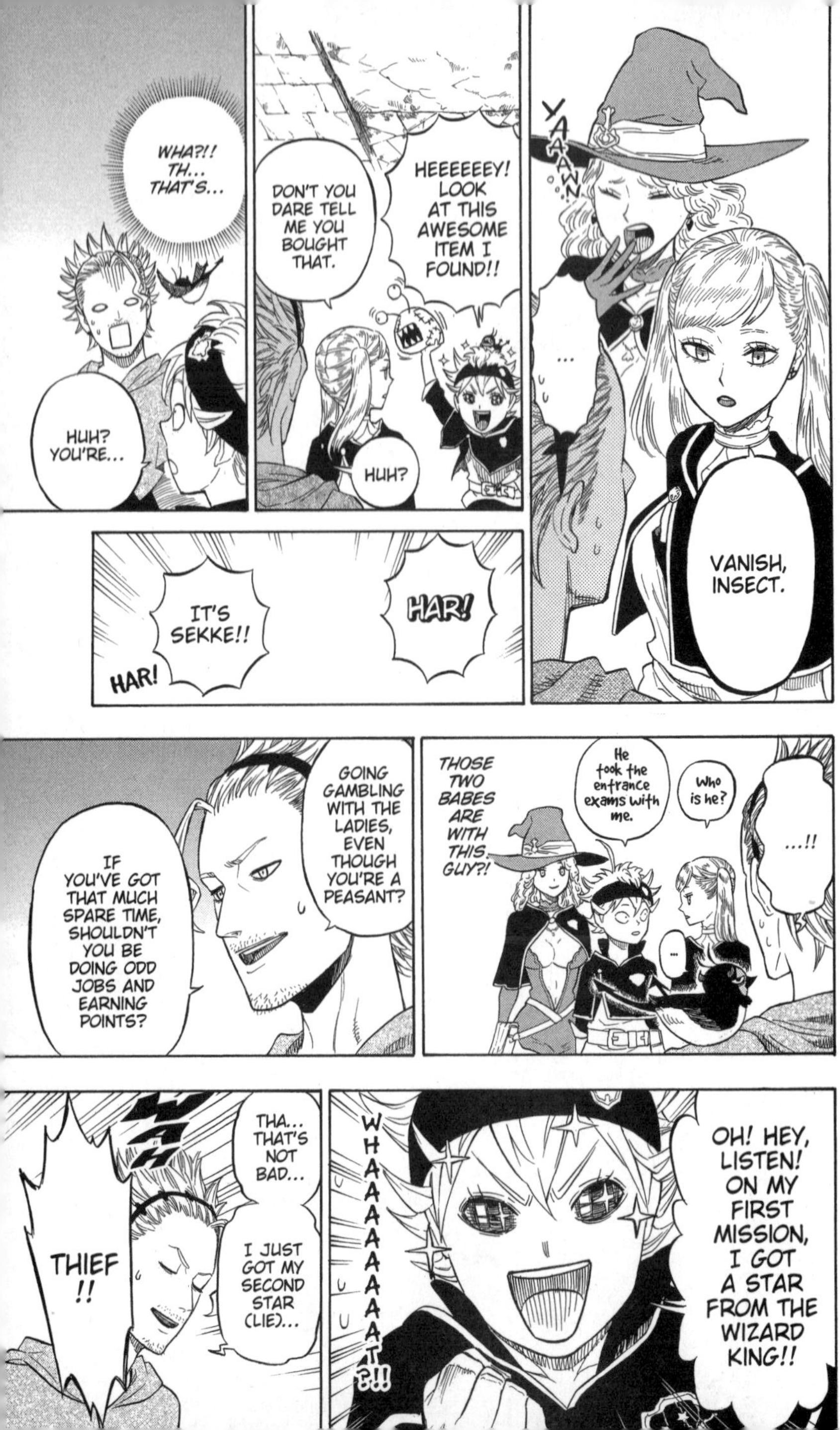
YAAAWN
...
VANISH, INSECT.
HEEEEEEY! LOOK AT THIS AWESOME ITEM I FOUND!!
DON'T YOU DARE TELL ME YOU BOUGHT THAT.
HUH?
WHA?!! TH... THAT'S...
HUH? YOU'RE...
HAR!
IT'S SEKKE!!
HAR!
...!!
Who is he?
He took the entrance exams with me.
THOSE TWO BABES ARE WITH THIS GUY?!
...
GOING GAMBLING WITH THE LADIES, EVEN THOUGH YOU'RE A PEASANT?
IF YOU'VE GOT THAT MUCH SPARE TIME, SHOULDN'T YOU BE DOING ODD JOBS AND EARNING POINTS?
OH! HEY, LISTEN! ON MY FIRST MISSION, I GOT A STAR FROM THE WIZARD KING!!
WHAAAAAAAAAAAT?!!
THA... THAT'S NOT BAD...
I JUST GOT MY SECOND STAR (LIE)...
WAH
THIEF!!

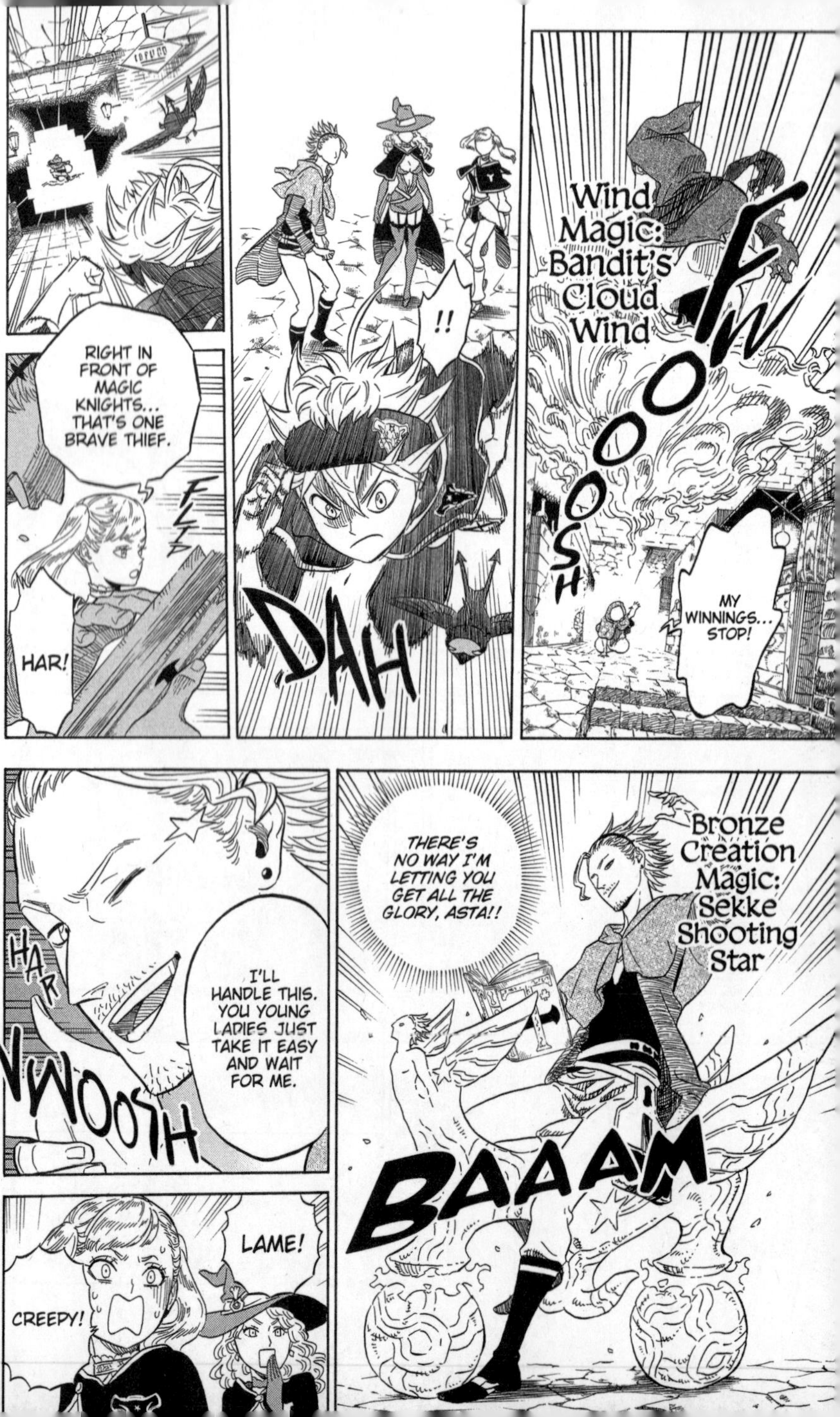

FWOOOOOSH
Wind Magic: Bandit's Cloud Wind
MY WINNINGS... STOP!
!!
DAH
RIGHT IN FRONT OF MAGIC KNIGHTS... THAT'S ONE BRAVE THIEF.
HAR!
Bronze Creation Magic: Sekke Shooting Star
THERE'S NO WAY I'M LETTING YOU GET ALL THE GLORY, ASTA!!
BAAAM
I'LL HANDLE THIS. YOU YOUNG LADIES JUST TAKE IT EASY AND WAIT FOR ME.
HAR
LAME!
CREEPY!

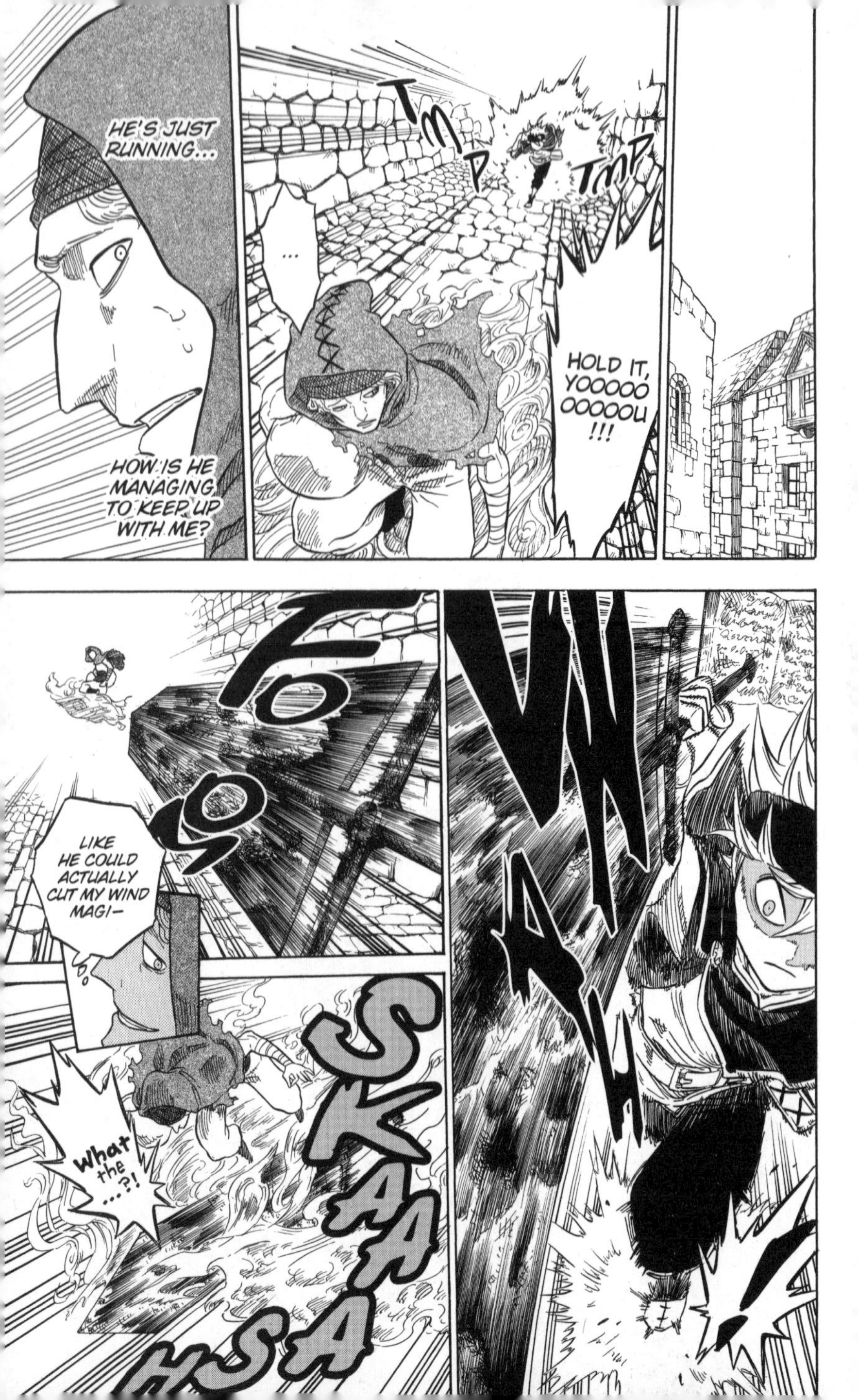
HOLD IT, YOOOOO OOOOOU!!!
TMP
TMP
...
HE'S JUST RUNNING...
HOW IS HE MANAGING TO KEEP UP WITH ME?
VWAAH
FOOM
LIKE HE COULD ACTUALLY CUT MY WIND MAGI-
SKAAA
HSA
What the...?!

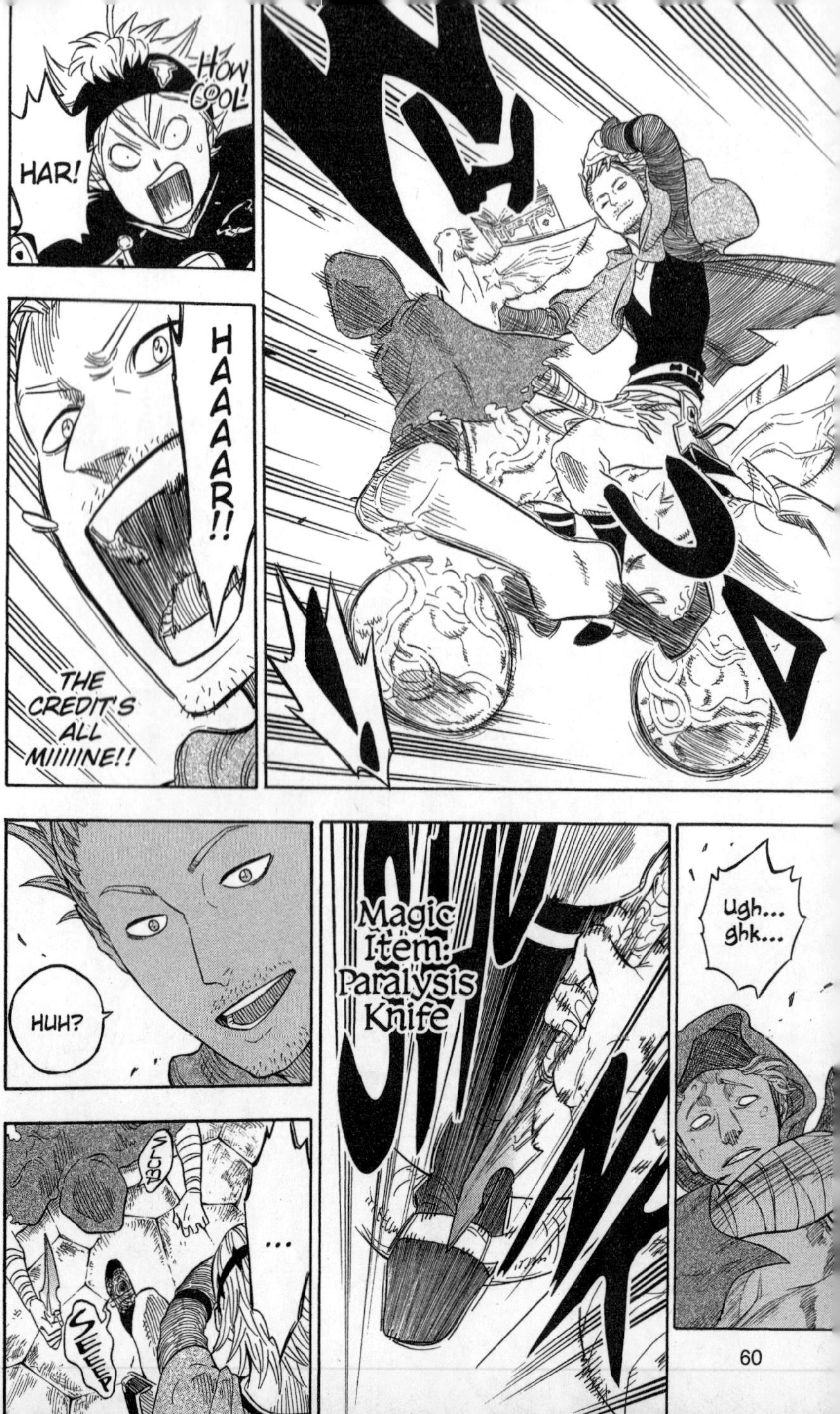
HOW COOL!
HAR!
HAAAAAR!!
THE CREDIT'S ALL MIIIIINE!!
Ugh... ghk...
Magic Item: Paralysis Knife
HUH?
SLUMP
...
SEEEP

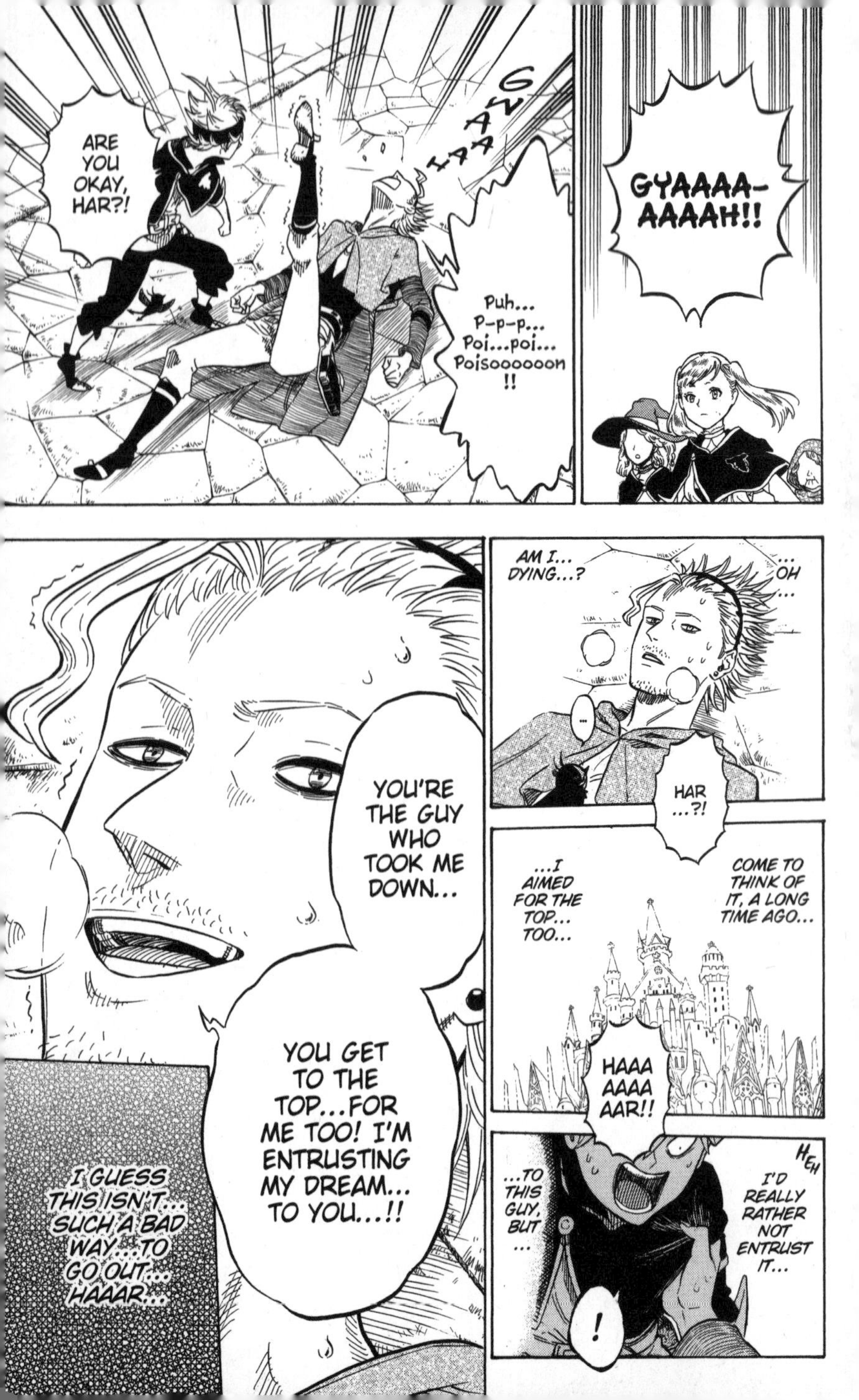
GYAAAA-AAAAH!!
GWAAAAH
Puh... P-p-p... Poi...poi... Poisoooooon!!
ARE YOU OKAY, HAR?!
...OH...
AM I... DYING...?
...
HAR...?!
COME TO THINK OF IT, A LONG TIME AGO...
...I AIMED FOR THE TOP... TOO...
HAAAAAAAAR!!
HEH
I'D REALLY RATHER NOT ENTRUST IT...
...TO THIS GUY, BUT...
!
YOU'RE THE GUY WHO TOOK ME DOWN...
YOU GET TO THE TOP...FOR ME TOO! I'M ENTRUSTING MY DREAM... TO YOU...!!
I GUESS THIS ISN'T... SUCH A BAD WAY... TO GO OUT... HAAAR...

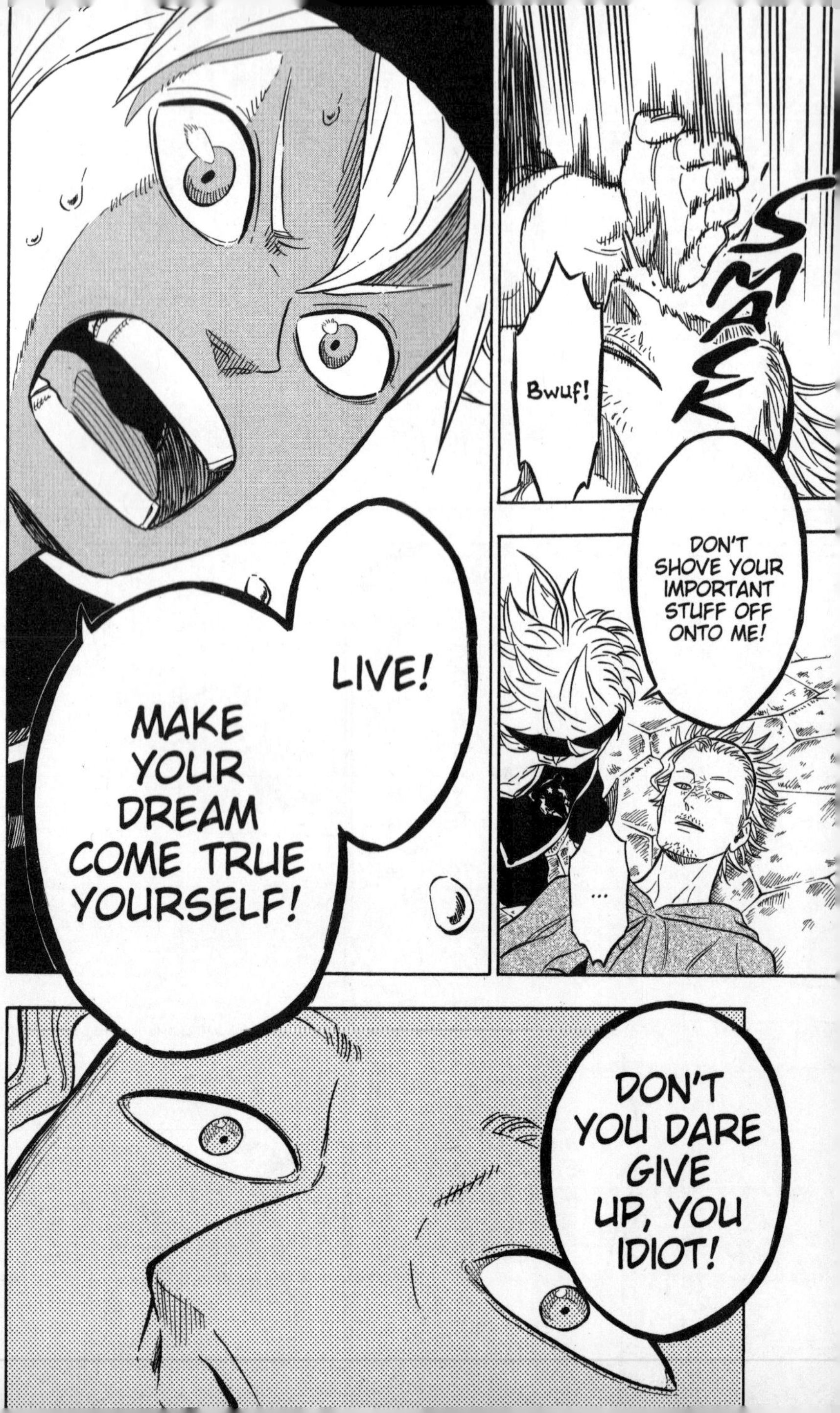
SMACK
Bwuf!
DON'T SHOVE YOUR IMPORTANT STUFF OFF ONTO ME!
...
LIVE!
MAKE YOUR DREAM COME TRUE YOURSELF!
DON'T YOU DARE GIVE UP, YOU IDIOT!

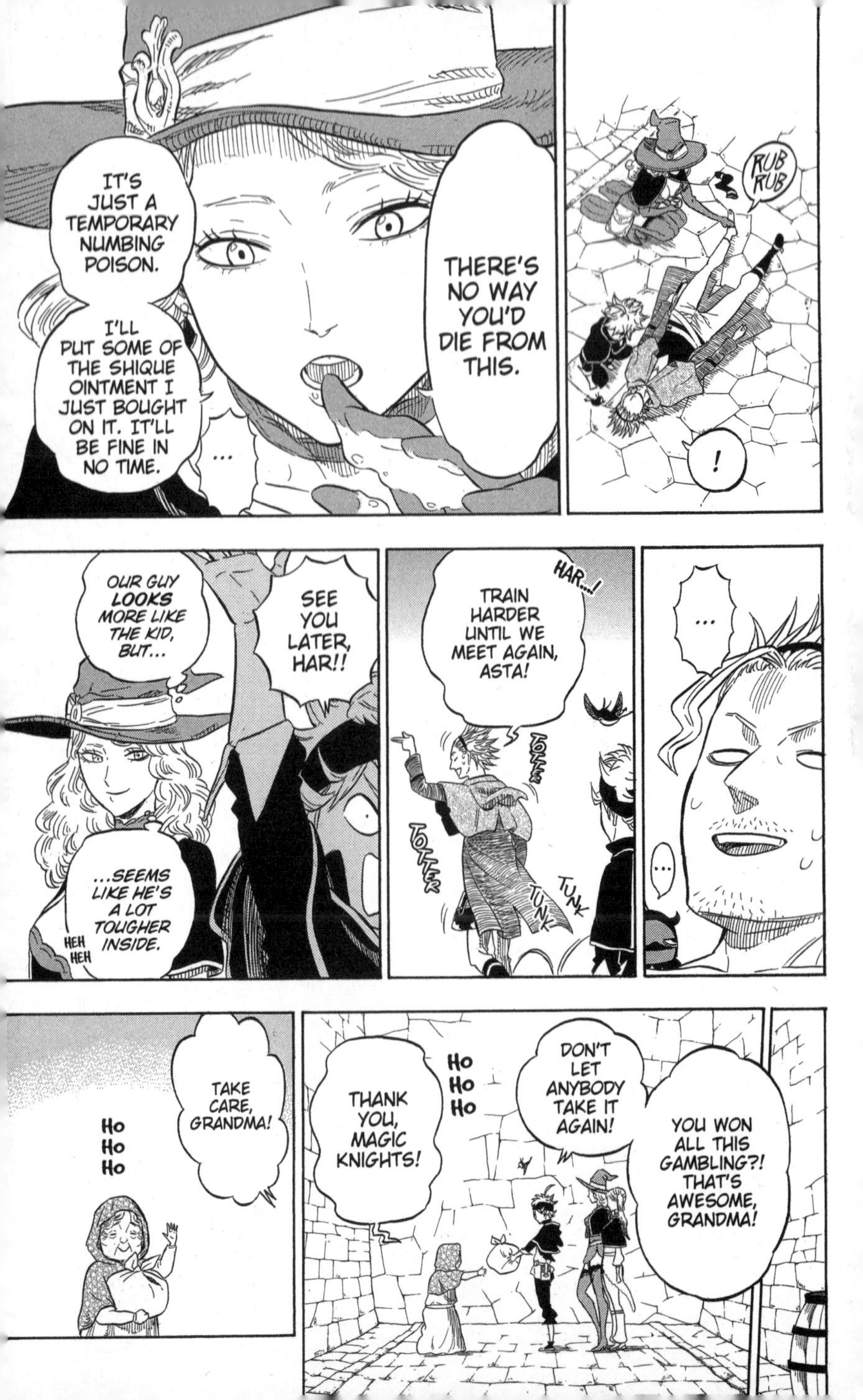
RUB RUB
!
THERE'S NO WAY YOU'D DIE FROM THIS.
IT'S JUST A TEMPORARY NUMBING POISON.
I'LL PUT SOME OF THE SHIQUE OINTMENT I JUST BOUGHT ON IT. IT'LL BE FINE IN NO TIME.
...
...
...
HAR...!
TRAIN HARDER UNTIL WE MEET AGAIN, ASTA!
TOTTER
TOTTER
TUNK
SEE YOU LATER, HAR!!
OUR GUY **LOOKS** MORE LIKE THE KID, BUT...
...SEEMS LIKE HE'S A LOT TOUGHER INSIDE.
HEH HEH
YOU WON ALL THIS GAMBLING?! THAT'S AWESOME, GRANDMA!
DON'T LET ANYBODY TAKE IT AGAIN!
Ho Ho Ho
THANK YOU, MAGIC KNIGHTS!
TAKE CARE, GRANDMA!
Ho Ho Ho

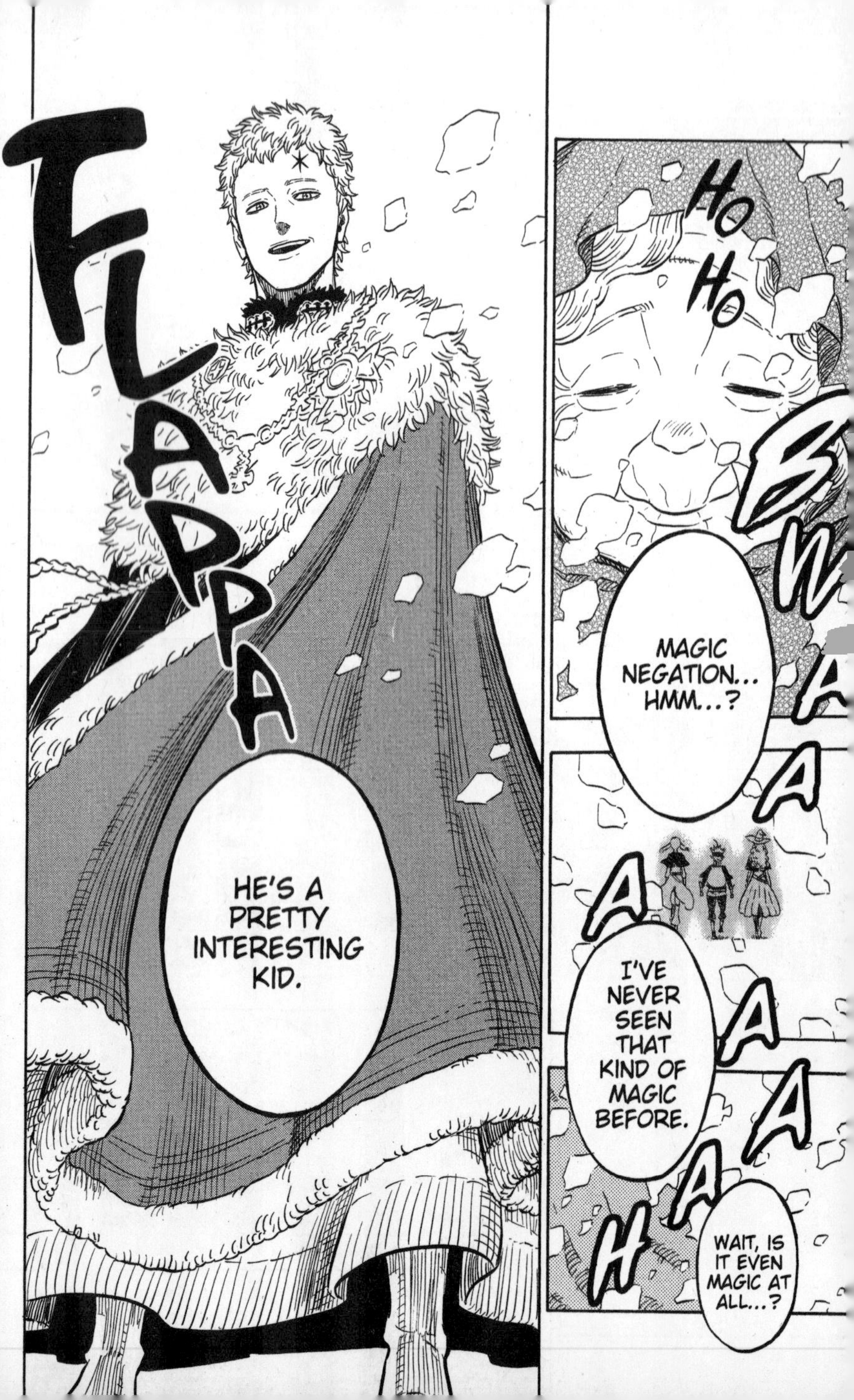
HO HO
MAGIC NEGATION... HMM...?
BWAAAAAAH
I'VE NEVER SEEN THAT KIND OF MAGIC BEFORE.
WAIT, IS IT EVEN MAGIC AT ALL...?
FLAPPA
HE'S A PRETTY INTERESTING KID.

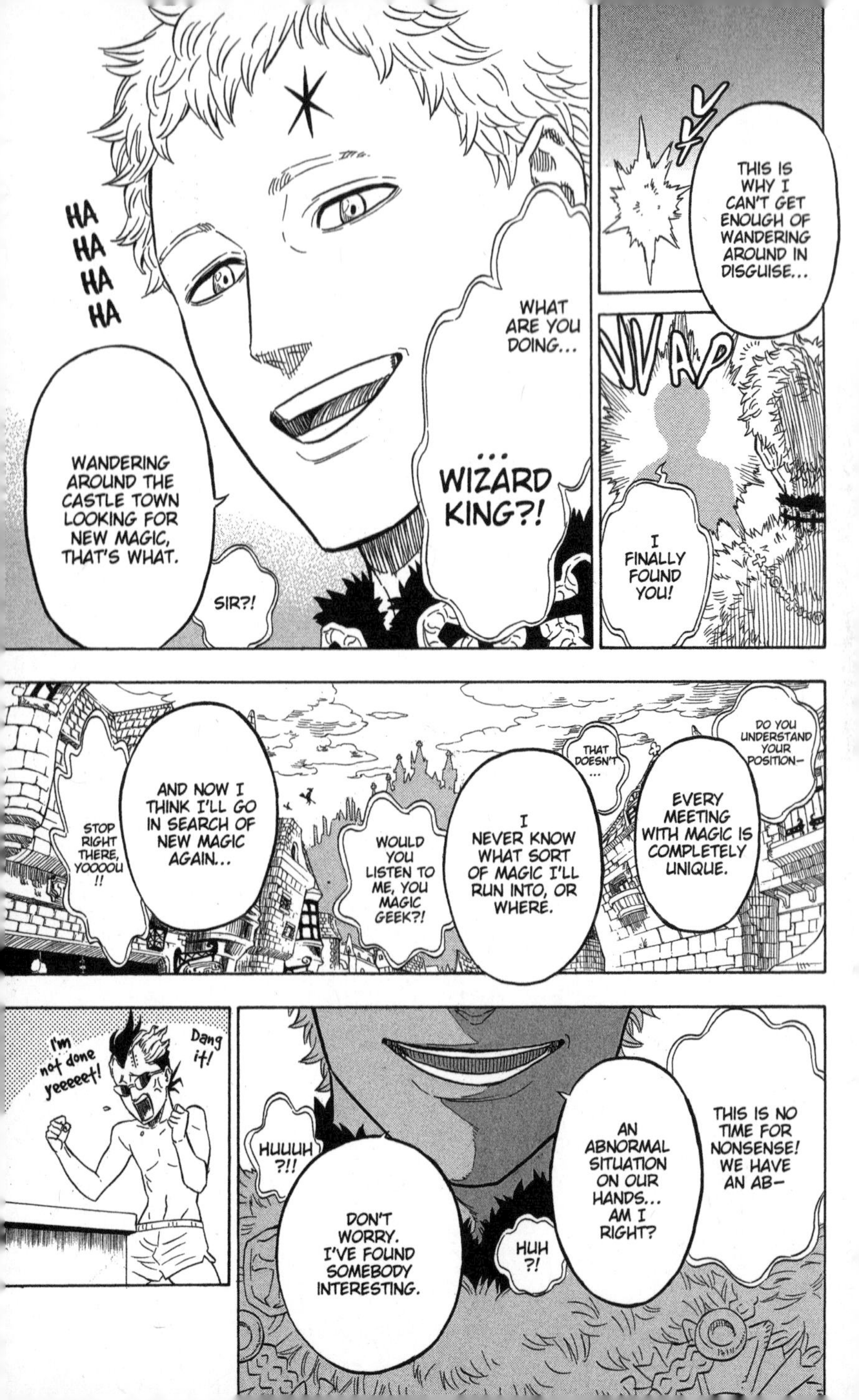
THIS IS WHY I CAN'T GET ENOUGH OF WANDERING AROUND IN DISGUISE...
WAP
I FINALLY FOUND YOU!
WHAT ARE YOU DOING...
...WIZARD KING?!
SIR?!
HA HA HA HA
WANDERING AROUND THE CASTLE TOWN LOOKING FOR NEW MAGIC, THAT'S WHAT.
DO YOU UNDERSTAND YOUR POSITION—
EVERY MEETING WITH MAGIC IS COMPLETELY UNIQUE.
THAT DOESN'T...
I NEVER KNOW WHAT SORT OF MAGIC I'LL RUN INTO, OR WHERE.
WOULD YOU LISTEN TO ME, YOU MAGIC GEEK?!
AND NOW I THINK I'LL GO IN SEARCH OF NEW MAGIC AGAIN...
STOP RIGHT THERE, YOOOOU!!
THIS IS NO TIME FOR NONSENSE! WE HAVE AN AB—
AN ABNORMAL SITUATION ON OUR HANDS... AM I RIGHT?
HUH?!
HUUUH?!!
DON'T WORRY. I'VE FOUND SOMEBODY INTERESTING.
Dang it!
I'm not done yeeeeet!

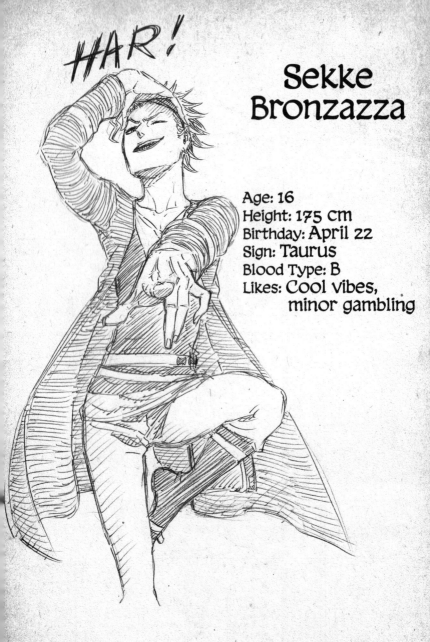

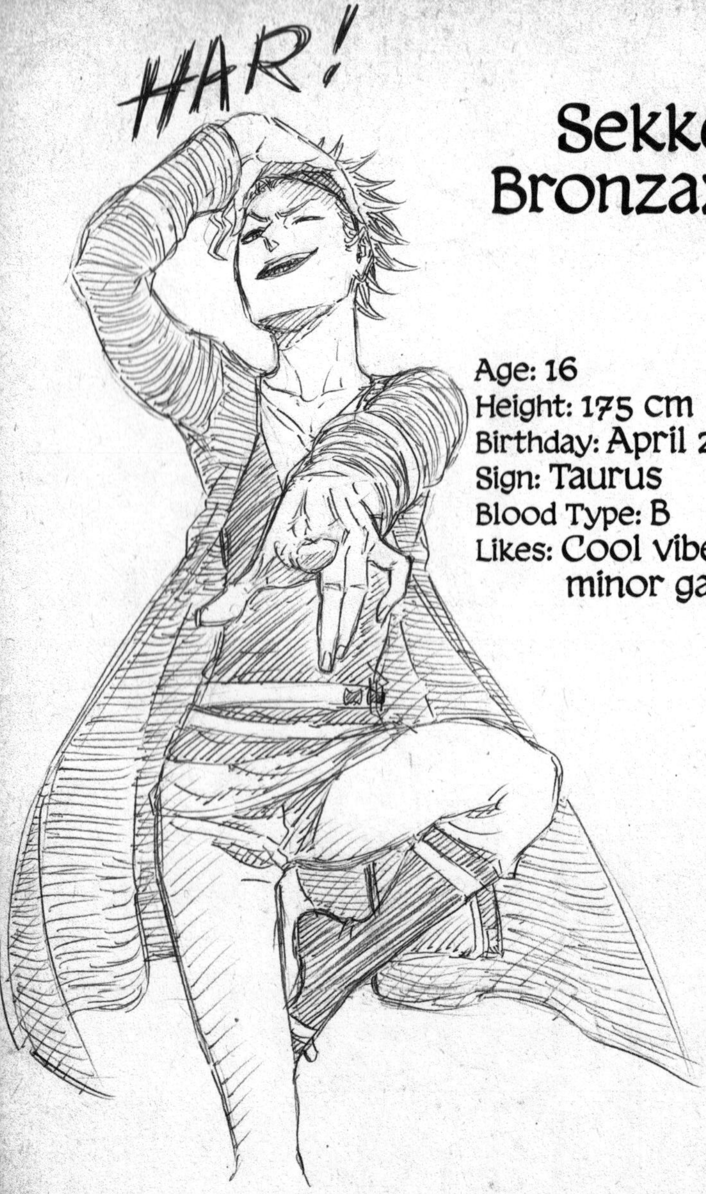
HAR!

Sekke Bronzazza

Age: 16
Height: 175 cm
Birthday: April 22
Sign: Taurus
Blood Type: B
Likes: Cool vibes, minor gambling

Character Profile

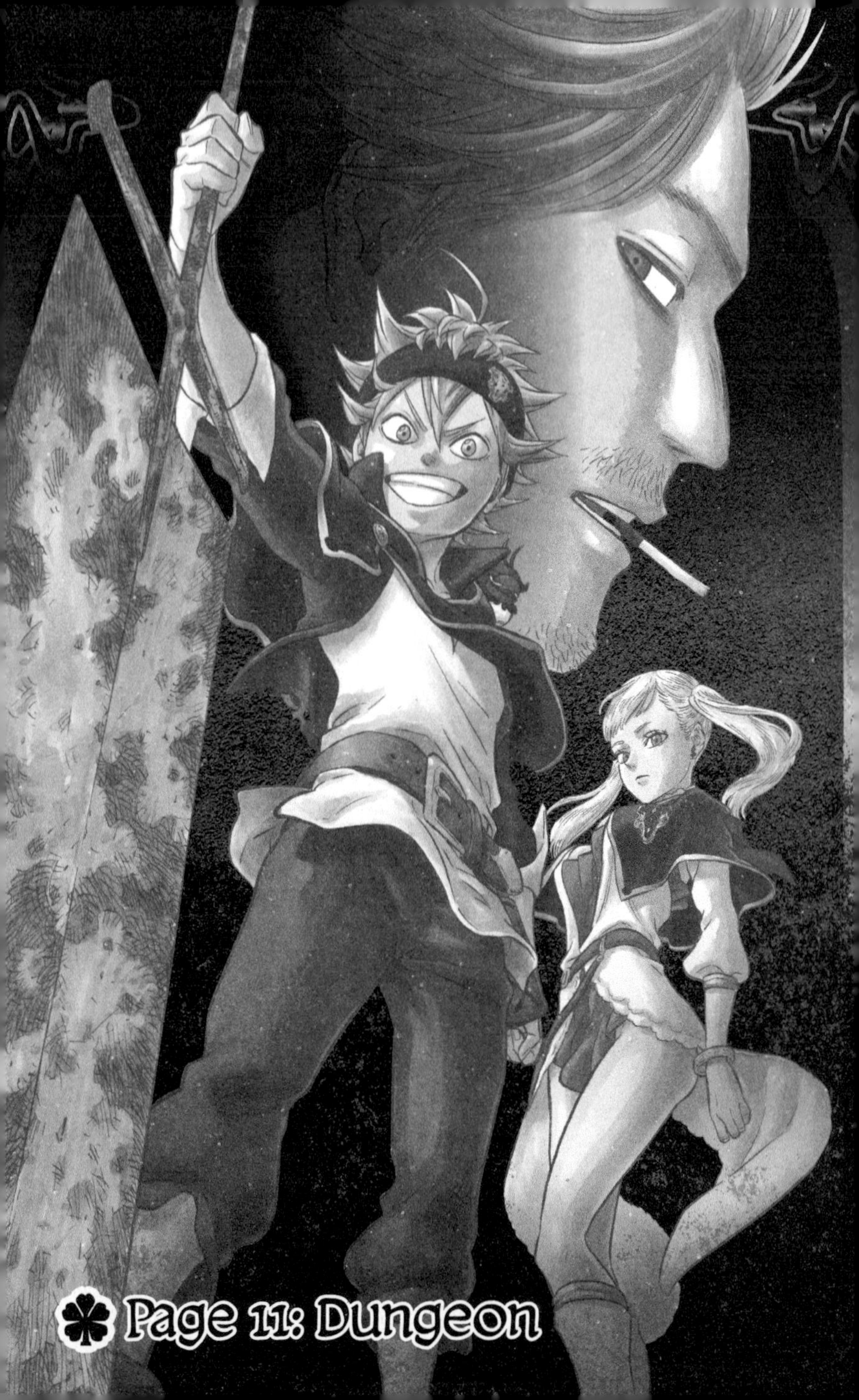

Page 11: Dungeon

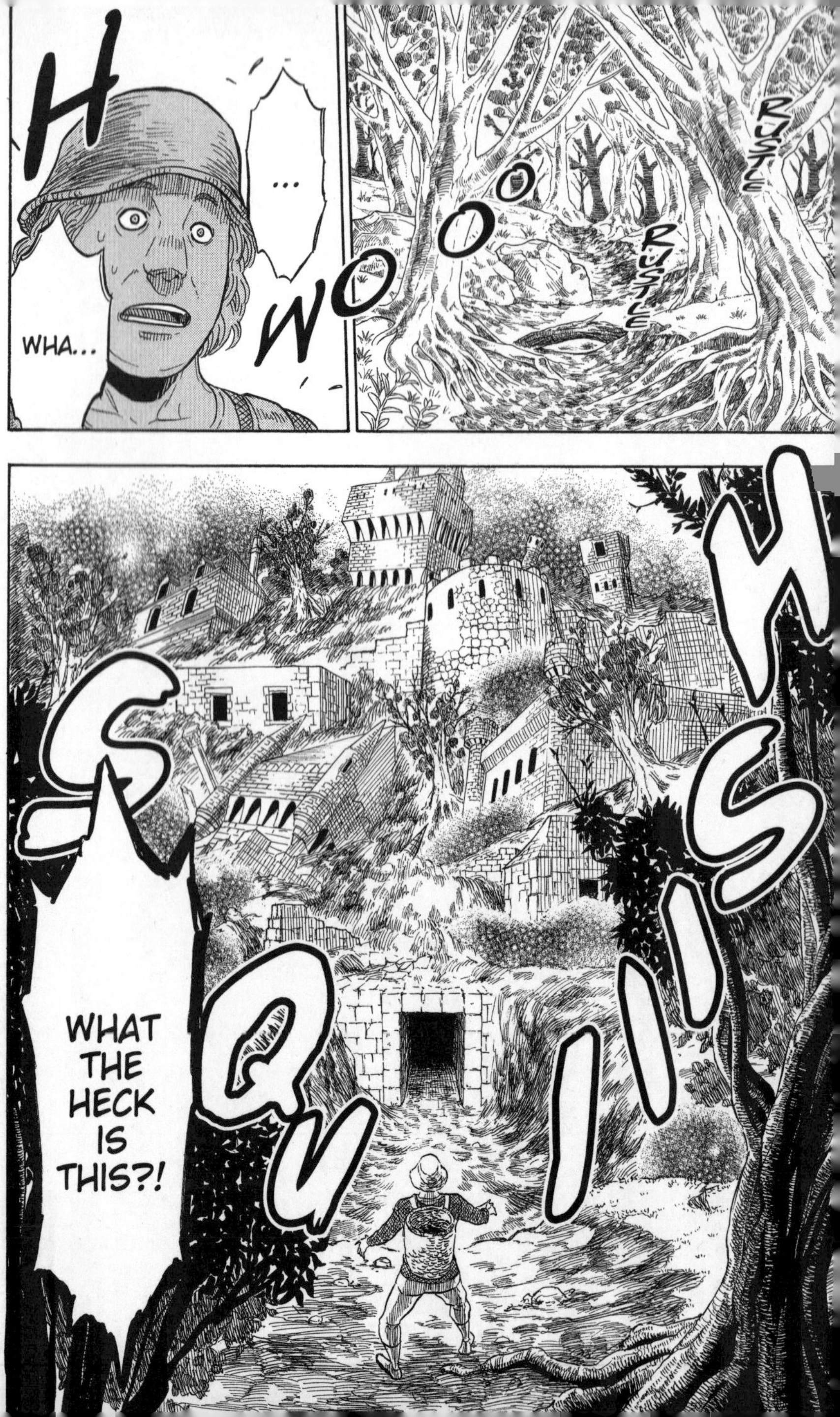
RUSTLE
RUSTLE
HWOOOO
...
WHA...
SQUIIISH
WHAT THE HECK IS THIS?!

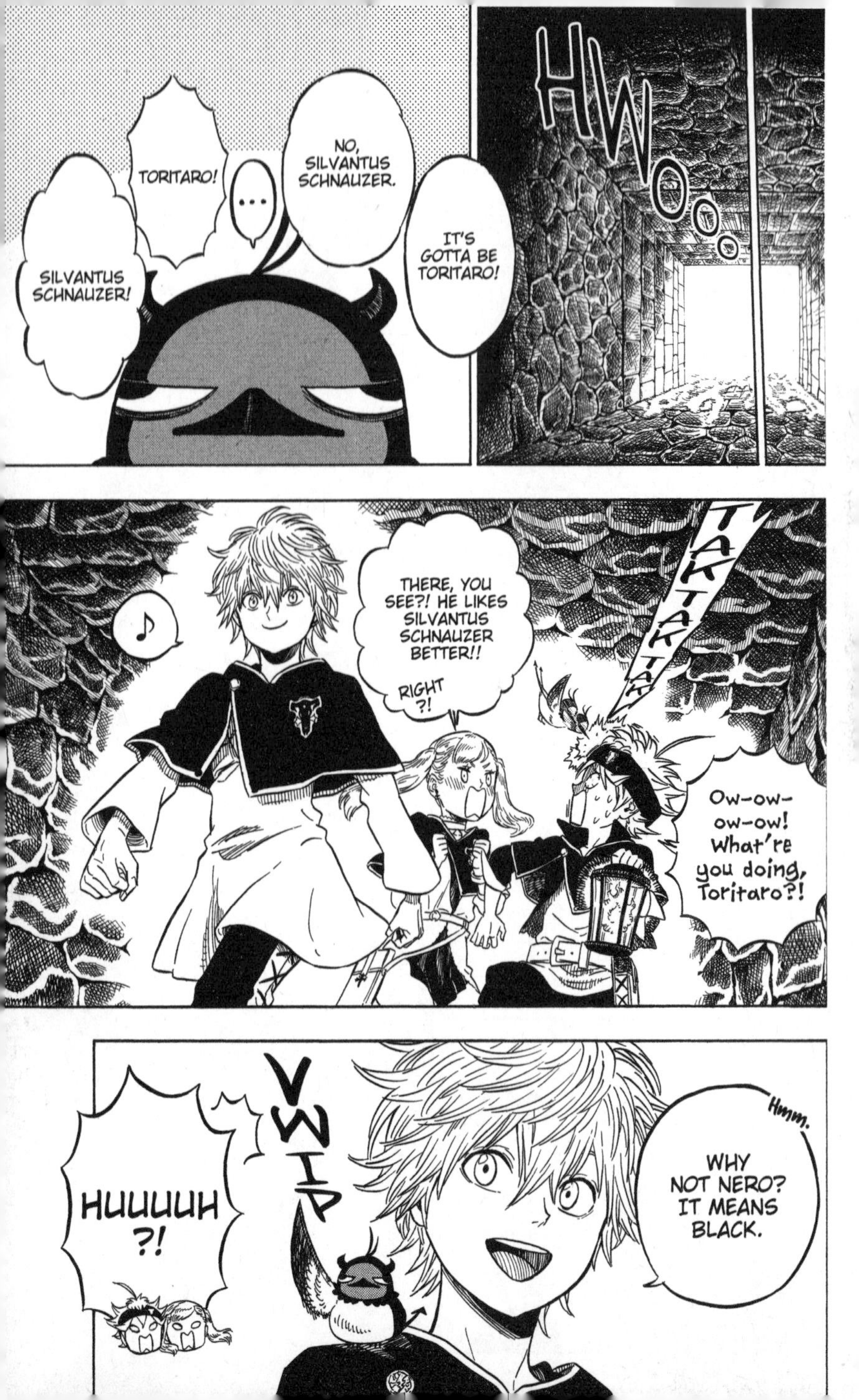
HWOOO
IT'S GOTTA BE TORITARO!
NO, SILVANTUS SCHNAUZER.
...
TORITARO!
SILVANTUS SCHNAUZER!
TAKTAKTAK
Ow-ow-ow-ow! What're you doing, Toritaro?!
THERE, YOU SEE?! HE LIKES SILVANTUS SCHNAUZER BETTER!!
RIGHT ?!
♪
Hmm.
WHY NOT NERO? IT MEANS BLACK.
VWIP
HUUUUH ?!

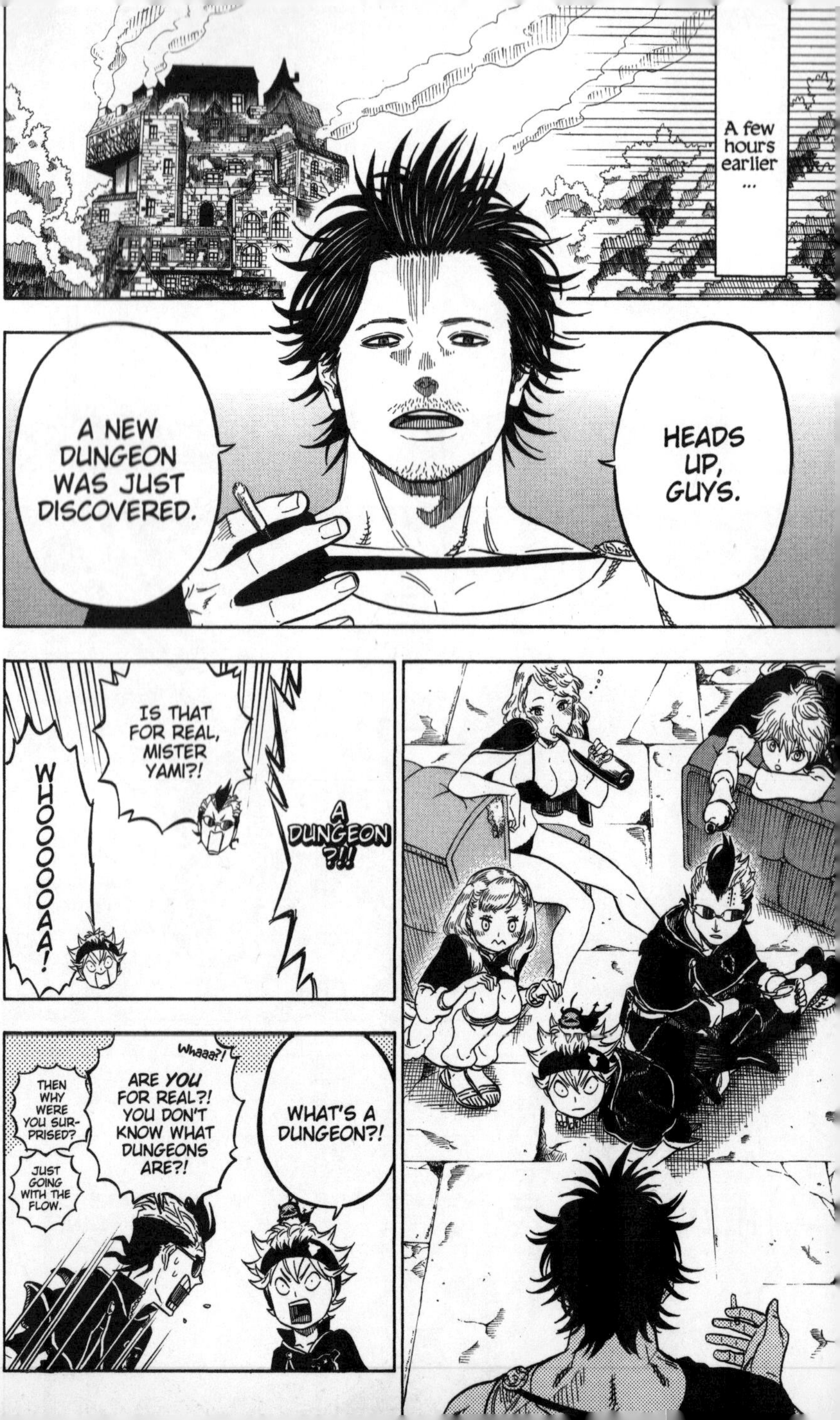
A few hours earlier ...
HEADS UP, GUYS.
A NEW DUNGEON WAS JUST DISCOVERED.
A DUNGEON ?!!
IS THAT FOR REAL, MISTER YAMI?!
WHOOOOOOAA!
WHAT'S A DUNGEON?!
Whaaa?!
ARE YOU FOR REAL?! YOU DON'T KNOW WHAT DUNGEONS ARE?!
THEN WHY WERE YOU SURPRISED?
JUST GOING WITH THE FLOW.

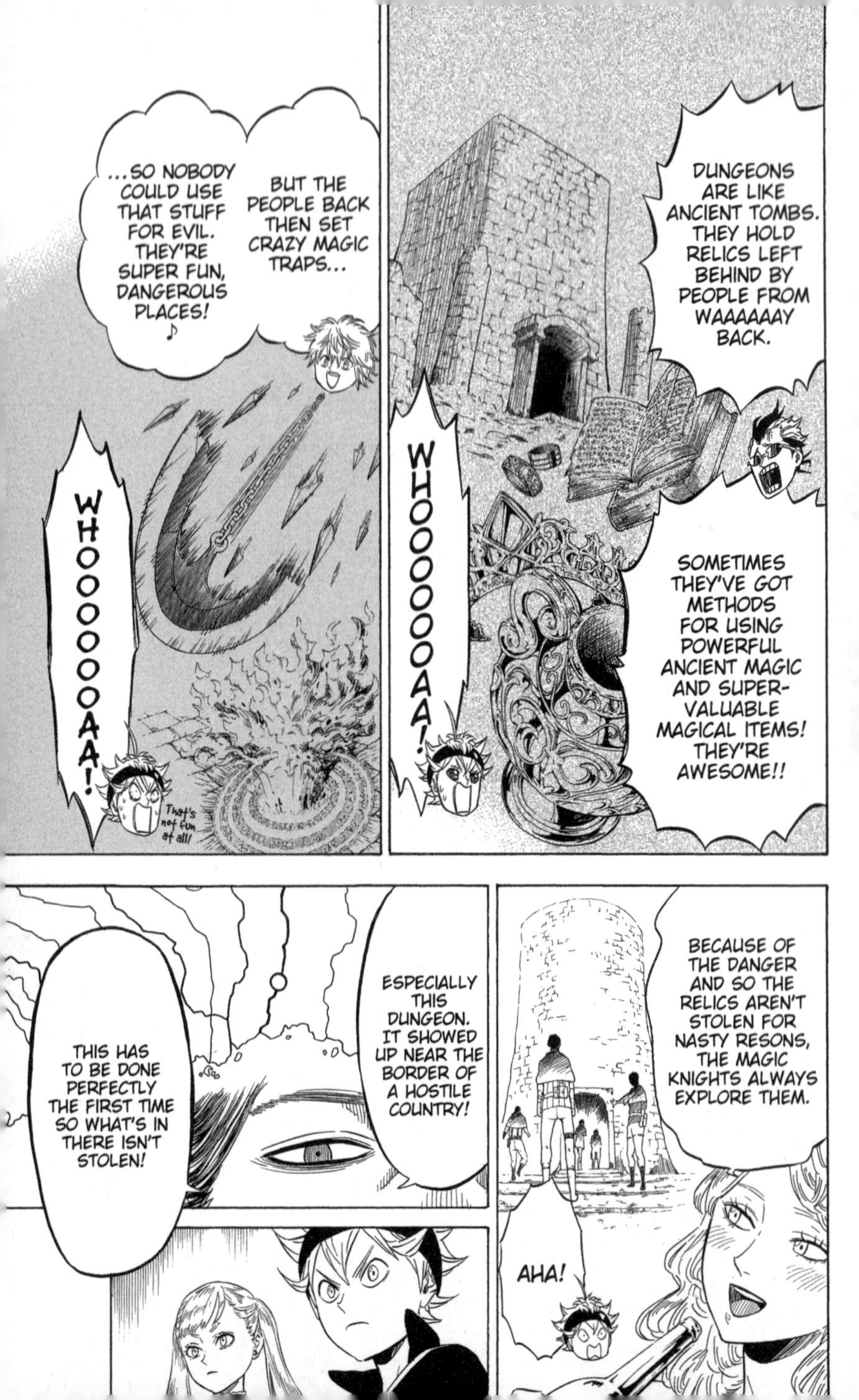
DUNGEONS ARE LIKE ANCIENT TOMBS. THEY HOLD RELICS LEFT BEHIND BY PEOPLE FROM WAAAAAAY BACK.
WHOOOOOOOAA!
SOMETIMES THEY'VE GOT METHODS FOR USING POWERFUL ANCIENT MAGIC AND SUPER-VALUABLE MAGICAL ITEMS! THEY'RE AWESOME!!
BUT THE PEOPLE BACK THEN SET CRAZY MAGIC TRAPS...
...SO NOBODY COULD USE THAT STUFF FOR EVIL. THEY'RE SUPER FUN, DANGEROUS PLACES! ♪
WHOOOOOOOAA!
That's not fun at all!
BECAUSE OF THE DANGER AND SO THE RELICS AREN'T STOLEN FOR NASTY RESONS, THE MAGIC KNIGHTS ALWAYS EXPLORE THEM.
AHA!
ESPECIALLY THIS DUNGEON. IT SHOWED UP NEAR THE BORDER OF A HOSTILE COUNTRY!
THIS HAS TO BE DONE PERFECTLY THE FIRST TIME SO WHAT'S IN THERE ISN'T STOLEN!

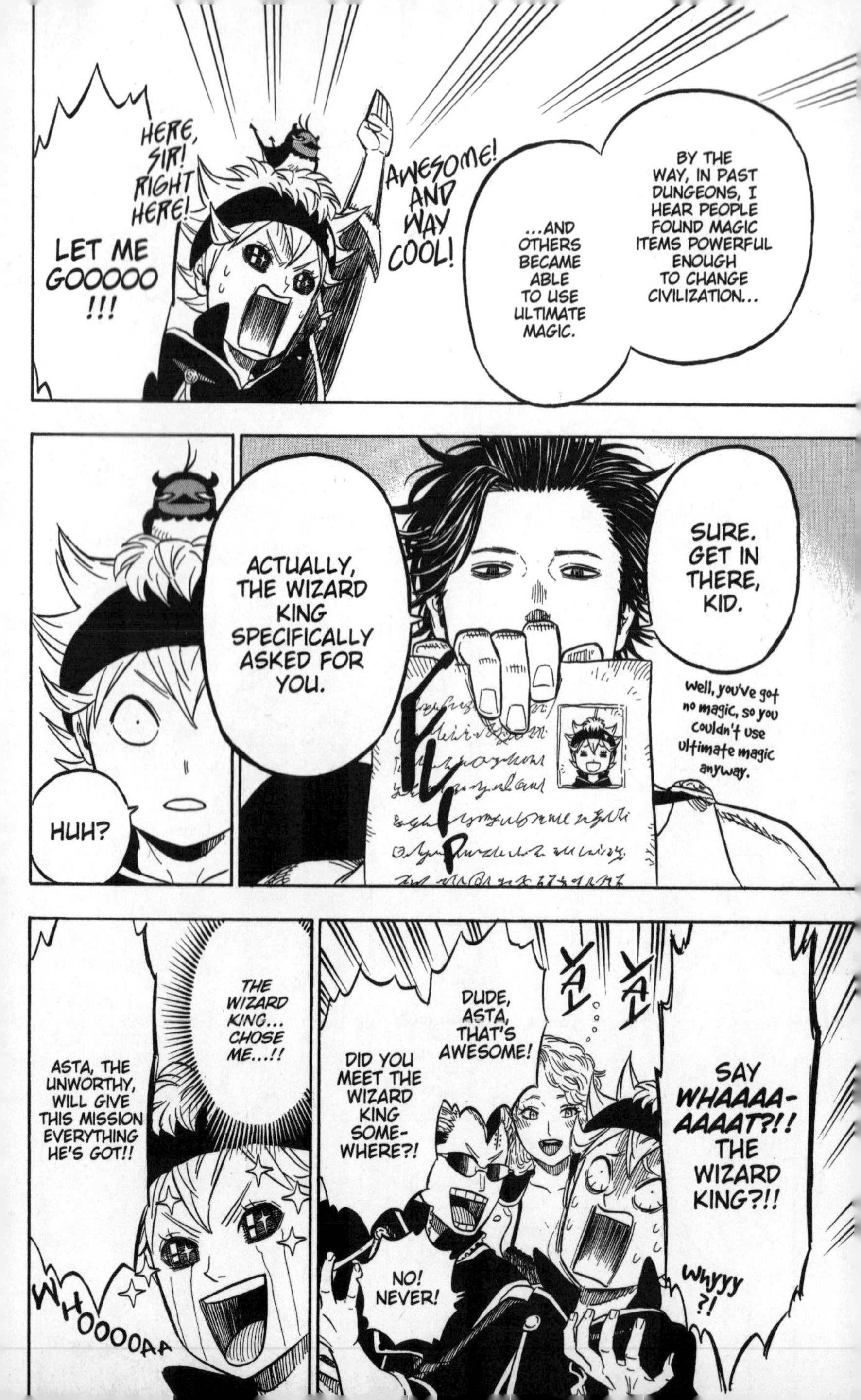
BY THE WAY, IN PAST DUNGEONS, I HEAR PEOPLE FOUND MAGIC ITEMS POWERFUL ENOUGH TO CHANGE CIVILIZATION...
...AND OTHERS BECAME ABLE TO USE ULTIMATE MAGIC.
AWESOME! AND WAY COOL!
HERE, SIR! RIGHT HERE!
LET ME GOOOOO!!!
SURE. GET IN THERE, KID.
Well, you've got no magic, so you couldn't use ultimate magic anyway.
FLIP
ACTUALLY, THE WIZARD KING SPECIFICALLY ASKED FOR YOU.
HUH?
SAY WHAAAA-AAAAT?!! THE WIZARD KING?!!
YAY
YAY
DUDE, ASTA, THAT'S AWESOME!
DID YOU MEET THE WIZARD KING SOME-WHERE?!
Whyyy ?!
NO! NEVER!
THE WIZARD KING... CHOSE ME...!!
ASTA, THE UNWORTHY, WILL GIVE THIS MISSION EVERYTHING HE'S GOT!!
WHOOOOAA

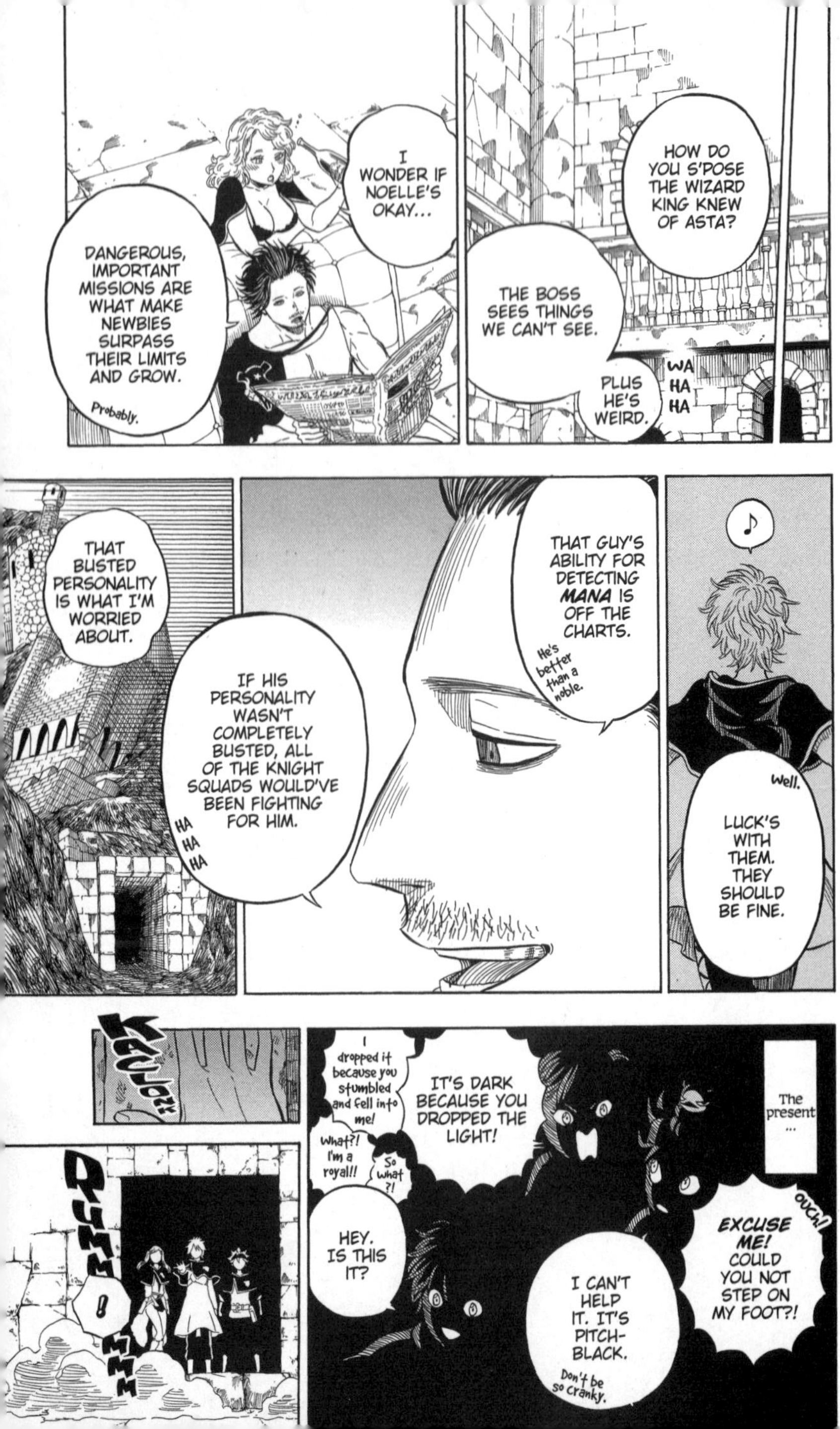
HOW DO YOU S'POSE THE WIZARD KING KNEW OF ASTA?
THE BOSS SEES THINGS WE CAN'T SEE.
PLUS HE'S WEIRD.
WA HA HA
I WONDER IF NOELLE'S OKAY...
DANGEROUS, IMPORTANT MISSIONS ARE WHAT MAKE NEWBIES SURPASS THEIR LIMITS AND GROW.
Probably.
♪
Well.
LUCK'S WITH THEM. THEY SHOULD BE FINE.
THAT GUY'S ABILITY FOR DETECTING ***MANA*** IS OFF THE CHARTS.
He's better than a noble.
IF HIS PERSONALITY WASN'T COMPLETELY BUSTED, ALL OF THE KNIGHT SQUADS WOULD'VE BEEN FIGHTING FOR HIM.
HA HA HA
THAT BUSTED PERSONALITY IS WHAT I'M WORRIED ABOUT.
The present...
IT'S DARK BECAUSE YOU DROPPED THE LIGHT!
I dropped it because you stumbled and fell into me!
What?! I'm a royal!!
So what?!
OUCH!
EXCUSE ME! COULD YOU NOT STEP ON MY FOOT?!
I CAN'T HELP IT. IT'S PITCH-BLACK.
Don't be so cranky.
HEY. IS THIS IT?
KACLONK
RUMMMMMMM

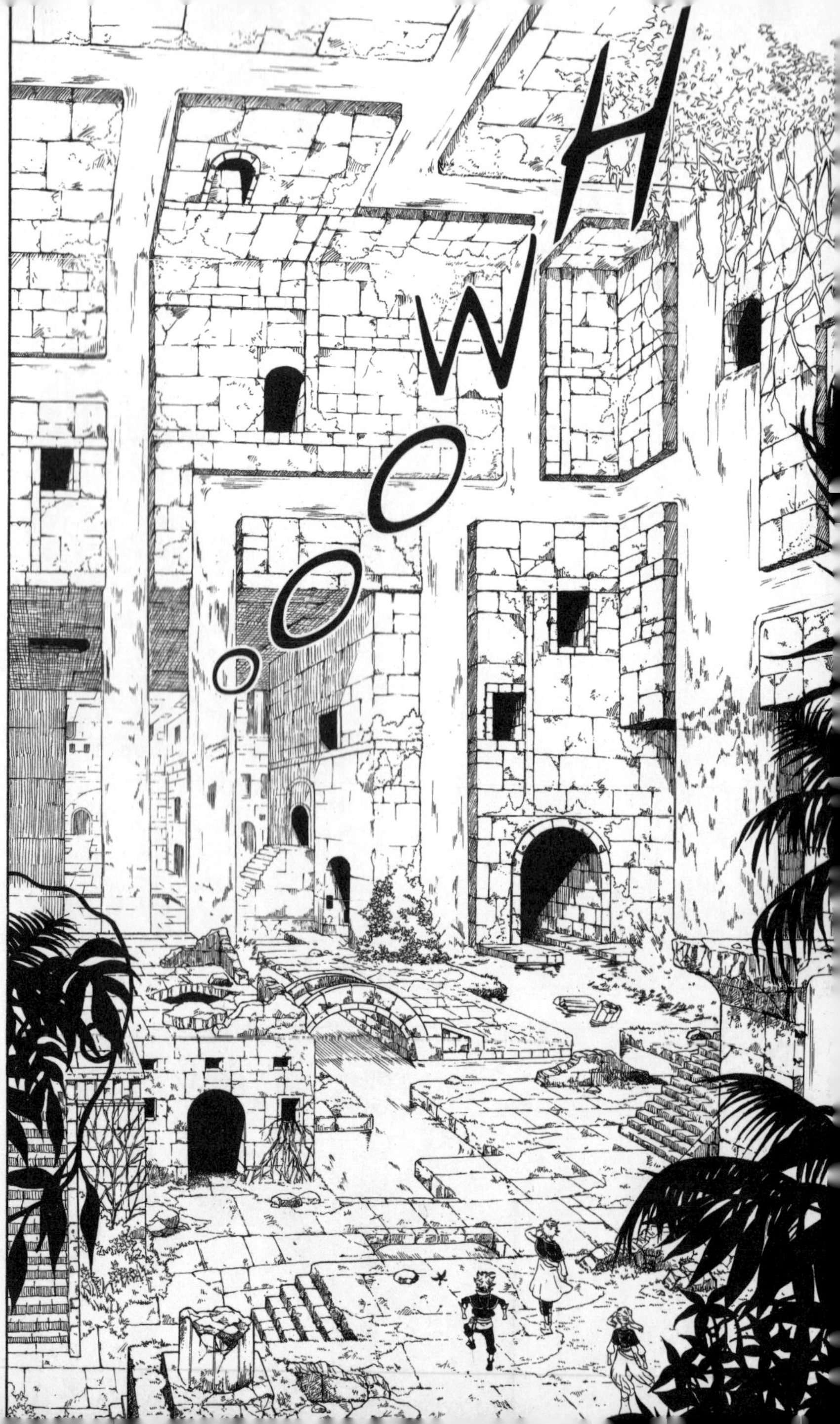
WHOOOO

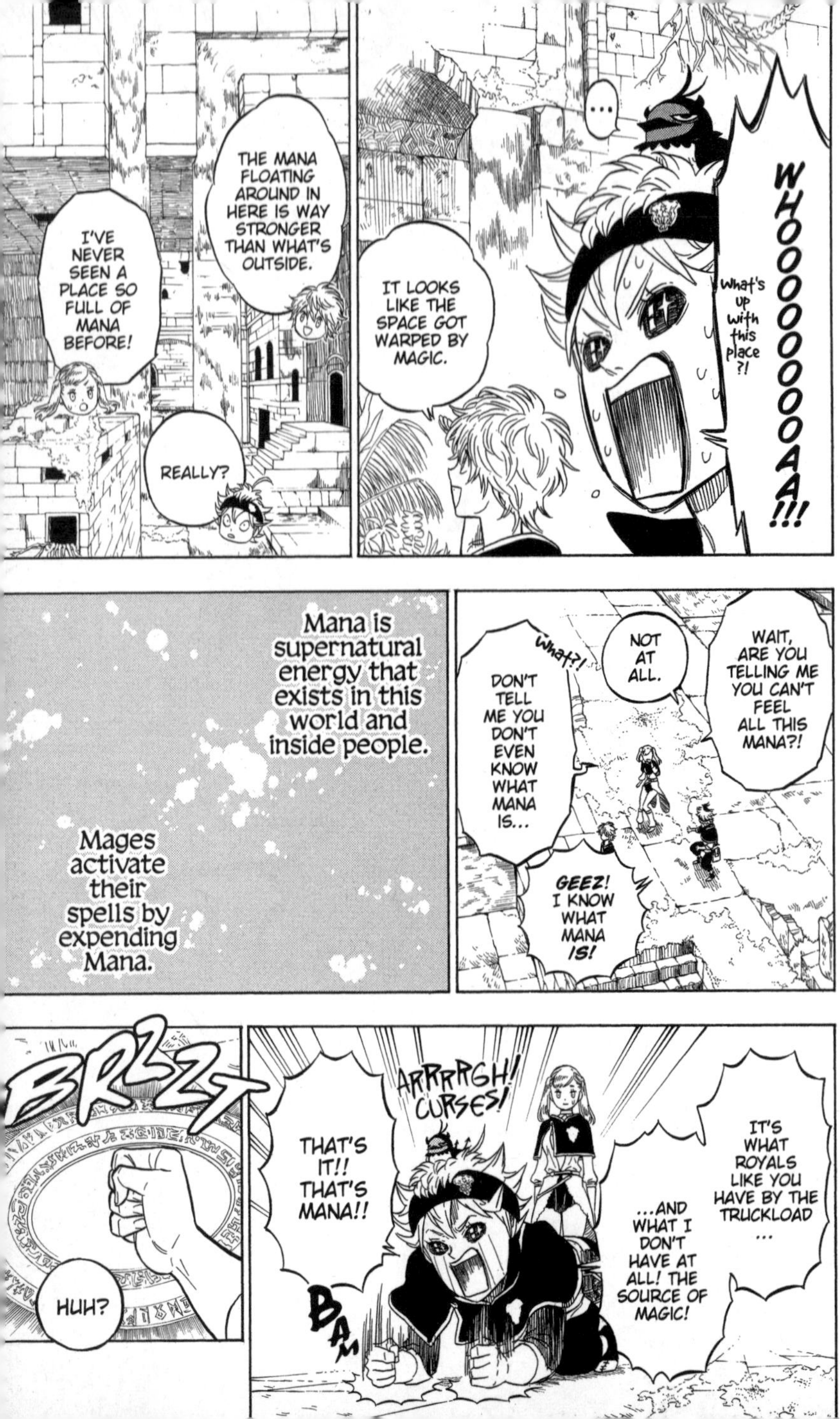
WHOOOOOOOOOAA!!!
What's up with this place?!
...
IT LOOKS LIKE THE SPACE GOT WARPED BY MAGIC.
THE MANA FLOATING AROUND IN HERE IS WAY STRONGER THAN WHAT'S OUTSIDE.
I'VE NEVER SEEN A PLACE SO FULL OF MANA BEFORE!
REALLY?
WAIT, ARE YOU TELLING ME YOU CAN'T FEEL ALL THIS MANA?!
NOT AT ALL.
What?!
DON'T TELL ME YOU DON'T EVEN KNOW WHAT MANA IS...
GEEZ! I KNOW WHAT MANA IS!
Mana is supernatural energy that exists in this world and inside people.
Mages activate their spells by expending Mana.
IT'S WHAT ROYALS LIKE YOU HAVE BY THE TRUCKLOAD...
...AND WHAT I DON'T HAVE AT ALL! THE SOURCE OF MAGIC!
ARRRRGH! CURSES!
THAT'S IT!! THAT'S MANA!!
BAM
BRZZT
HUH?

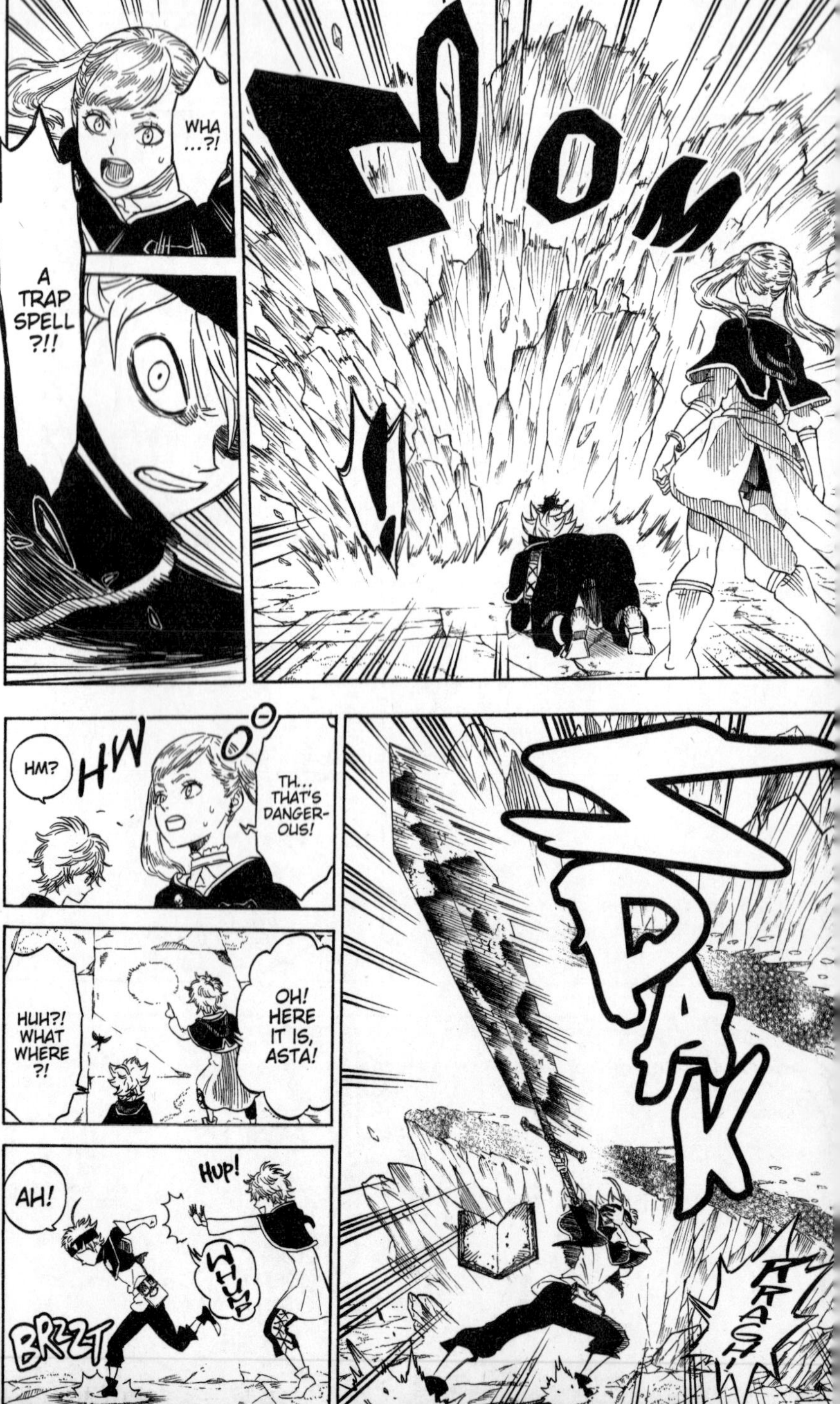
FOOM
!
WHA ...?!
A TRAP SPELL ?!!
ZDAK
RRASH!
HWOO
HM?
TH... THAT'S DANGER-OUS!
OH! HERE IT IS, ASTA!
HUH?! WHAT WHERE ?!
HUP!
WHUMP
AH!
BRZZT

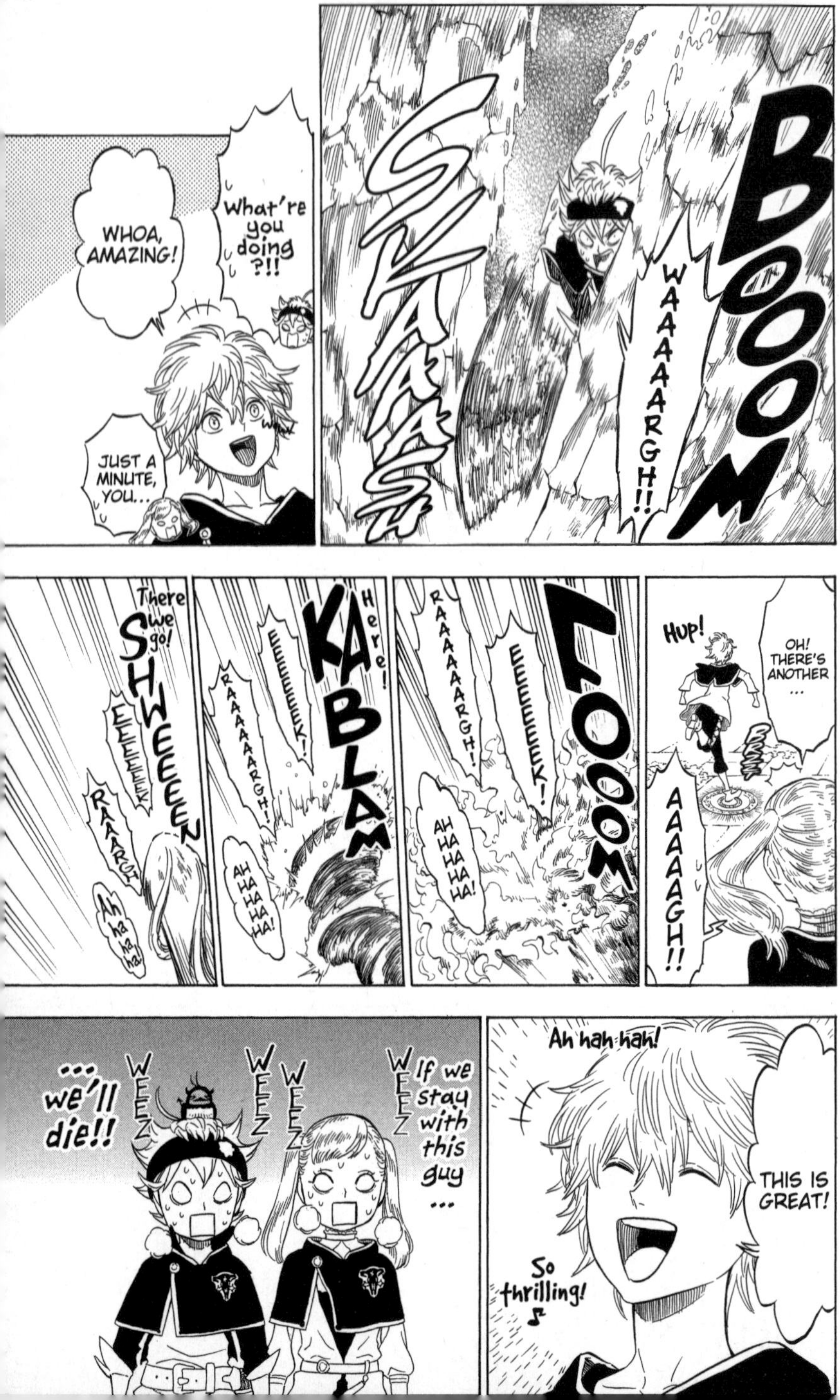
BOOOM
WAAAAAARGH!!
SHAAAASH
What're you doing?!!
WHOA, AMAZING!
JUST A MINUTE, YOU...
OH! THERE'S ANOTHER...
HUP!
AAAAAAGH!!
FOOOM
EEEEEEEK!
RAAAAAAARGH!
AH HA HA HA HA!
Here!
KABLAM
EEEEEEEK!
RAAAAAAARGH!
AH HA HA HA HA!
There we go!
SHWEEEEN
EEEEEEEK
RAAARGH
Ah ha ha ha
Ah hah hah!
THIS IS GREAT!
So thrilling! ♪
WEEZ
If we stay with this guy...
WEEZ
WEEZ
WEEZ
...we'll die!!

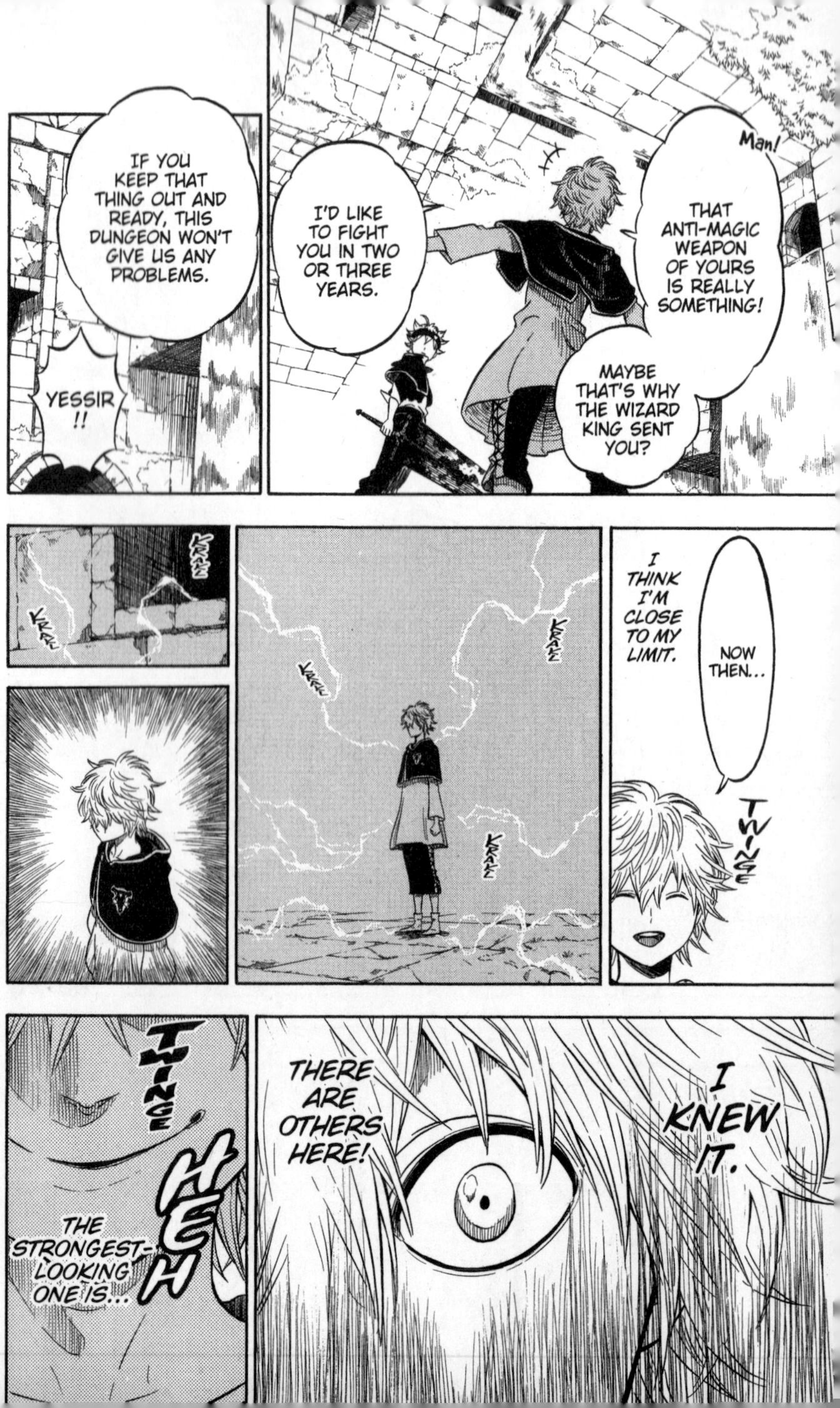
Man!
THAT ANTI-MAGIC WEAPON OF YOURS IS REALLY SOMETHING!
MAYBE THAT'S WHY THE WIZARD KING SENT YOU?
I'D LIKE TO FIGHT YOU IN TWO OR THREE YEARS.
IF YOU KEEP THAT THING OUT AND READY, THIS DUNGEON WON'T GIVE US ANY PROBLEMS.
YESSIR!!
NOW THEN...
I THINK I'M CLOSE TO MY LIMIT.
TWINGE
KRAKK
KRAKK
KRAKK
KRAKK
KRAKK
I KNEW IT.
THERE ARE OTHERS HERE!
TWINGE
HEH
THE STRONGEST-LOOKING ONE IS...

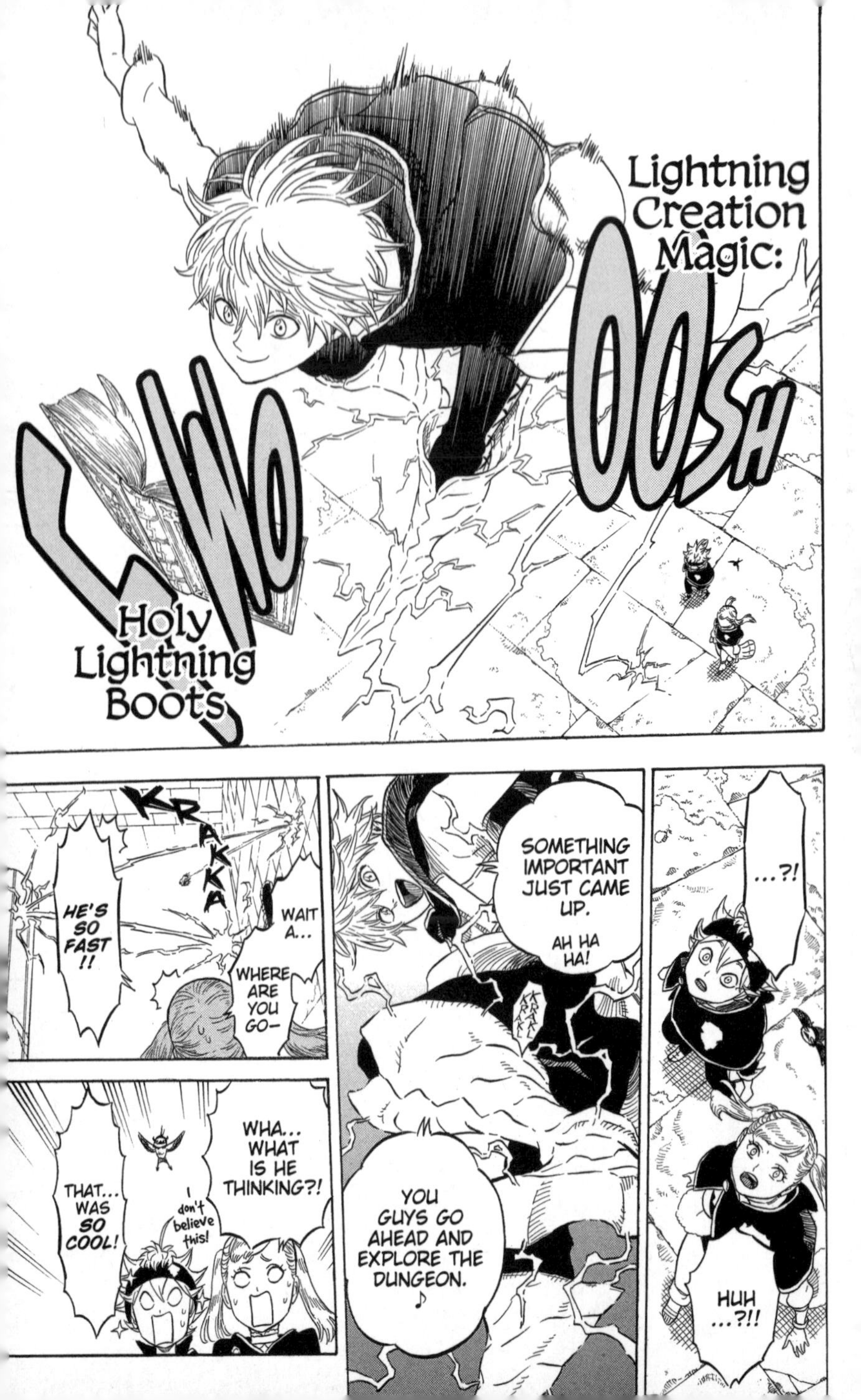
Lightning Creation Magic:
SWOOOSH
Holy Lightning Boots
...?!
HUH ...?!!
SOMETHING IMPORTANT JUST CAME UP.
AH HA HA!
KRAK KRAK
YOU GUYS GO AHEAD AND EXPLORE THE DUNGEON. ♪
KRAKKA
WAIT A...
WHERE ARE YOU GO—
HE'S SO FAST!!
WHA... WHAT IS HE THINKING?!
I don't believe this!
THAT... WAS SO COOL!

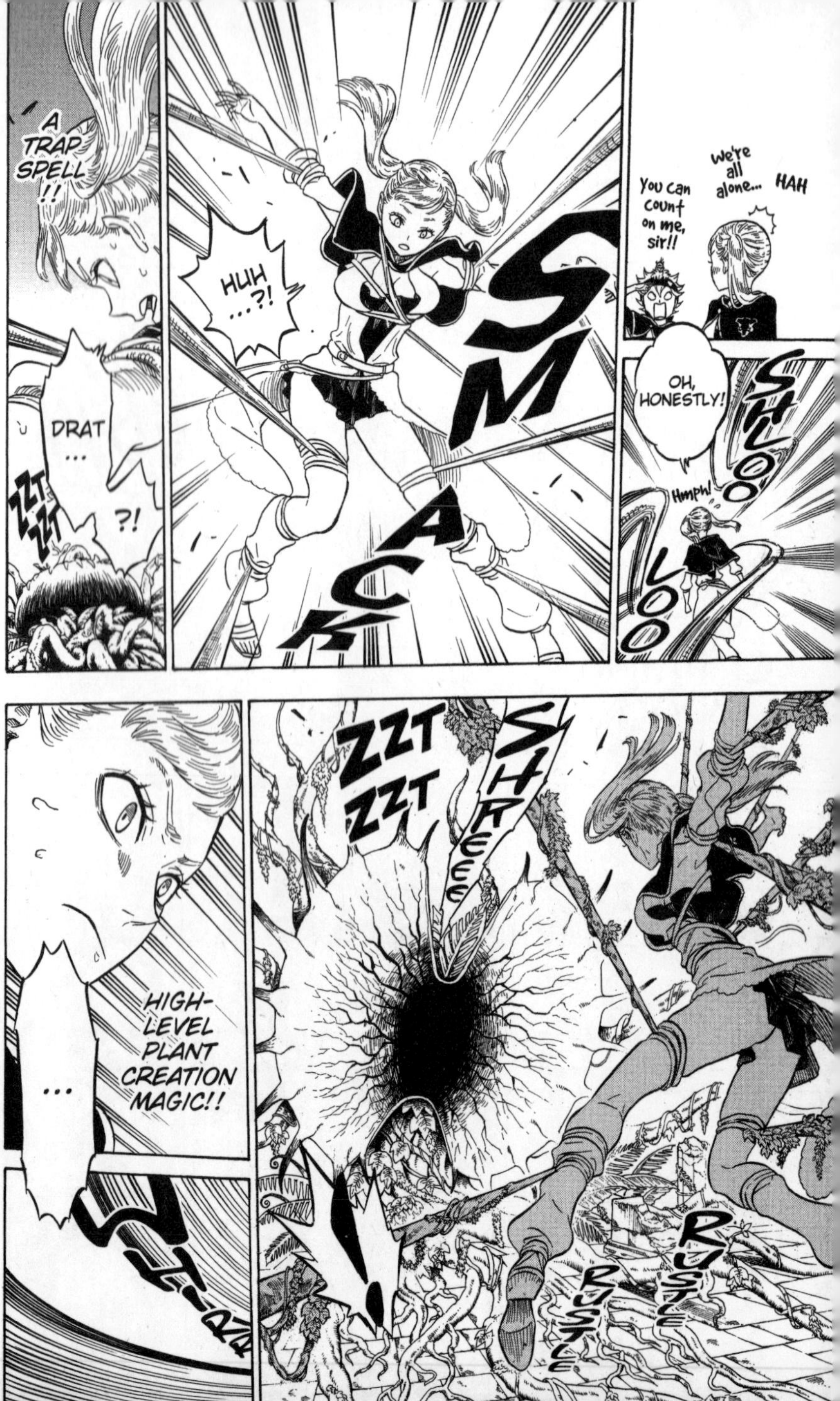
HAH
We're all alone...
You can count on me, sir!!
OH, HONESTLY!
SHLOOOO
Hmph!
LOOO
SMACK
HUH ...?!
A TRAP SPELL!!
DRAT ...
ZZT ZZT
?!
SHREEEE
ZZT ZZT
RUSTLE
RUSTLE
!
HIGH-LEVEL PLANT CREATION MAGIC!!
...

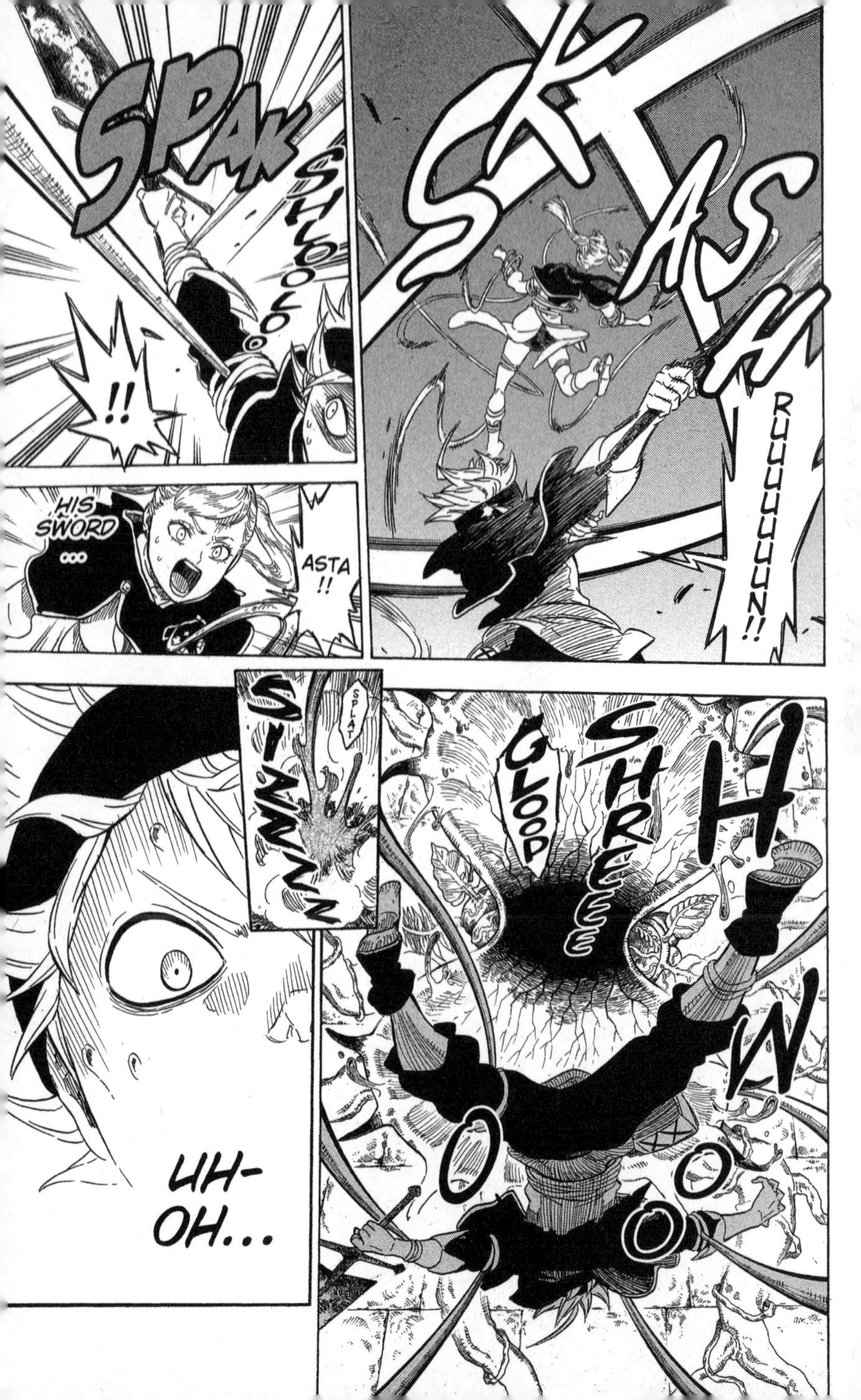
SKASH
RUUUUUUUUUN!!
SPAK
SHOOOOOO
!!
HIS SWORD...
ASTA!!
HWOOO
SHREEEEE
GLOOP
SPLAT
SIZZZZZ
UH-OH...

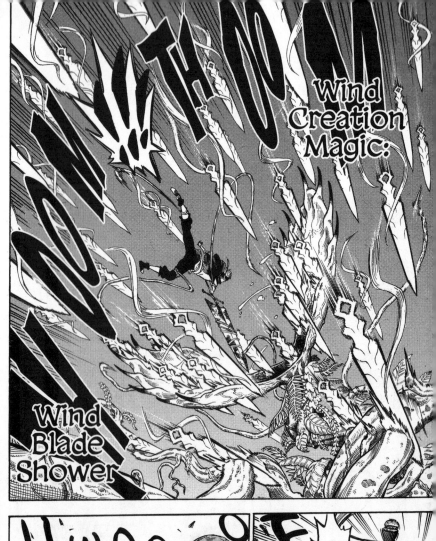

Wind Creation Magic:

Wind Blade Shower

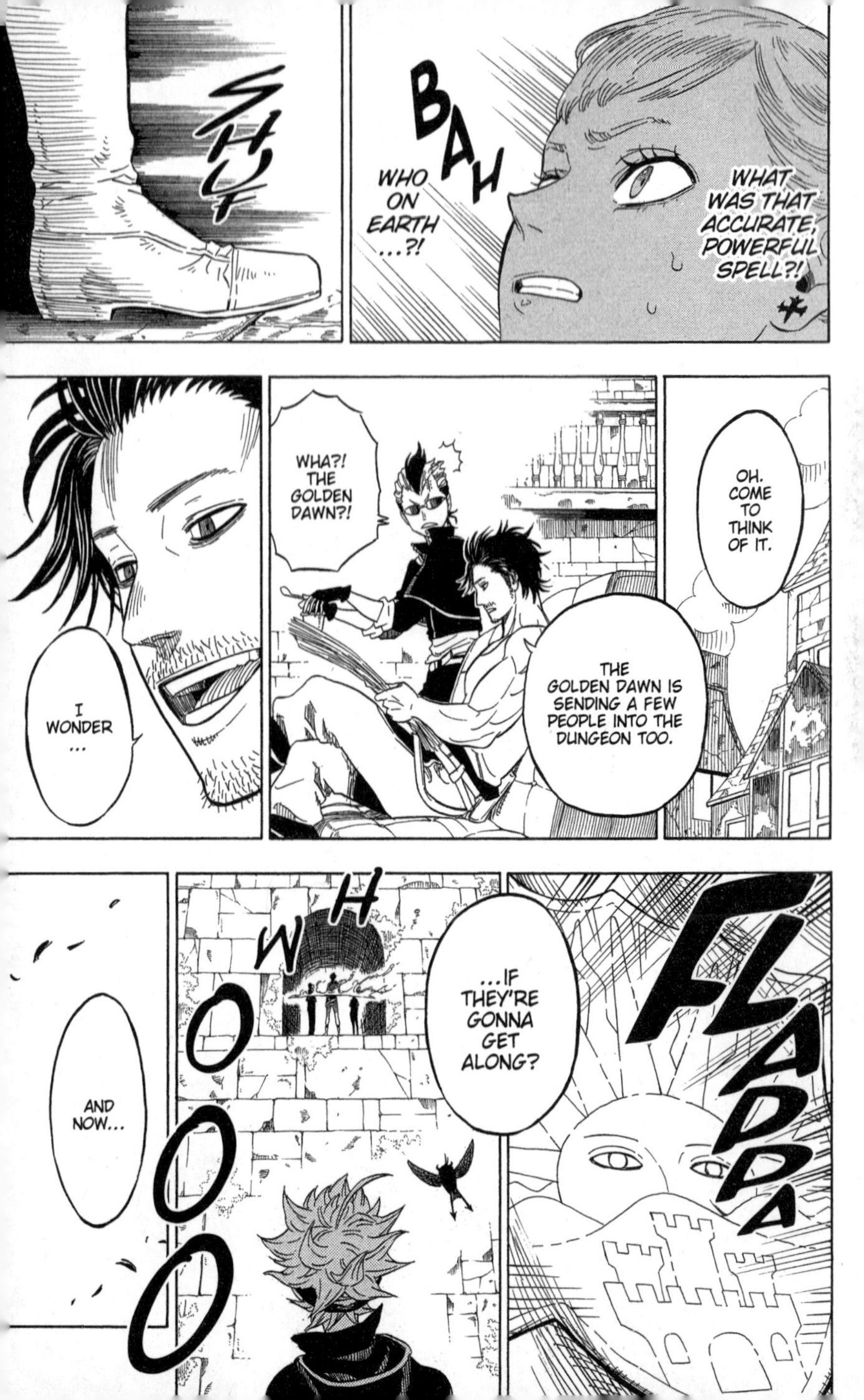
BAH
WHAT WAS THAT ACCURATE, POWERFUL SPELL?!
WHO ON EARTH ...?!
SHUF
OH. COME TO THINK OF IT.
THE GOLDEN DAWN IS SENDING A FEW PEOPLE INTO THE DUNGEON TOO.
WHA?! THE GOLDEN DAWN?!
I WONDER ...
FLAPPA
...IF THEY'RE GONNA GET ALONG?
WHOOOO
AND NOW...

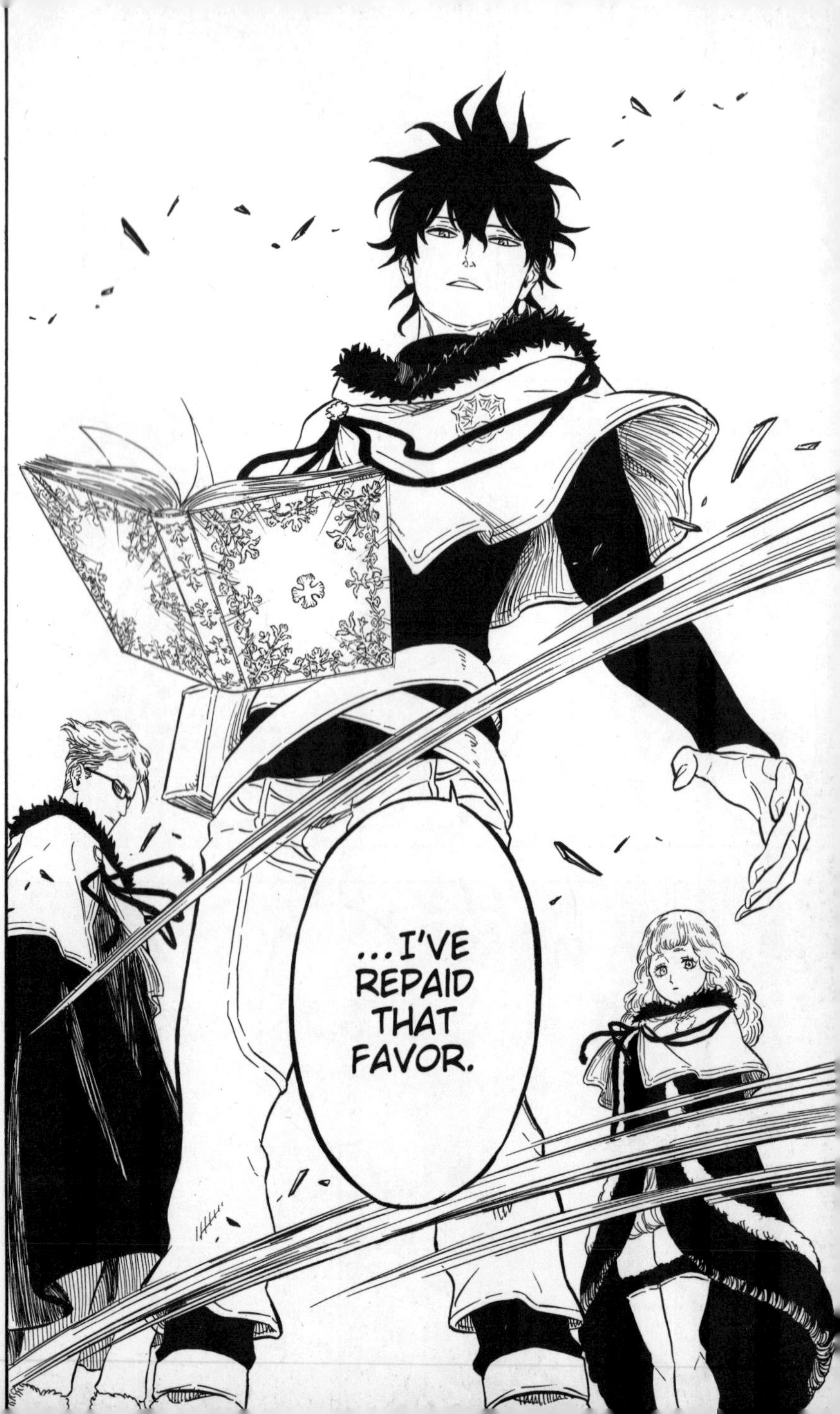
...I'VE REPAID THAT FAVOR.

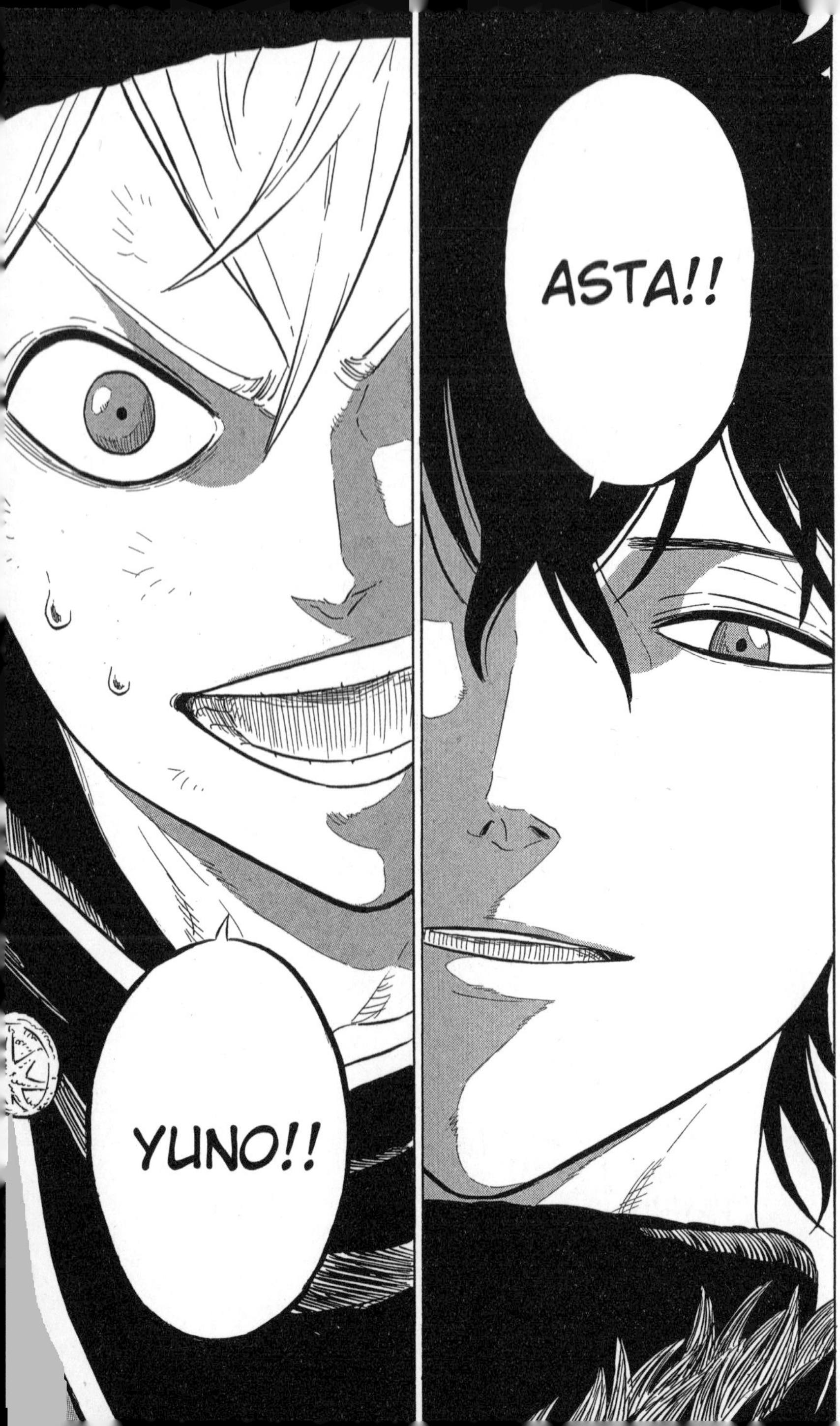
ASTA!!
YUNO!!

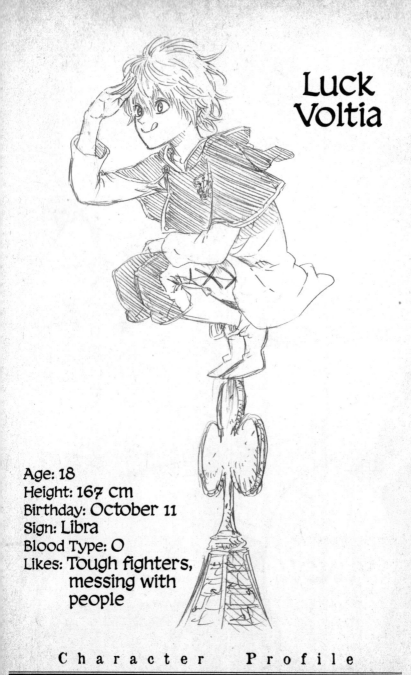

Luck Voltia

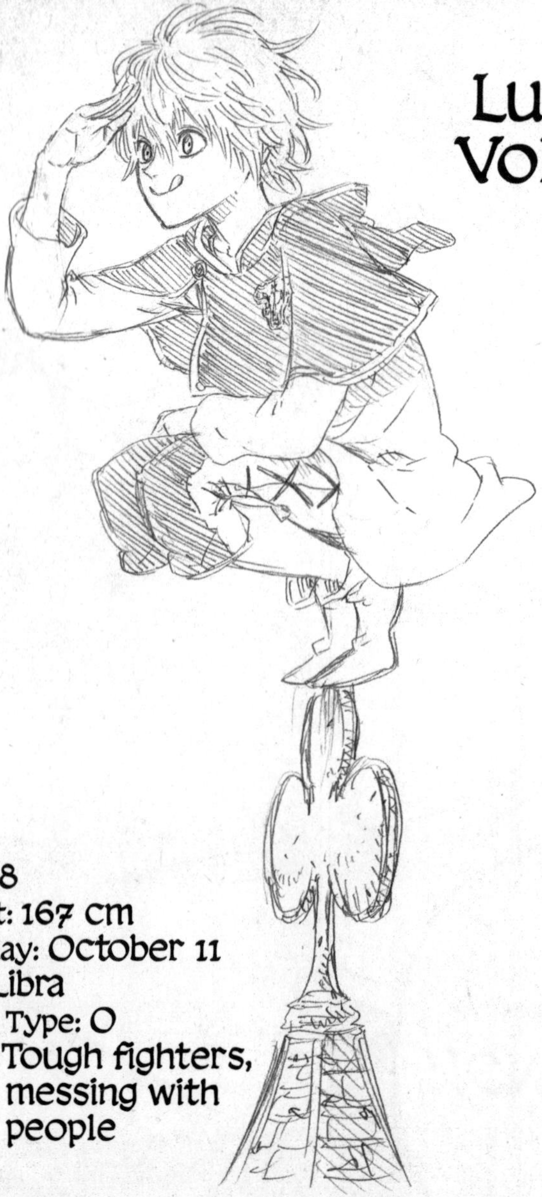

Age: 18
Height: 167 cm
Birthday: October 11
Sign: Libra
Blood Type: O
Likes: Tough fighters, messing with people

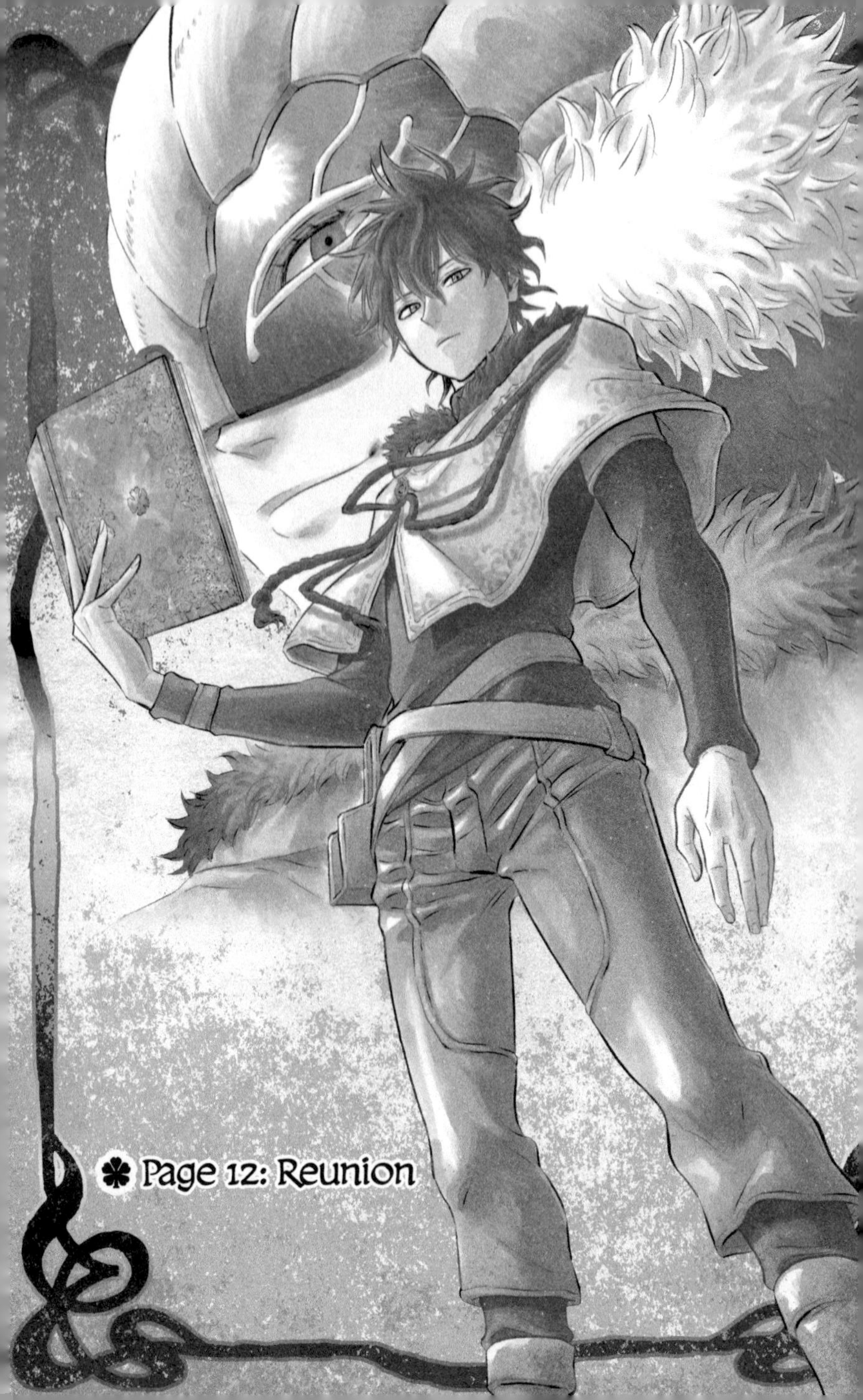
Page 12: Reunion

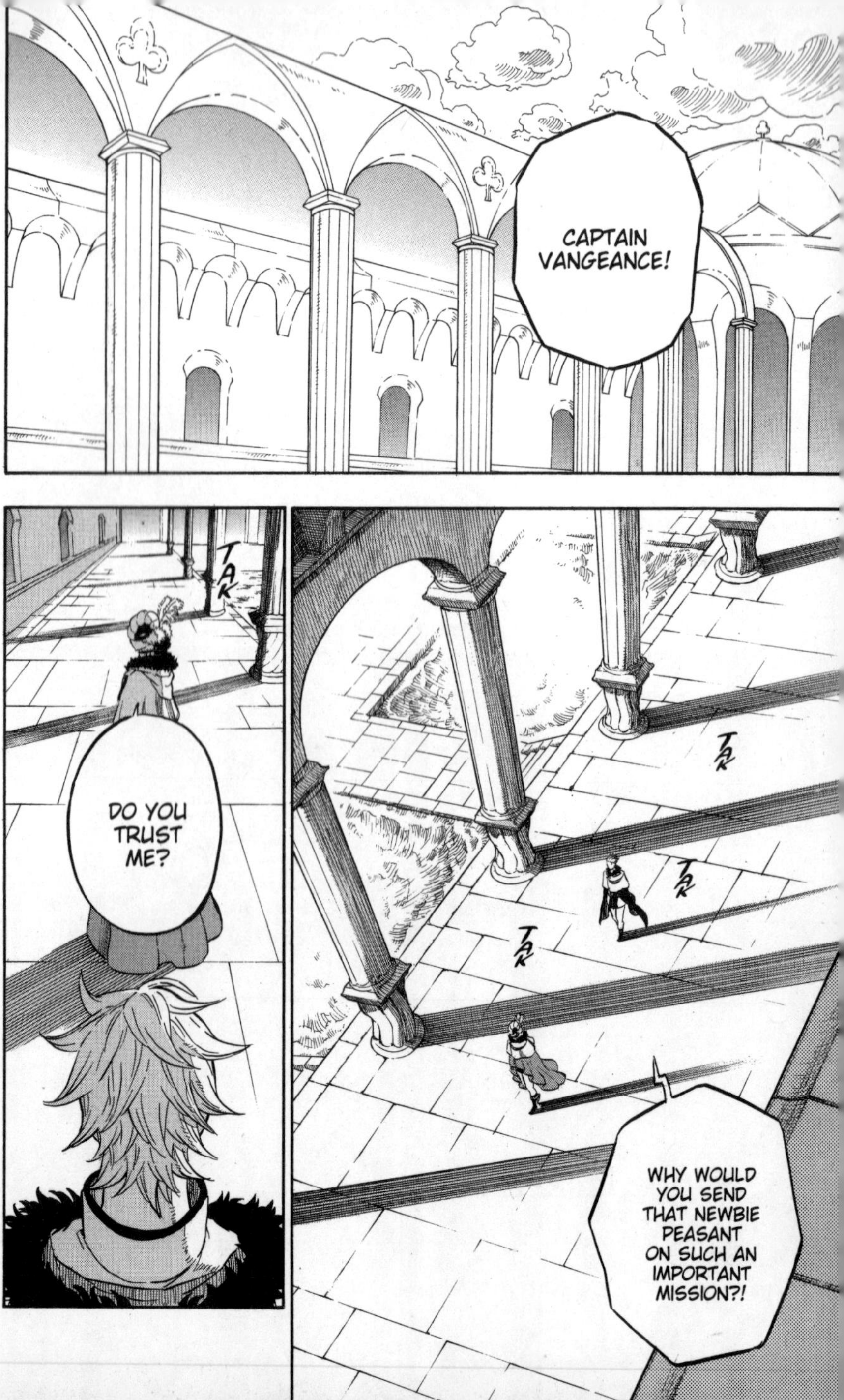
CAPTAIN VANGEANCE!
TAK
TAK
TAK
WHY WOULD YOU SEND THAT NEWBIE PEASANT ON SUCH AN IMPORTANT MISSION?!
TAK
DO YOU TRUST ME?

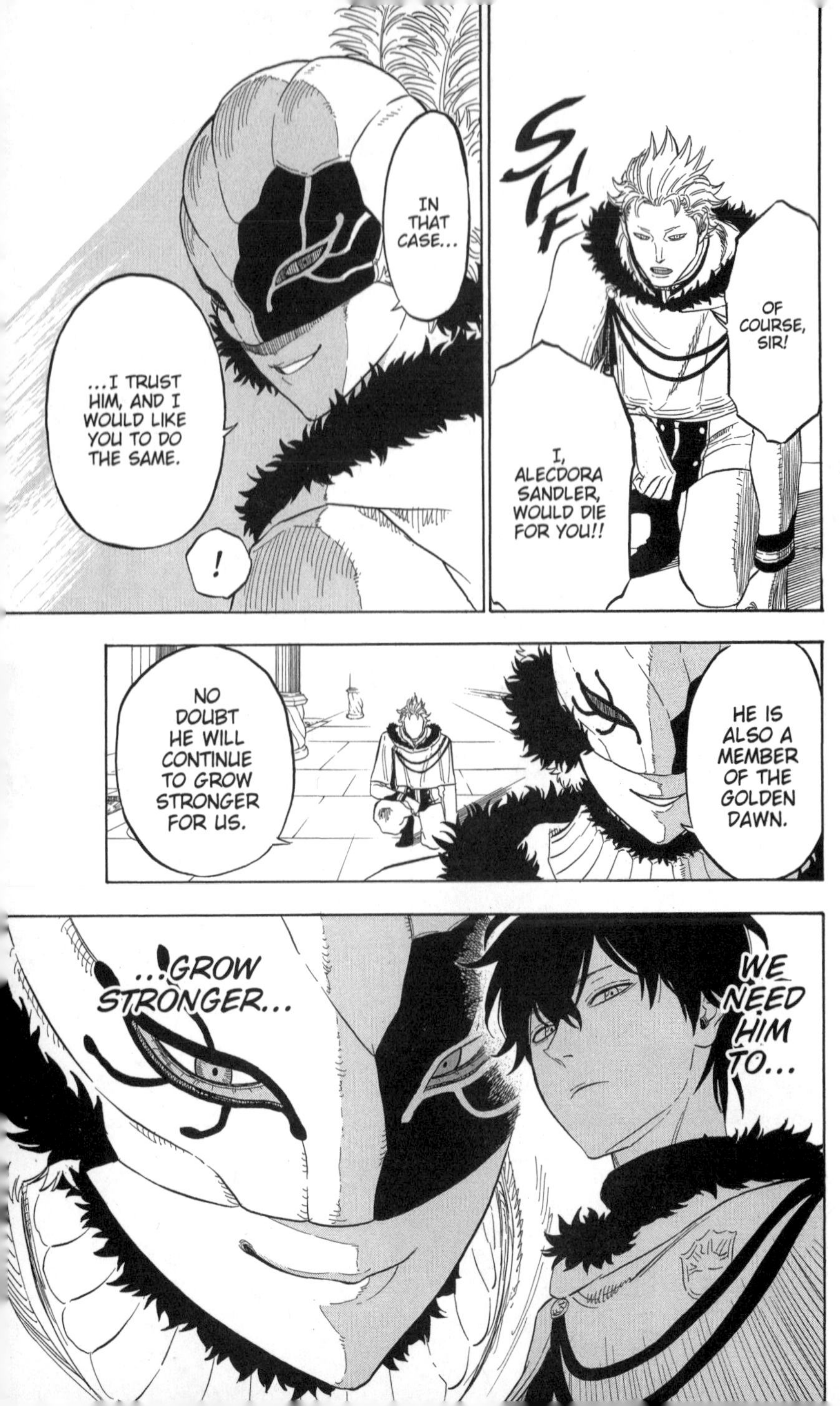
SHF
OF COURSE, SIR!
I, ALECDORA SANDLER, WOULD DIE FOR YOU!!
IN THAT CASE...
...I TRUST HIM, AND I WOULD LIKE YOU TO DO THE SAME.
!
HE IS ALSO A MEMBER OF THE GOLDEN DAWN.
NO DOUBT HE WILL CONTINUE TO GROW STRONGER FOR US.
WE NEED HIM TO...
...GROW STRONGER...

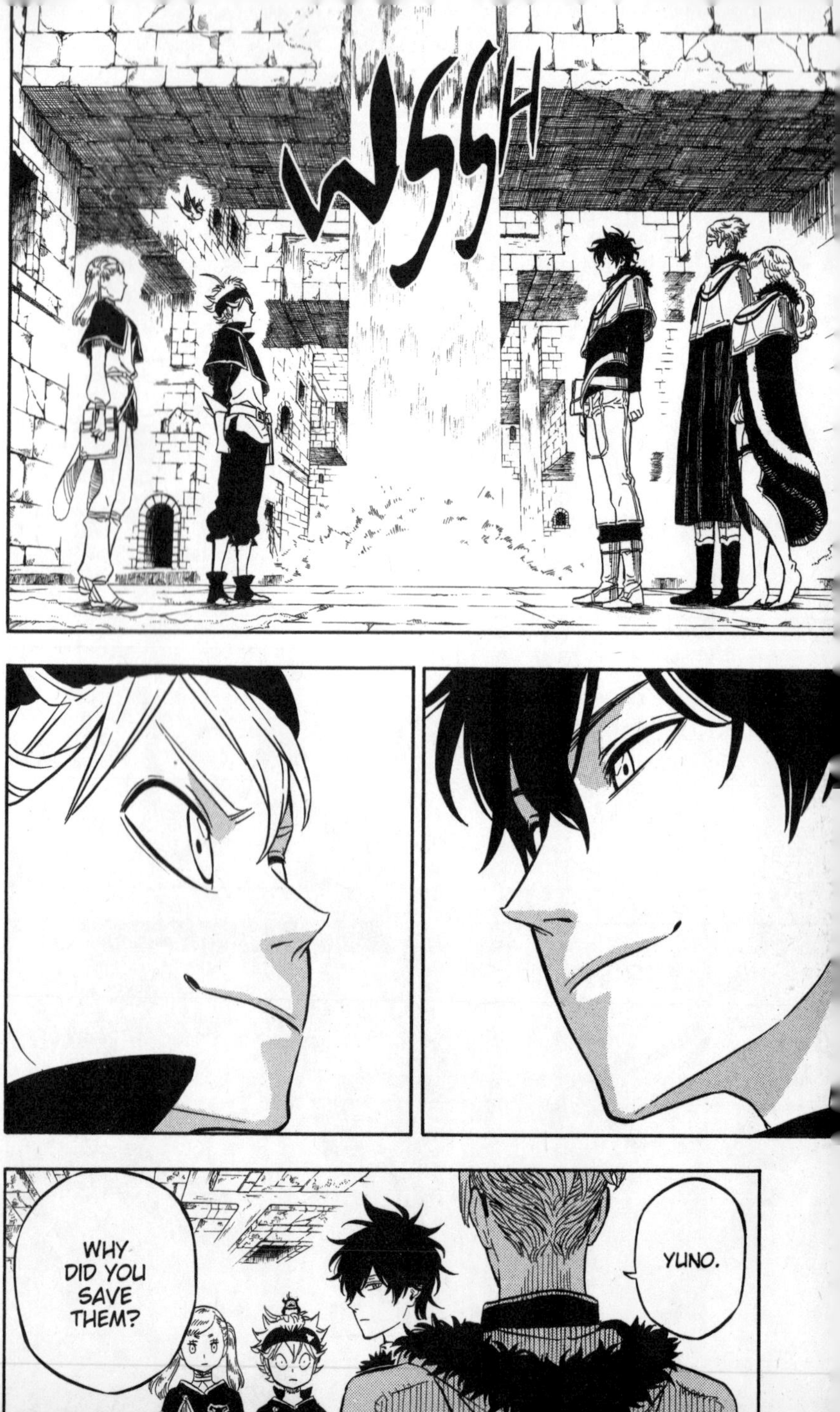
WSSH
YUNO.
WHY DID YOU SAVE THEM?

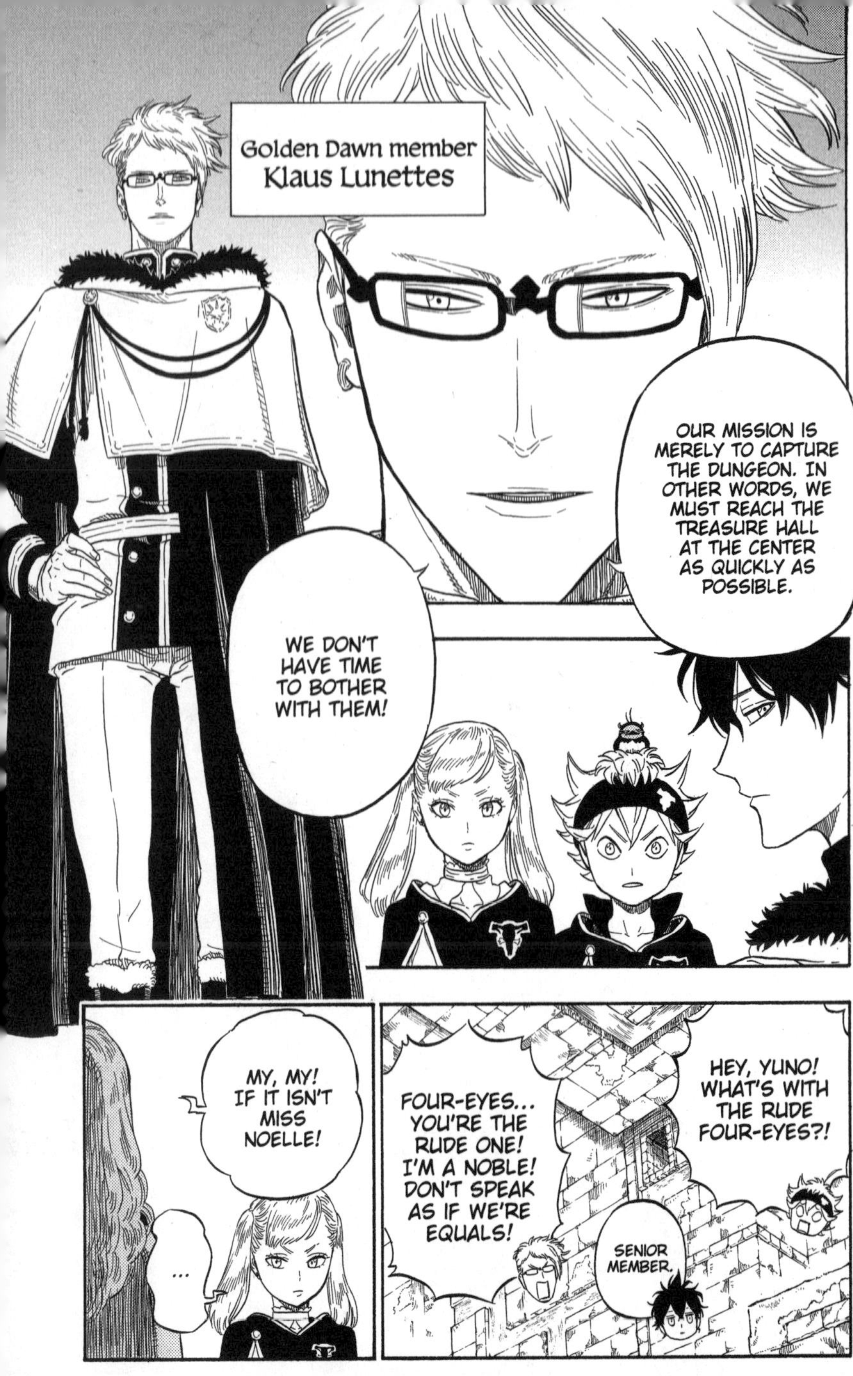

OUR MISSION IS MERELY TO CAPTURE THE DUNGEON. IN OTHER WORDS, WE MUST REACH THE TREASURE HALL AT THE CENTER AS QUICKLY AS POSSIBLE.
WE DON'T HAVE TIME TO BOTHER WITH THEM!
Golden Dawn member
Klaus Lunettes
HEY, YUNO! WHAT'S WITH THE RUDE FOUR-EYES?!
FOUR-EYES... YOU'RE THE RUDE ONE! I'M A NOBLE! DON'T SPEAK AS IF WE'RE EQUALS!
SENIOR MEMBER.
MY, MY! IF IT ISN'T MISS NOELLE!
...

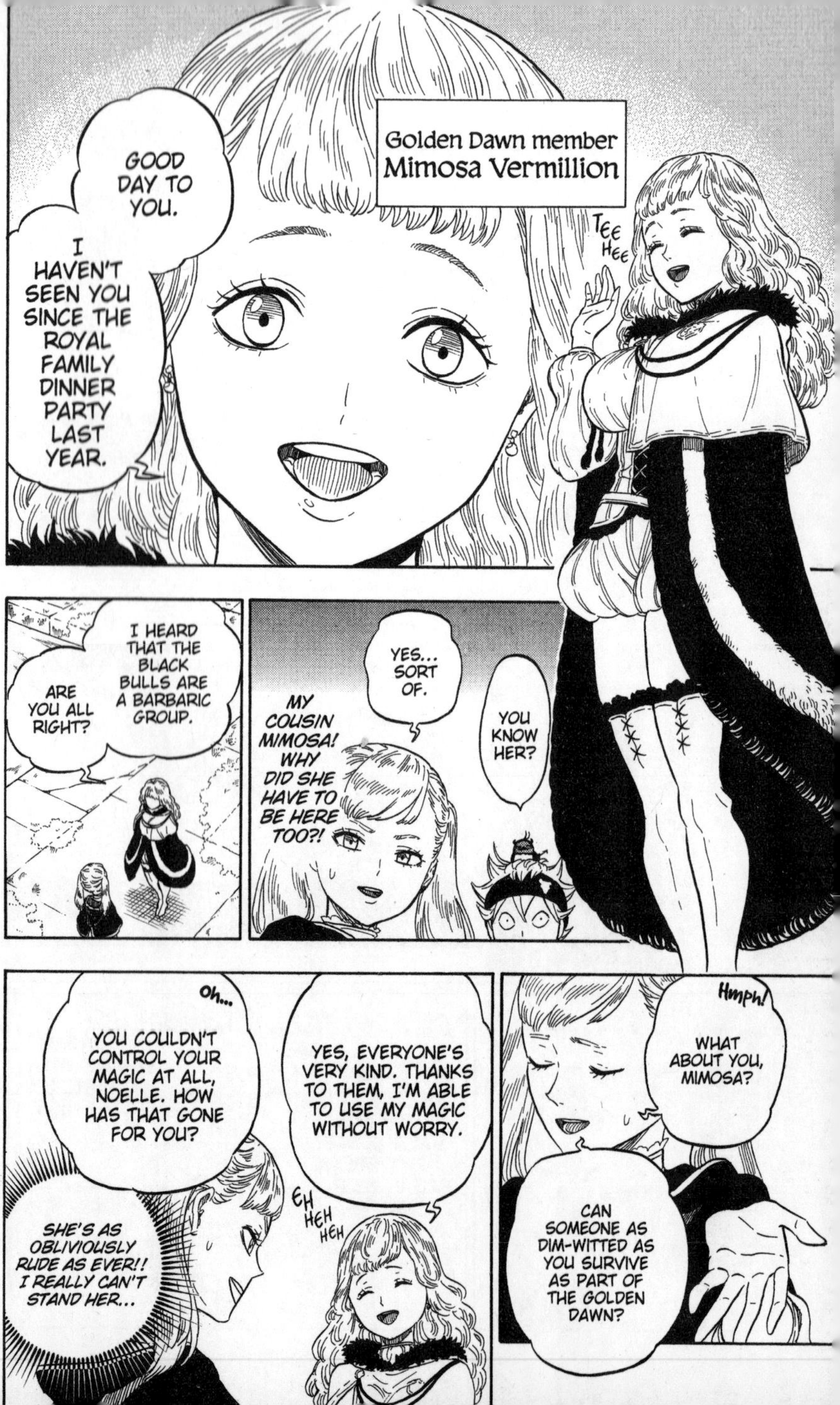
Golden Dawn member Mimosa Vermillion
TEE HEE
GOOD DAY TO YOU.
I HAVEN'T SEEN YOU SINCE THE ROYAL FAMILY DINNER PARTY LAST YEAR.
YOU KNOW HER?
YES... SORT OF.
MY COUSIN MIMOSA! WHY DID SHE HAVE TO BE HERE TOO?!
I HEARD THAT THE BLACK BULLS ARE A BARBARIC GROUP.
ARE YOU ALL RIGHT?
Hmph!
WHAT ABOUT YOU, MIMOSA?
CAN SOMEONE AS DIM-WITTED AS YOU SURVIVE AS PART OF THE GOLDEN DAWN?
YES, EVERYONE'S VERY KIND. THANKS TO THEM, I'M ABLE TO USE MY MAGIC WITHOUT WORRY.
Oh...
YOU COULDN'T CONTROL YOUR MAGIC AT ALL, NOELLE. HOW HAS THAT GONE FOR YOU?
EH HEH HEH
SHE'S AS OBLIVIOUSLY RUDE AS EVER!! I REALLY CAN'T STAND HER...

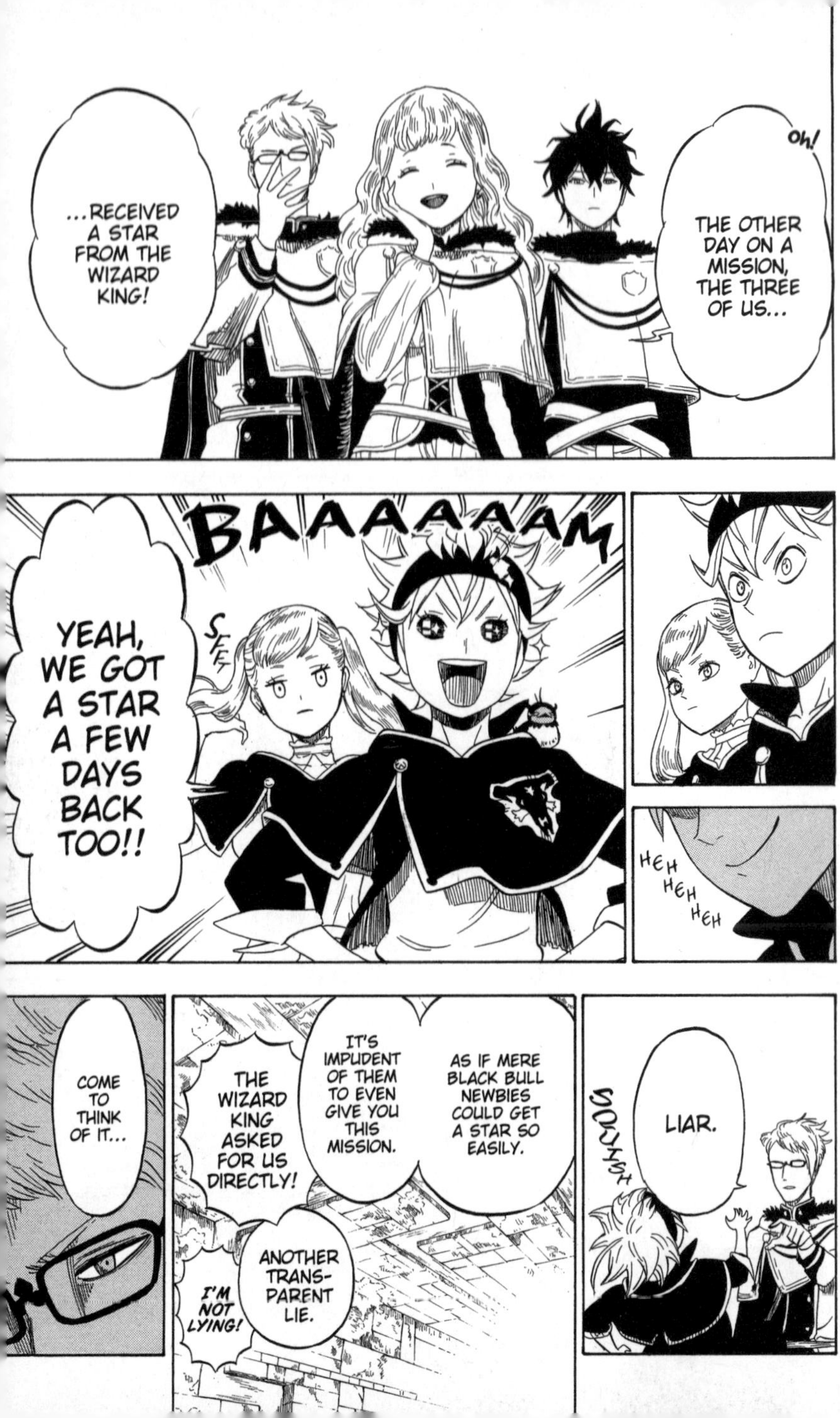

Oh!
THE OTHER DAY ON A MISSION, THE THREE OF US...
...RECEIVED A STAR FROM THE WIZARD KING!
HEH HEH HEH
BAAAAAAM
SFFT
YEAH, WE GOT A STAR A FEW DAYS BACK TOO!!
WHOOSH
LIAR.
AS IF MERE BLACK BULL NEWBIES COULD GET A STAR SO EASILY.
IT'S IMPUDENT OF THEM TO EVEN GIVE YOU THIS MISSION.
THE WIZARD KING ASKED FOR US DIRECTLY!
ANOTHER TRANS-PARENT LIE.
I'M NOT LYING!
COME TO THINK OF IT...

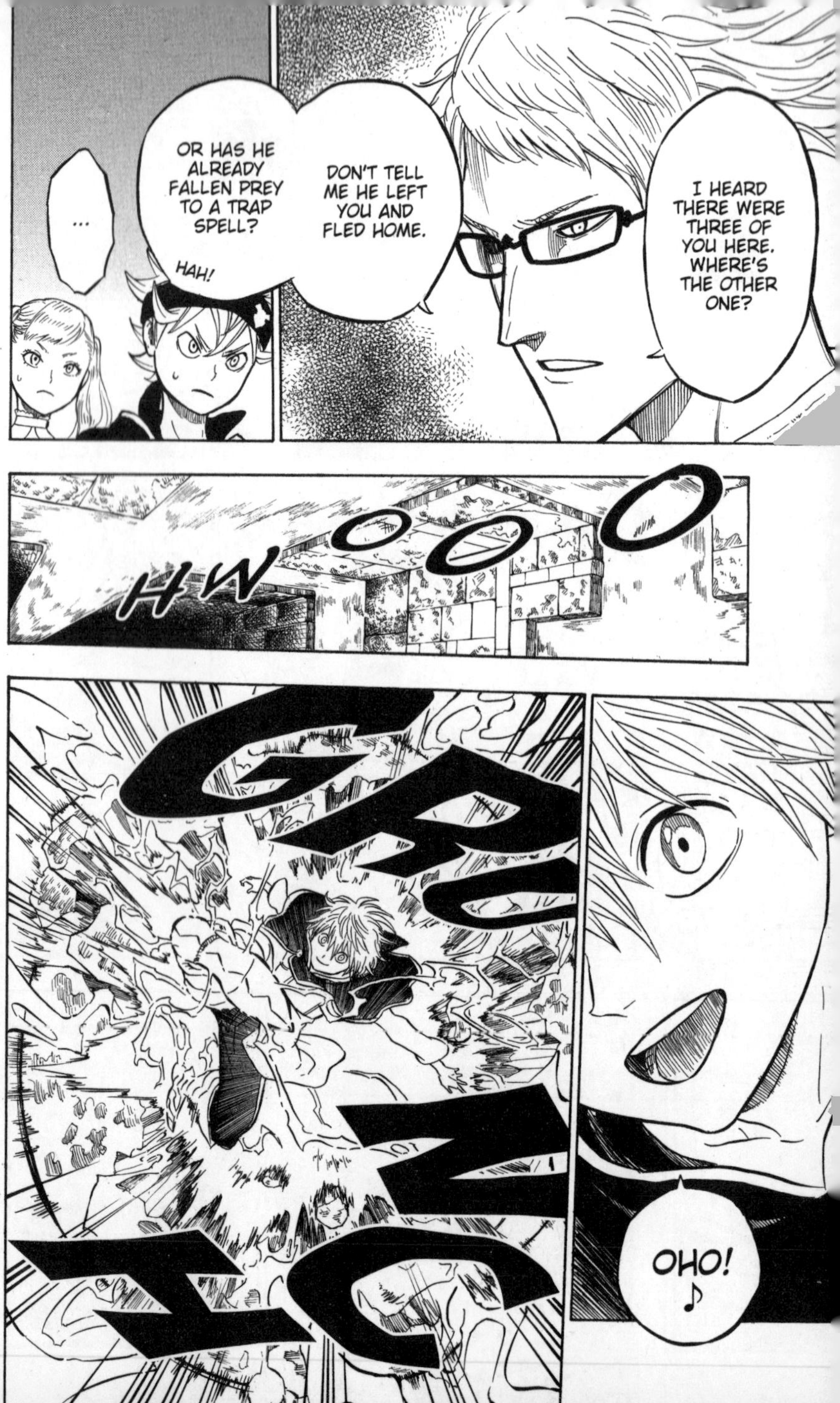

I HEARD THERE WERE THREE OF YOU HERE. WHERE'S THE OTHER ONE?
DON'T TELL ME HE LEFT YOU AND FLED HOME.
OR HAS HE ALREADY FALLEN PREY TO A TRAP SPELL?
HAH!
...
HWOOOO
OHO! ♪
CRUNCH

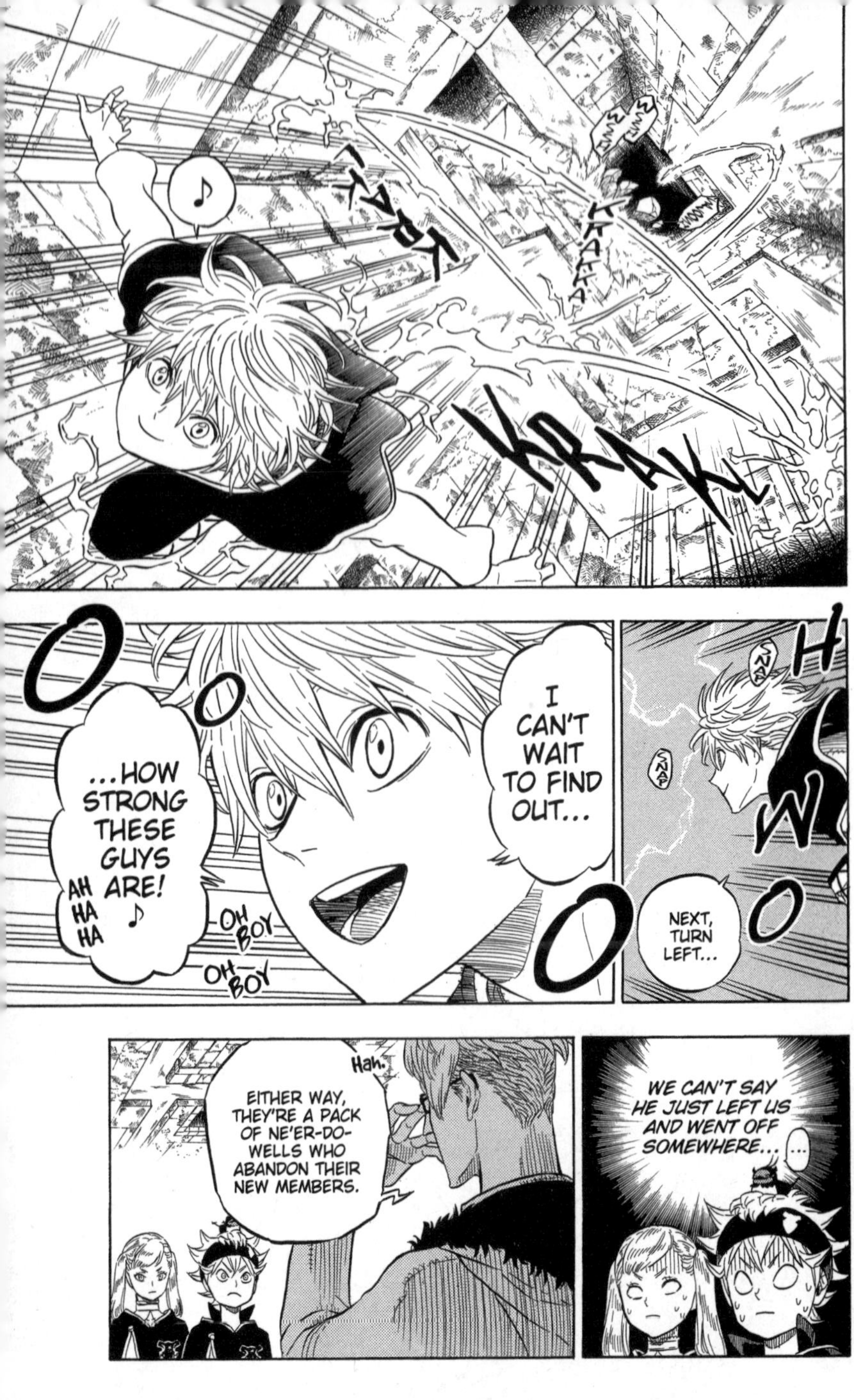
KRAKKA
♪
KRAK
KRAK
SNAP
SNAP
NEXT, TURN LEFT...
WHOOOO
I CAN'T WAIT TO FIND OUT...
...HOW STRONG THESE GUYS ARE! ♪
AH HA HA
OH BOY
OH BOY
WE CAN'T SAY HE JUST LEFT US AND WENT OFF SOMEWHERE...
...
Hah.
EITHER WAY, THEY'RE A PACK OF NE'ER-DO-WELLS WHO ABANDON THEIR NEW MEMBERS.

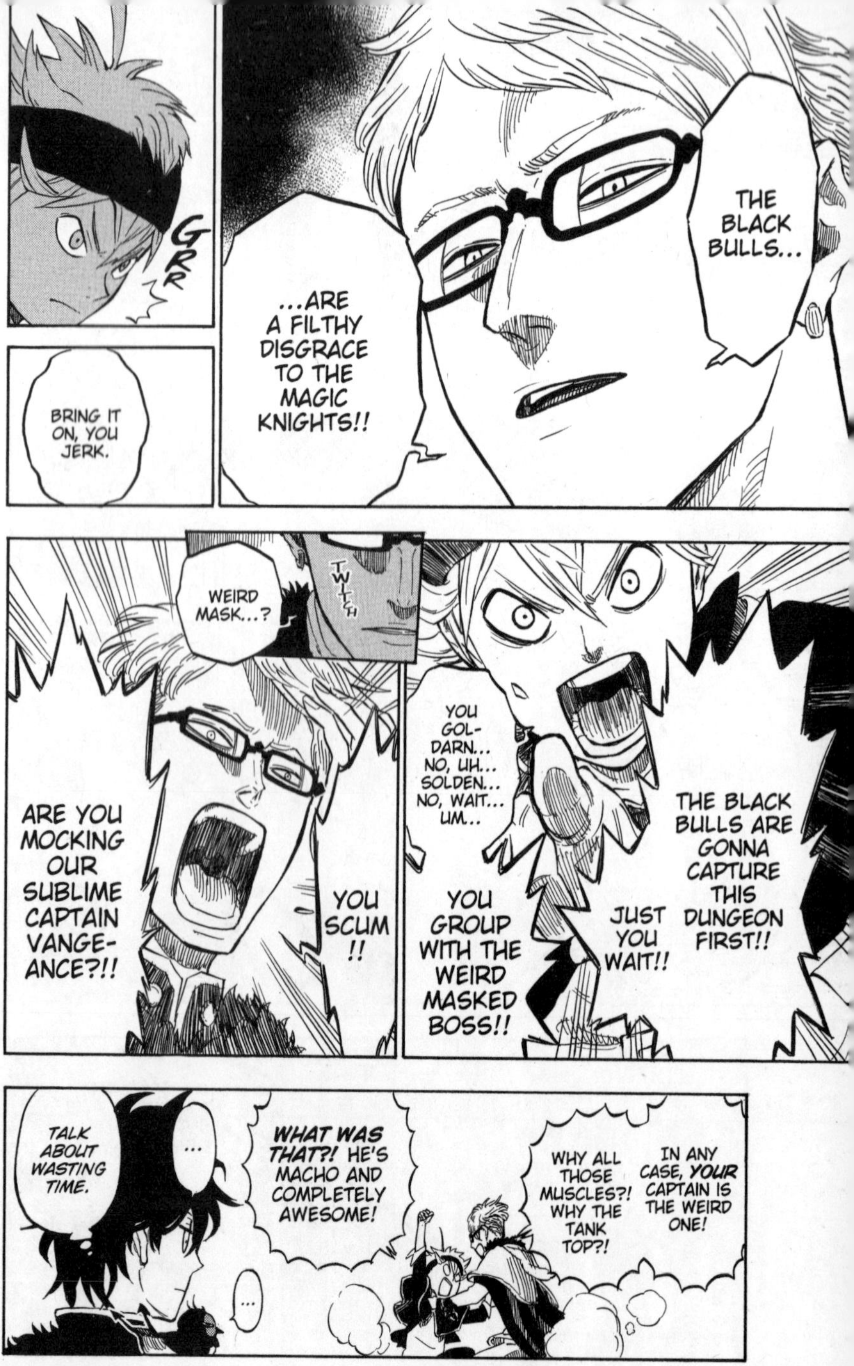
THE BLACK BULLS...
...ARE A FILTHY DISGRACE TO THE MAGIC KNIGHTS!!
GRR
BRING IT ON, YOU JERK.
THE BLACK BULLS ARE GONNA CAPTURE THIS DUNGEON FIRST!!
JUST YOU WAIT!!
YOU GROUP WITH THE WEIRD MASKED BOSS!!
YOU GOL-DARN... NO, UH... SOLDEN... NO, WAIT... UM..
WEIRD MASK...?
TWITCH
YOU SCUM!!
ARE YOU MOCKING OUR SUBLIME CAPTAIN VANGE-ANCE?!!
IN ANY CASE, *YOUR* CAPTAIN IS THE WEIRD ONE!
WHY ALL THOSE MUSCLES?! WHY THE TANK TOP?!
WHAT WAS THAT?! HE'S MACHO AND COMPLETELY AWESOME!
...
TALK ABOUT WASTING TIME.
...

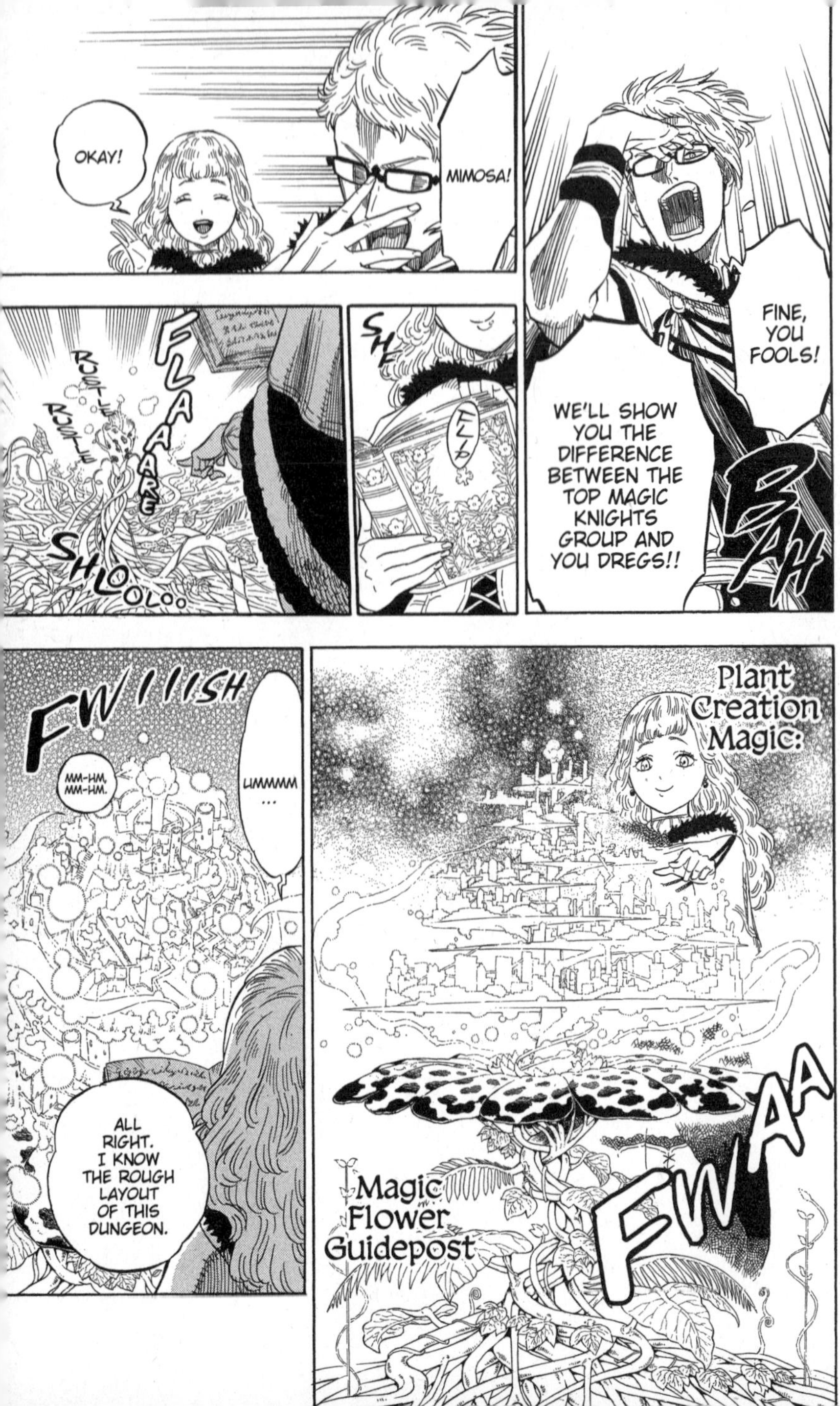
FINE, YOU FOOLS!
WE'LL SHOW YOU THE DIFFERENCE BETWEEN THE TOP MAGIC KNIGHTS GROUP AND YOU DREGS!!
BAH
MIMOSA!
OKAY!
SHF
FLAAARE
RUSTLE
RUSTLE
SHLOOLOO
Plant Creation Magic:
Magic Flower Guidepost
FWAA
FWIIISH
UMMMM...
MM-HM, MM-HM.
ALL RIGHT. I KNOW THE ROUGH LAYOUT OF THIS DUNGEON.

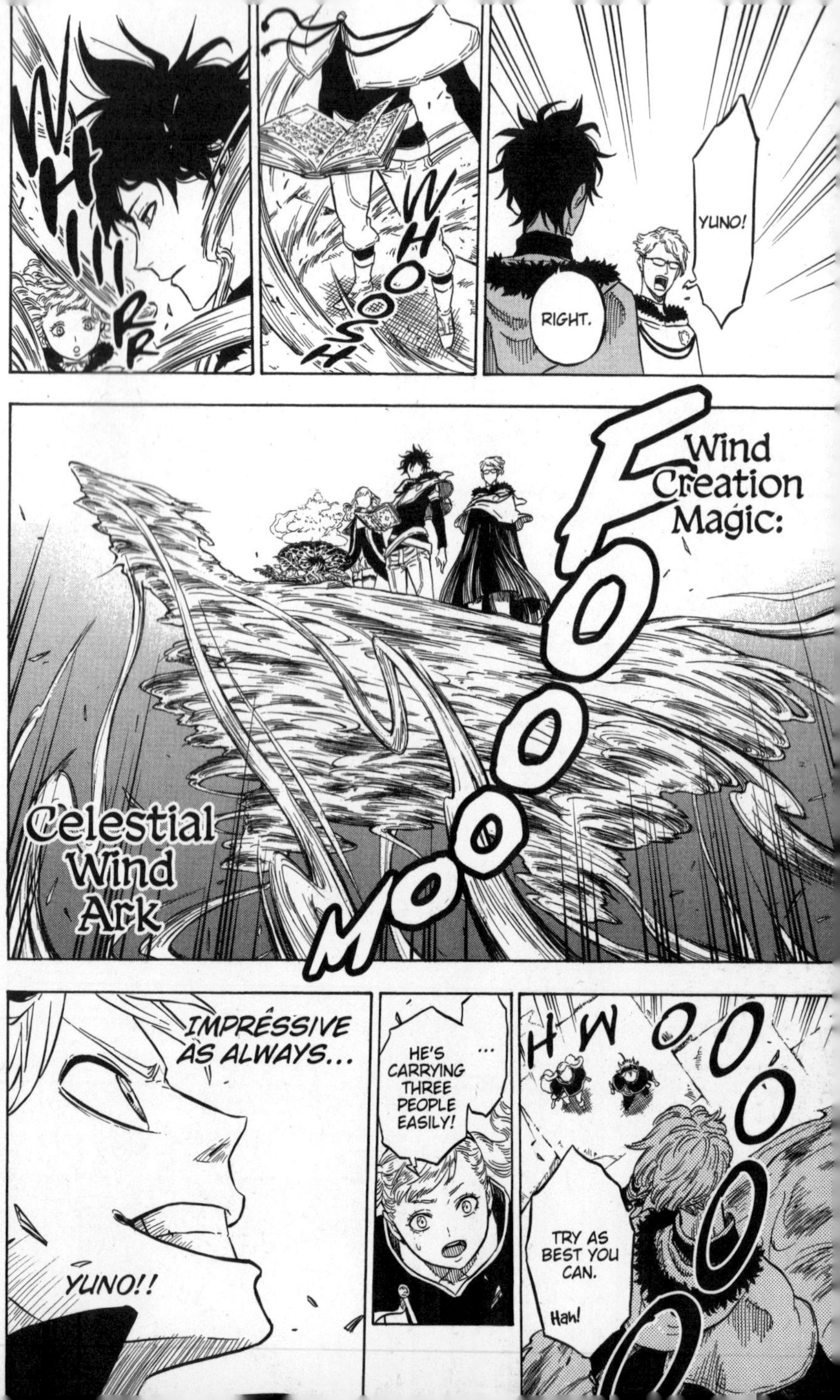
YUNO!
RIGHT.
WHOOOSH
WHIIRR
Wind Creation Magic:
Celestial Wind Ark
HWOOOOOO
TRY AS BEST YOU CAN.
Hah!
...
HE'S CARRYING THREE PEOPLE EASILY!
IMPRESSIVE AS ALWAYS...
YUNO!!

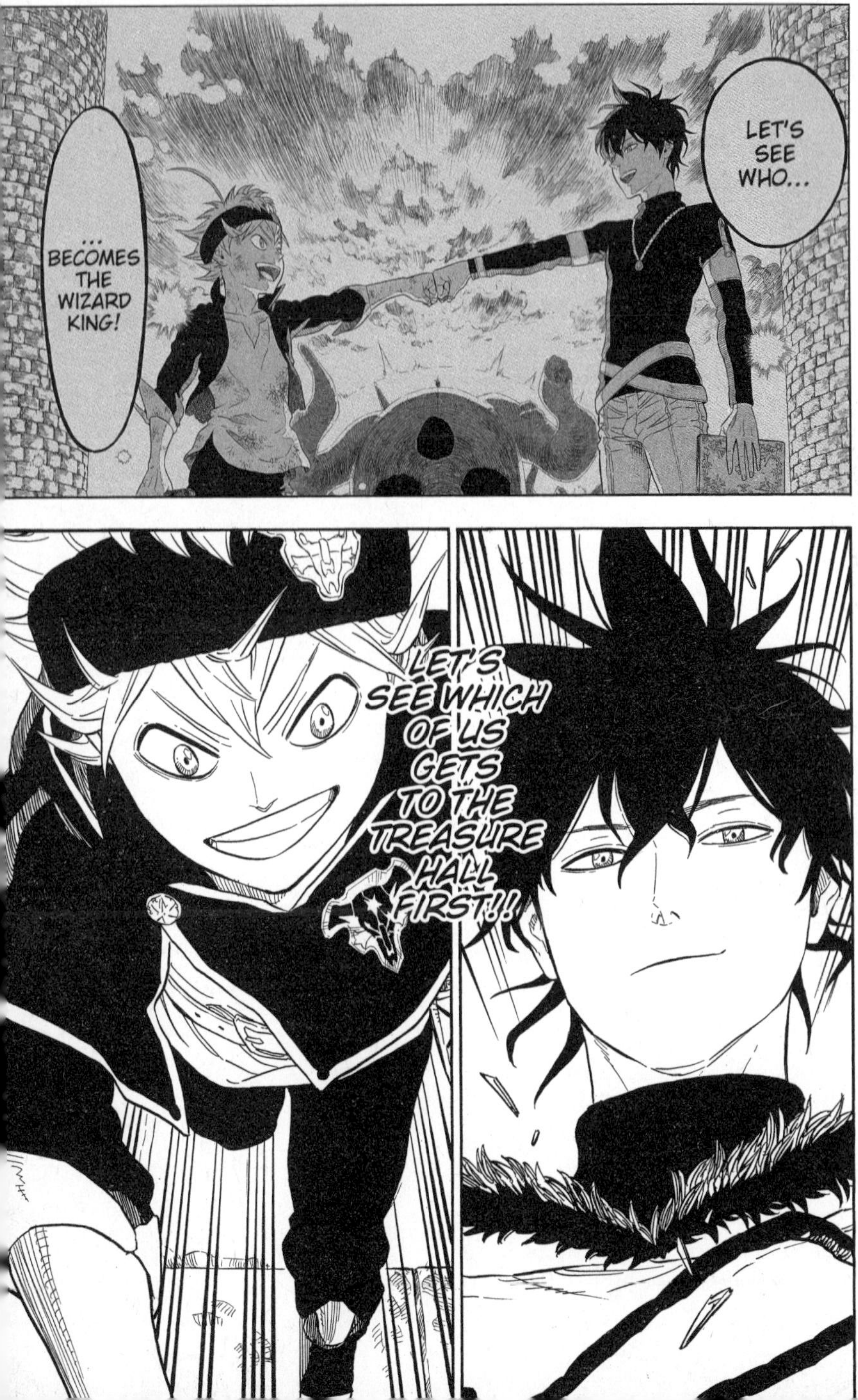
LET'S SEE WHO...
...BECOMES THE WIZARD KING!
LET'S SEE WHICH OF US GETS TO THE TREASURE HALL FIRST!!

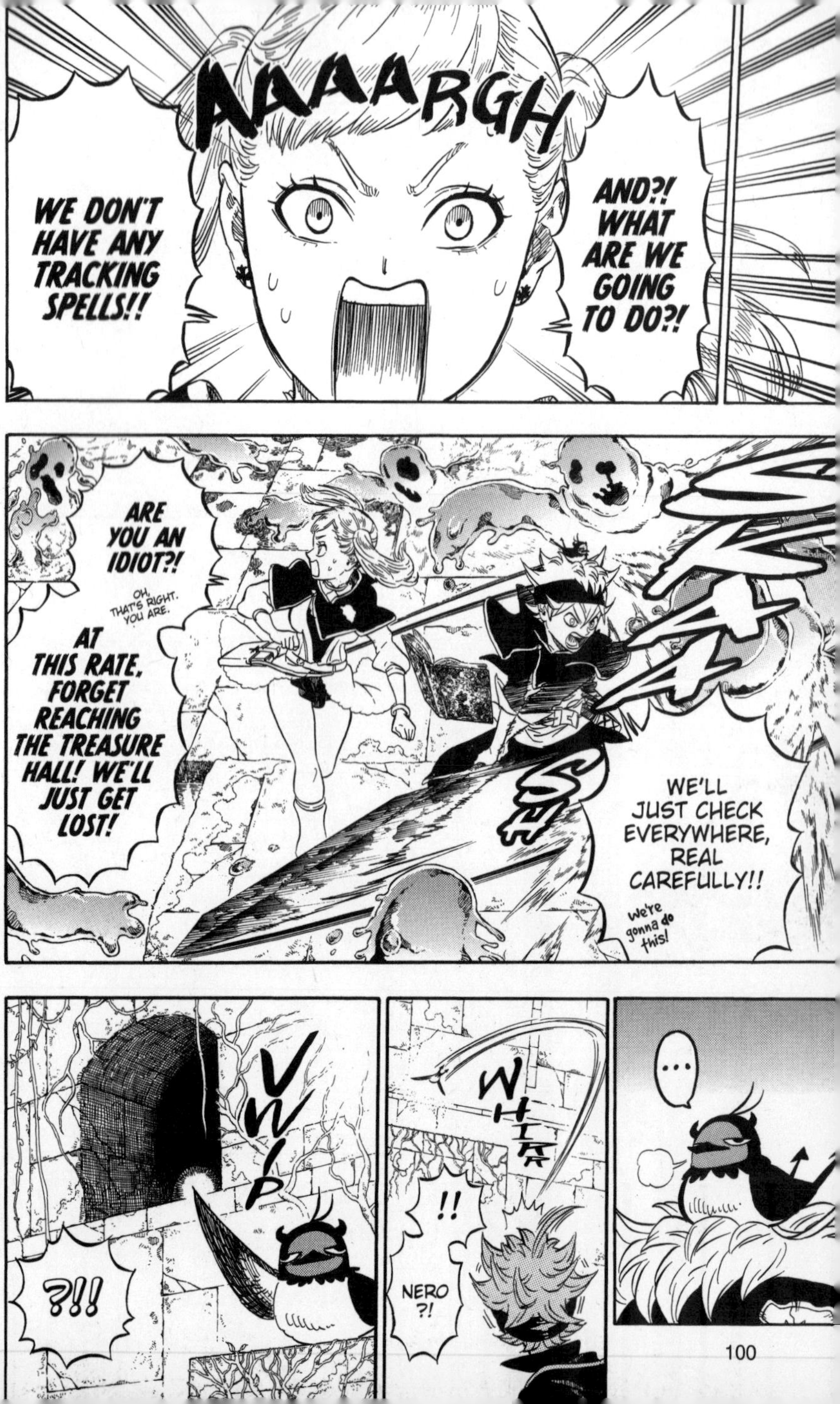
AAAARGH
AND?! WHAT ARE WE GOING TO DO?!
WE DON'T HAVE ANY TRACKING SPELLS!!
WE'LL JUST CHECK EVERYWHERE, REAL CAREFULLY!!
we're gonna do this!
ARE YOU AN IDIOT?!
OH, THAT'S RIGHT. YOU ARE.
AT THIS RATE, FORGET REACHING THE TREASURE HALL! WE'LL JUST GET LOST!
...
WHIRR
!!
NERO ?!
VWIP
?!!

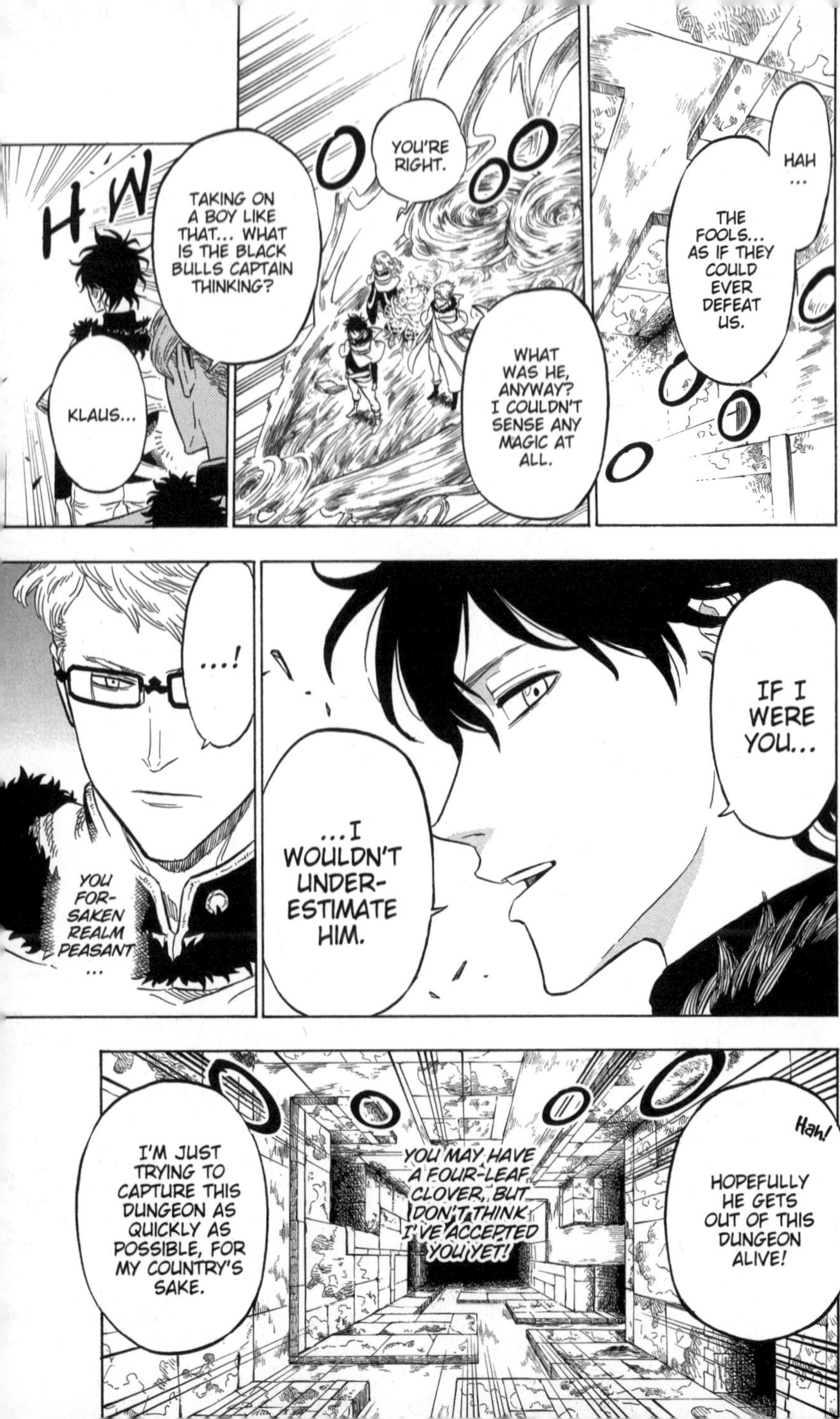
HAH... THE FOOLS... AS IF THEY COULD EVER DEFEAT US.
YOU'RE RIGHT.
WHAT WAS HE, ANYWAY? I COULDN'T SENSE ANY MAGIC AT ALL.
TAKING ON A BOY LIKE THAT... WHAT IS THE BLACK BULLS CAPTAIN THINKING?
HW
KLAUS...
IF I WERE YOU...
...I WOULDN'T UNDER-ESTIMATE HIM.
...!
YOU FOR-SAKEN REALM PEASANT...
Hah!
HOPEFULLY HE GETS OUT OF THIS DUNGEON ALIVE!
YOU MAY HAVE A FOUR-LEAF CLOVER, BUT DON'T THINK I'VE ACCEPTED YOU YET!
I'M JUST TRYING TO CAPTURE THIS DUNGEON AS QUICKLY AS POSSIBLE, FOR MY COUNTRY'S SAKE.

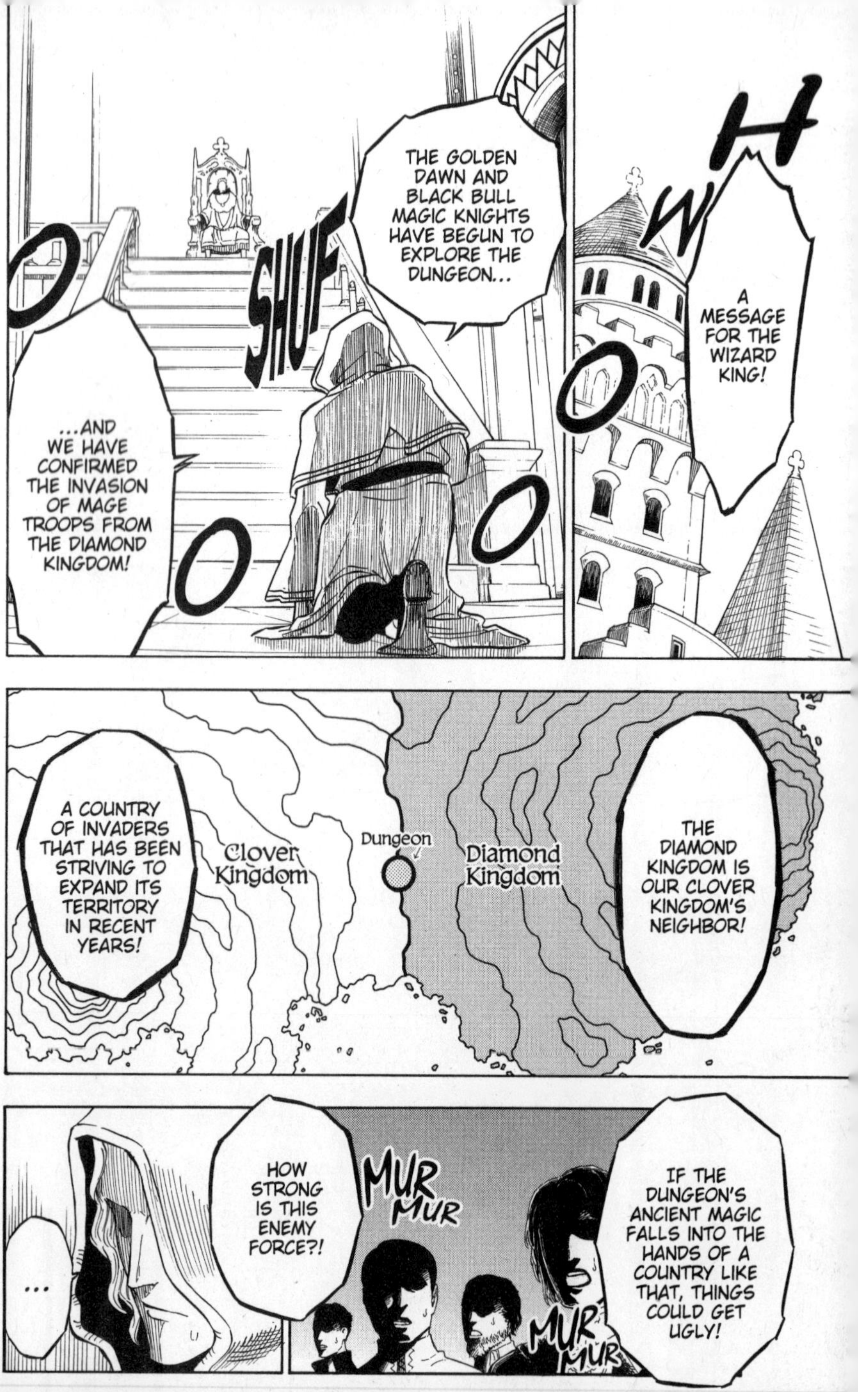
WHOOOO
A MESSAGE FOR THE WIZARD KING!
THE GOLDEN DAWN AND BLACK BULL MAGIC KNIGHTS HAVE BEGUN TO EXPLORE THE DUNGEON...
SHUF
...AND WE HAVE CONFIRMED THE INVASION OF MAGE TROOPS FROM THE DIAMOND KINGDOM!
THE DIAMOND KINGDOM IS OUR CLOVER KINGDOM'S NEIGHBOR!
Diamond Kingdom
Dungeon
Clover Kingdom
A COUNTRY OF INVADERS THAT HAS BEEN STRIVING TO EXPAND ITS TERRITORY IN RECENT YEARS!
IF THE DUNGEON'S ANCIENT MAGIC FALLS INTO THE HANDS OF A COUNTRY LIKE THAT, THINGS COULD GET UGLY!
MUR MUR
MUR MUR
HOW STRONG IS THIS ENEMY FORCE?!
...

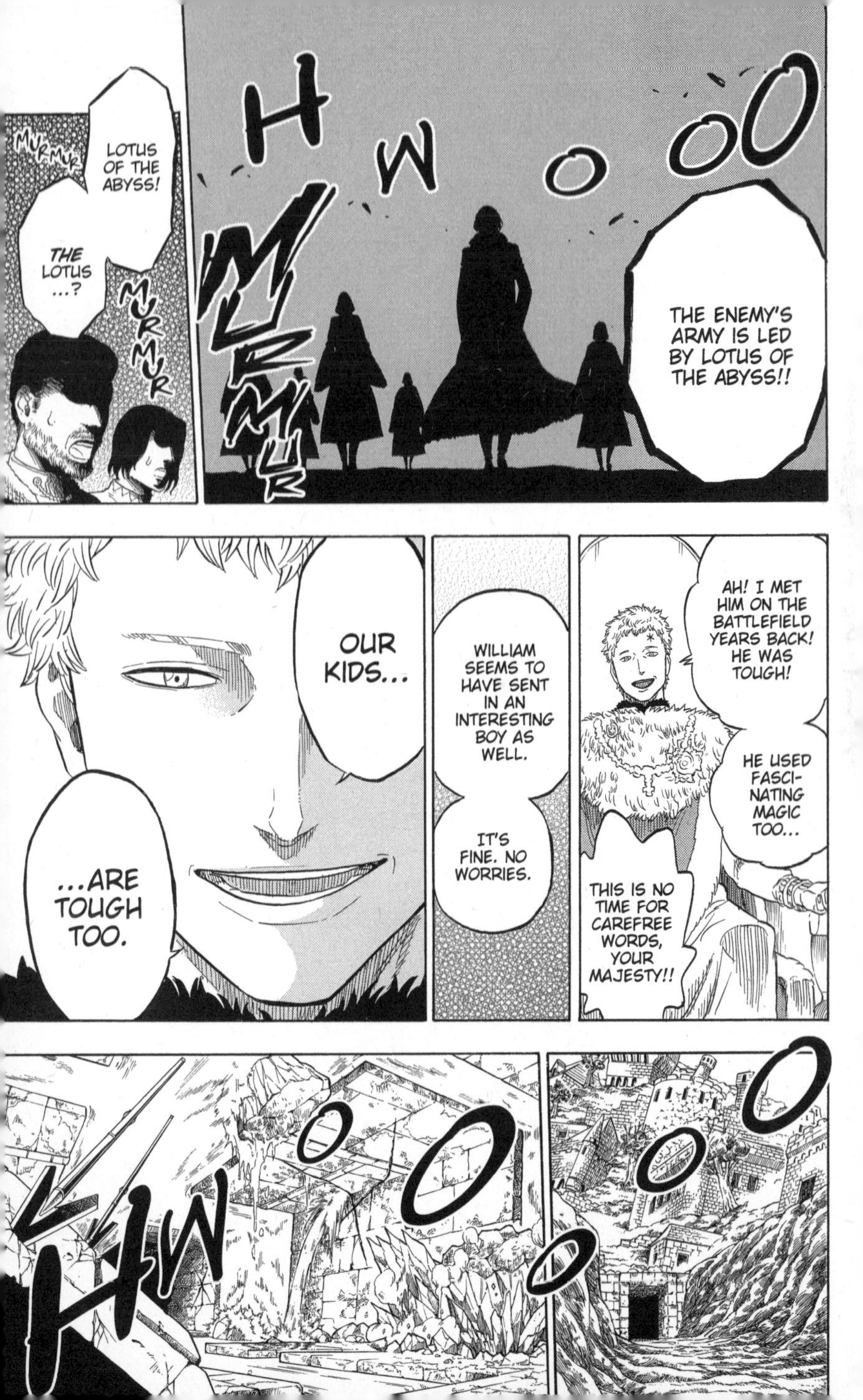
HWOOOO
MURMUR
THE ENEMY'S ARMY IS LED BY LOTUS OF THE ABYSS!!
MURMUR
LOTUS OF THE ABYSS!
THE LOTUS ...?
MURMUR
AH! I MET HIM ON THE BATTLEFIELD YEARS BACK! HE WAS TOUGH!
HE USED FASCINATING MAGIC TOO...
THIS IS NO TIME FOR CAREFREE WORDS, YOUR MAJESTY!!
WILLIAM SEEMS TO HAVE SENT IN AN INTERESTING BOY AS WELL.
IT'S FINE. NO WORRIES.
OUR KIDS...
...ARE TOUGH TOO.
OOOOO
HWOOOO

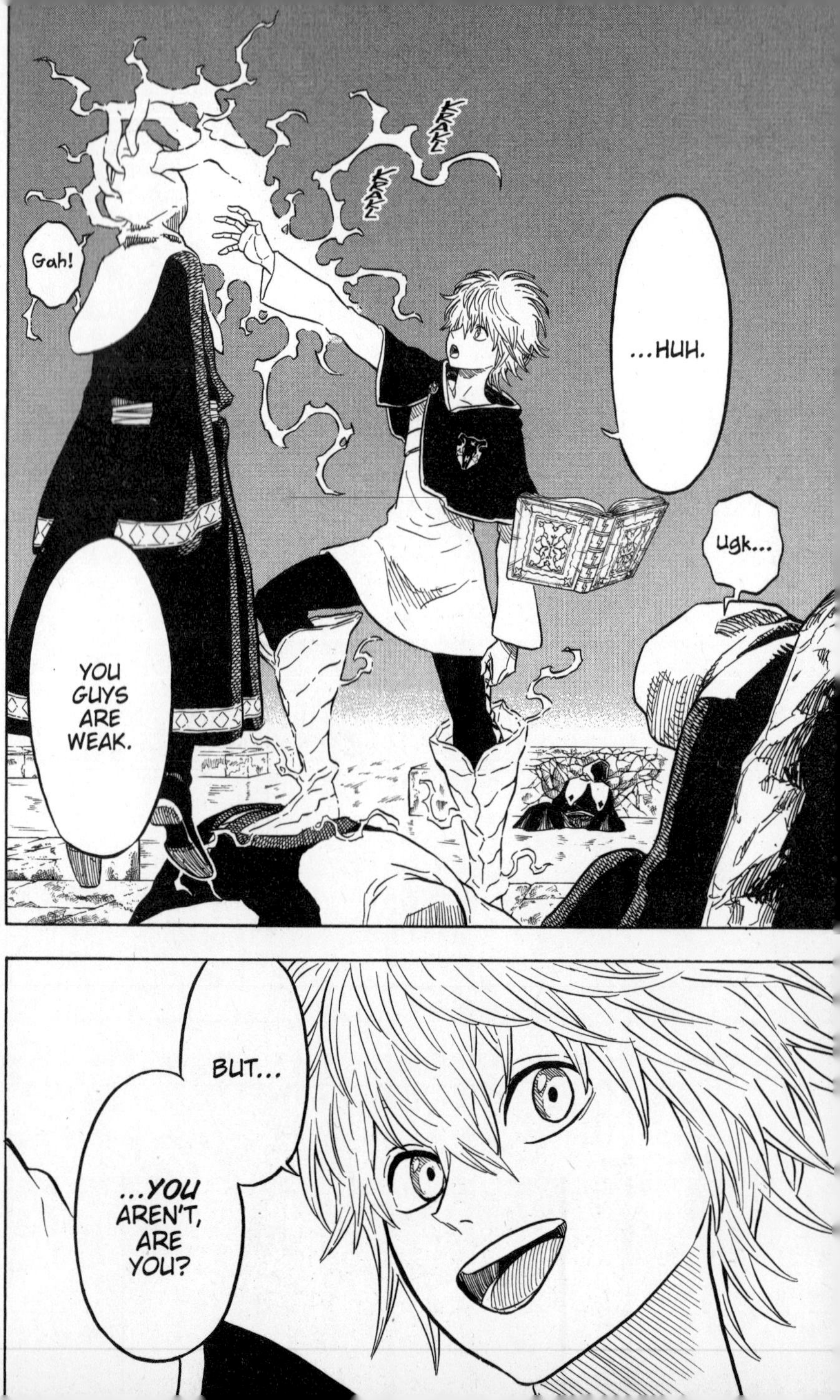

KRAK
KRAK
...HUH.
Gah!
Ugk...
YOU GUYS ARE WEAK.
BUT...
...YOU AREN'T, ARE YOU?

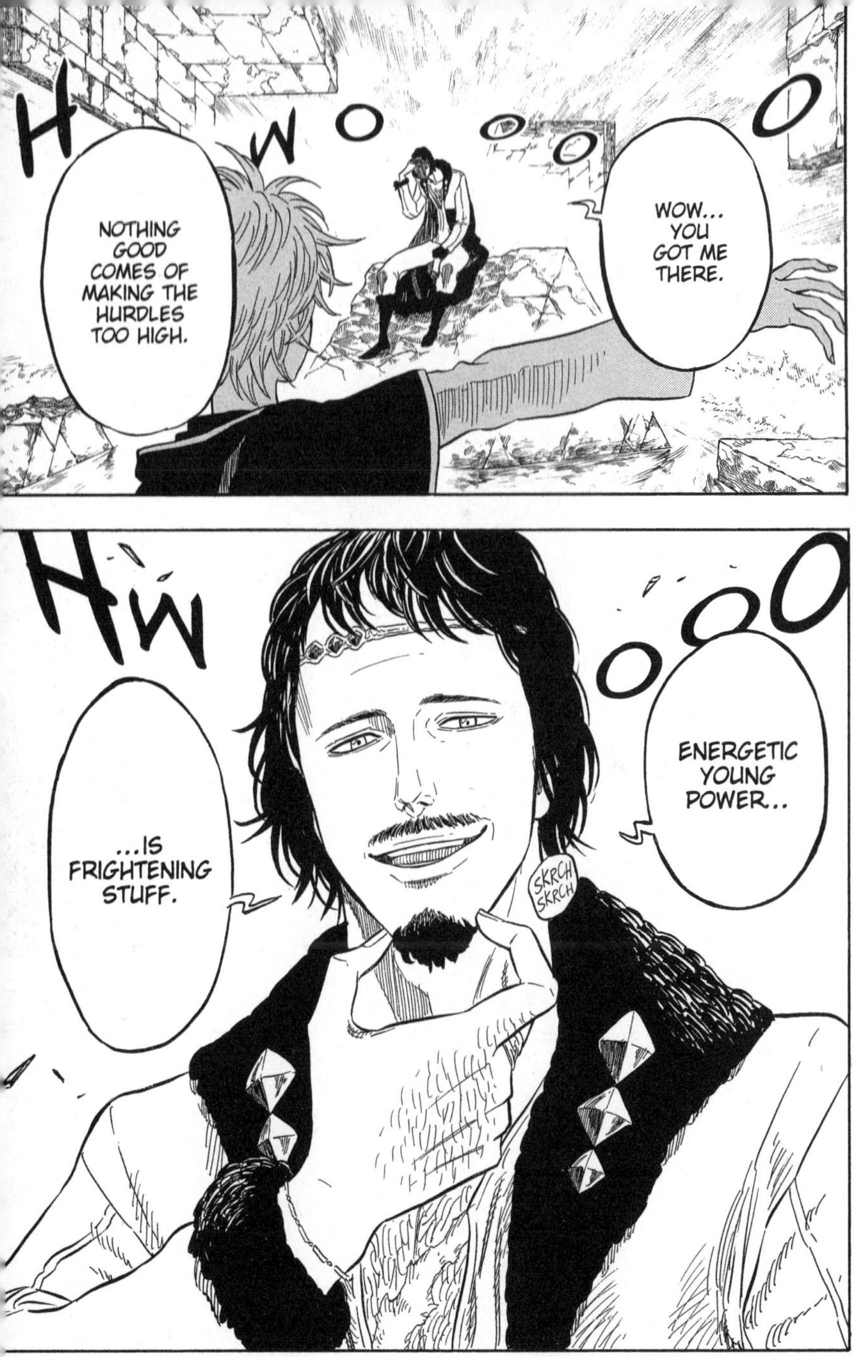
HWOOOOO
WOW... YOU GOT ME THERE.
NOTHING GOOD COMES OF MAKING THE HURDLES TOO HIGH.
HWOOOO
ENERGETIC YOUNG POWER...
SKRCH SKRCH
...IS FRIGHTENING STUFF.

Nero

**A mysterious bird
that follows Asta.**

Page 13: The Diamond Mage

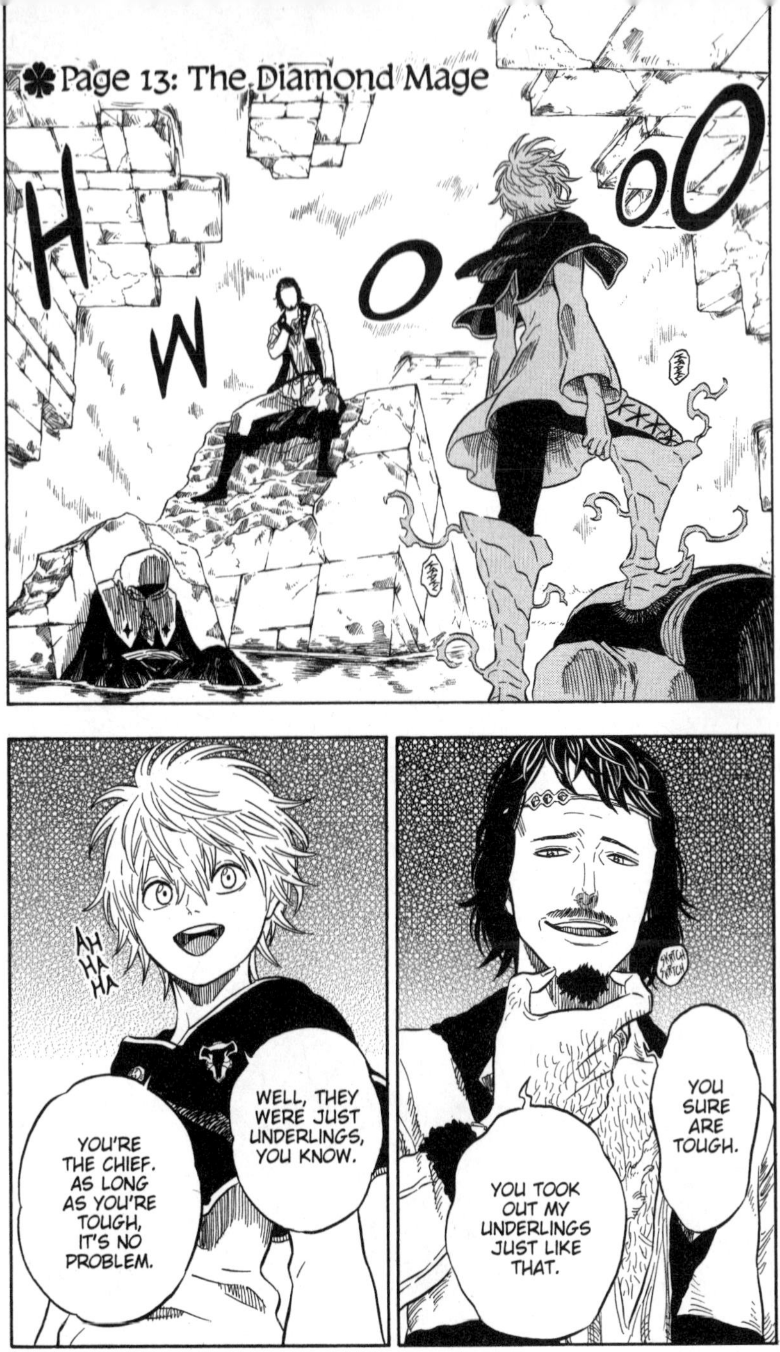
HWOOOOO
YOU SURE ARE TOUGH.
YOU TOOK OUT MY UNDERLINGS JUST LIKE THAT.
AH HA HA
WELL, THEY WERE JUST UNDERLINGS, YOU KNOW.
YOU'RE THE CHIEF. AS LONG AS YOU'RE TOUGH, IT'S NO PROBLEM.

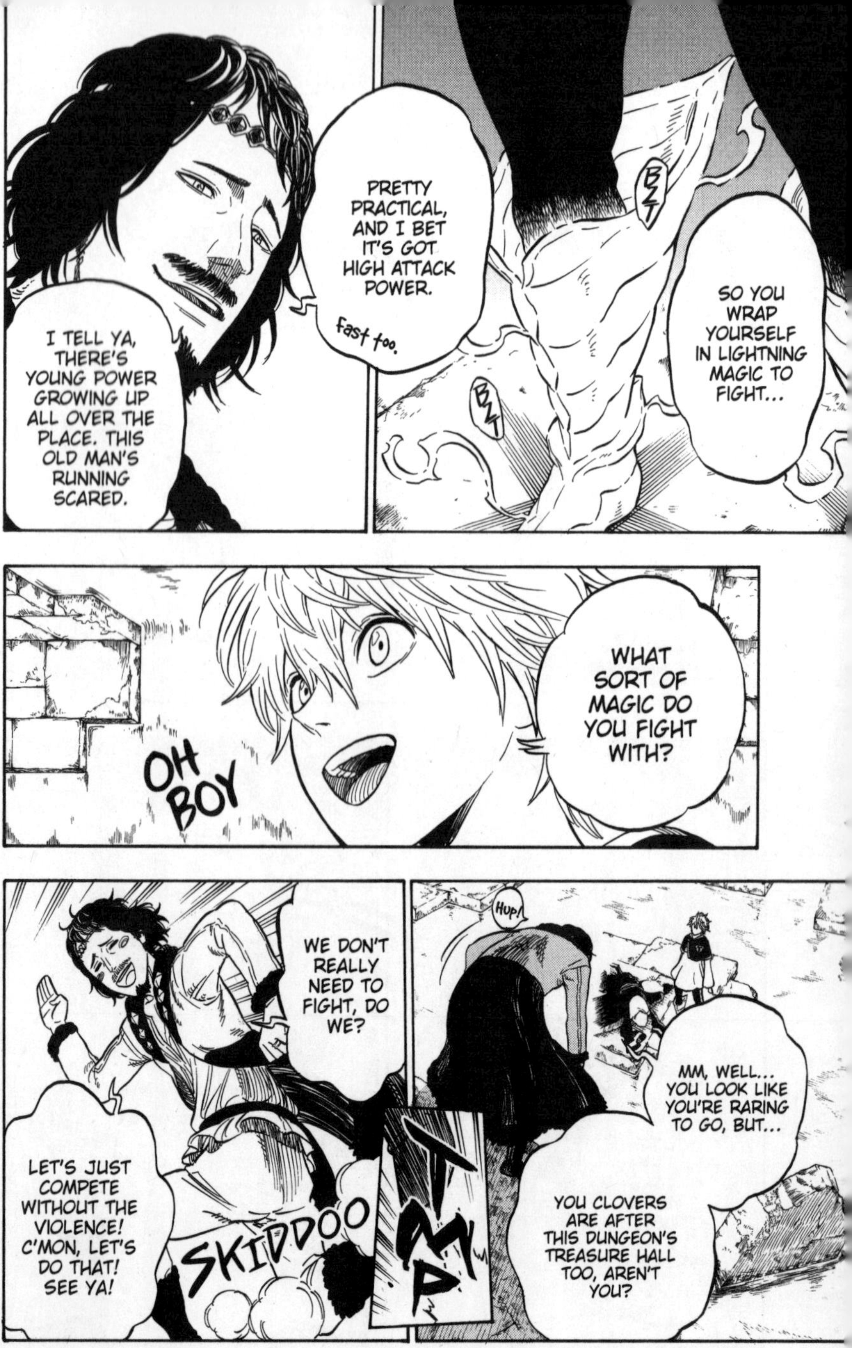
BZT
SO YOU WRAP YOURSELF IN LIGHTNING MAGIC TO FIGHT...
BZT
PRETTY PRACTICAL, AND I BET IT'S GOT HIGH ATTACK POWER.
fast too.
I TELL YA, THERE'S YOUNG POWER GROWING UP ALL OVER THE PLACE. THIS OLD MAN'S RUNNING SCARED.
WHAT SORT OF MAGIC DO YOU FIGHT WITH?
OH BOY
Hup!
MM, WELL... YOU LOOK LIKE YOU'RE RARING TO GO, BUT...
YOU CLOVERS ARE AFTER THIS DUNGEON'S TREASURE HALL TOO, AREN'T YOU?
TMP
WE DON'T REALLY NEED TO FIGHT, DO WE?
LET'S JUST COMPETE WITHOUT THE VIOLENCE! C'MON, LET'S DO THAT! SEE YA!
SKIDDOO

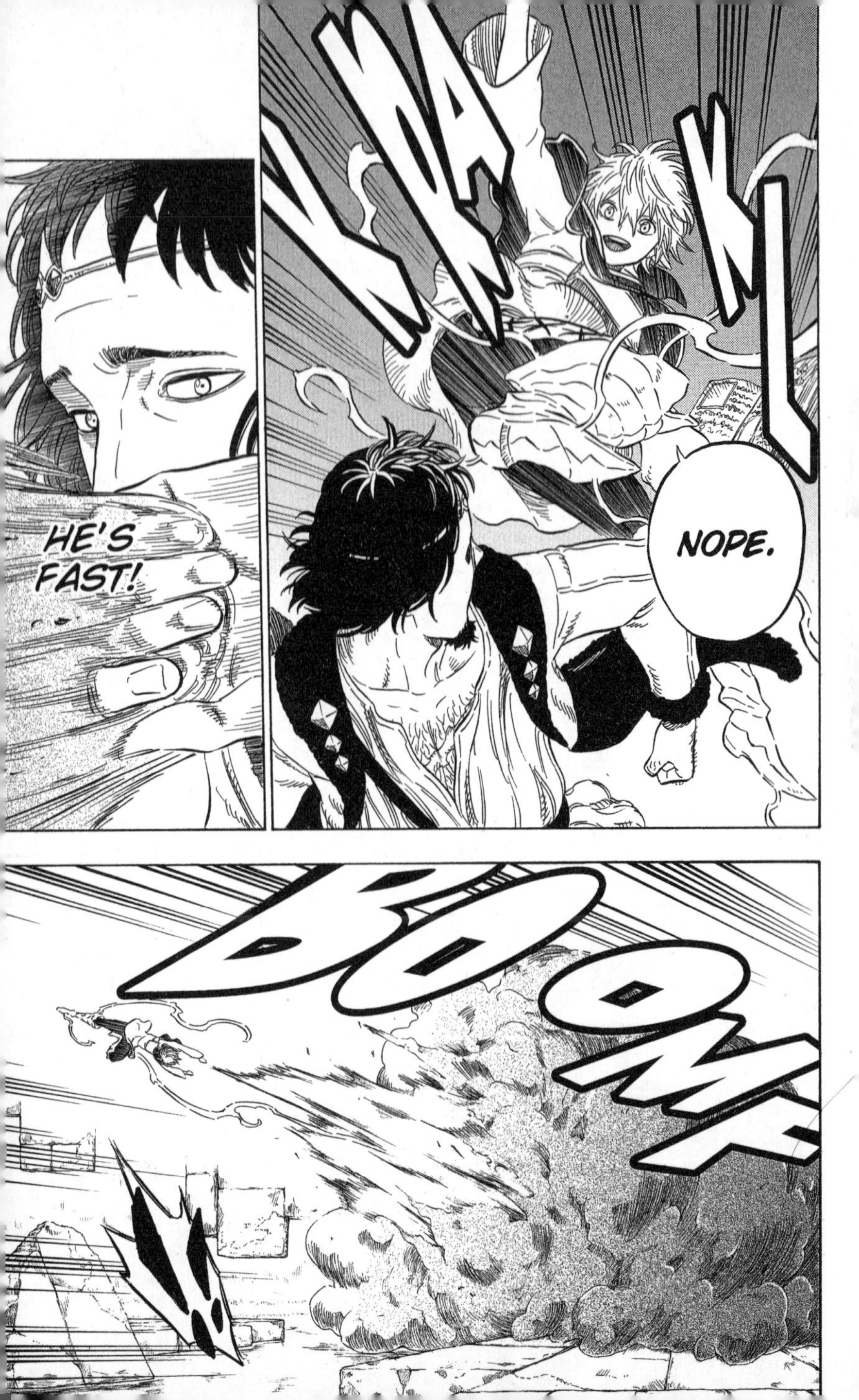
NOPE.
HE'S FAST!

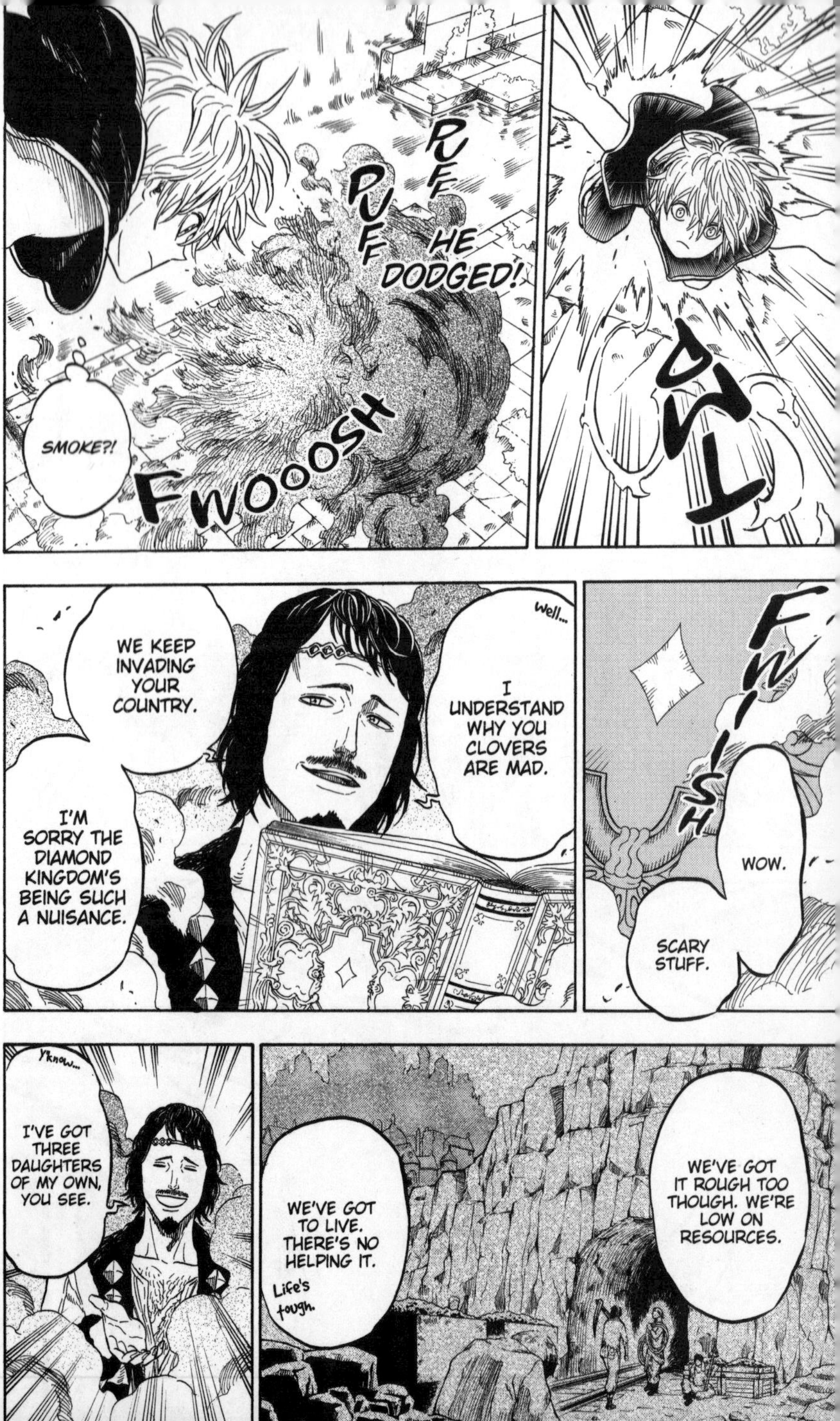
HE DODGED!
PUFF PUFF
FWOOOSH
SMOKE?!
FWI-I-ISH
WOW.
SCARY STUFF.
Well...
I UNDERSTAND WHY YOU CLOVERS ARE MAD.
WE KEEP INVADING YOUR COUNTRY.
I'M SORRY THE DIAMOND KINGDOM'S BEING SUCH A NUISANCE.
WE'VE GOT IT ROUGH TOO THOUGH. WE'RE LOW ON RESOURCES.
WE'VE GOT TO LIVE. THERE'S NO HELPING IT.
Life's tough.
Y'know...
I'VE GOT THREE DAUGHTERS OF MY OWN, YOU SEE.

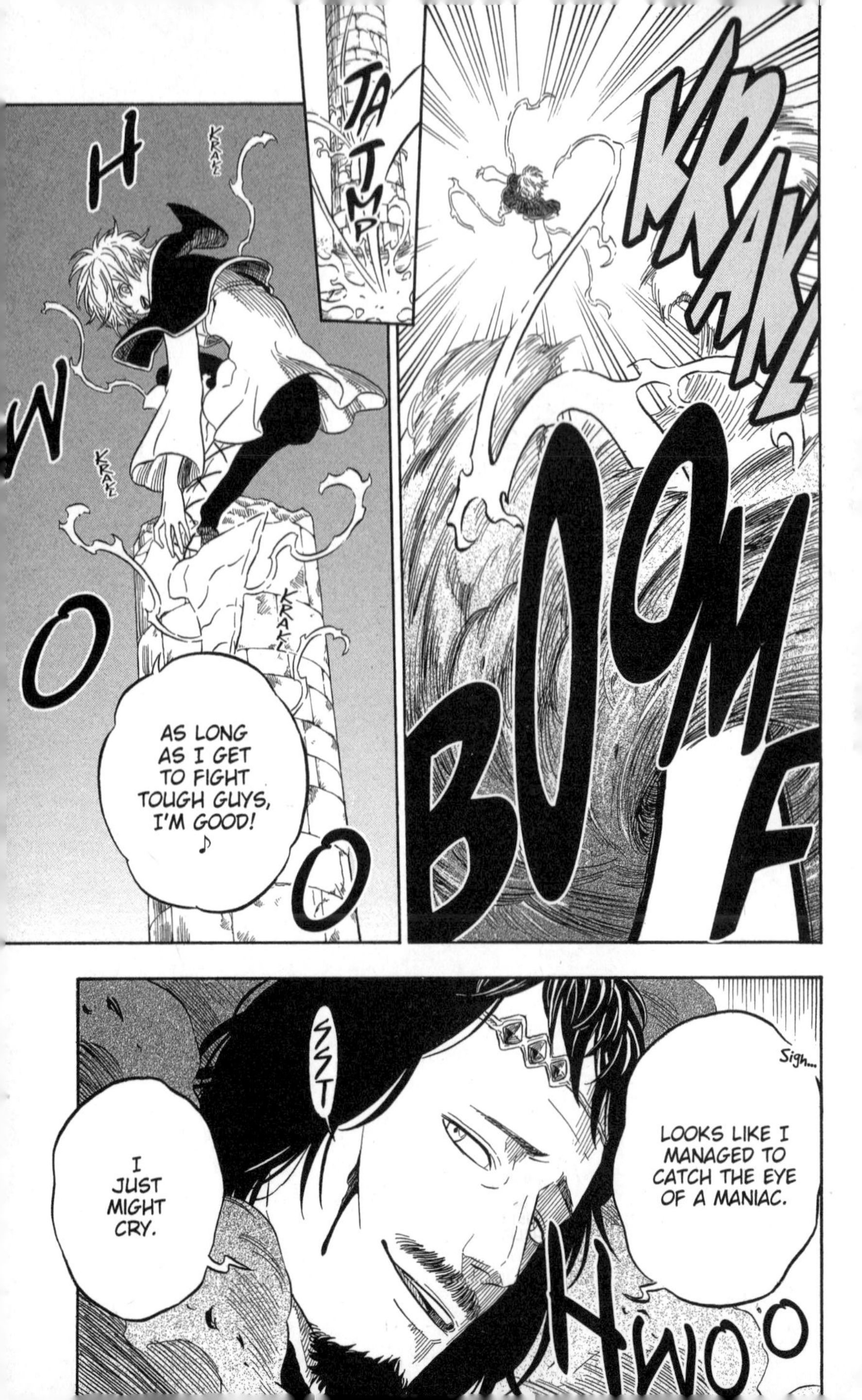

BOOM
TA
TMP
KRAK
KRAK
KRAK
AS LONG AS I GET TO FIGHT TOUGH GUYS, I'M GOOD! ♪
Sigh...
LOOKS LIKE I MANAGED TO CATCH THE EYE OF A MANIAC.
SST
I JUST MIGHT CRY.

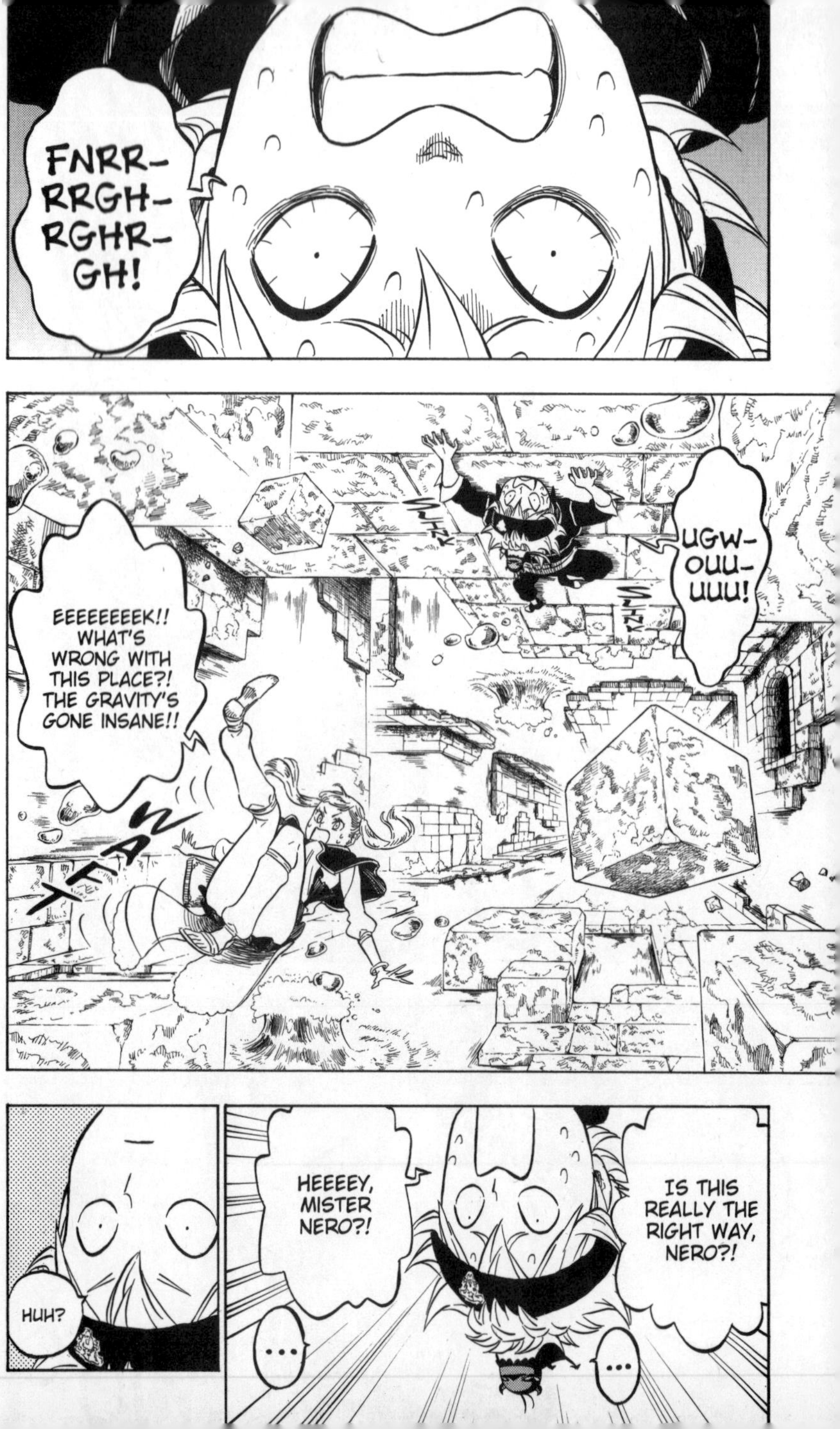
FNRR-RRGH-RGHR-GH!
UGW-OUUU-UUU!
EEEEEEEEK!! WHAT'S WRONG WITH THIS PLACE?! THE GRAVITY'S GONE INSANE!!
IS THIS REALLY THE RIGHT WAY, NERO?!
HEEEEY, MISTER NERO?!
...
...
HUH?

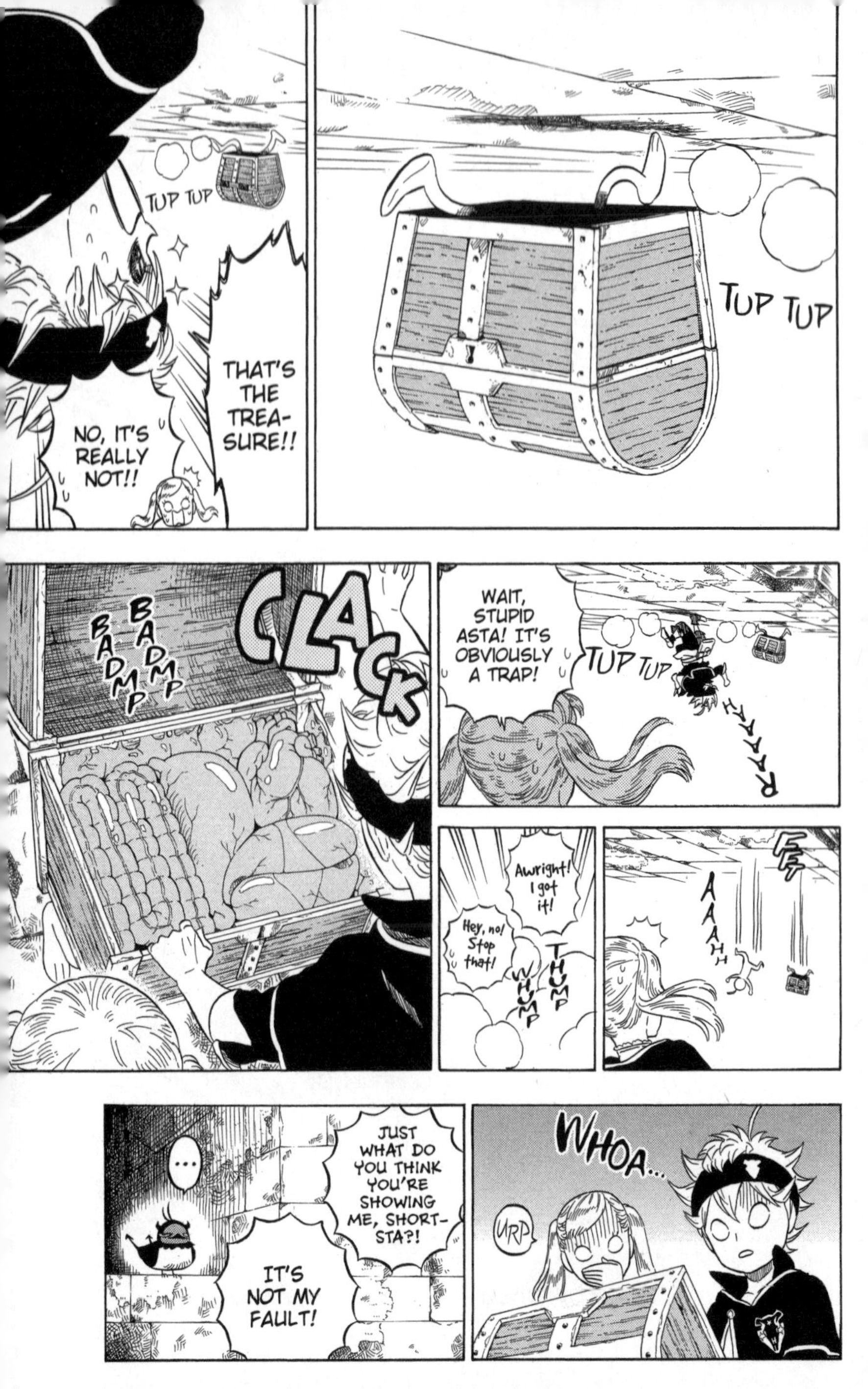
TUP TUP
TUP TUP
THAT'S THE TREASURE!!
NO, IT'S REALLY NOT!!
WAIT, STUPID ASTA! IT'S OBVIOUSLY A TRAP!
TUP TUP
RAAAAH
CLACK
BADMP BADMP
FF
AAAAHH
Awright! I got it!
Hey, no! Stop that!
THUMP
WHUMP
WHOA...
URP
JUST WHAT DO YOU THINK YOU'RE SHOWING ME, SHORT-STA?!
IT'S NOT MY FAULT!
...

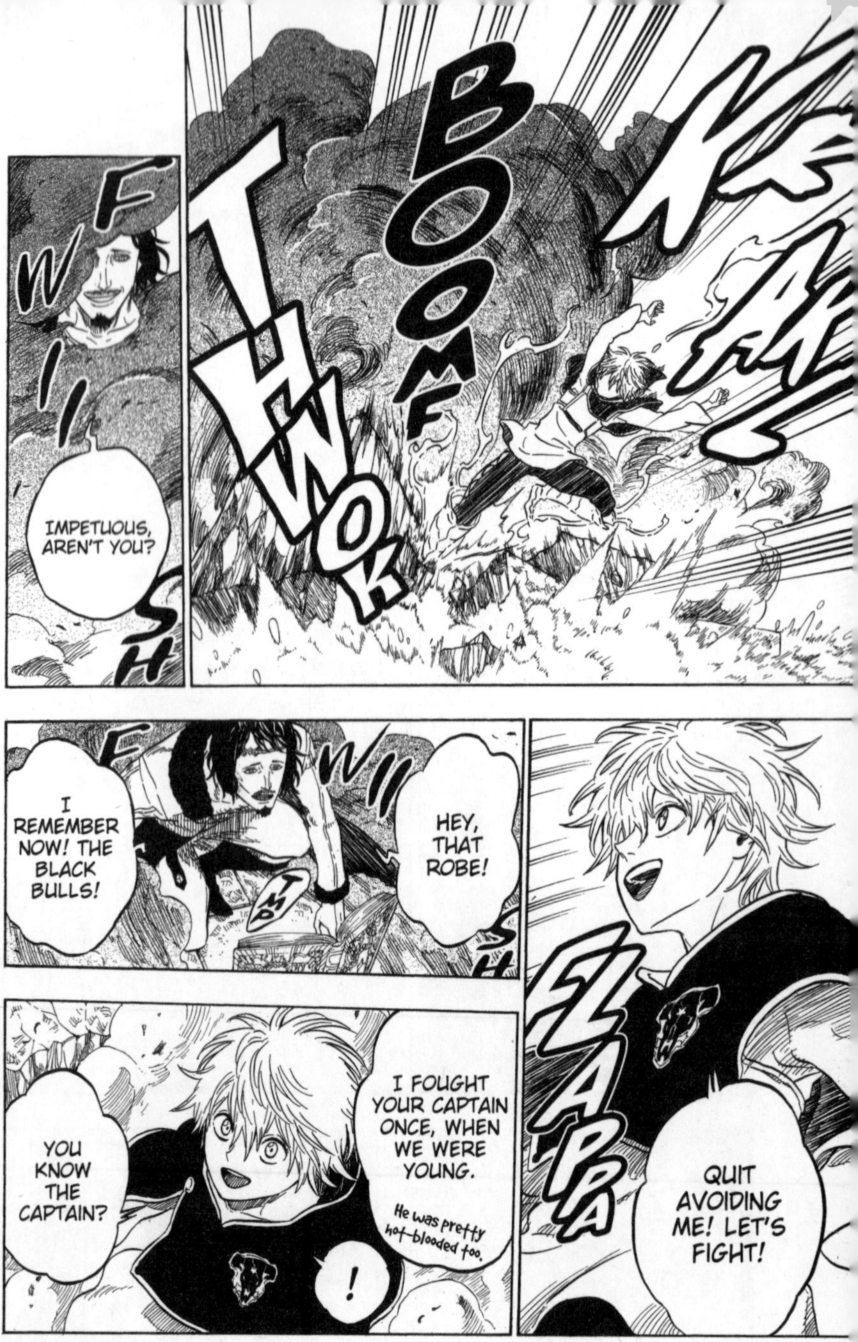
BOOMF
THWOK
FWIISH
IMPETUOUS, AREN'T YOU?
QUIT AVOIDING ME! LET'S FIGHT!
HEY, THAT ROBE!
FWIISH
TMP
I REMEMBER NOW! THE BLACK BULLS!
I FOUGHT YOUR CAPTAIN ONCE, WHEN WE WERE YOUNG.
He was pretty hot-blooded too.
!
YOU KNOW THE CAPTAIN?

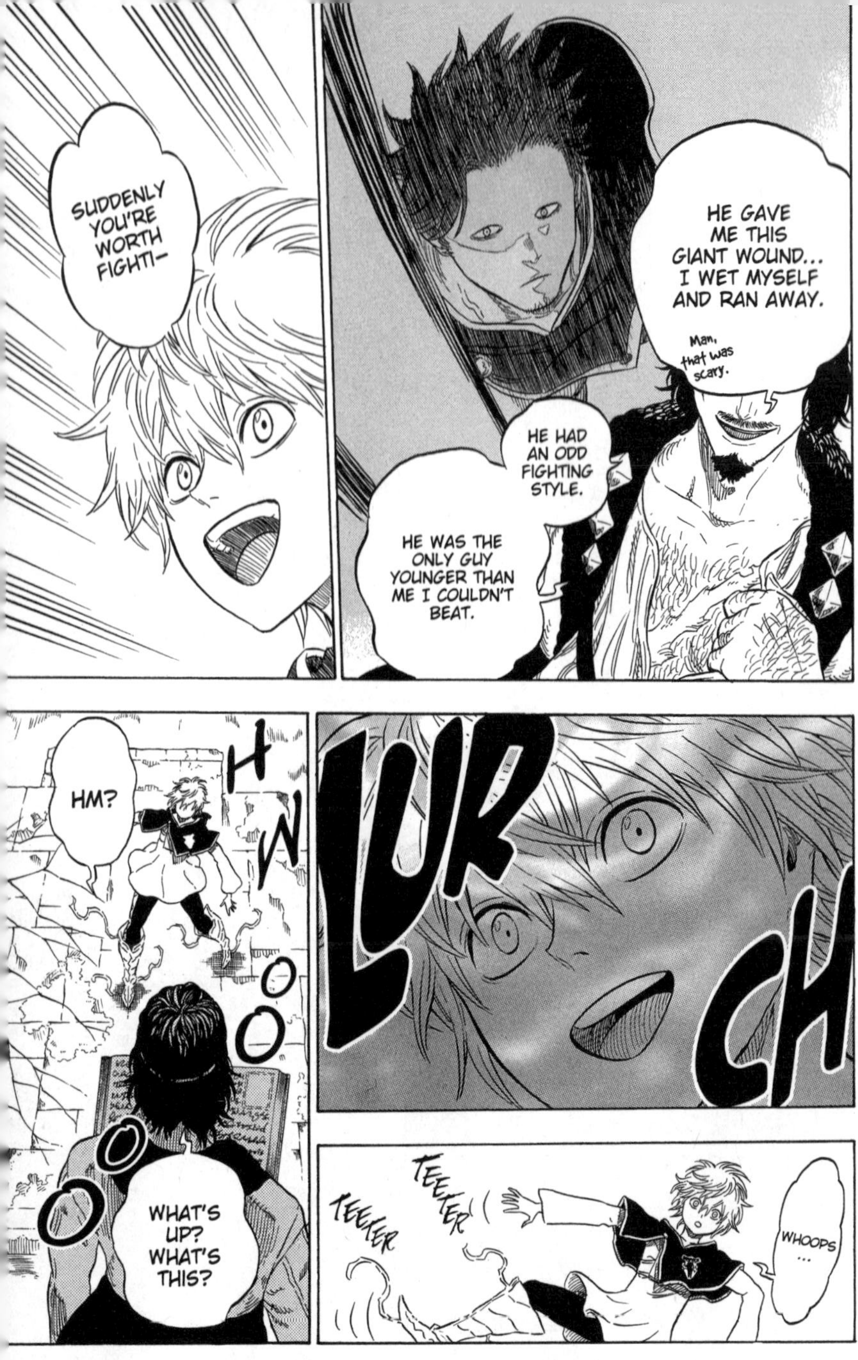
HE GAVE ME THIS GIANT WOUND... I WET MYSELF AND RAN AWAY.
Man, that was scary.
HE HAD AN ODD FIGHTING STYLE.
HE WAS THE ONLY GUY YOUNGER THAN ME I COULDN'T BEAT.
SUDDENLY YOU'RE WORTH FIGHTI–
LUR
CH
WHOOPS...
TEETER
TEETER
HM?
HWOOO
OOO
WHAT'S UP? WHAT'S THIS?

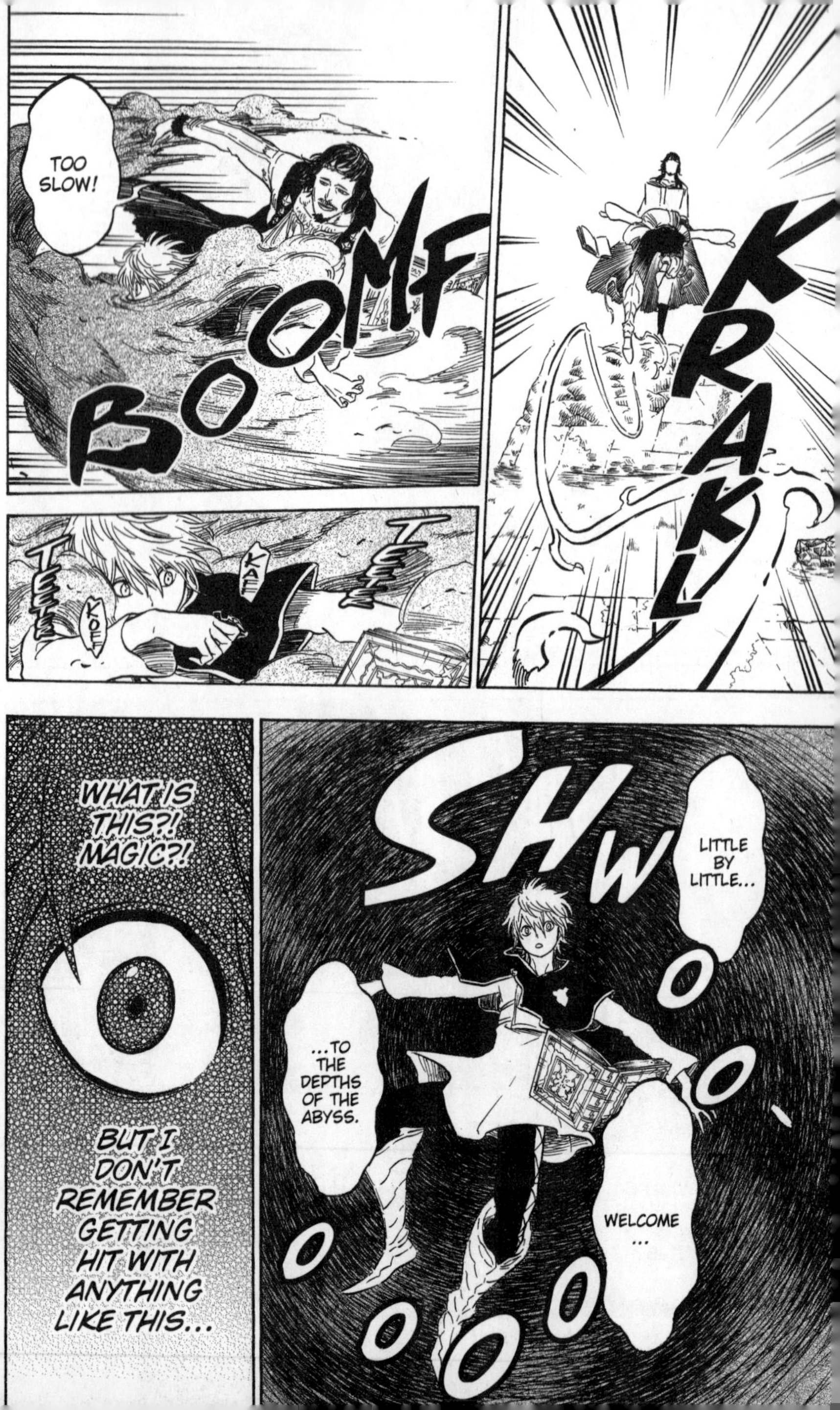
KRAKL
TOO SLOW!
BOOMF
TETETE
KAFF
KOFF
TETETE
SHWOOOOOOOOO
LITTLE BY LITTLE...
...TO THE DEPTHS OF THE ABYSS.
WELCOME...
WHAT IS THIS?! MAGIC?!
BUT I DON'T REMEMBER GETTING HIT WITH ANYTHING LIKE THIS...

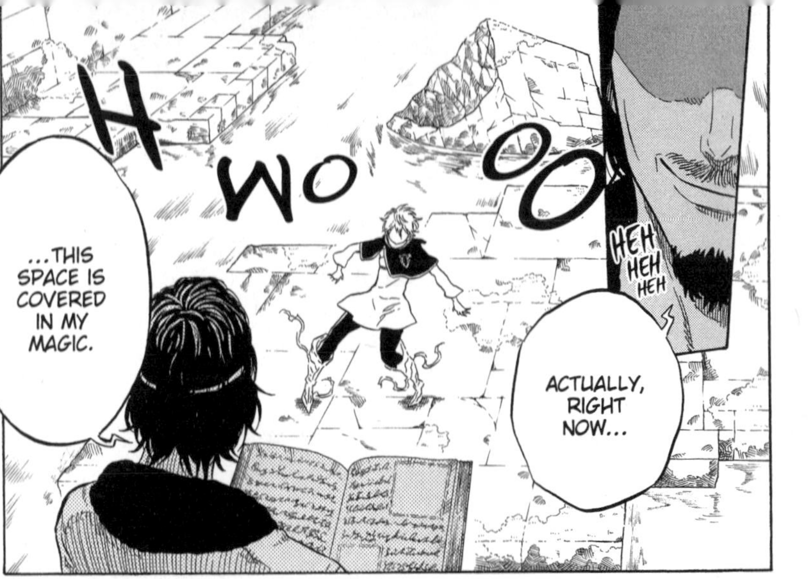
HWOOO
HEH HEH HEH
ACTUALLY, RIGHT NOW...
...THIS SPACE IS COVERED IN MY MAGIC.

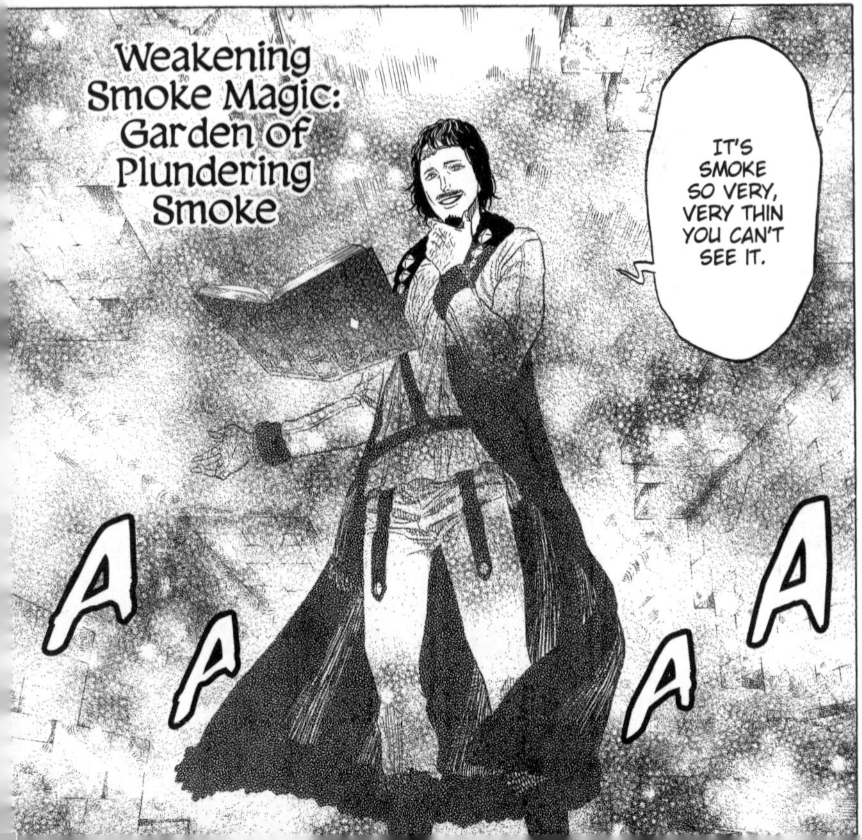
IT'S SMOKE SO VERY, VERY THIN YOU CAN'T SEE IT.
Weakening Smoke Magic: Garden of Plundering Smoke
AAAAA

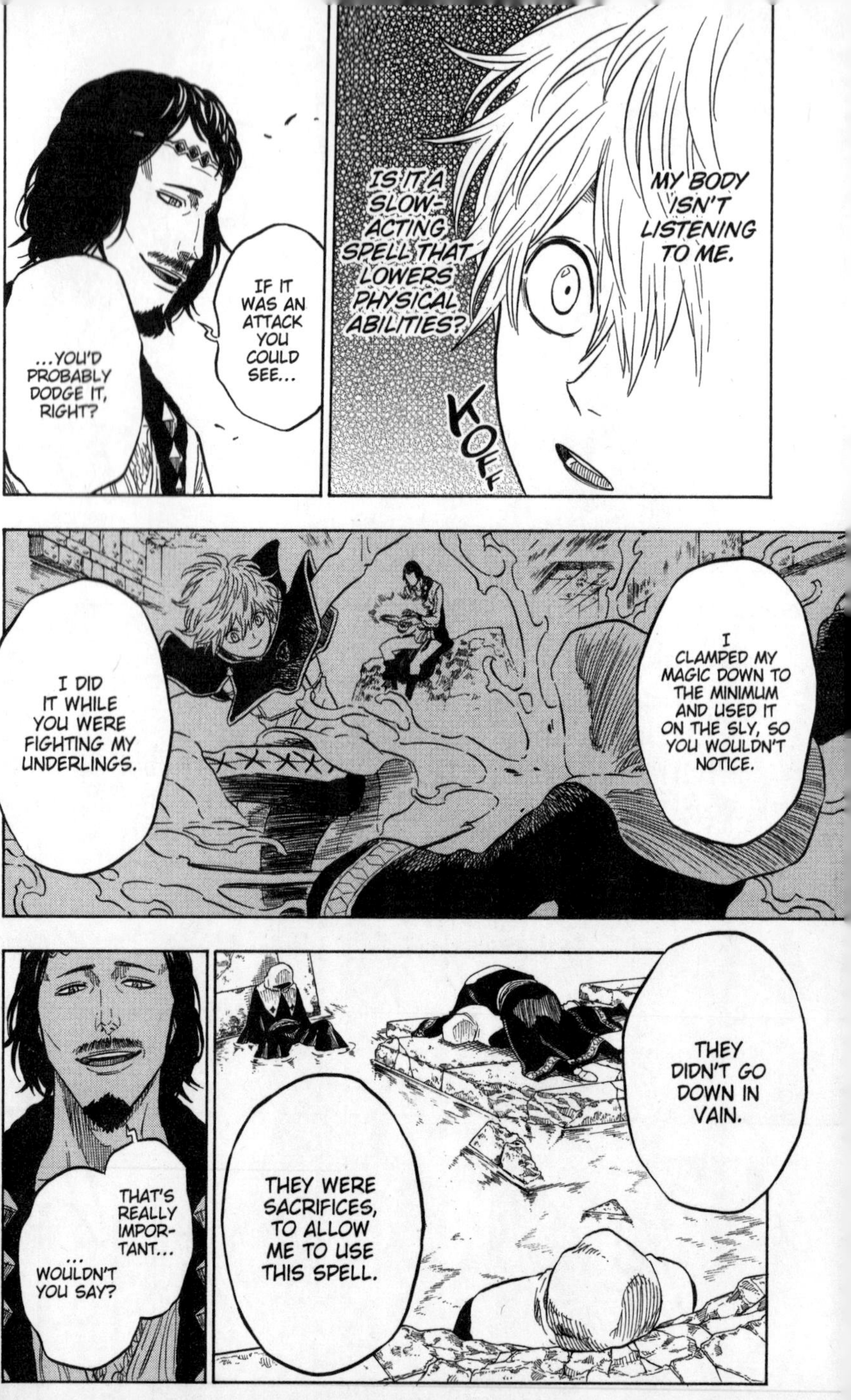
MY BODY ISN'T LISTENING TO ME.
IS IT A SLOW-ACTING SPELL THAT LOWERS PHYSICAL ABILITIES?
KOFF
IF IT WAS AN ATTACK YOU COULD SEE...
...YOU'D PROBABLY DODGE IT, RIGHT?
I CLAMPED MY MAGIC DOWN TO THE MINIMUM AND USED IT ON THE SLY, SO YOU WOULDN'T NOTICE.
I DID IT WHILE YOU WERE FIGHTING MY UNDERLINGS.
THEY DIDN'T GO DOWN IN VAIN.
THEY WERE SACRIFICES, TO ALLOW ME TO USE THIS SPELL.
THAT'S REALLY IMPOR-TANT... ...WOULDN'T YOU SAY?

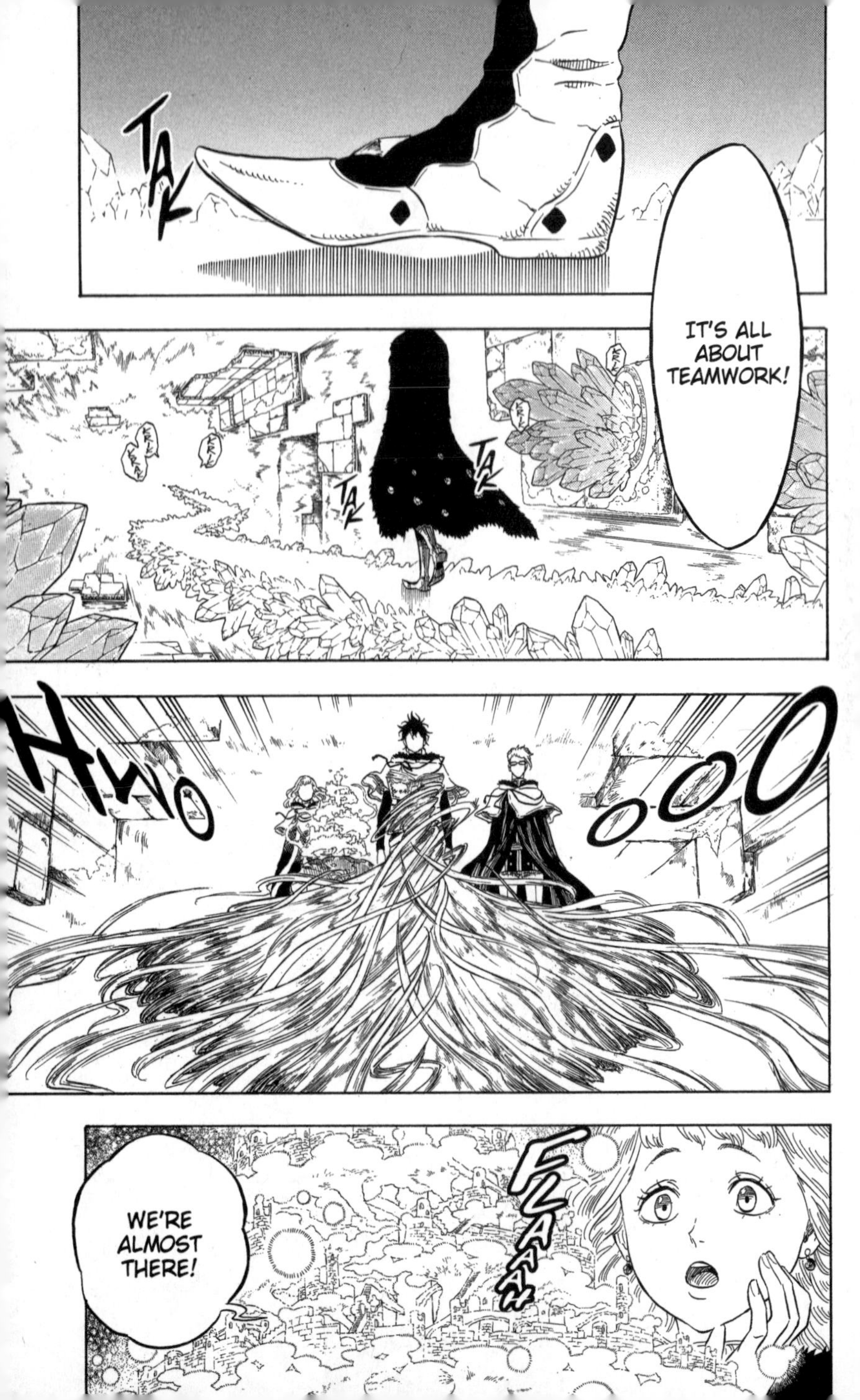
TAK
IT'S ALL ABOUT TEAMWORK!
KRIK
KRIK
TAK
TAK
HWOOOOO
FLAAAAH
WE'RE ALMOST THERE!

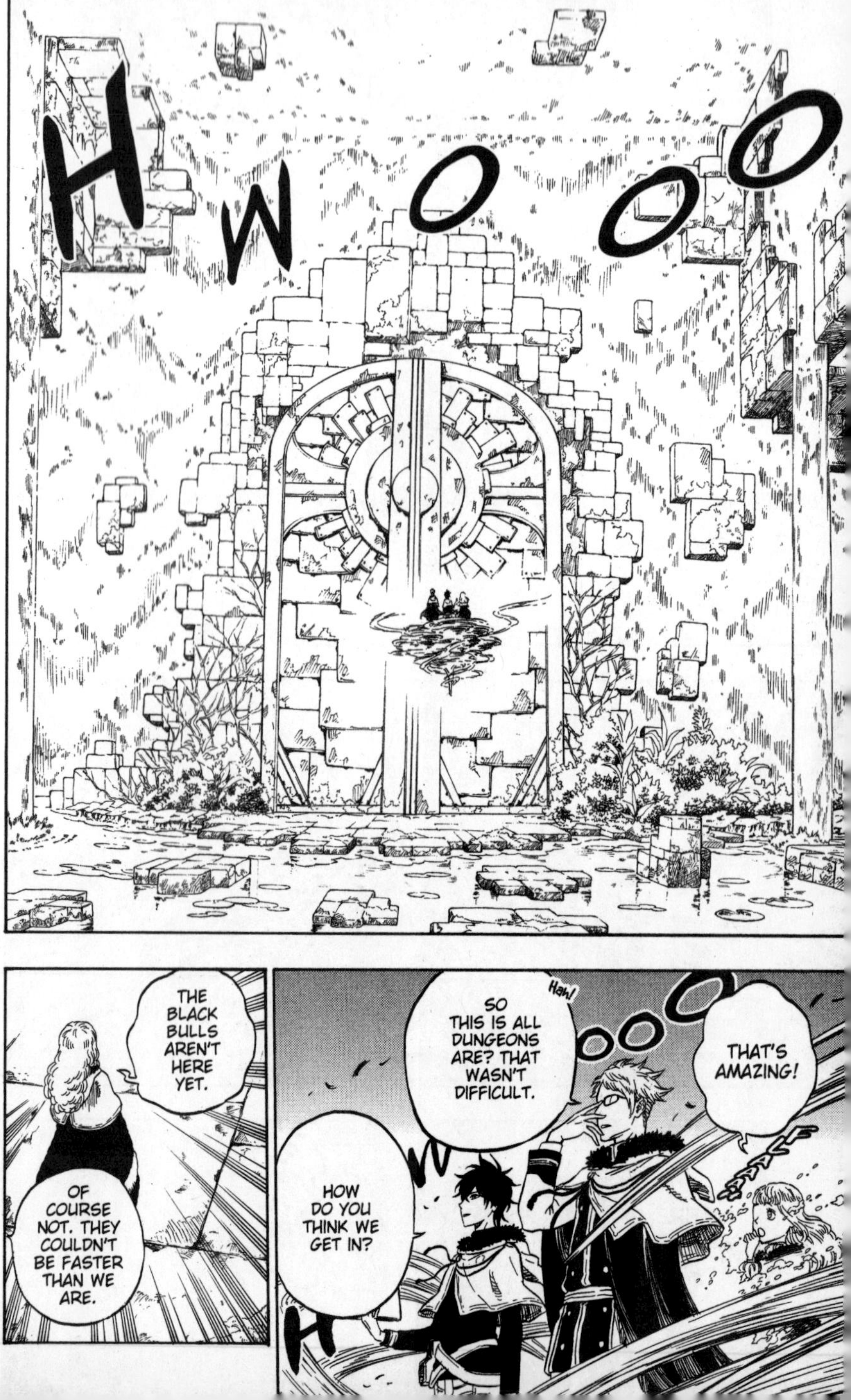
HWOOOO
THAT'S AMAZING!
Hah!
SO THIS IS ALL DUNGEONS ARE? THAT WASN'T DIFFICULT.
OOO
HOW DO YOU THINK WE GET IN?
THE BLACK BULLS AREN'T HERE YET.
OF COURSE NOT. THEY COULDN'T BE FASTER THAN WE ARE.

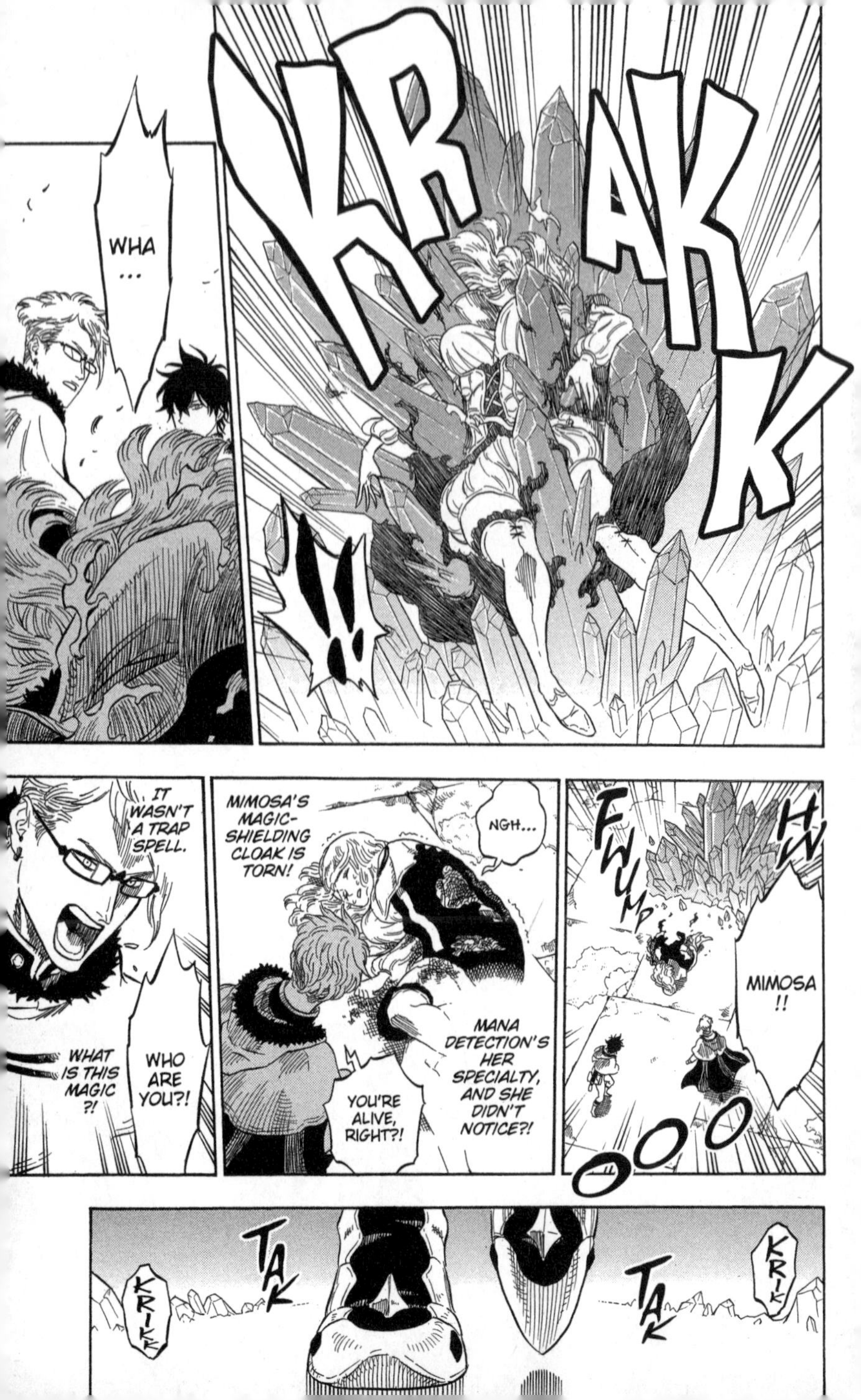
KRAKK
!!
WHA ...
NGH...
MIMOSA'S MAGIC-SHIELDING CLOAK IS TORN!
MANA DETECTION'S HER SPECIALTY, AND SHE DIDN'T NOTICE?!
YOU'RE ALIVE, RIGHT?!
FWUMP
MIMOSA !!
OOOO
IT WASN'T A TRAP SPELL.
WHO ARE YOU?!
WHAT IS THIS MAGIC ?!
KRIK
TAK
TAK
KRIKK

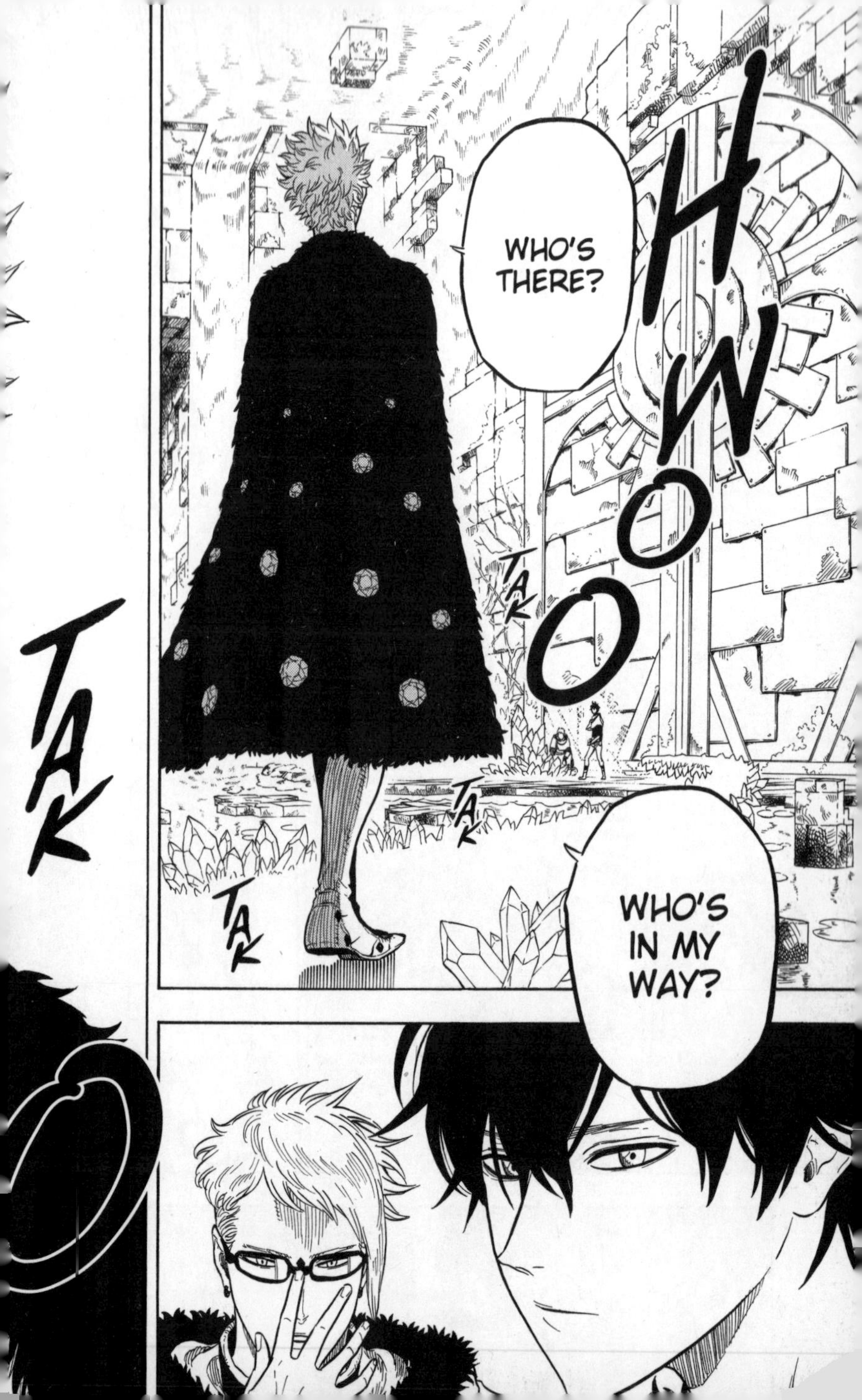
HWOOO
WHO'S THERE?
TAK
TAK
TAK
TAK
WHO'S IN MY WAY?

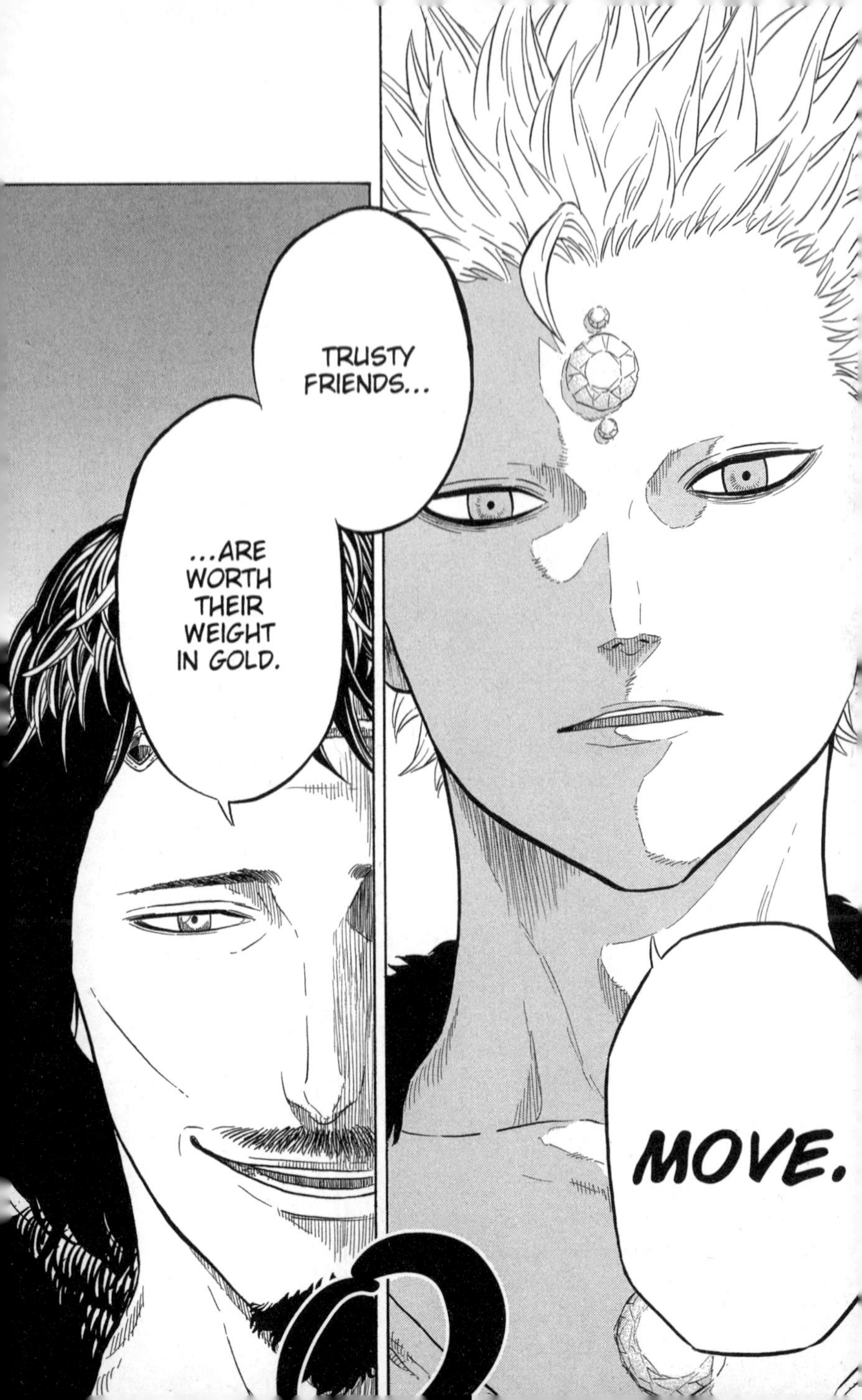
TRUSTY FRIENDS...
...ARE WORTH THEIR WEIGHT IN GOLD.
MOVE.

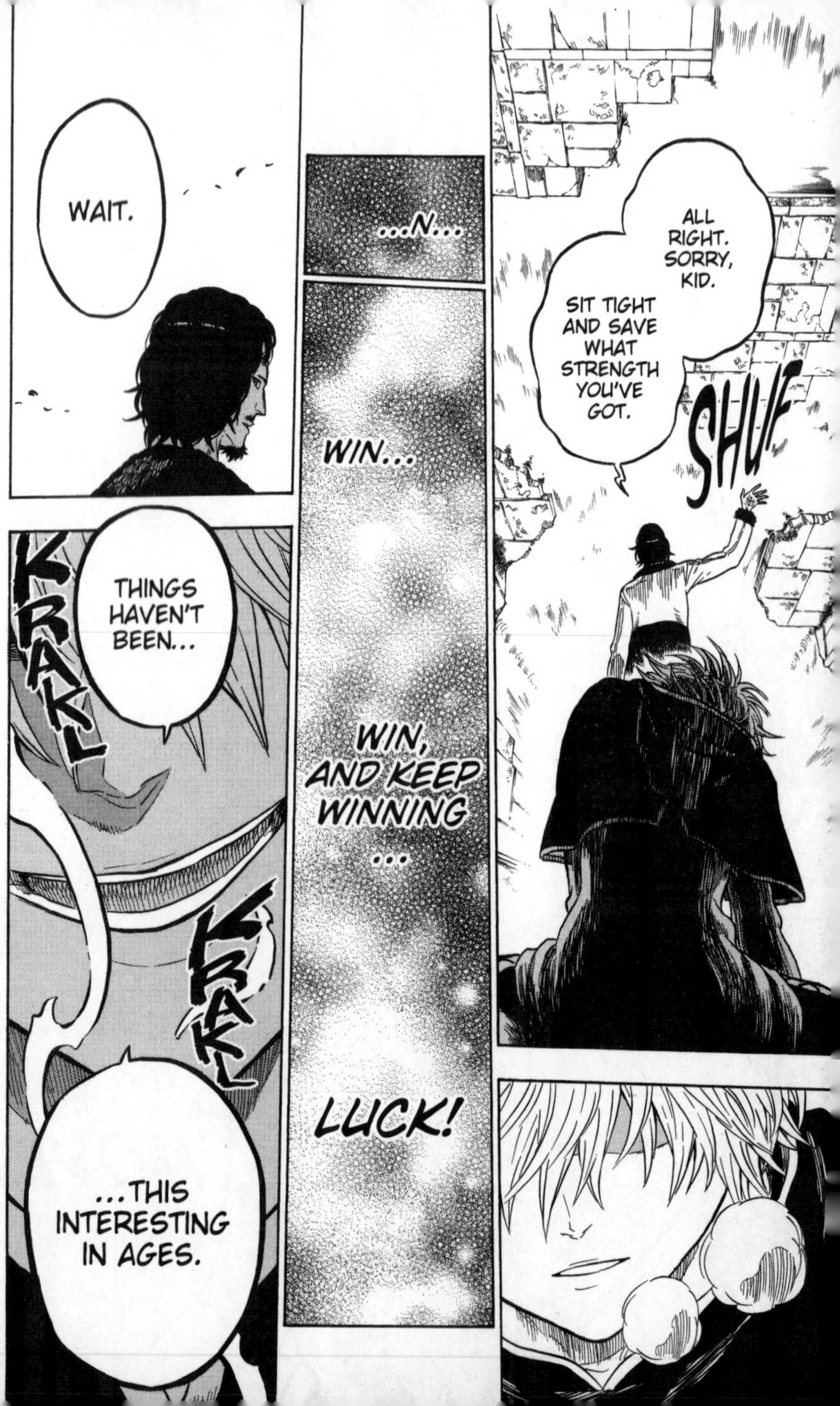
ALL RIGHT. SORRY, KID.
SIT TIGHT AND SAVE WHAT STRENGTH YOU'VE GOT.
SHUF
...N...
WIN...
WIN, AND KEEP WINNING...
LUCK!
WAIT.
THINGS HAVEN'T BEEN...
KRAKL
KRAKL
...THIS INTERESTING IN AGES.

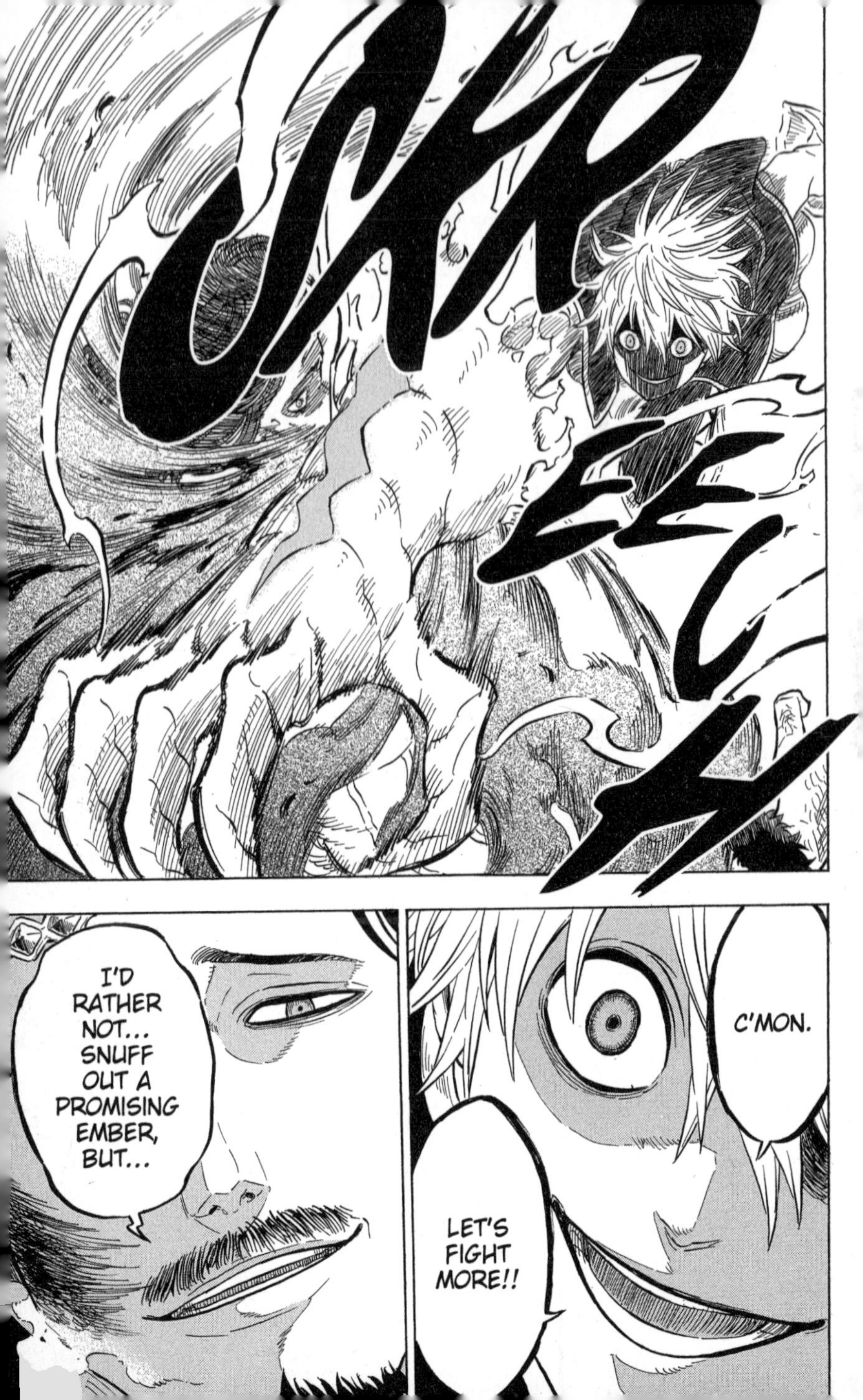
C'MON.
LET'S FIGHT MORE!!
I'D RATHER NOT... SNUFF OUT A PROMISING EMBER, BUT...

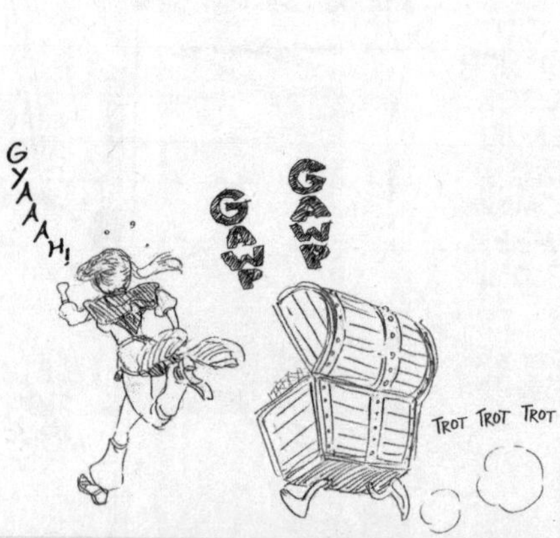
GYAAAH!
GAWP
GAWP
TROT TROT TROT

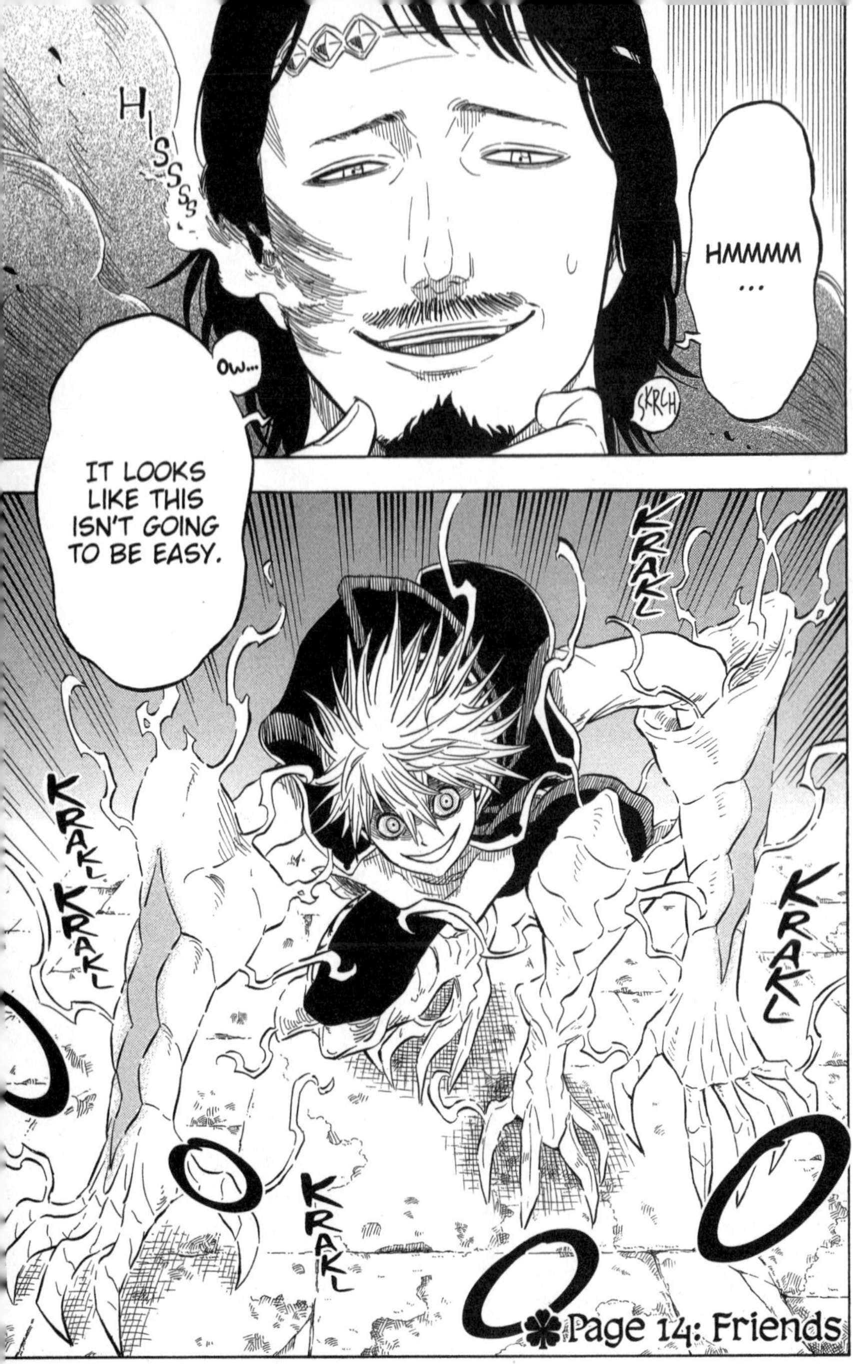
HMMMM ...
SKRCH
HISSSSS
OW...
IT LOOKS LIKE THIS ISN'T GOING TO BE EASY.
KRAKL
KRAKL
KRAKL KRAKL
KRAKL
Page 14: Friends

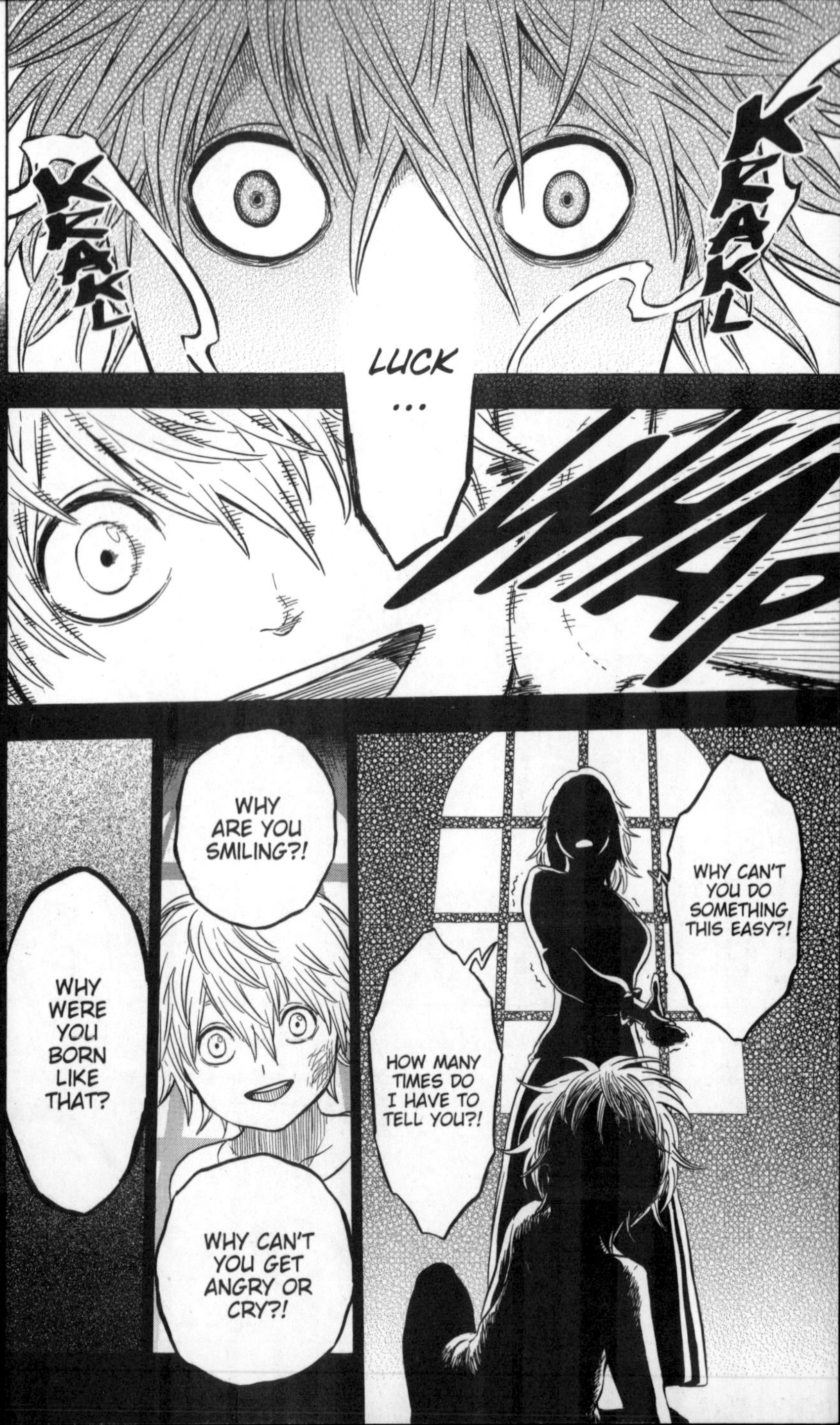
KRAKL
KRAKL
LUCK...
WHAP
WHY CAN'T YOU DO SOMETHING THIS EASY?!
HOW MANY TIMES DO I HAVE TO TELL YOU?!
WHY ARE YOU SMILING?!
WHY CAN'T YOU GET ANGRY OR CRY?!
WHY WERE YOU BORN LIKE THAT?

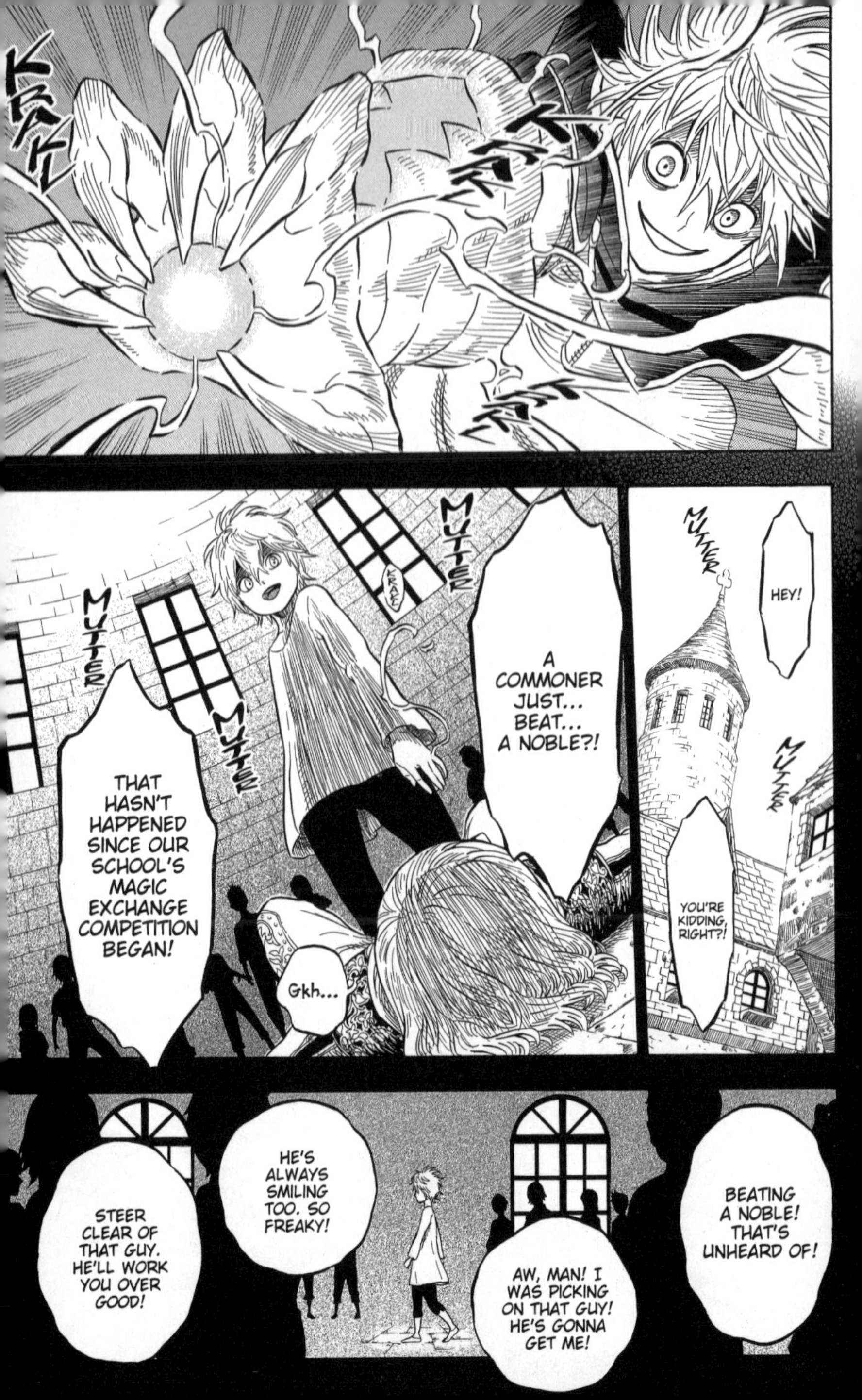
KRAKL
HEY!
MUTTER
MUTTER
YOU'RE KIDDING, RIGHT?!
A COMMONER JUST... BEAT... A NOBLE?!
MUTTER
KRAK
MUTTER
MUTTER
THAT HASN'T HAPPENED SINCE OUR SCHOOL'S MAGIC EXCHANGE COMPETITION BEGAN!
Gkh...
BEATING A NOBLE! THAT'S UNHEARD OF!
AW, MAN! I WAS PICKING ON THAT GUY! HE'S GONNA GET ME!
HE'S ALWAYS SMILING TOO. SO FREAKY!
STEER CLEAR OF THAT GUY. HE'LL WORK YOU OVER GOOD!

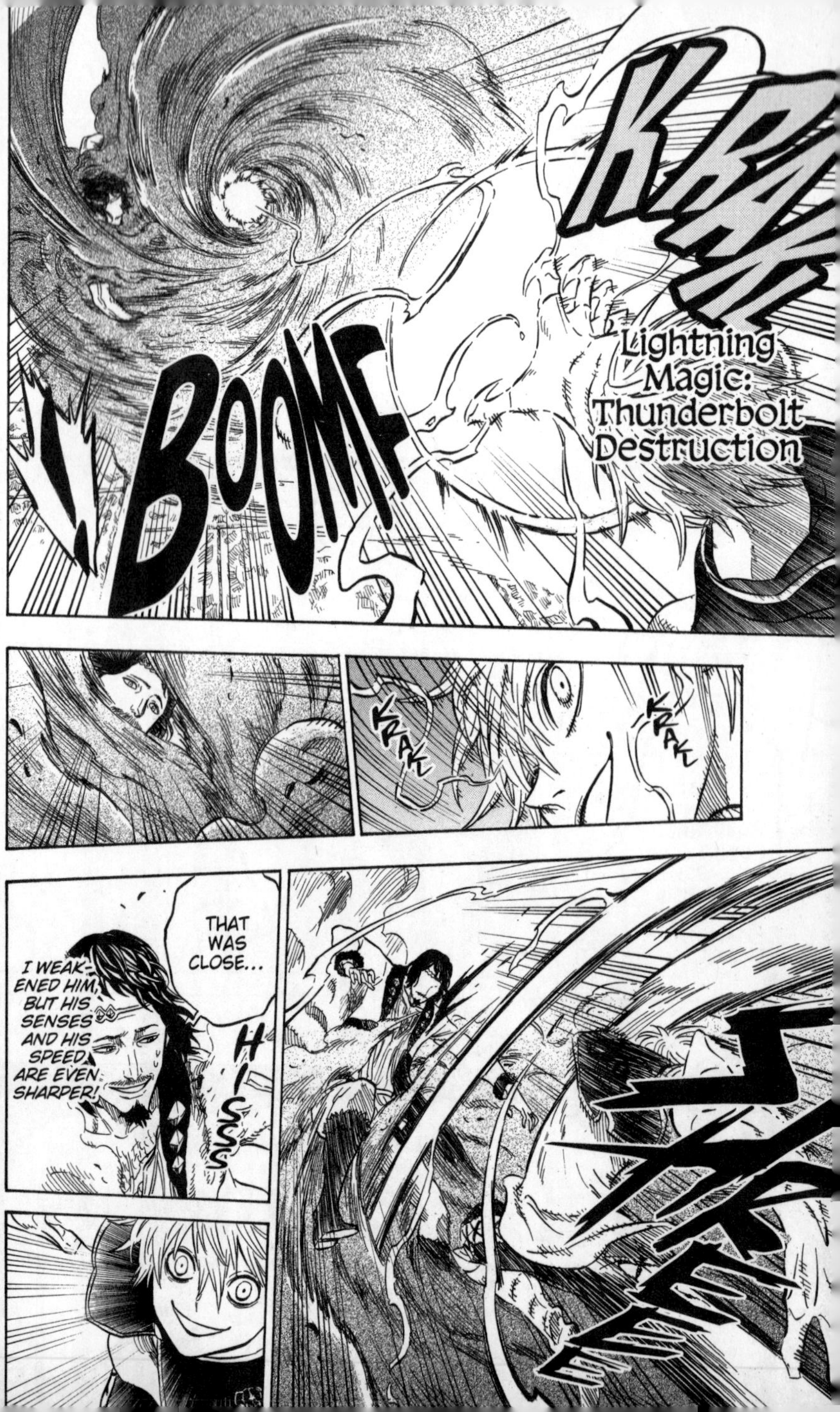
KRAK
Lightning Magic: Thunderbolt Destruction
BOOMF
KRAKL
KRAKL
THAT WAS CLOSE...
I WEAKENED HIM, BUT HIS SENSES AND HIS SPEED ARE EVEN SHARPER!
HISSS

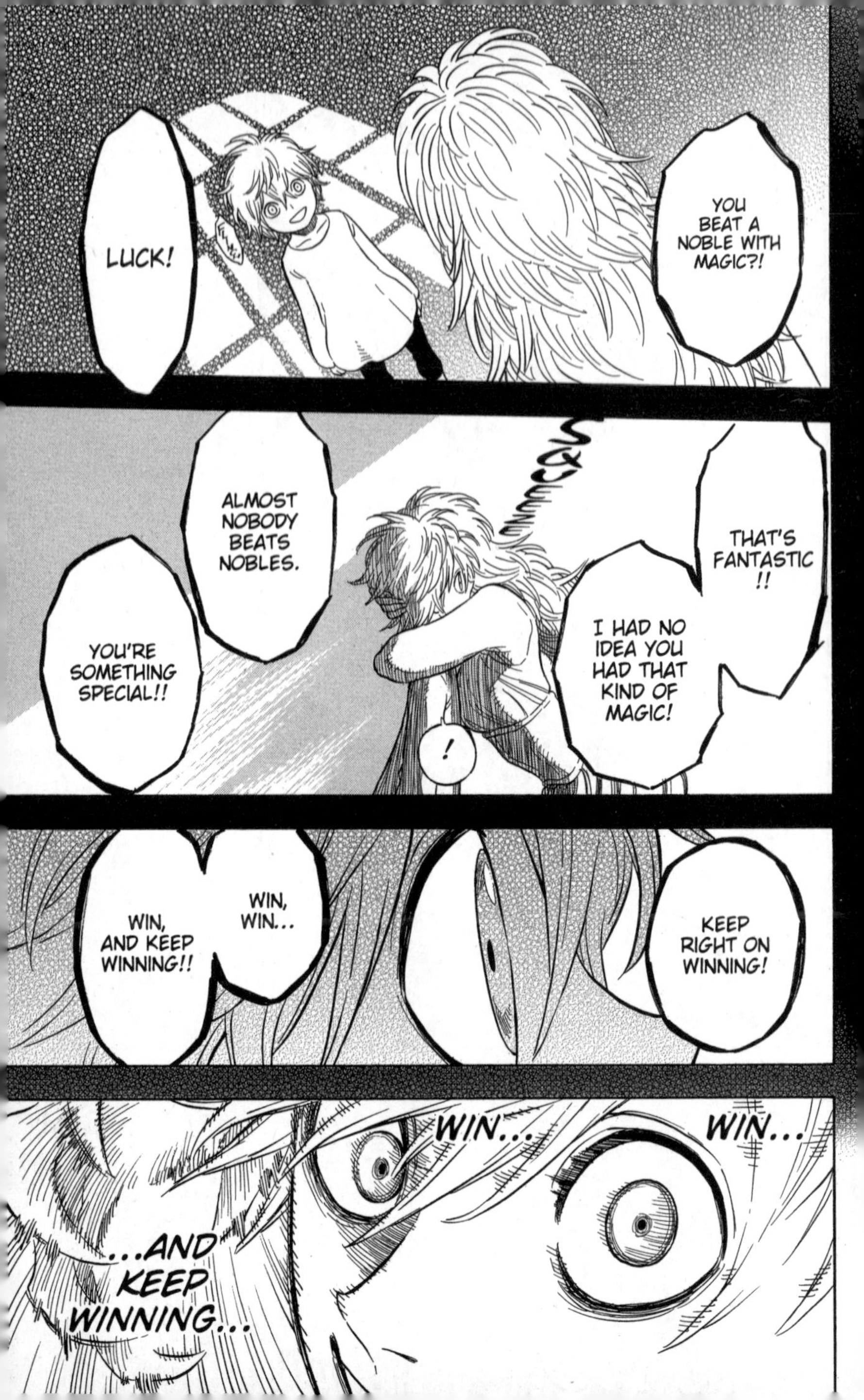
YOU BEAT A NOBLE WITH MAGIC?!
LUCK!
THAT'S FANTASTIC!!
I HAD NO IDEA YOU HAD THAT KIND OF MAGIC!
ALMOST NOBODY BEATS NOBLES.
YOU'RE SOMETHING SPECIAL!!
!
KEEP RIGHT ON WINNING!
WIN, WIN...
WIN, AND KEEP WINNING!!
WIN...
WIN...
...AND KEEP WINNING...

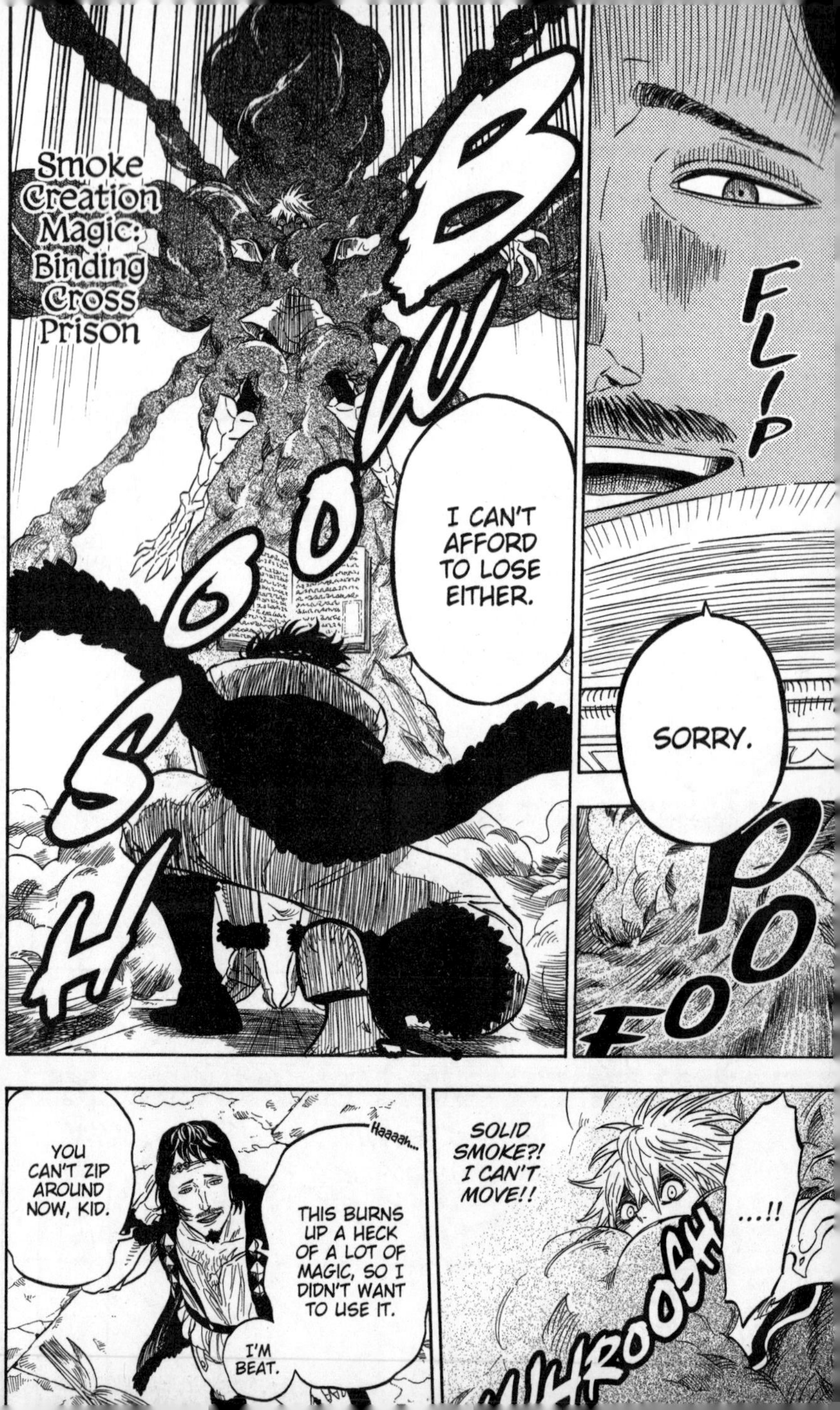
FLIP
SORRY.
FOOP
I CAN'T AFFORD TO LOSE EITHER.
Smoke Creation Magic: Binding Cross Prison
BWOOSH
...!!
SOLID SMOKE?! I CAN'T MOVE!!
WHROOSH
YOU CAN'T ZIP AROUND NOW, KID.
Haaaah...
THIS BURNS UP A HECK OF A LOT OF MAGIC, SO I DIDN'T WANT TO USE IT.
I'M BEAT.

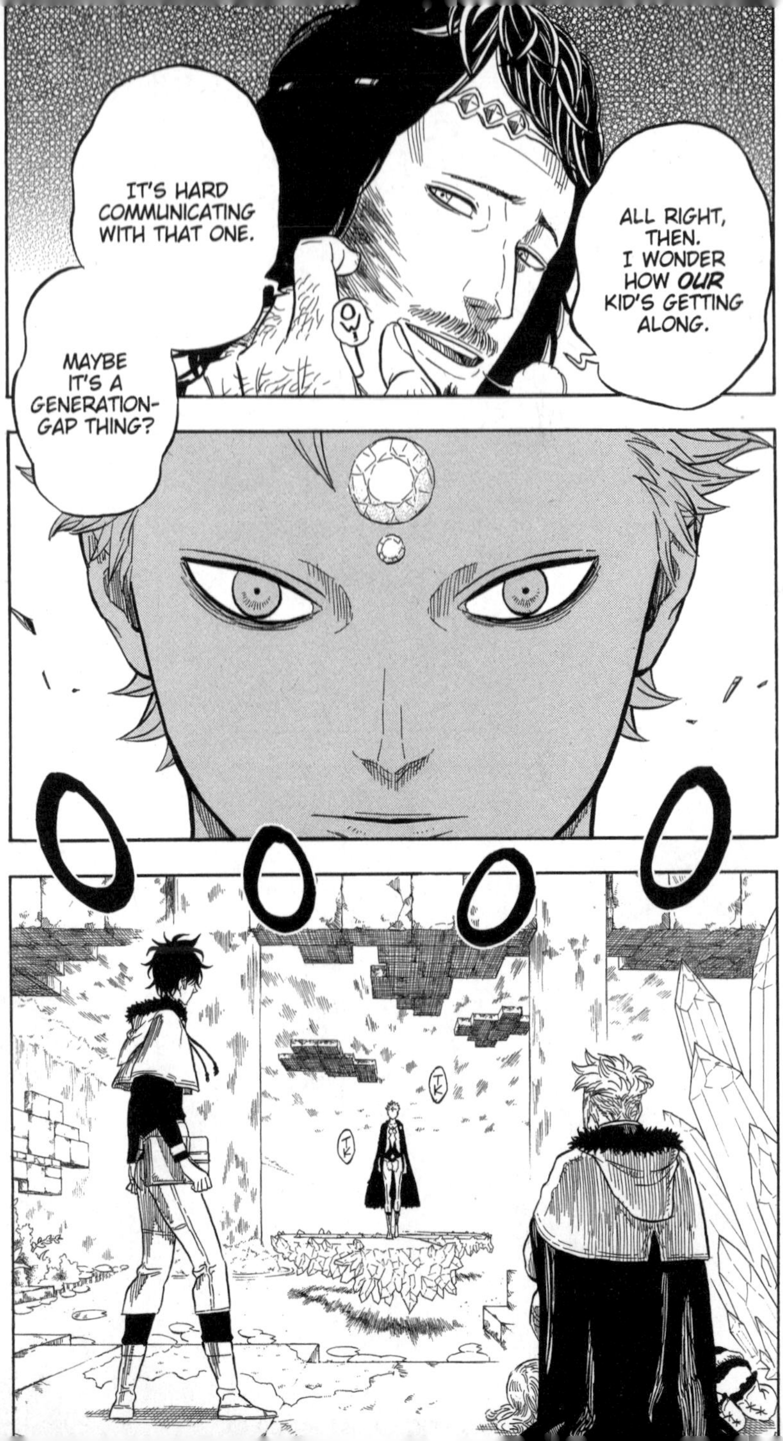
ALL RIGHT, THEN. I WONDER HOW ***OUR*** KID'S GETTING ALONG.
IT'S HARD COMMUNICATING WITH THAT ONE.
OW
MAYBE IT'S A GENERATION-GAP THING?
TK
TK

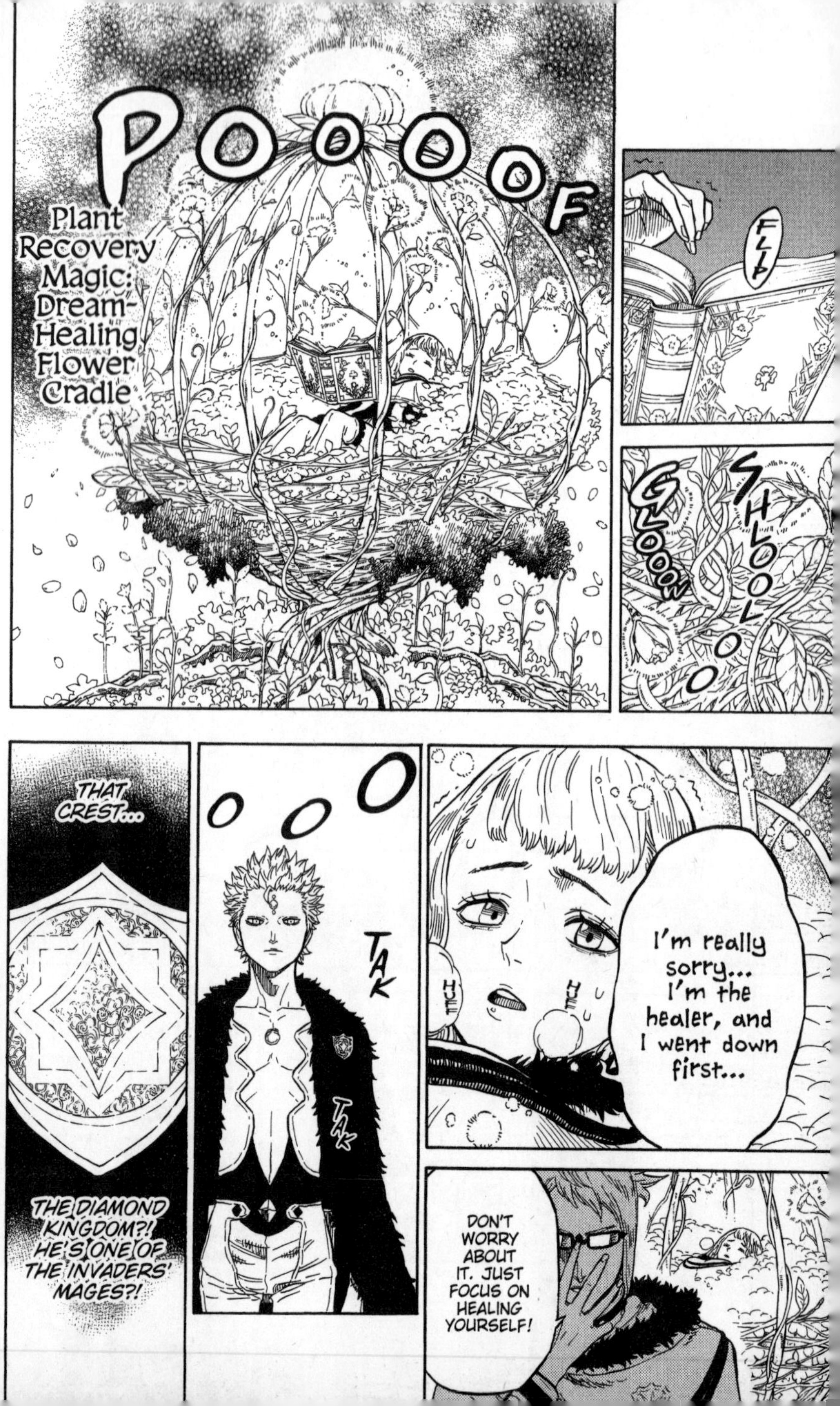
FLIP
SHLOOLOO
GLOOOOW
POOOOOF
Plant Recovery Magic: Dream-Healing Flower Cradle
HUF
HUF
I'm really sorry... I'm the healer, and I went down first...
DON'T WORRY ABOUT IT. JUST FOCUS ON HEALING YOURSELF!
OOO
TAK
TAK
THAT CREST...
THE DIAMOND KINGDOM?! HE'S ONE OF THE INVADERS' MAGES?!

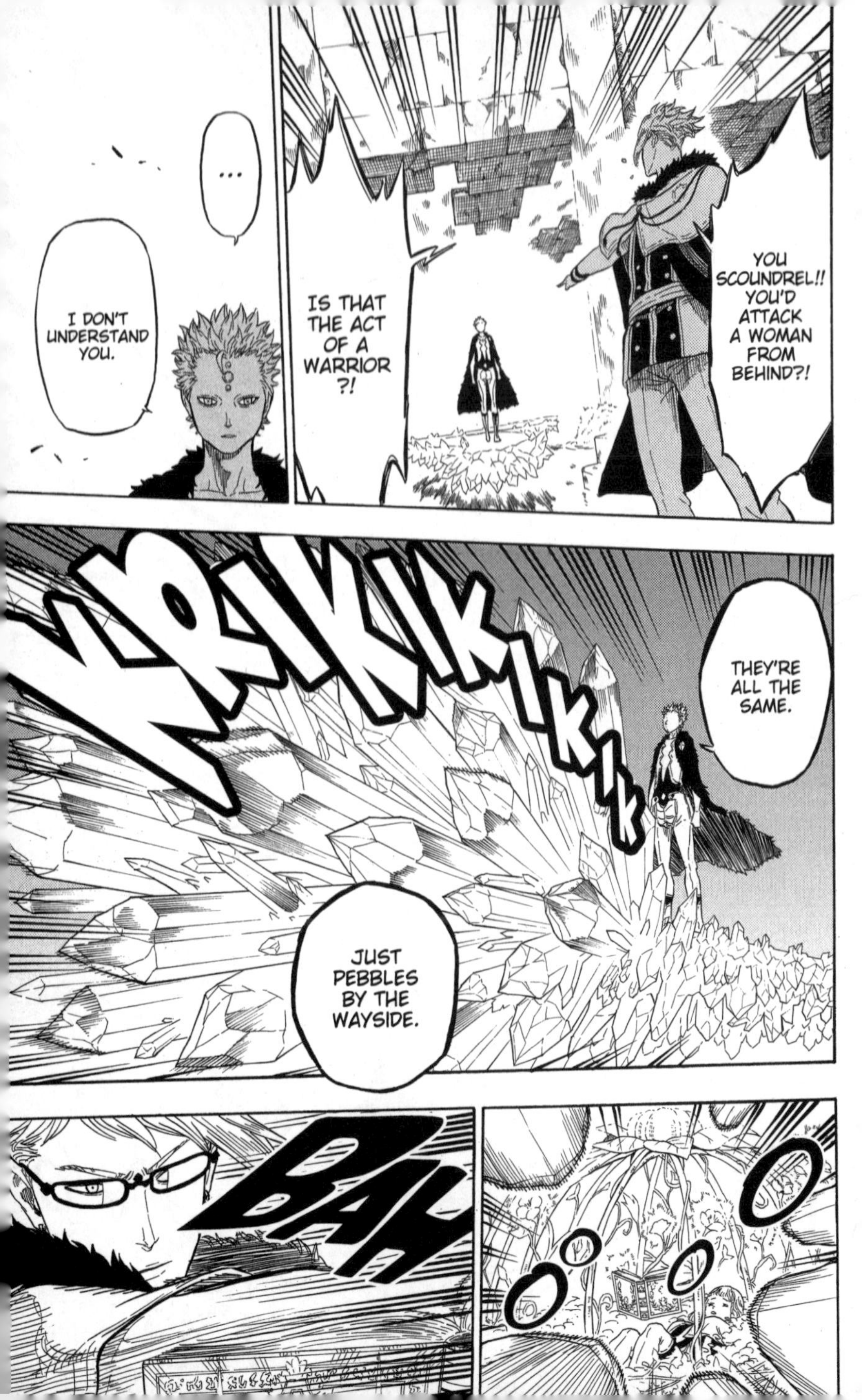

YOU SCOUNDREL!! YOU'D ATTACK A WOMAN FROM BEHIND?!
IS THAT THE ACT OF A WARRIOR?!
...
I DON'T UNDERSTAND YOU.
KRIKIKIKIK
THEY'RE ALL THE SAME.
JUST PEBBLES BY THE WAYSIDE.
BAH

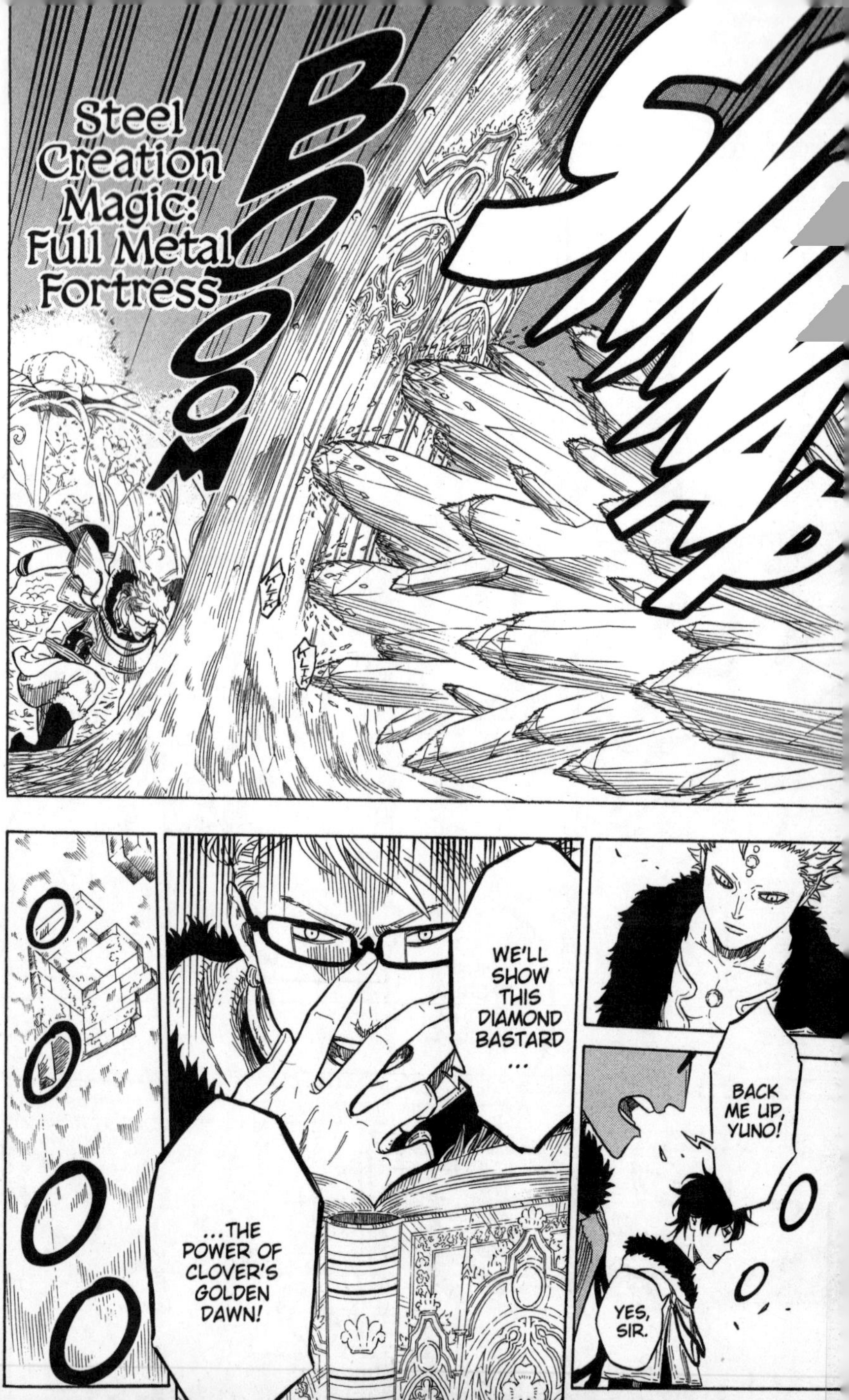
SHNAP
BOOOM
Steel Creation Magic: Full Metal Fortress
KLIK
KLIK
BACK ME UP, YUNO!
YES, SIR.
WE'LL SHOW THIS DIAMOND BASTARD...
...THE POWER OF CLOVER'S GOLDEN DAWN!

AWRIGHT!! THIS WAY'S A LOT EASIER!!

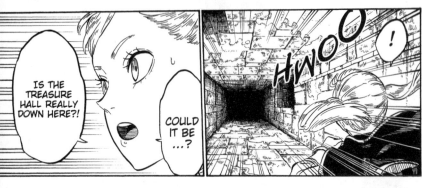

IS THE TREASURE HALL REALLY DOWN HERE?!

COULD IT BE...?

HWOO

!

IT'S PROBABLY LUCK.

I THINK HE'S FIGHTING WITH SOMEONE!

HUH? WAZZAT?!

THIS MAGIC...

BOOOM

!

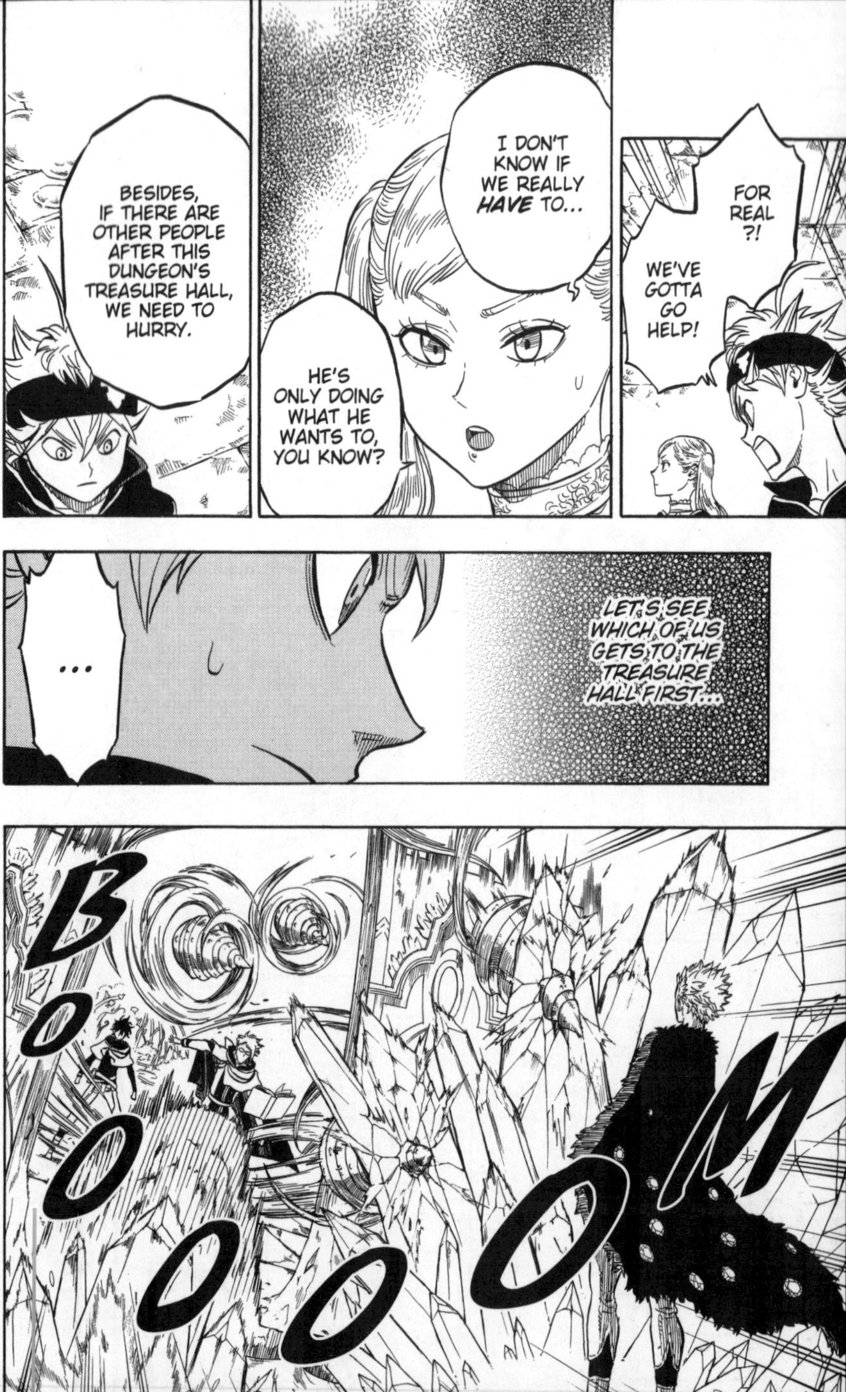

FOR REAL?!
WE'VE GOTTA GO HELP!
I DON'T KNOW IF WE REALLY HAVE TO...
HE'S ONLY DOING WHAT HE WANTS TO, YOU KNOW?
BESIDES, IF THERE ARE OTHER PEOPLE AFTER THIS DUNGEON'S TREASURE HALL, WE NEED TO HURRY.
LET'S SEE WHICH OF US GETS TO THE TREASURE HALL FIRST...
...
BOOOOOOOM

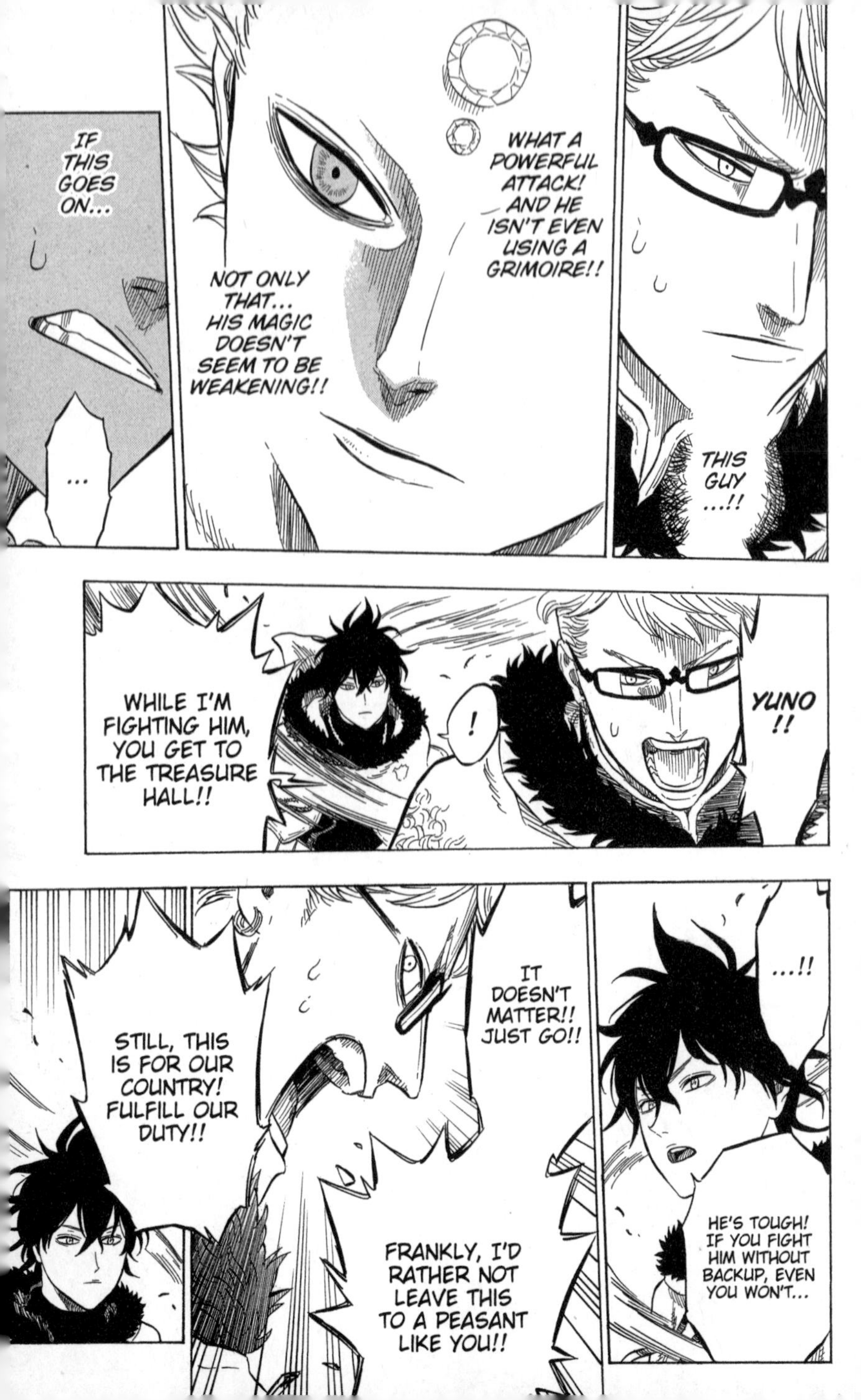
THIS GUY ...!!
WHAT A POWERFUL ATTACK! AND HE ISN'T EVEN USING A GRIMOIRE!!
NOT ONLY THAT... HIS MAGIC DOESN'T SEEM TO BE WEAKENING!!
IF THIS GOES ON...
...
YUNO !!
!
WHILE I'M FIGHTING HIM, YOU GET TO THE TREASURE HALL!!
...!!
HE'S TOUGH! IF YOU FIGHT HIM WITHOUT BACKUP, EVEN YOU WON'T...
IT DOESN'T MATTER!! JUST GO!!
FRANKLY, I'D RATHER NOT LEAVE THIS TO A PEASANT LIKE YOU!!
STILL, THIS IS FOR OUR COUNTRY! FULFILL OUR DUTY!!

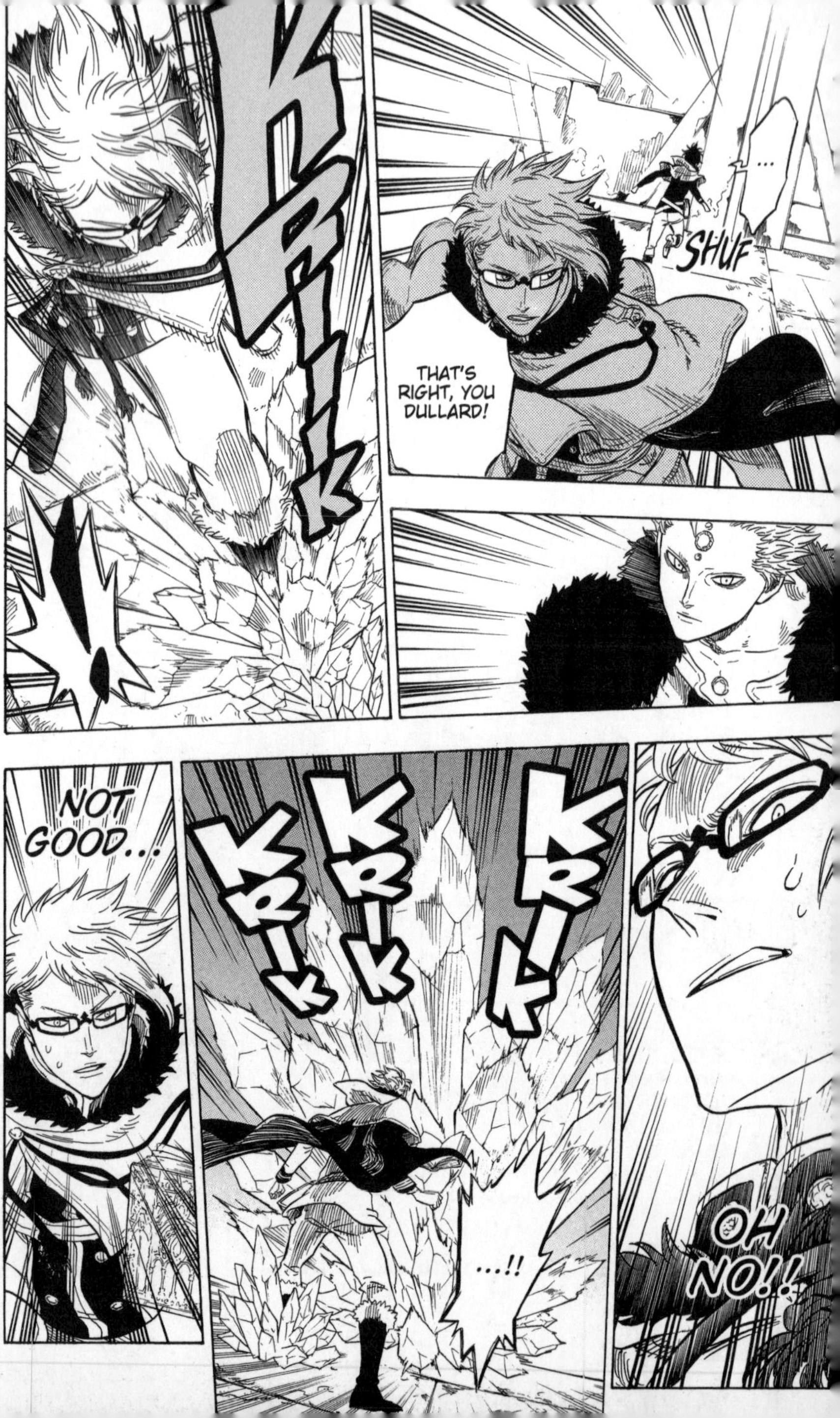
...
SHUF
THAT'S RIGHT, YOU DULLARD!
KRIK
OH NO!!
KRIK
KRIK
KRIK
...!!
NOT GOOD...

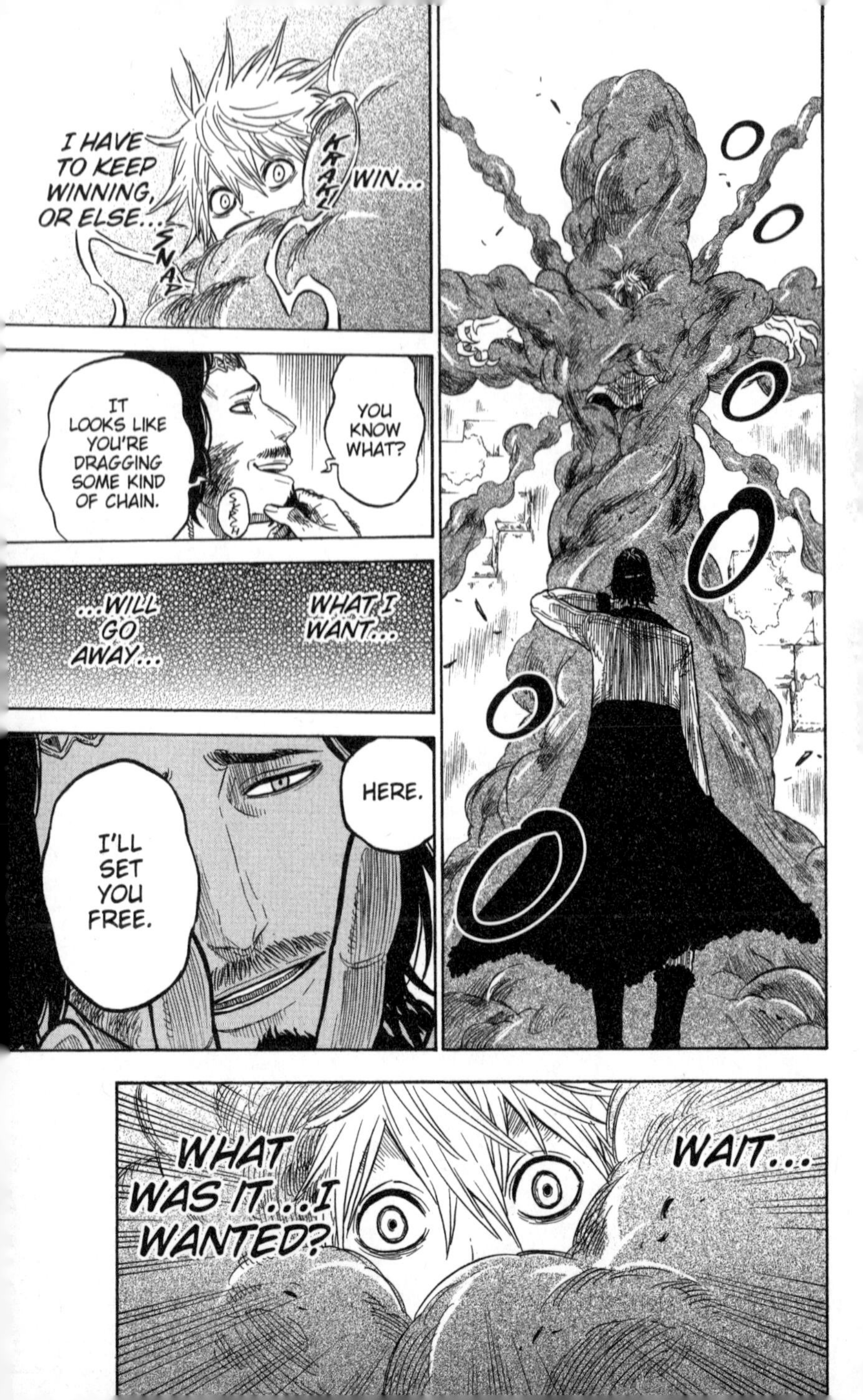
WIN...
KRAK!!
I HAVE TO KEEP WINNING, OR ELSE...
SNAP
YOU KNOW WHAT?
IT LOOKS LIKE YOU'RE DRAGGING SOME KIND OF CHAIN.
WHAT I WANT...
...WILL GO AWAY...
HERE.
I'LL SET YOU FREE.
WAIT...
WHAT WAS IT...I WANTED?

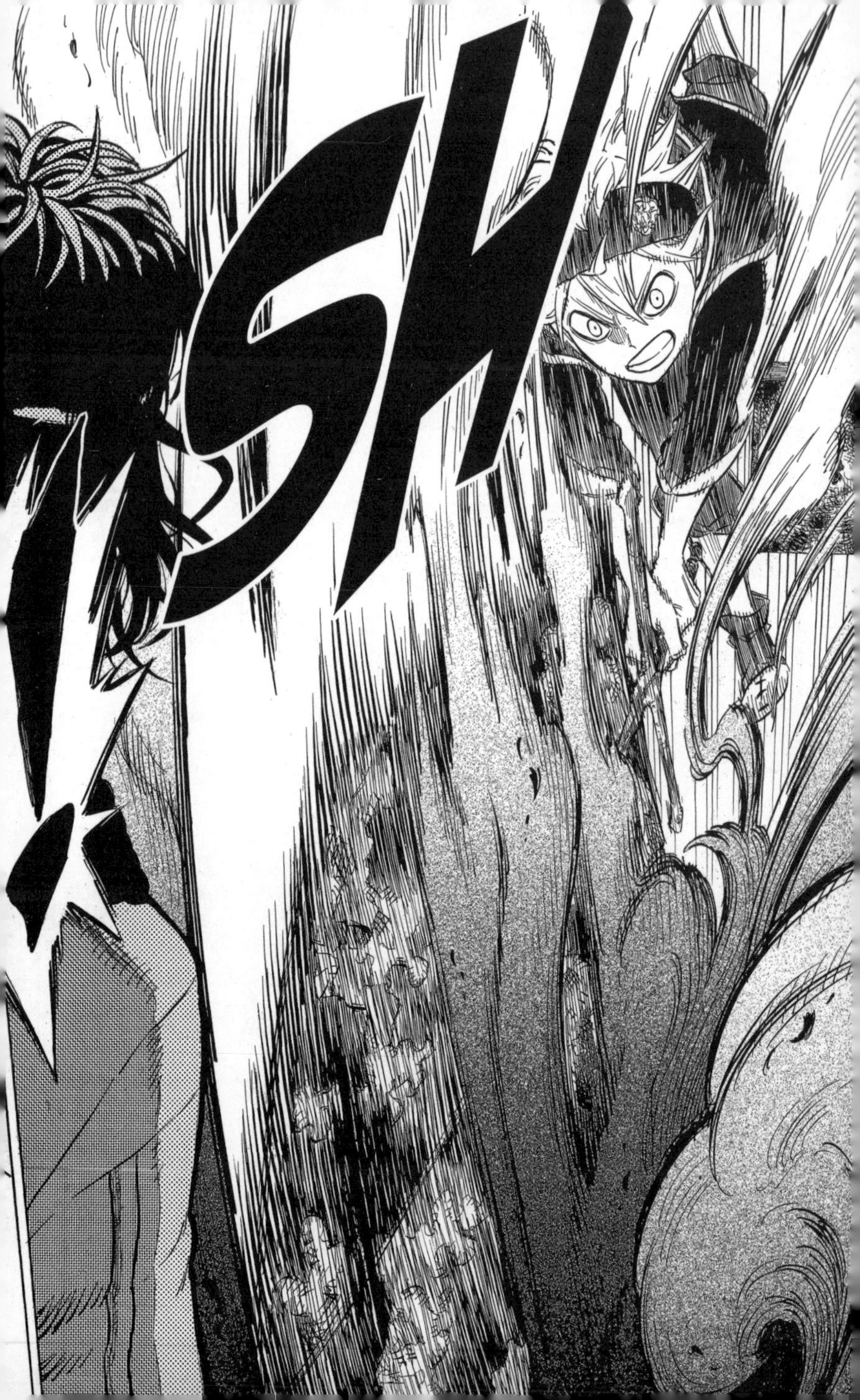
SH

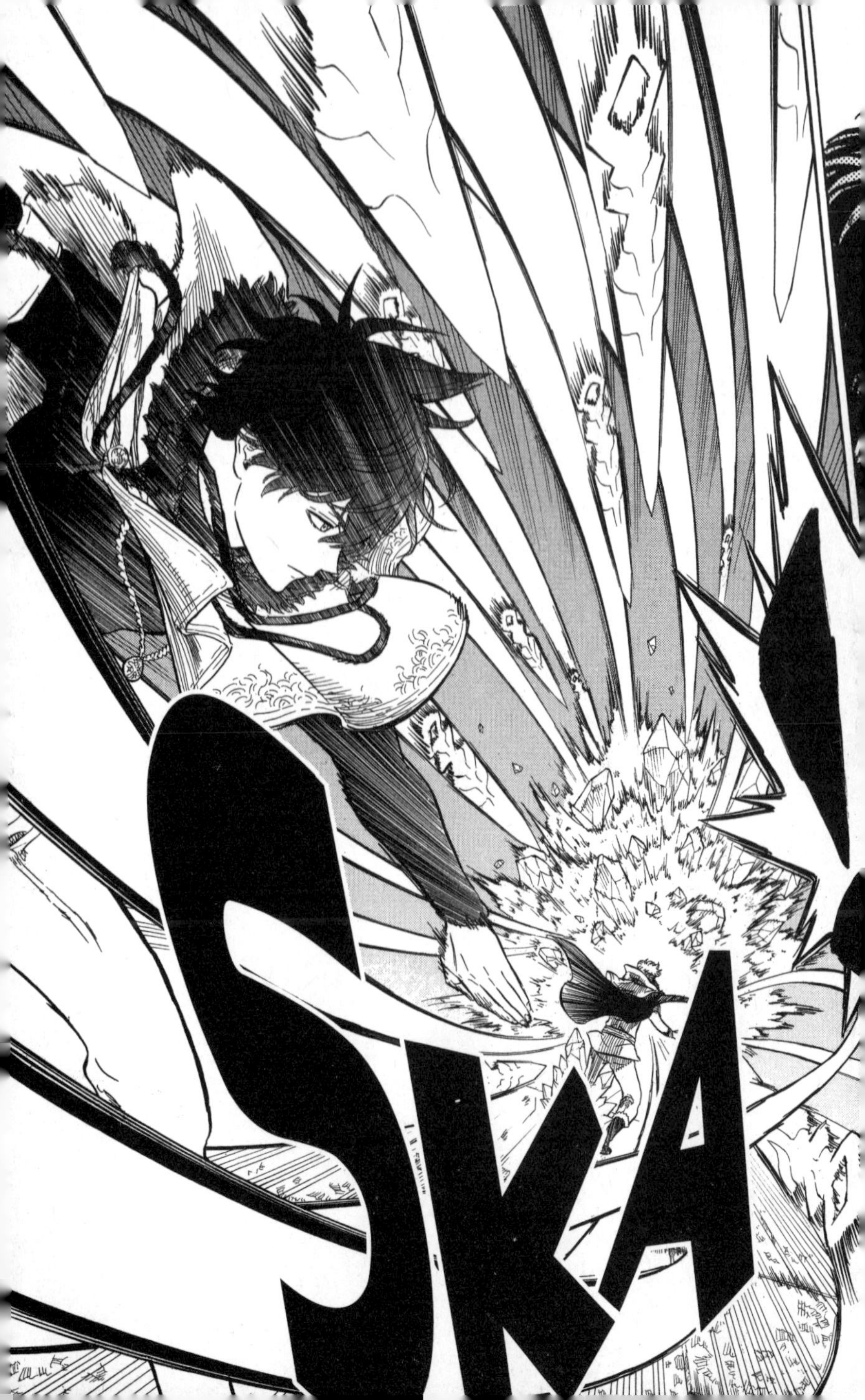
SKA

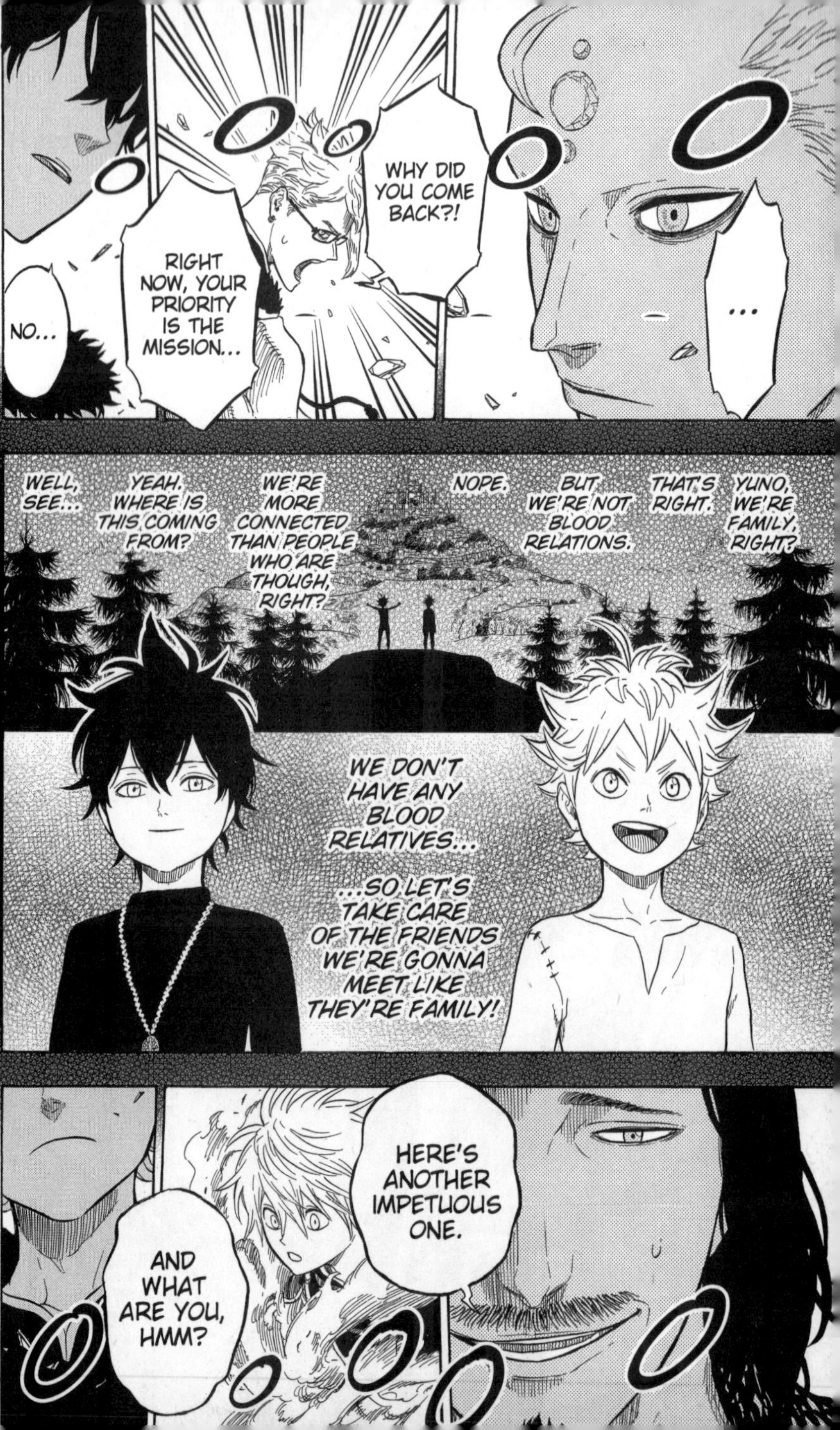
...
WHY DID YOU COME BACK?!
RIGHT NOW, YOUR PRIORITY IS THE MISSION...
NO...
YUNO, WE'RE FAMILY, RIGHT?
THAT'S RIGHT.
BUT WE'RE NOT BLOOD RELATIONS.
NOPE.
WE'RE MORE CONNECTED THAN PEOPLE WHO ARE THOUGH, RIGHT?
YEAH. WHERE IS THIS COMING FROM?
WELL, SEE...
WE DON'T HAVE ANY BLOOD RELATIVES...
...SO LET'S TAKE CARE OF THE FRIENDS WE'RE GONNA MEET LIKE THEY'RE FAMILY!
HERE'S ANOTHER IMPETUOUS ONE.
AND WHAT ARE YOU, HMM?

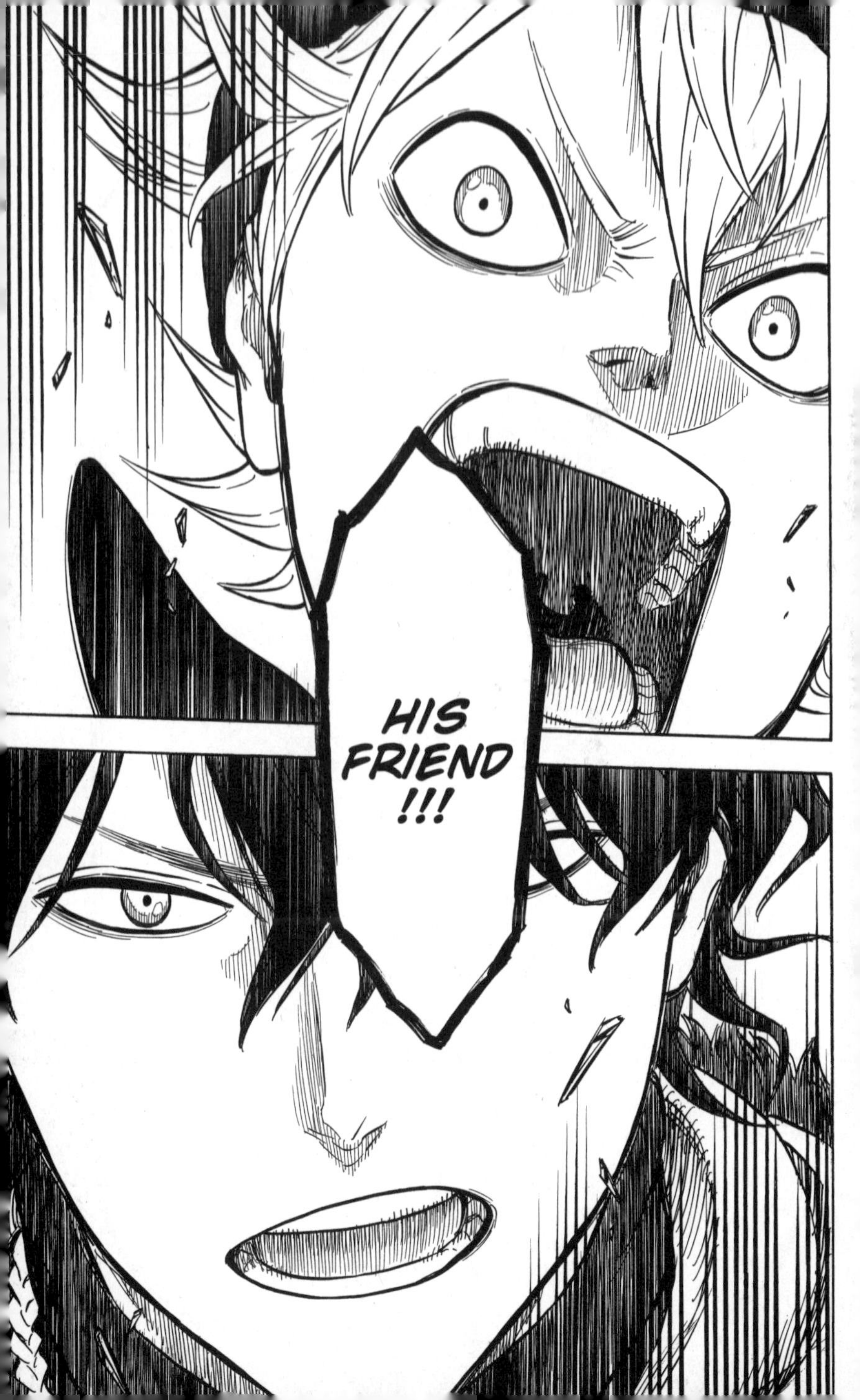
HIS FRIEND!!!

These are pictures I drew for the Special Jump Japan Map Poster in the 22-23 issue of *Weekly Shonen Jump* in 2015.

I drew the legendary Yamata-no-Orochi snake for Shimane Prefecture and a snow crab for Fukui Prefecture.

By the way, I'm from Fukuoka Prefecture.

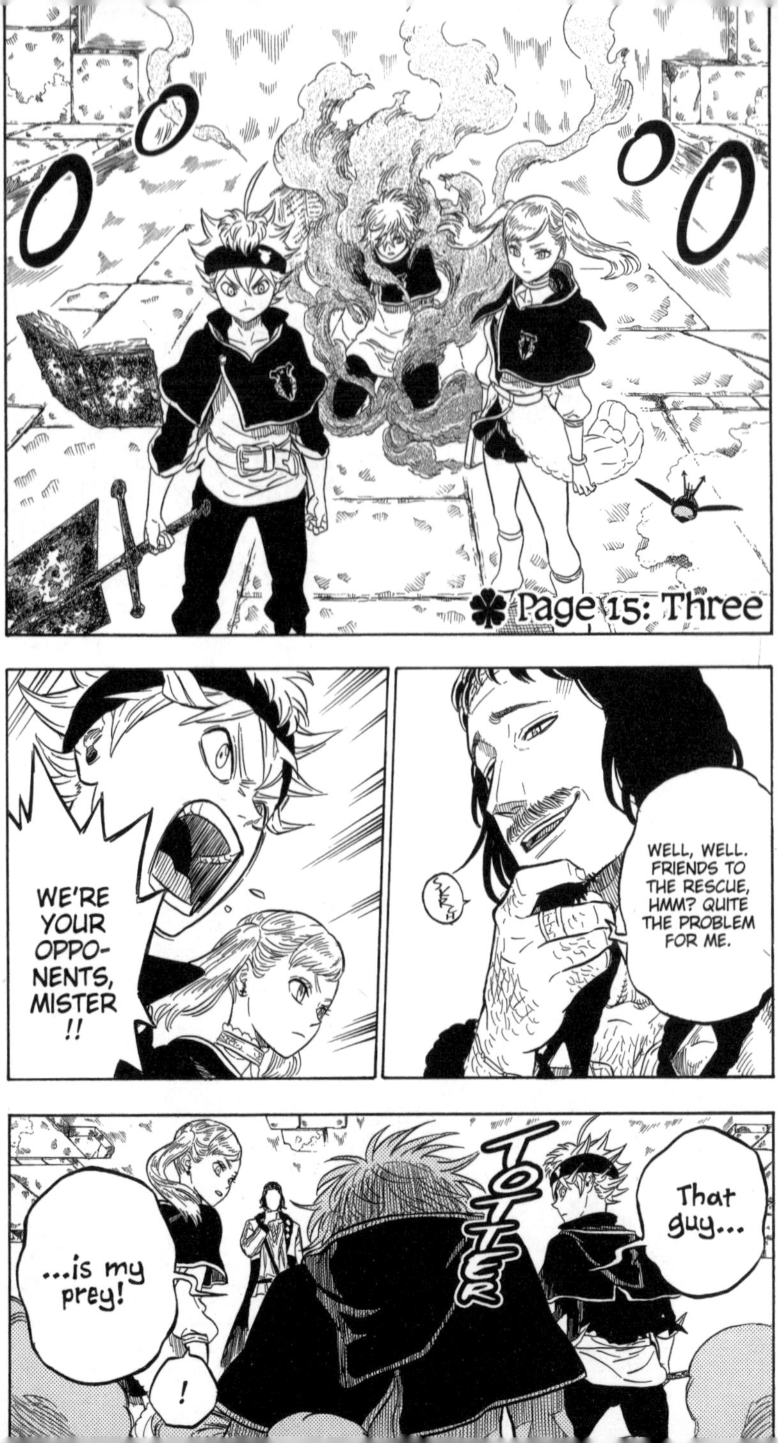
Page 15: Three
WELL, WELL. FRIENDS TO THE RESCUE, HMM? QUITE THE PROBLEM FOR ME.
WE'RE YOUR OPPONENTS, MISTER!!
That guy...
TOTTER
...is my prey!
!

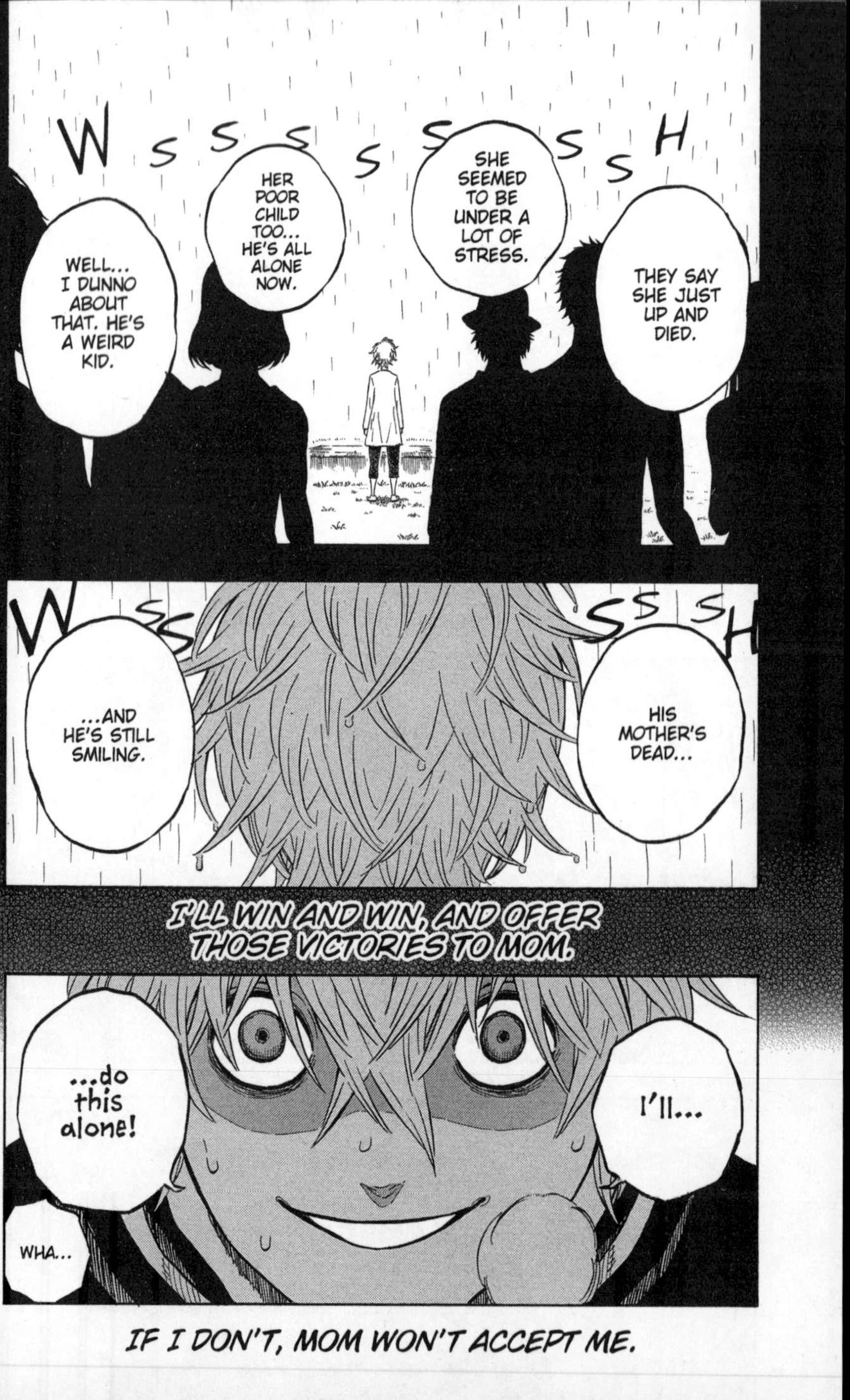
WSSSSSSSH
THEY SAY SHE JUST UP AND DIED.
SHE SEEMED TO BE UNDER A LOT OF STRESS.
HER POOR CHILD TOO... HE'S ALL ALONE NOW.
WELL... I DUNNO ABOUT THAT. HE'S A WEIRD KID.
WSSSSH
HIS MOTHER'S DEAD...
...AND HE'S STILL SMILING.
I'LL WIN AND WIN, AND OFFER THOSE VICTORIES TO MOM.
I'll...
...do this alone!
WHA...
IF I DON'T, MOM WON'T ACCEPT ME.

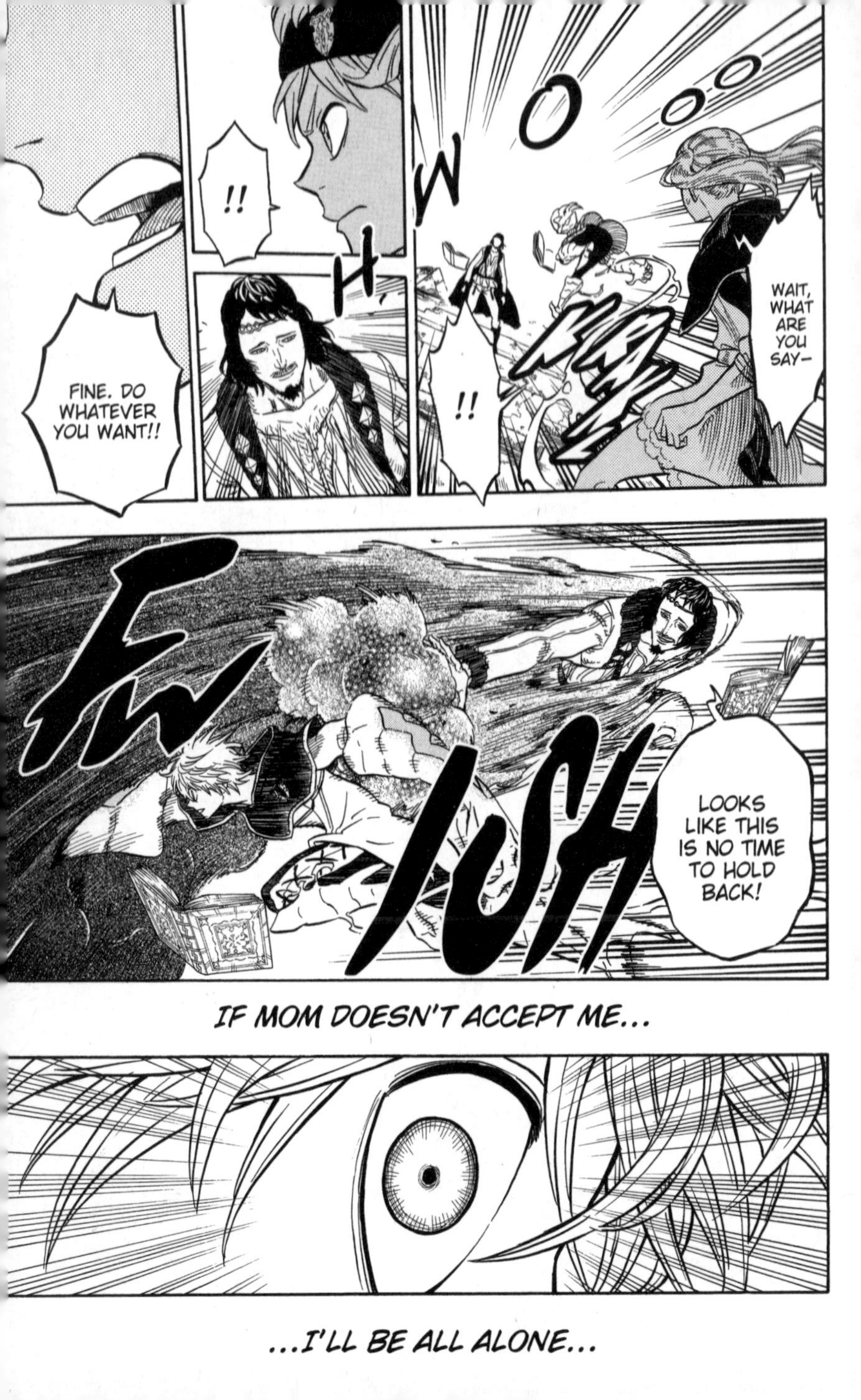
WHOOOSH
WAIT, WHAT ARE YOU SAY—
!!
!!
FINE. DO WHATEVER YOU WANT!!
LOOKS LIKE THIS IS NO TIME TO HOLD BACK!
FWUSH
IF MOM DOESN'T ACCEPT ME...
...I'LL BE ALL ALONE...

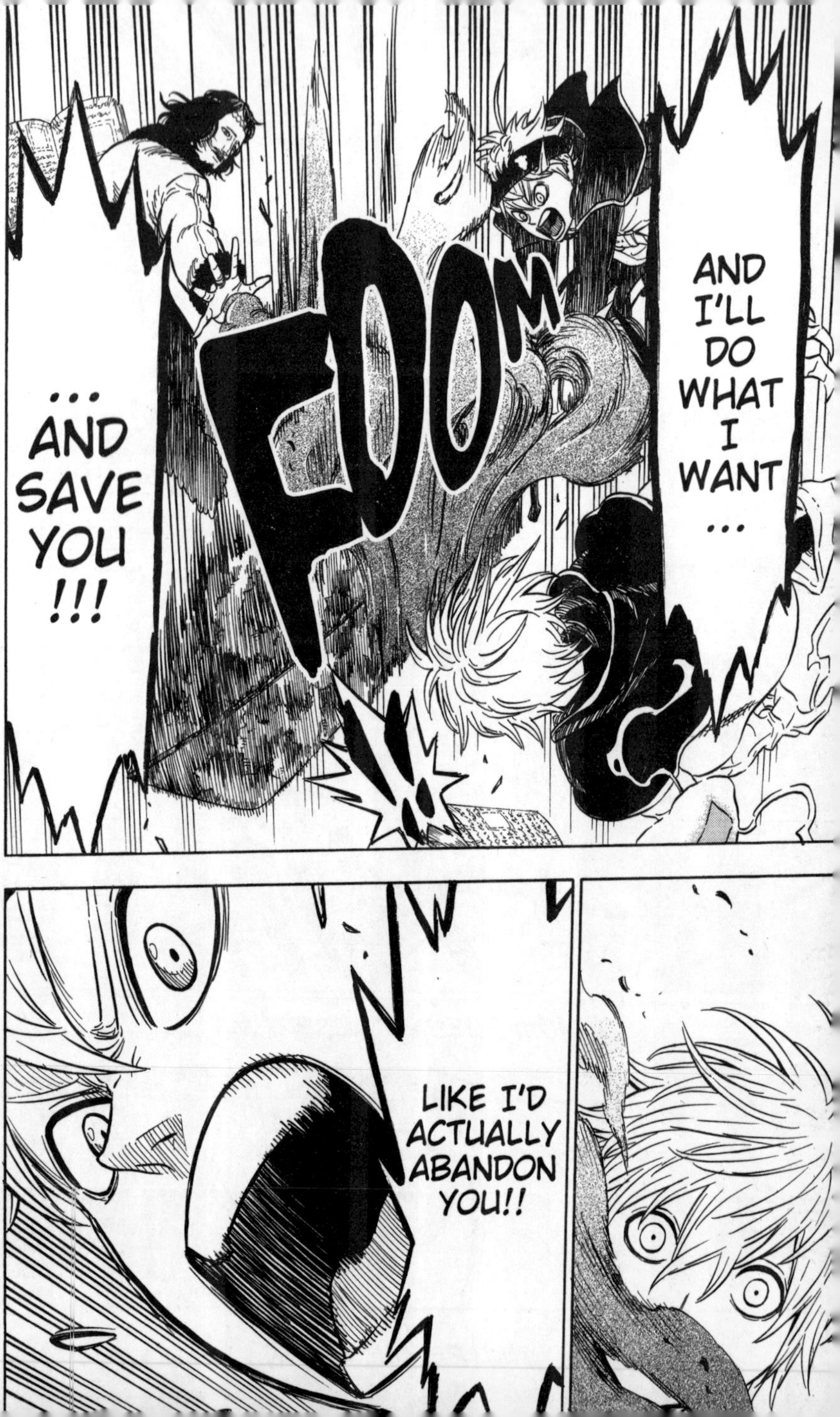
AND I'LL DO WHAT I WANT...
FDOOM
...AND SAVE YOU!!!
LIKE I'D ACTUALLY ABANDON YOU!!

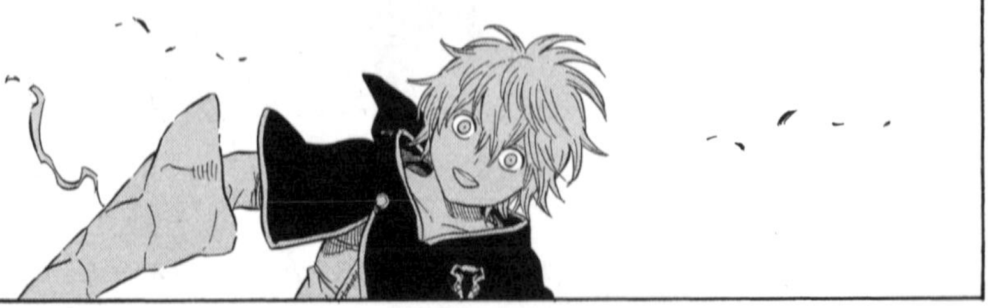

I THINK...

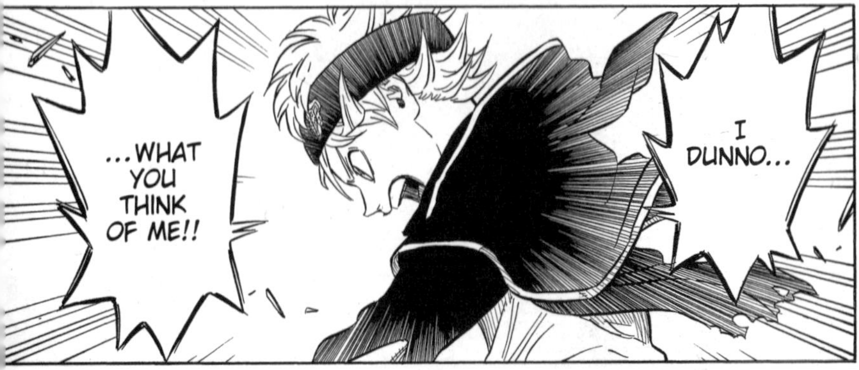
I DUNNO...
...WHAT YOU THINK OF ME!!

...I WAS TRYING NOT TO NOTICE.

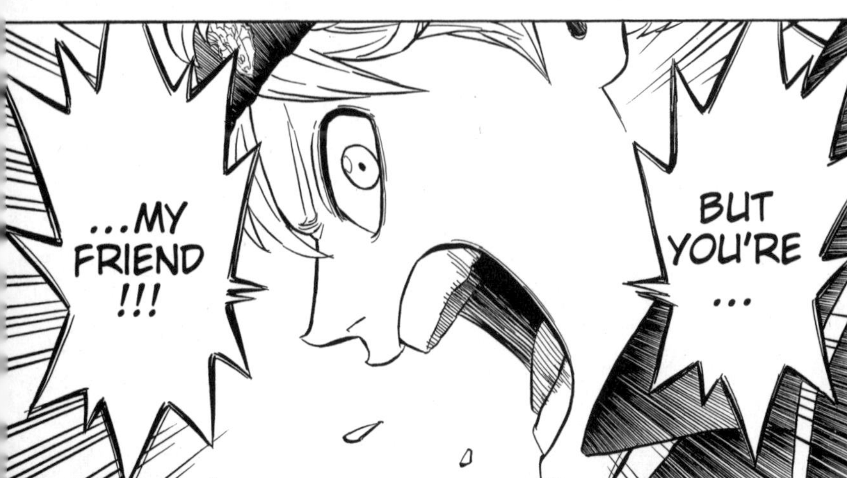
BUT YOU'RE ...
...MY FRIEND !!!

I HAVE THEM TOO NOW.

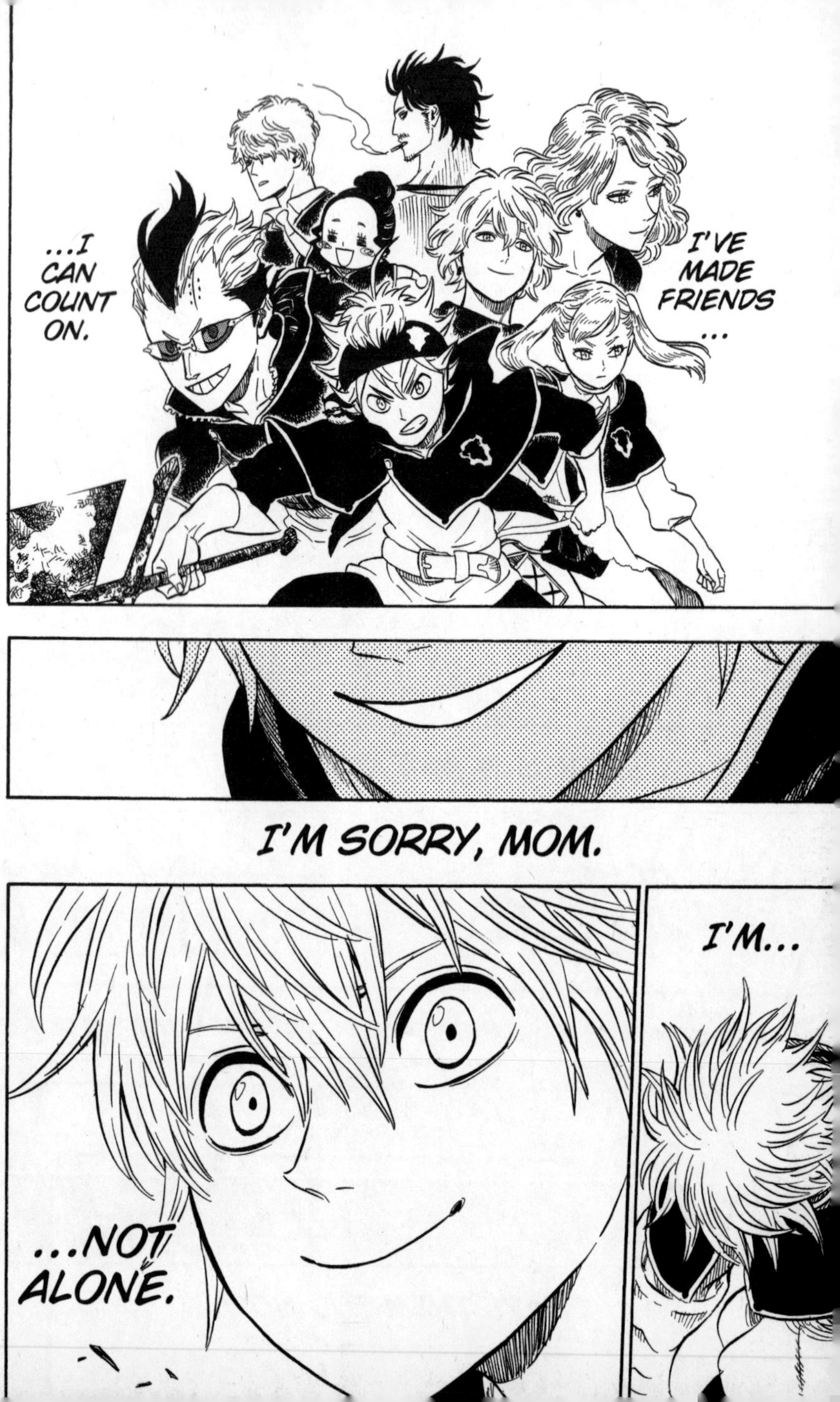
I'VE MADE FRIENDS...
...I CAN COUNT ON.
I'M SORRY, MOM.
I'M...
...NOT ALONE.

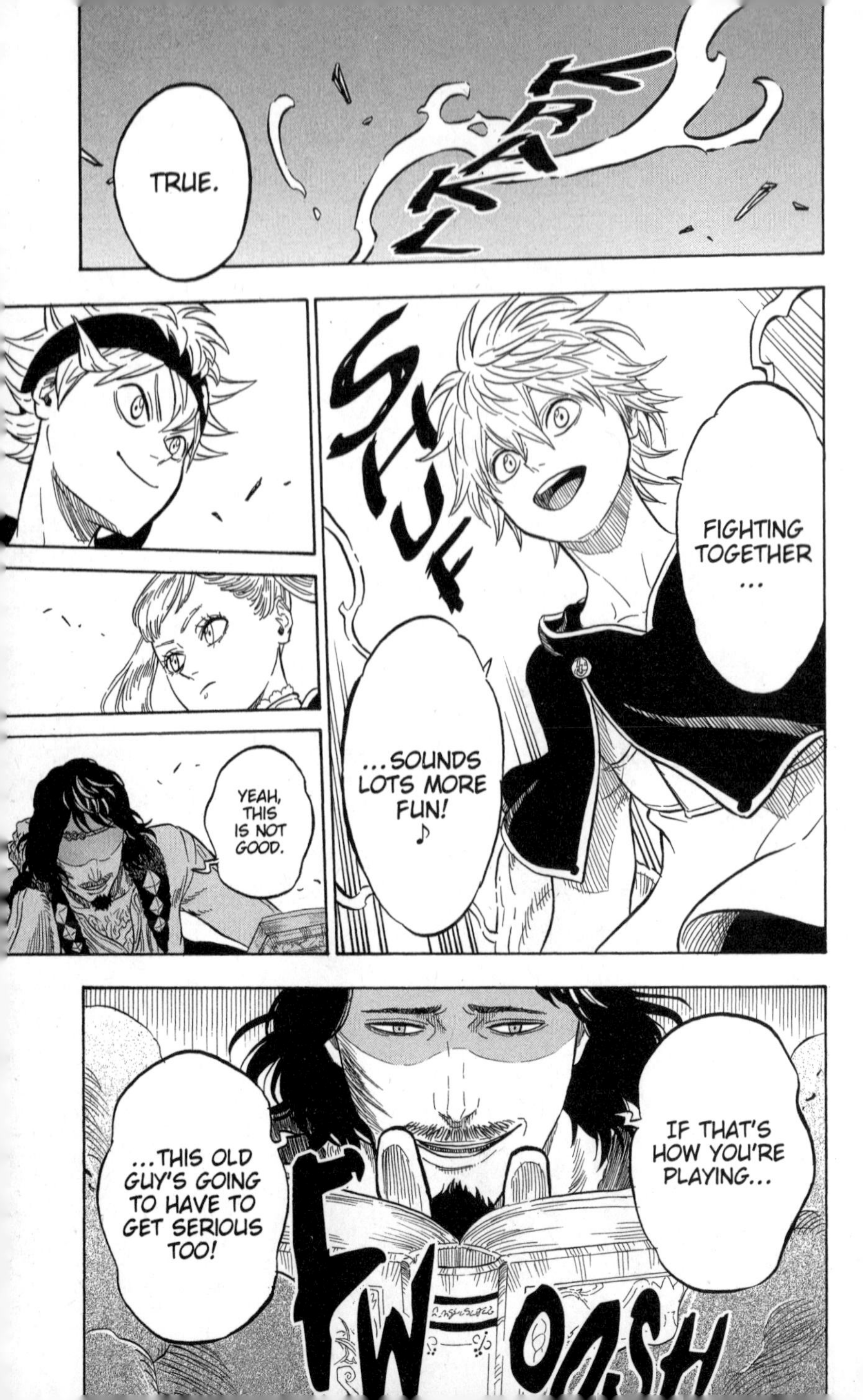
KRAK
TRUE.
FIGHTING TOGETHER...
SHUF
...SOUNDS LOTS MORE FUN! ♪
YEAH, THIS IS NOT GOOD.
IF THAT'S HOW YOU'RE PLAYING...
...THIS OLD GUY'S GOING TO HAVE TO GET SERIOUS TOO!
FWOOSH

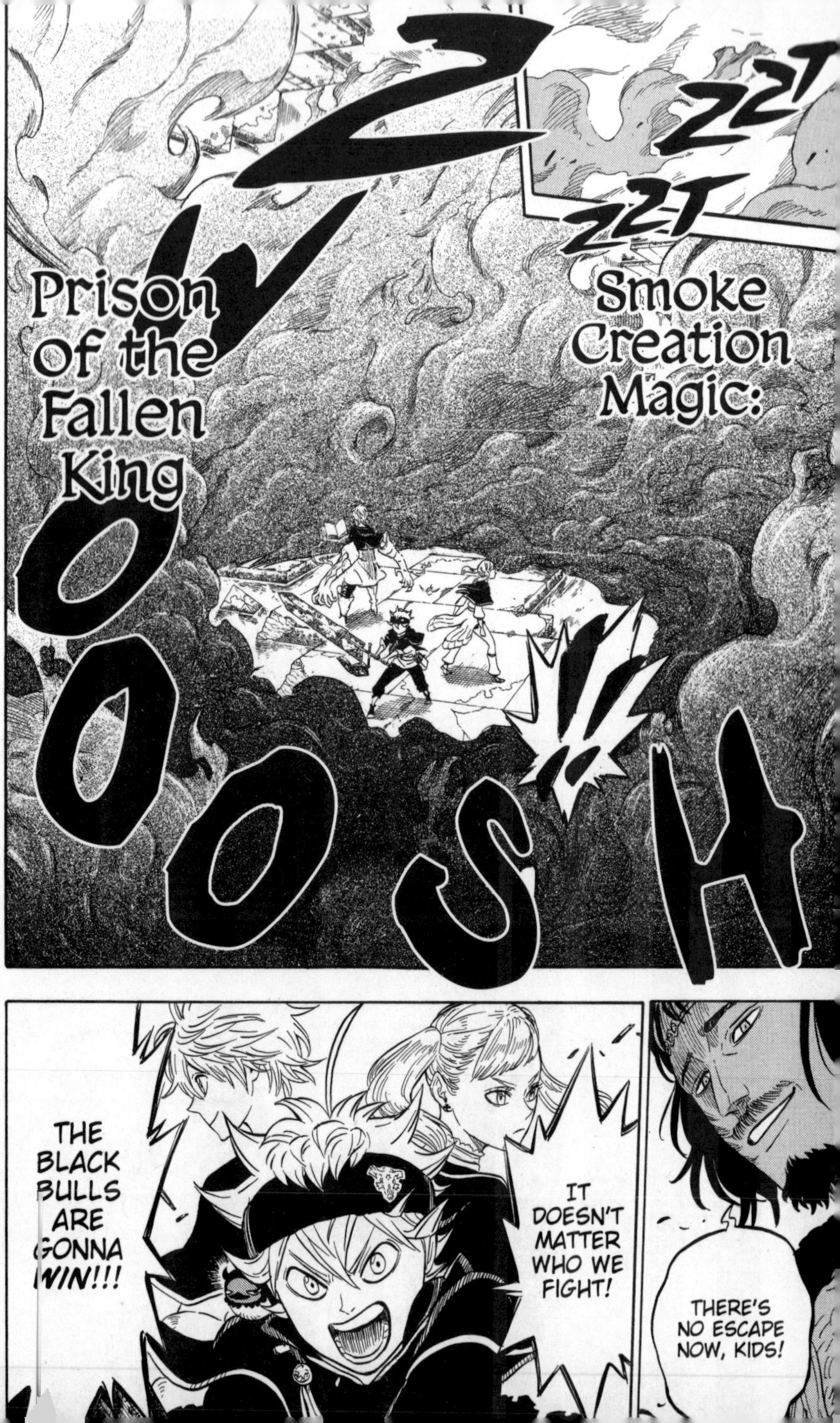
ZZZT
ZZT
Smoke Creation Magic:
Prison of the Fallen King
WOOOSH!!
THERE'S NO ESCAPE NOW, KIDS!
IT DOESN'T MATTER WHO WE FIGHT!
THE BLACK BULLS ARE GONNA WIN!!!

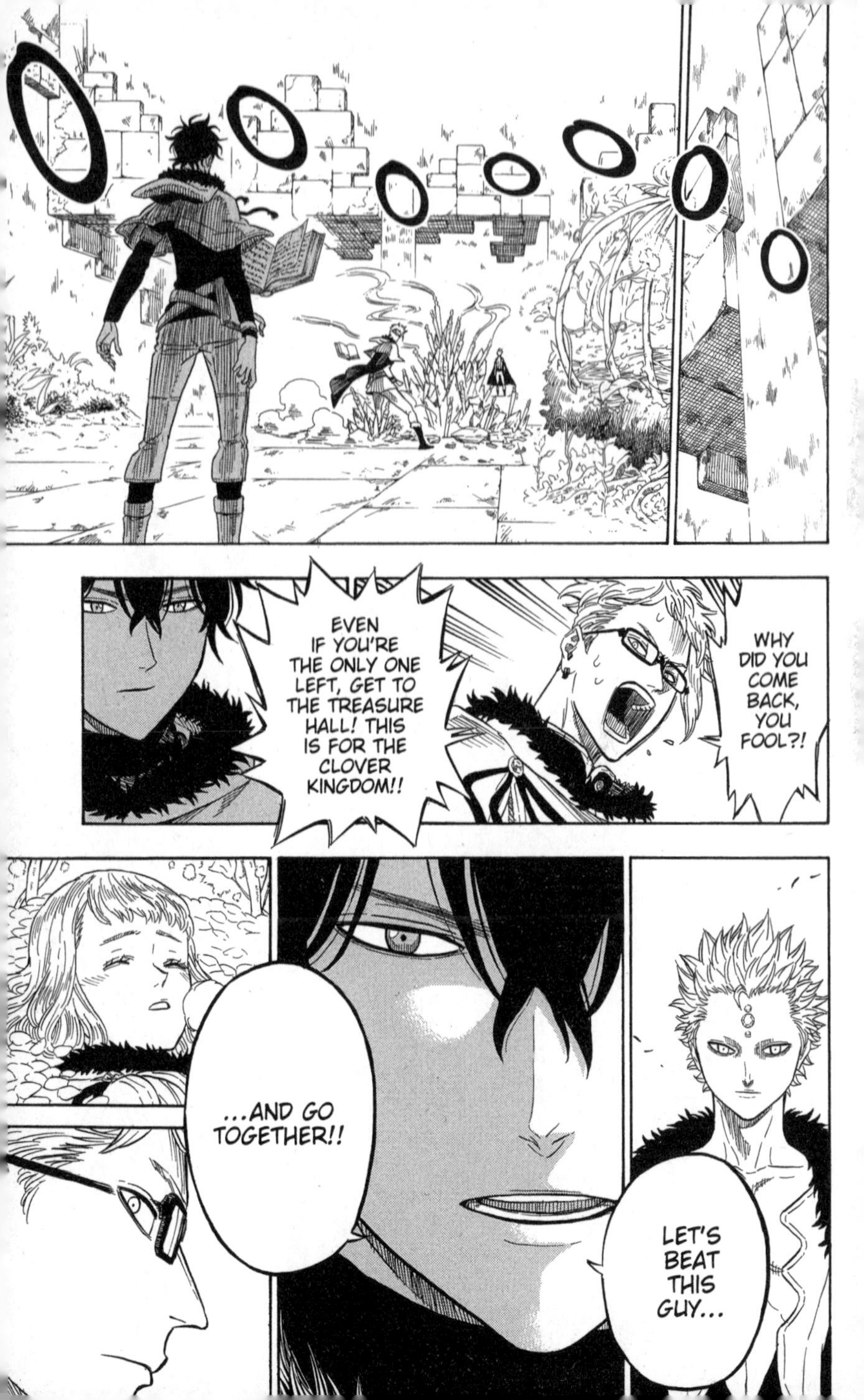
WHY DID YOU COME BACK, YOU FOOL?!
EVEN IF YOU'RE THE ONLY ONE LEFT, GET TO THE TREASURE HALL! THIS IS FOR THE CLOVER KINGDOM!!
LET'S BEAT THIS GUY...
...AND GO TOGETHER!!

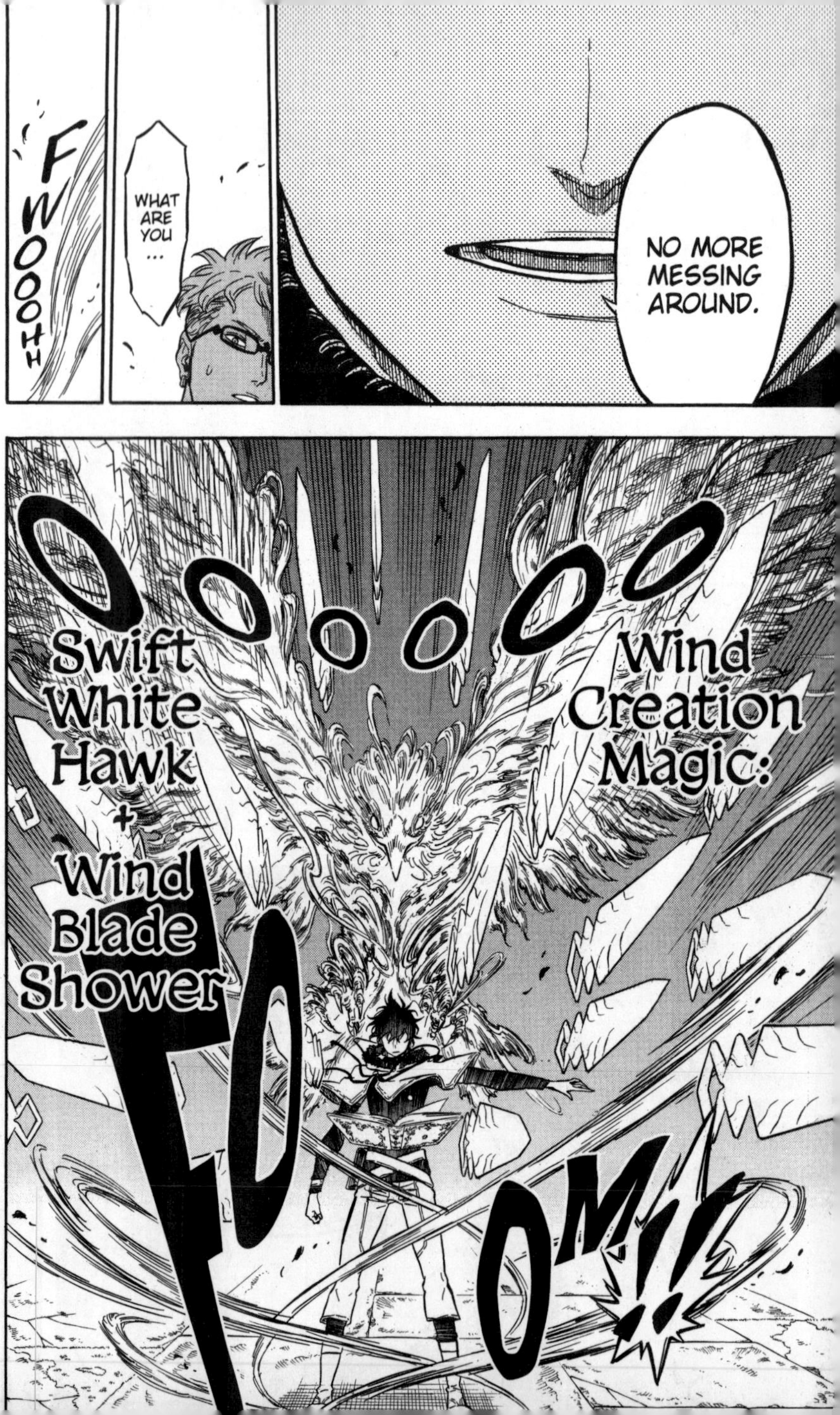
NO MORE MESSING AROUND.
WHAT ARE YOU...
FWOOOOHH
Wind Creation Magic:
Swift White Hawk + Wind Blade Shower
FOOOOOOOOOOM!!

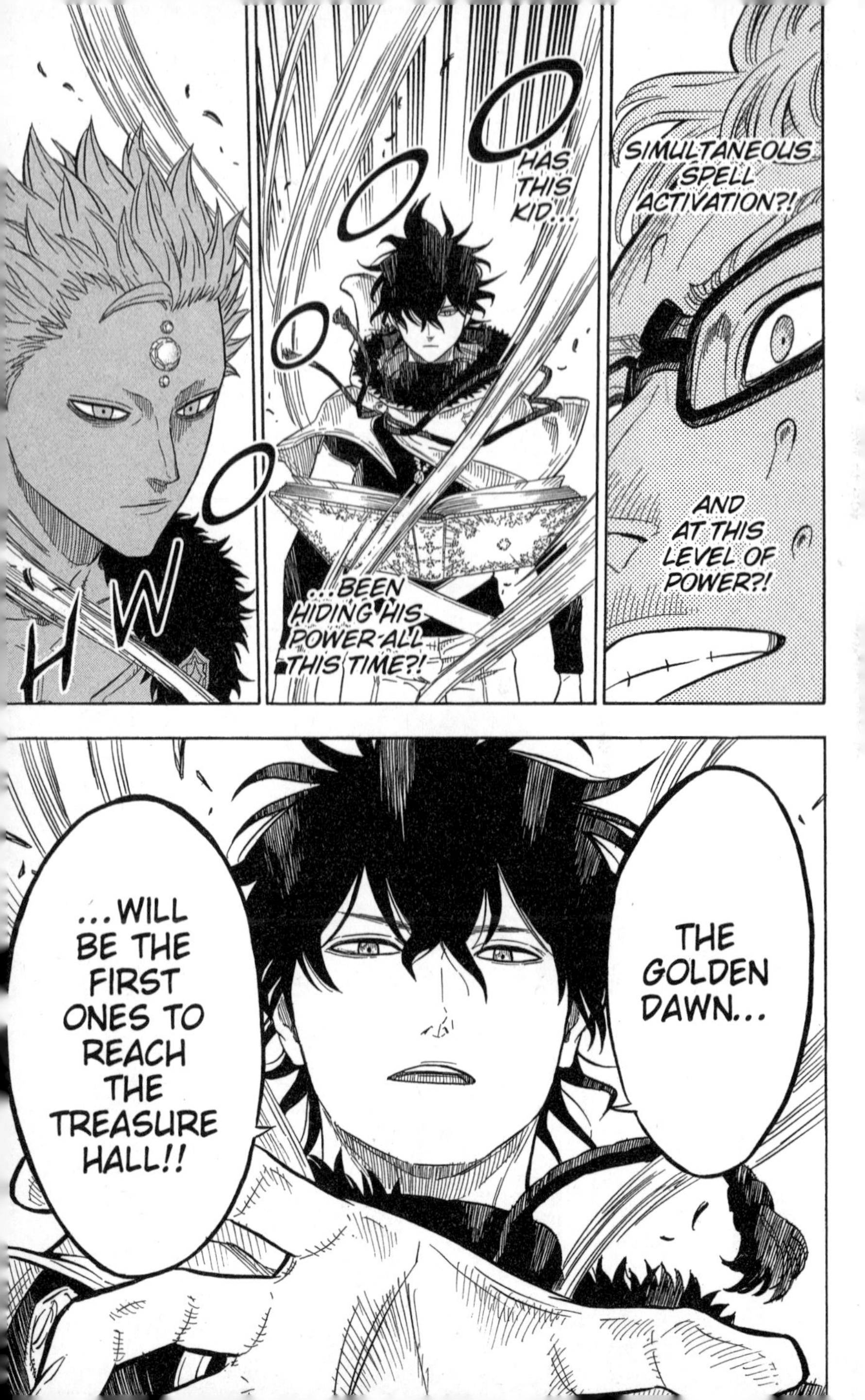
SIMULTANEOUS SPELL ACTIVATION?!
AND AT THIS LEVEL OF POWER?!
HAS THIS KID...
...BEEN HIDING HIS POWER ALL THIS TIME?!
HW
THE GOLDEN DAWN...
...WILL BE THE FIRST ONES TO REACH THE TREASURE HALL!!

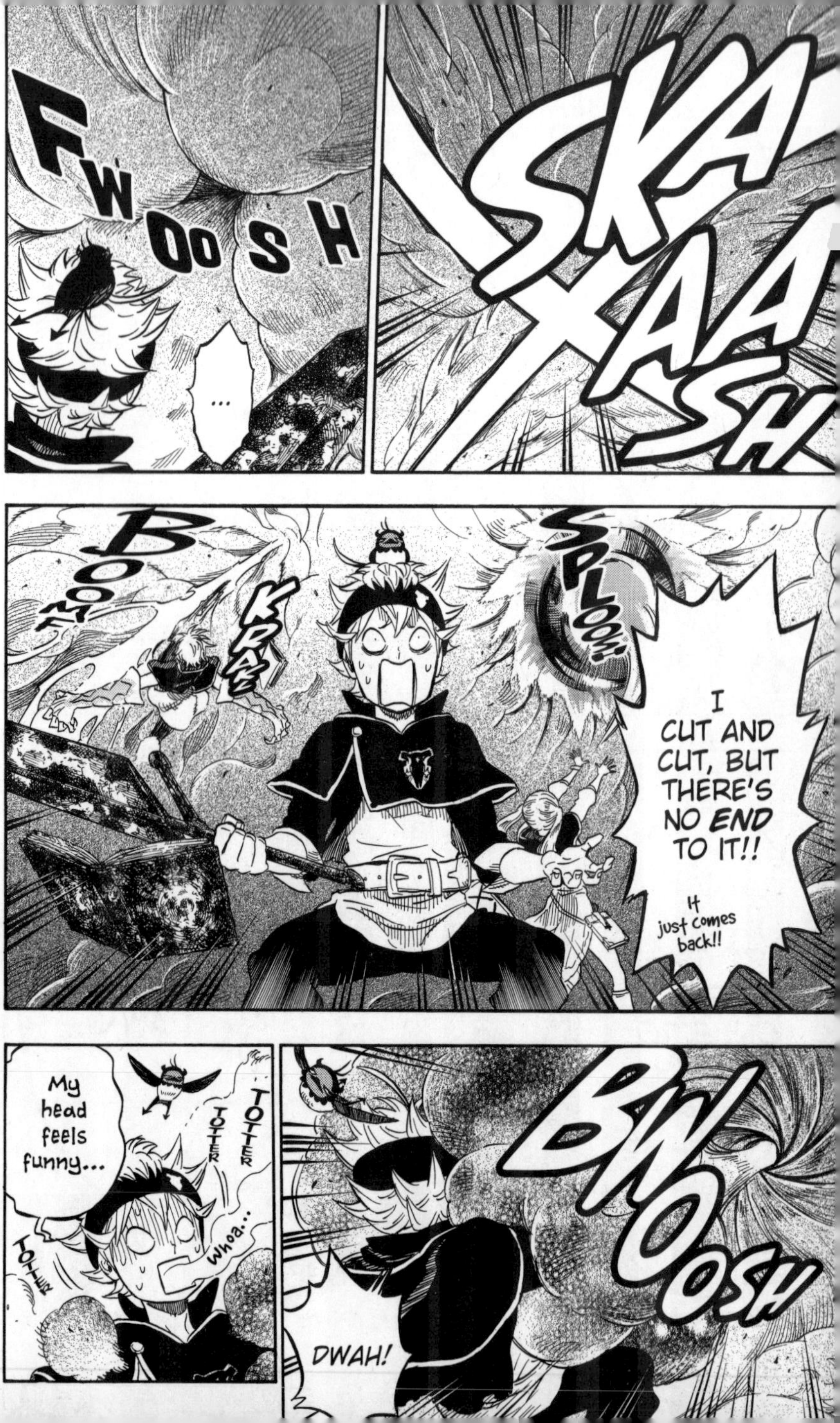
SKAAASH
FWOOSH
...
SPLOOSH
I CUT AND CUT, BUT THERE'S NO END TO IT!!
It just comes back!!
KRAK
BOOMF
BWOOOSH
DWAH!
My head feels funny...
TOTTER TOTTER
Whoa...
TOTTER

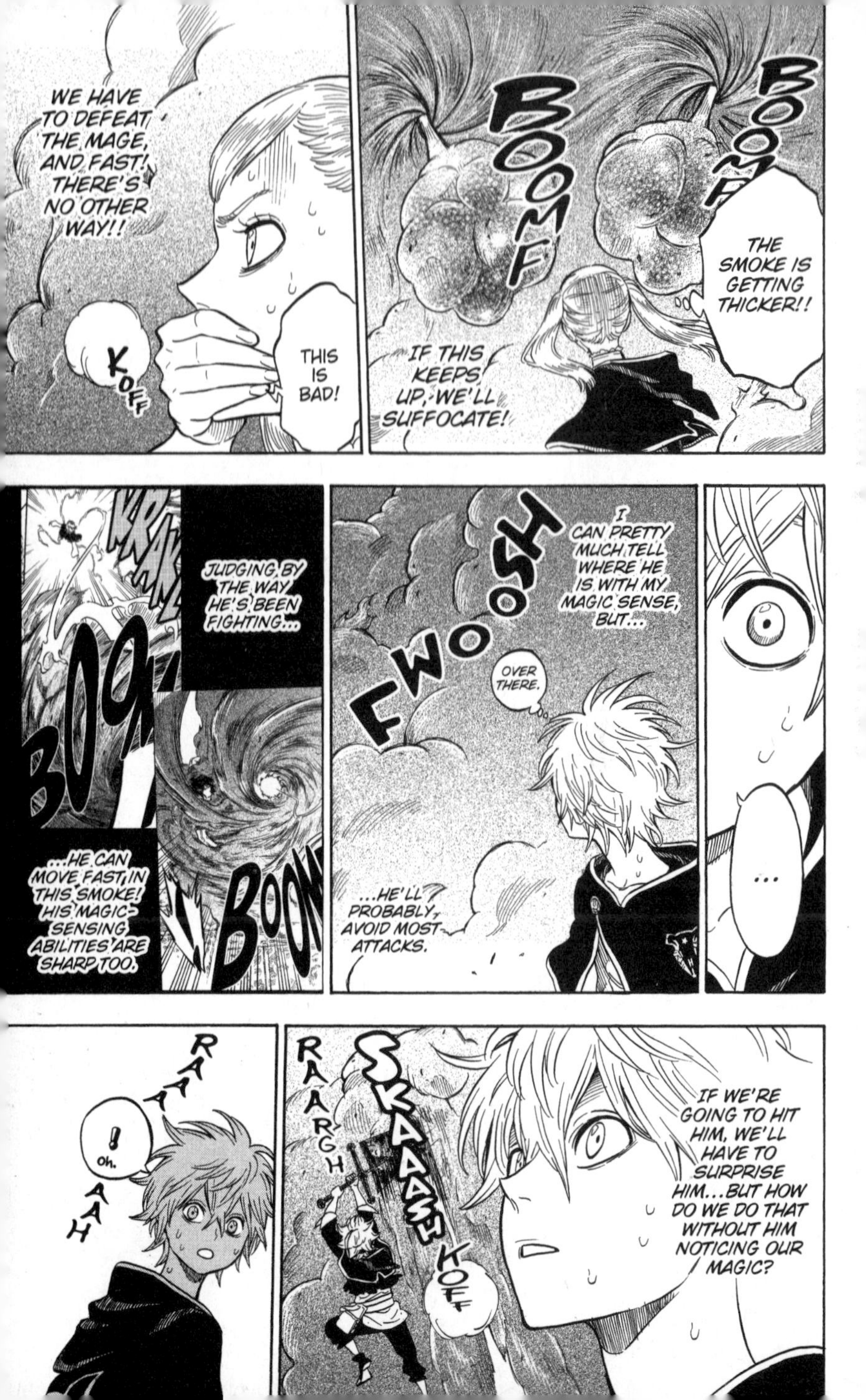
BOOMF
BOOMF
THE SMOKE IS GETTING THICKER!!
IF THIS KEEPS UP, WE'LL SUFFOCATE!
KOFF
THIS IS BAD!
WE HAVE TO DEFEAT THE MAGE, AND FAST! THERE'S NO OTHER WAY!!
...
I CAN PRETTY MUCH TELL WHERE HE IS WITH MY MAGIC SENSE, BUT...
FWOOSH
OVER THERE.
...HE'LL PROBABLY AVOID MOST ATTACKS.
JUDGING BY THE WAY HE'S BEEN FIGHTING...
...HE CAN MOVE FAST IN THIS SMOKE! HIS MAGIC-SENSING ABILITIES ARE SHARP TOO.
IF WE'RE GOING TO HIT HIM, WE'LL HAVE TO SURPRISE HIM...BUT HOW DO WE DO THAT WITHOUT HIM NOTICING OUR MAGIC?
SKAAASH
RAARGH
KOFF
RAAAAAH
!
oh.

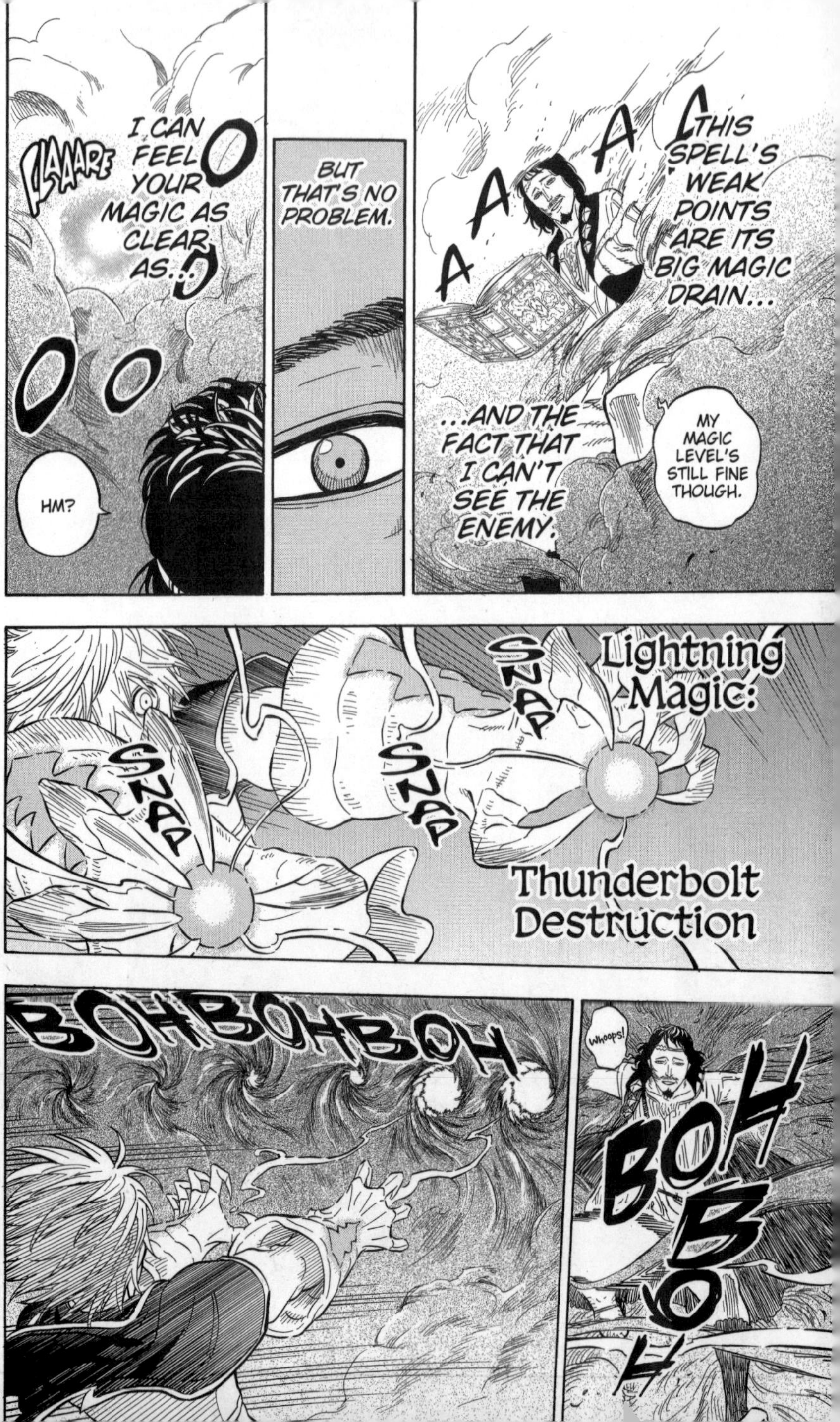
AAAA
THIS SPELL'S WEAK POINTS ARE ITS BIG MAGIC DRAIN...
...AND THE FACT THAT I CAN'T SEE THE ENEMY.
MY MAGIC LEVEL'S STILL FINE THOUGH.
BUT THAT'S NO PROBLEM.
GLAAARE
I CAN FEEL YOUR MAGIC AS CLEAR AS...
OOOO
HM?
Lightning Magic:
SNAP
SNAP
SNAP
Thunderbolt Destruction
Whoops!
BOH
BOHBOHBOH

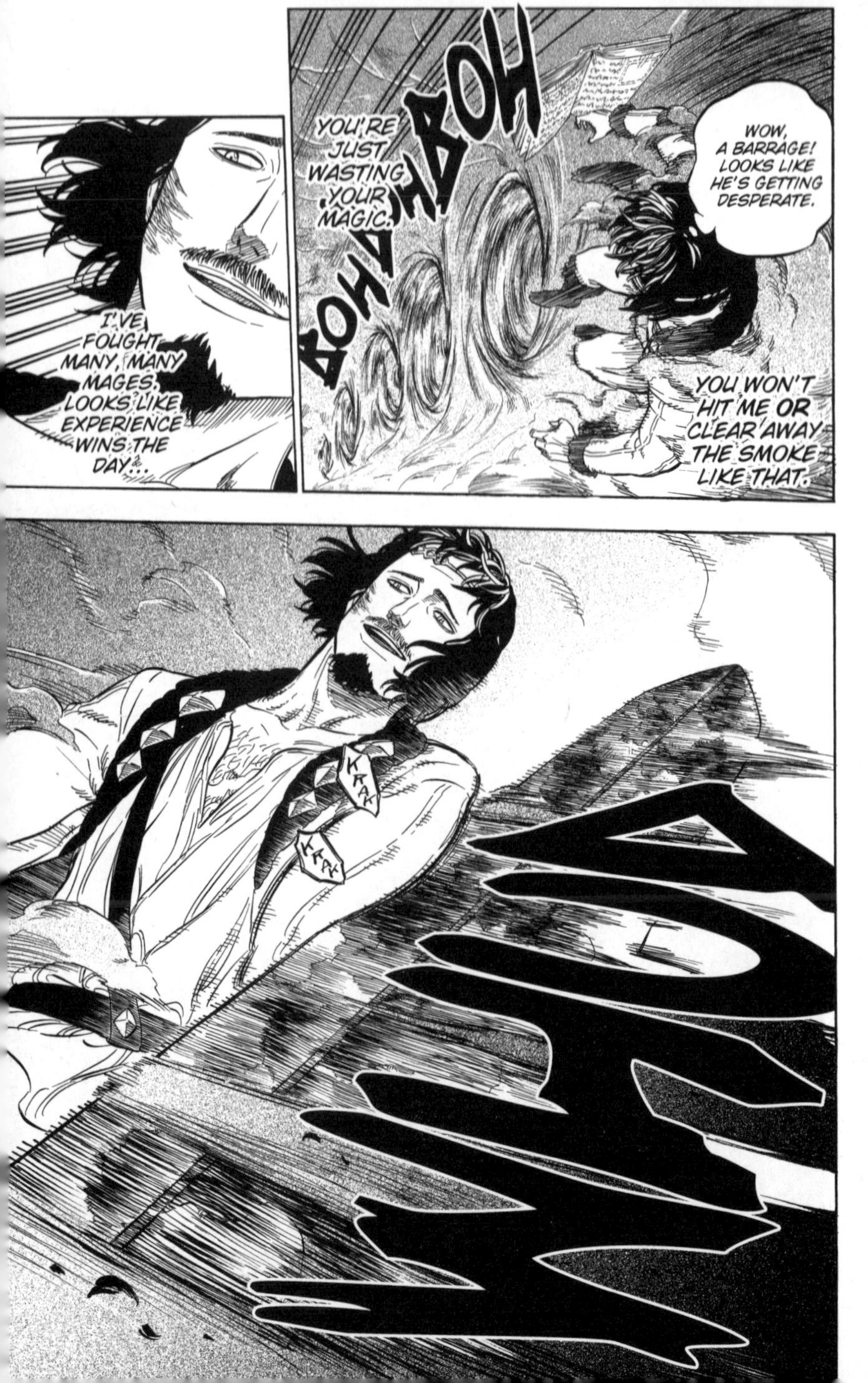
WOW, A BARRAGE! LOOKS LIKE HE'S GETTING DESPERATE.
YOU'RE JUST WASTING YOUR MAGIC.
BOH BOH BOH
YOU WON'T HIT ME OR CLEAR AWAY THE SMOKE LIKE THAT.
I'VE FOUGHT MANY, MANY MAGES. LOOKS LIKE EXPERIENCE WINS THE DAY...
KRAK
KRAK

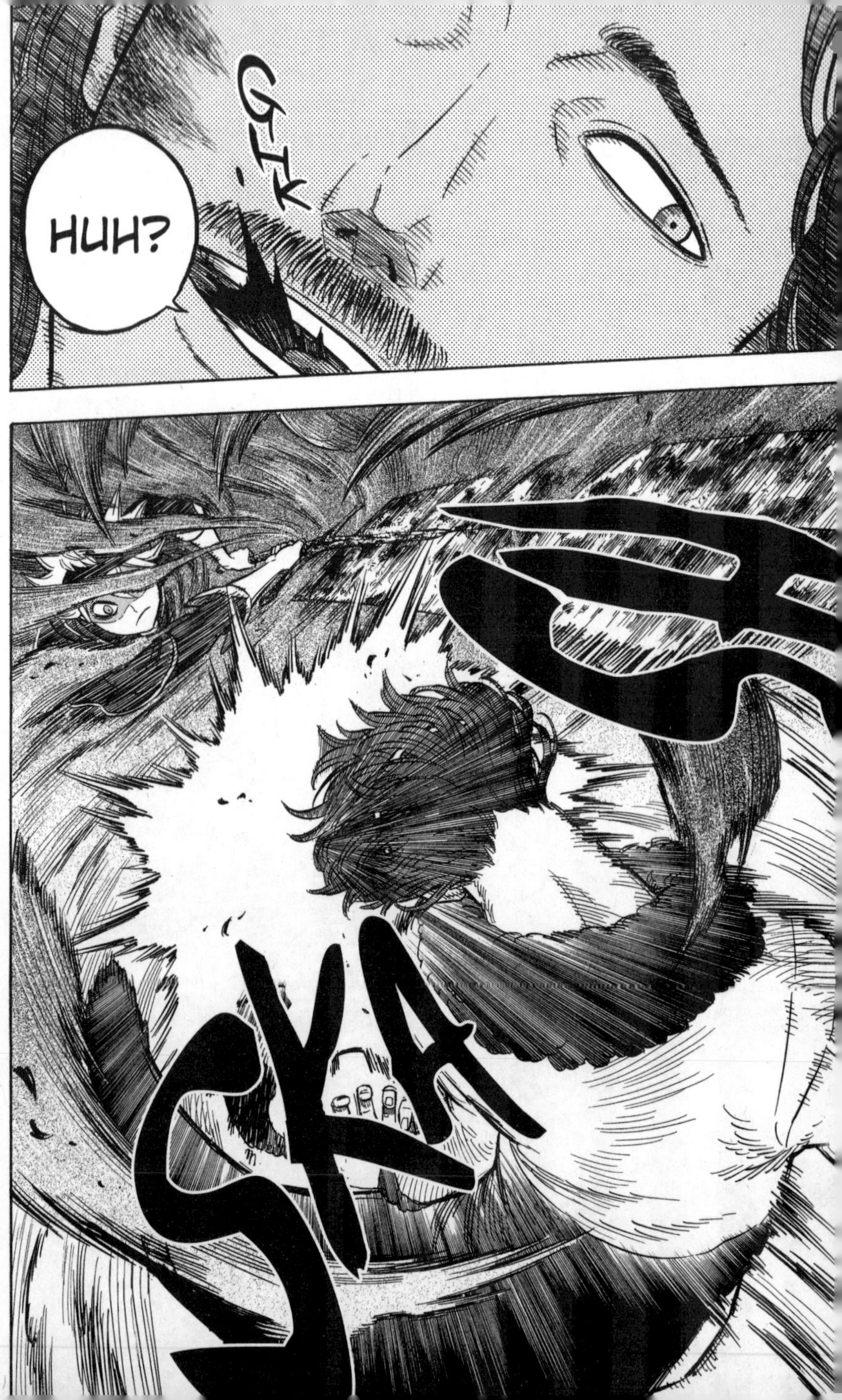
GIK
HUH?
SKA

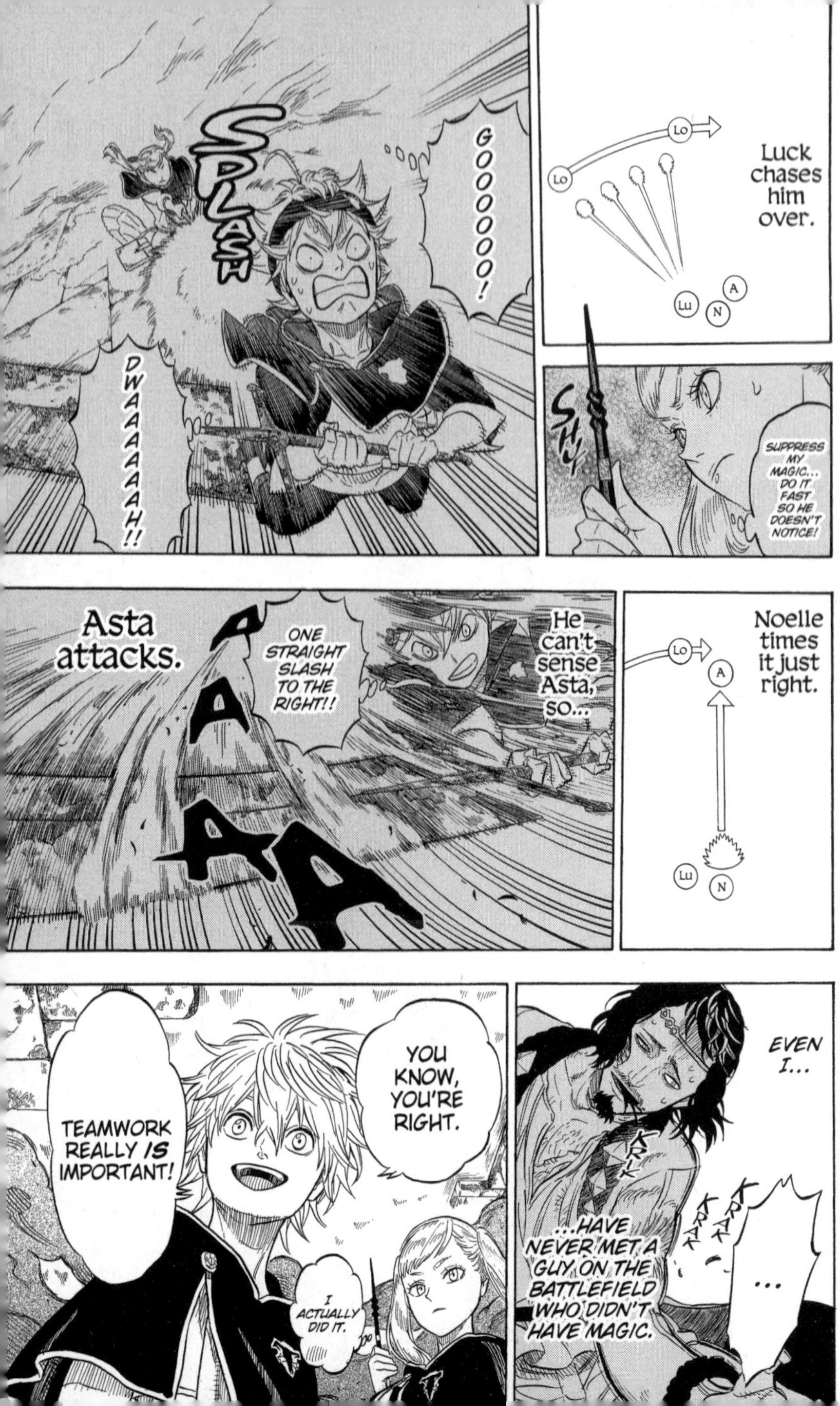
Luck chases him over.
Lo
Lo
Lu
N
A
SUPPRESS MY MAGIC... DO IT FAST SO HE DOESN'T NOTICE!
GOOOOOOO!
SPLASH
DWAAAAAAAAH!!
Noelle times it just right.
Lo
A
Lu
N
He can't sense Asta, so...
ONE STRAIGHT SLASH TO THE RIGHT!!
Asta attacks.
AAAAA
EVEN I...
KRIK
...HAVE NEVER MET A GUY ON THE BATTLEFIELD WHO DIDN'T HAVE MAGIC.
KRAK KRAK
...
YOU KNOW, YOU'RE RIGHT.
TEAMWORK REALLY IS IMPORTANT!
I ACTUALLY DID IT.

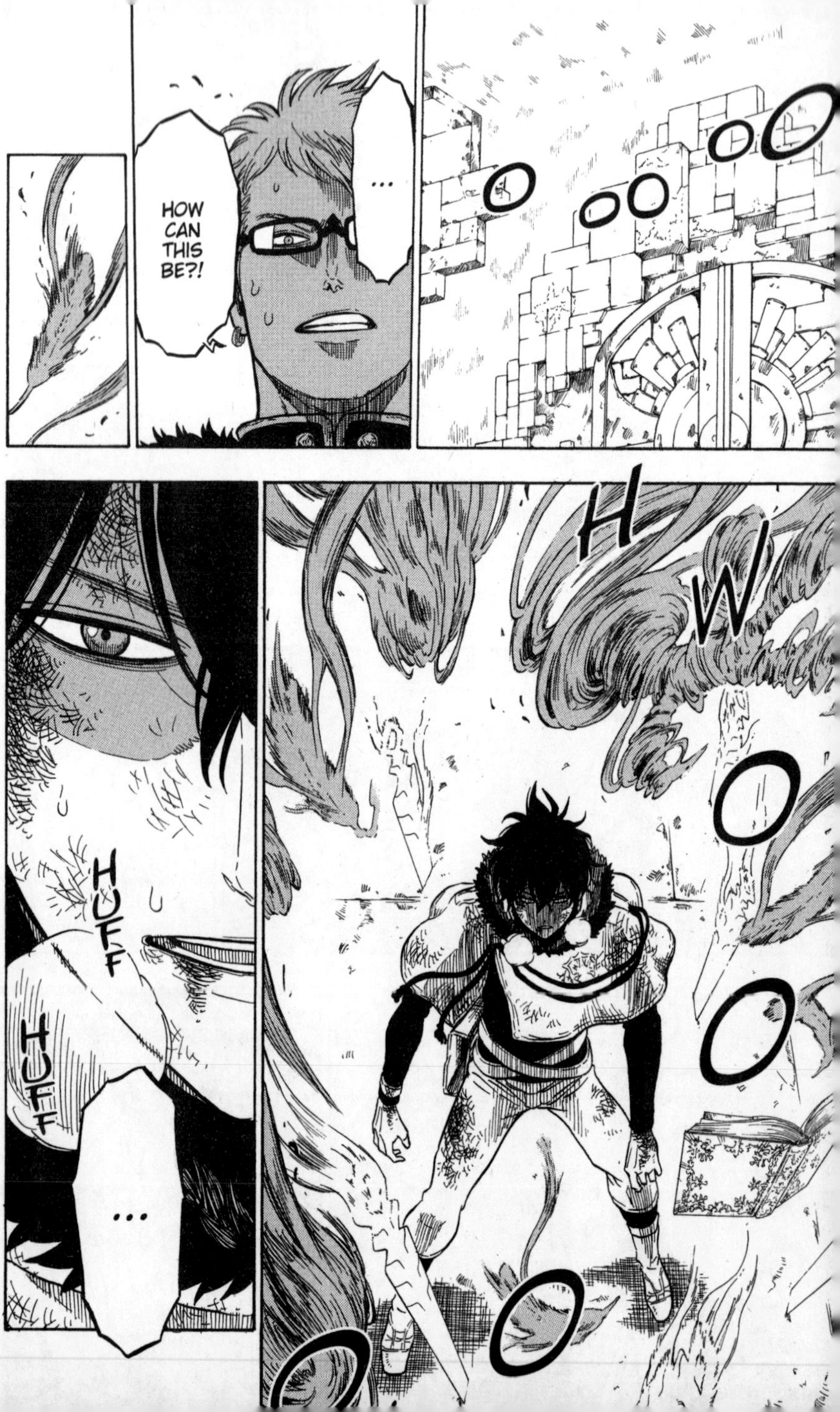
OOOOOO
...
HOW CAN THIS BE?!
HWOOOO
HUFF
HUFF
...

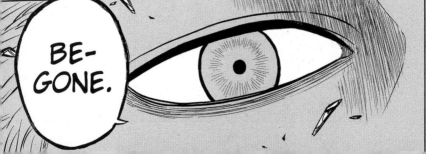

BE-
GONE.

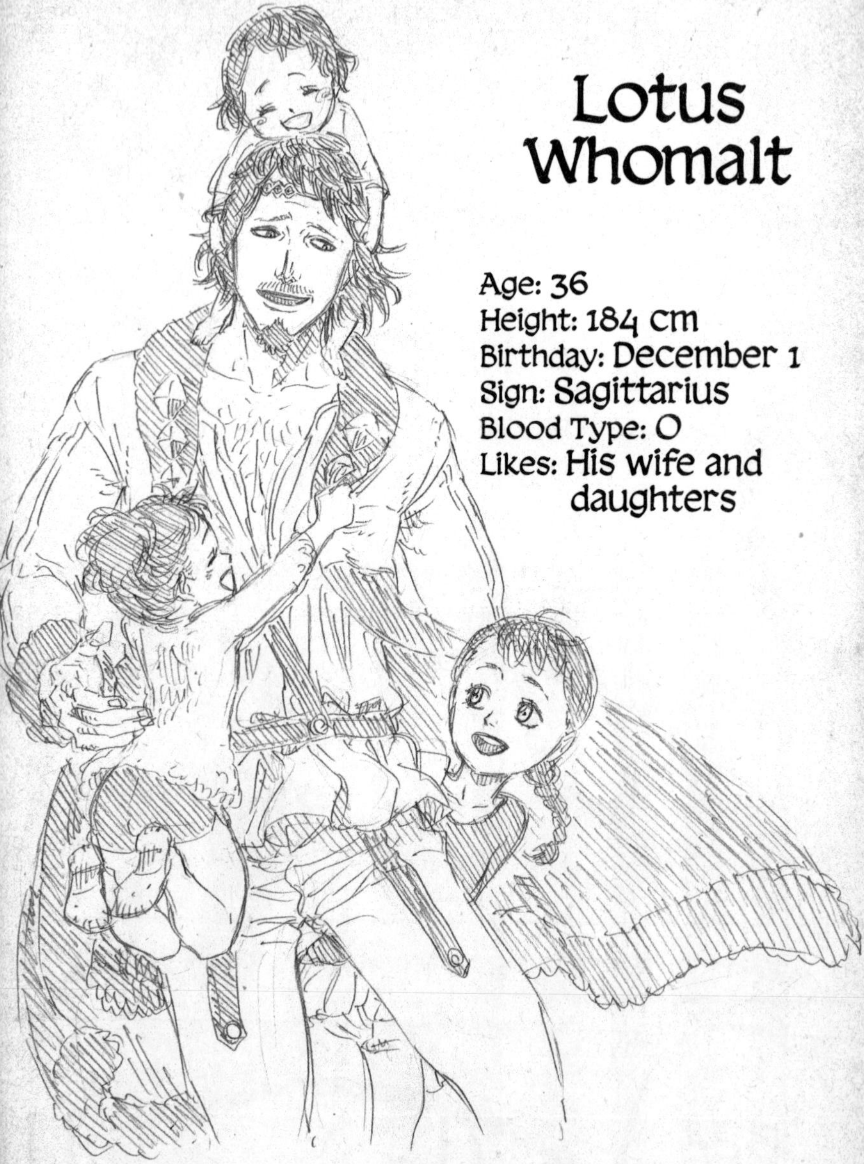

Lotus Whomalt

Age: 36
Height: 184 cm
Birthday: December 1
Sign: Sagittarius
Blood Type: O
Likes: His wife and daughters

Character Profile

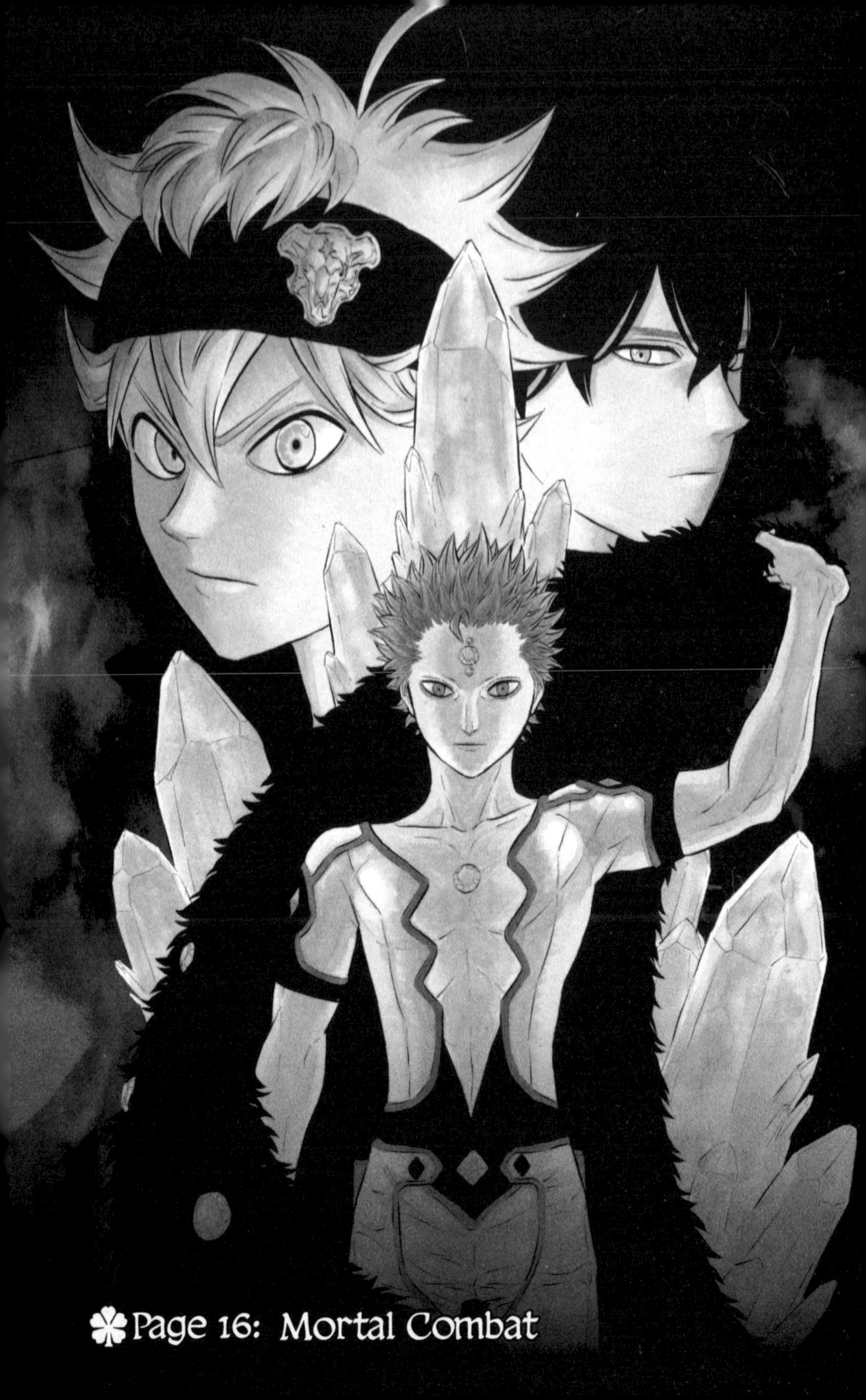
Page 16: Mortal Combat

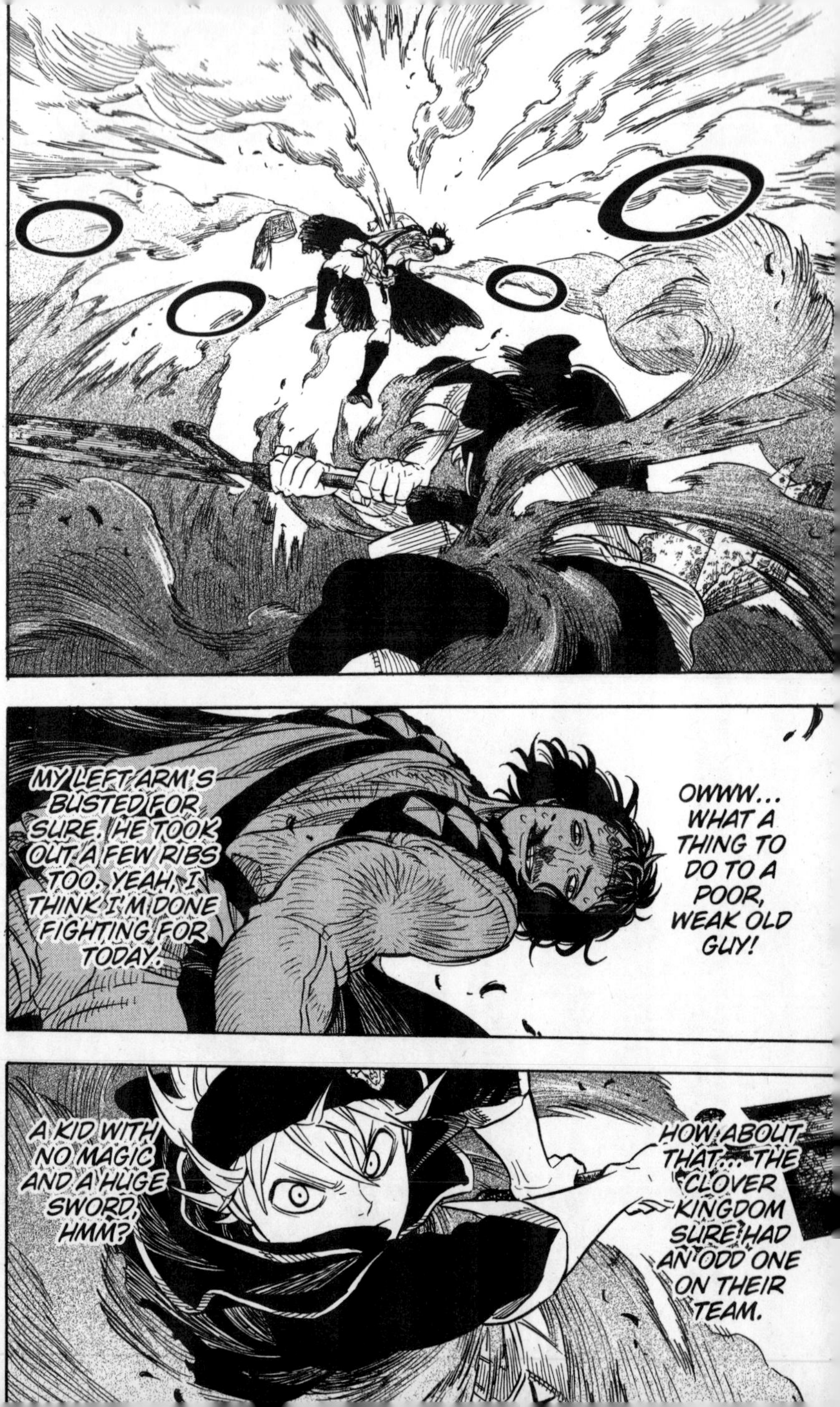
OWWW... WHAT A THING TO DO TO A POOR, WEAK OLD GUY!
MY LEFT ARM'S BUSTED FOR SURE. HE TOOK OUT A FEW RIBS TOO. YEAH, I THINK I'M DONE FIGHTING FOR TODAY.
HOW ABOUT THAT... THE CLOVER KINGDOM SURE HAD AN ODD ONE ON THEIR TEAM.
A KID WITH NO MAGIC AND A HUGE SWORD, HMM?

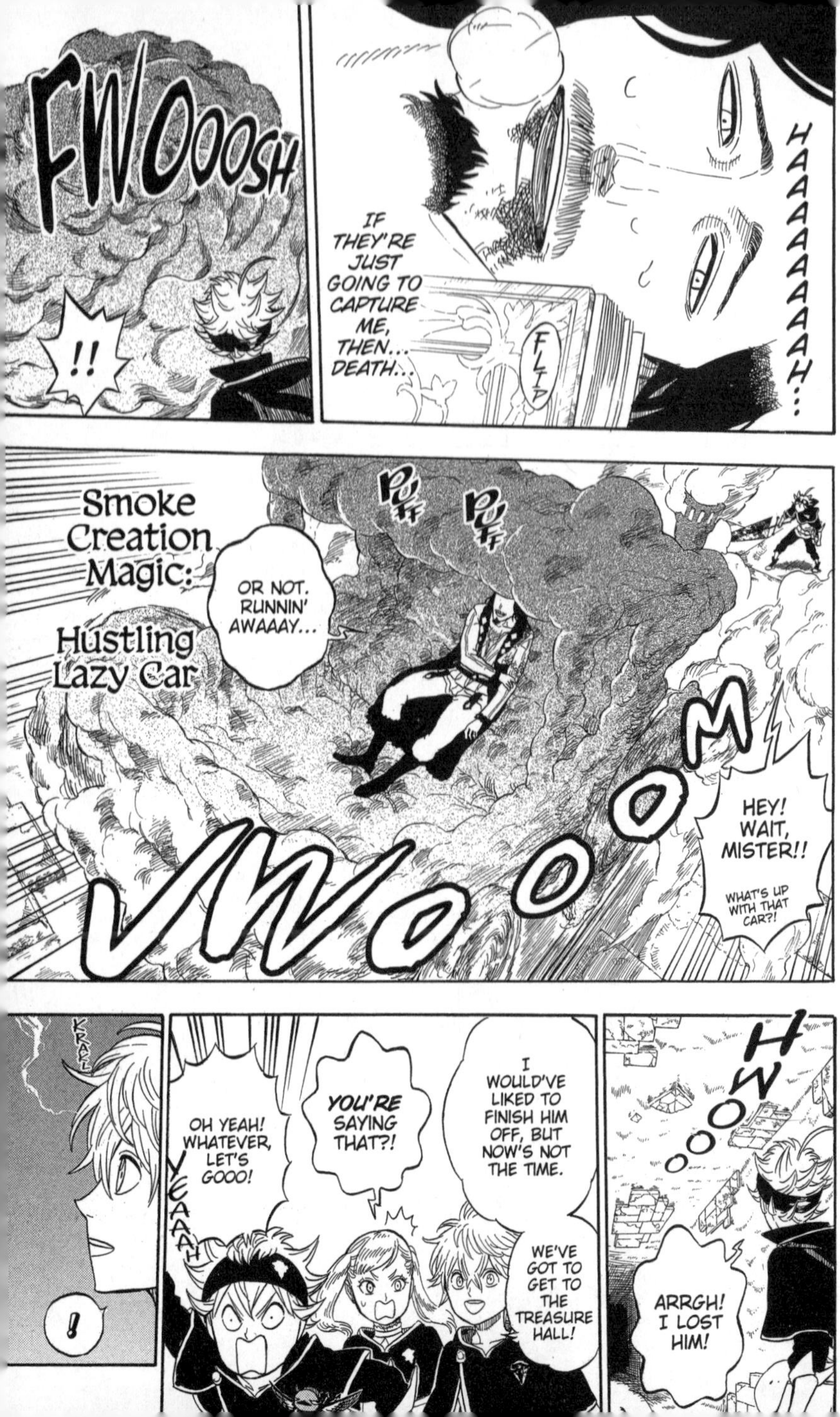
HAAAAAAAAAAH...
IF THEY'RE JUST GOING TO CAPTURE ME, THEN... DEATH...
FLIP
FWOOOSH
!!
HEY! WAIT, MISTER!!
WHAT'S UP WITH THAT CAR?!
VWOOOOM
PUFF
PUFF
OR NOT. RUNNIN' AWAAAY...
Smoke Creation Magic: Hustling Lazy Car
HWOOOO
ARRGH! I LOST HIM!
I WOULD'VE LIKED TO FINISH HIM OFF, BUT NOW'S NOT THE TIME.
WE'VE GOT TO GET TO THE TREASURE HALL!
YOU'RE SAYING THAT?!
OH YEAH! WHATEVER, LET'S GOOO!
YEAAAAH
KRAKL
!

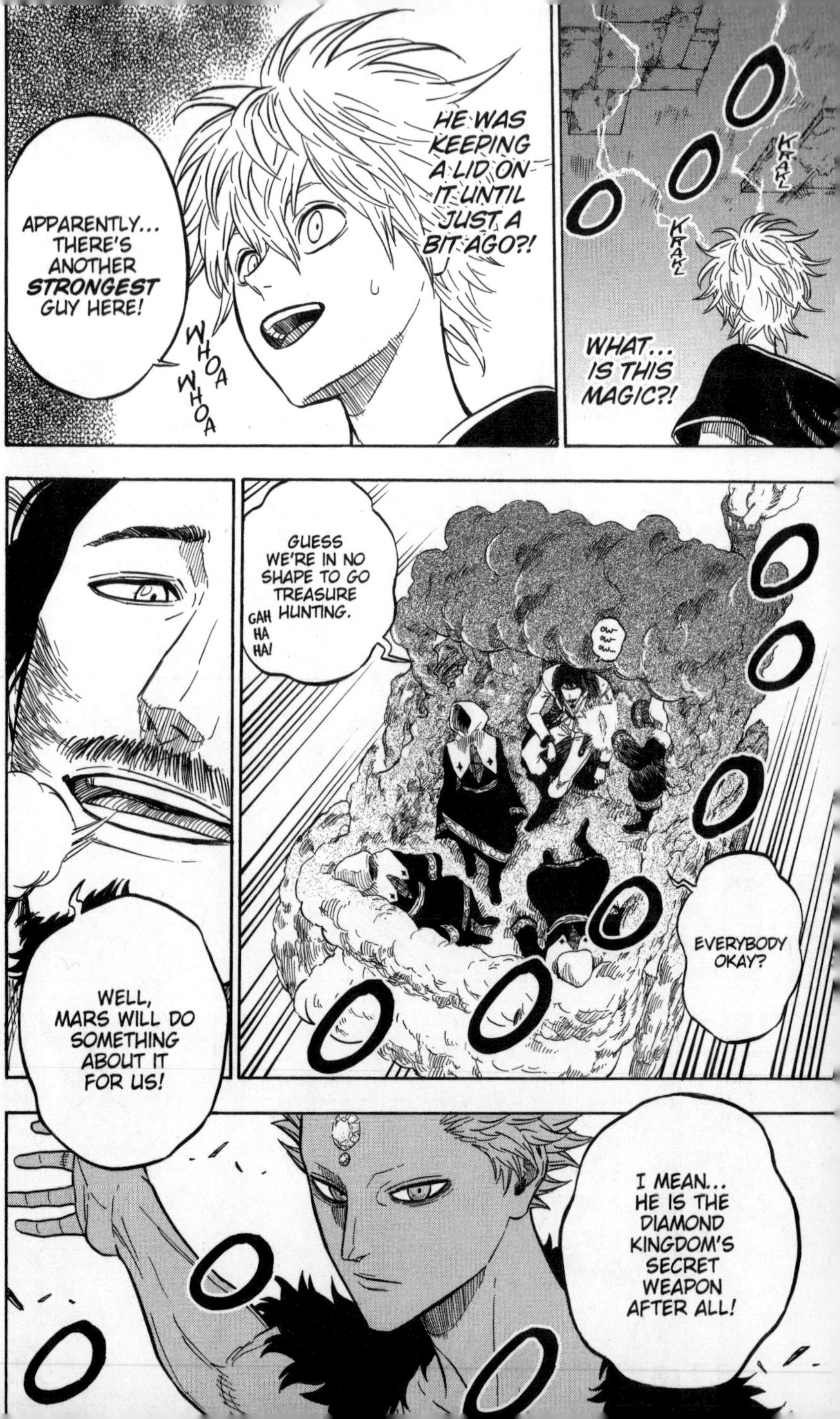
KRAK
KRAK
WHAT... IS THIS MAGIC?!
HE WAS KEEPING A LID ON IT UNTIL JUST A BIT AGO?!
APPARENTLY... THERE'S ANOTHER STRONGEST GUY HERE!
WHOA WHOA
EVERYBODY OKAY?
OW OW OW...
GUESS WE'RE IN NO SHAPE TO GO TREASURE HUNTING.
GAH HA HA!
WELL, MARS WILL DO SOMETHING ABOUT IT FOR US!
I MEAN... HE IS THE DIAMOND KINGDOM'S SECRET WEAPON AFTER ALL!

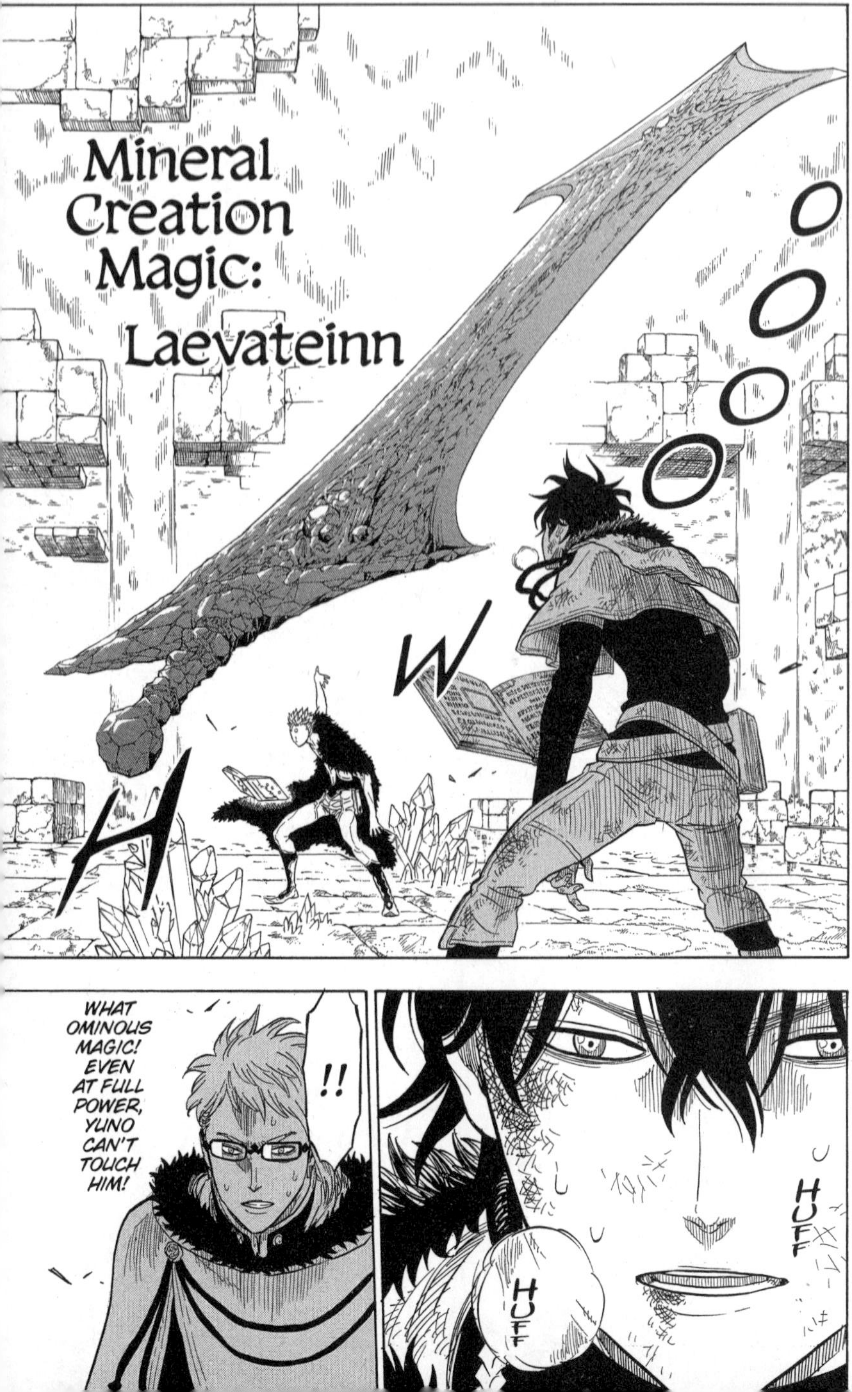
Mineral Creation Magic: Laevateinn
HWOOOO
HUFF
HUFF
!!
WHAT OMINOUS MAGIC! EVEN AT FULL POWER, YUNO CAN'T TOUCH HIM!

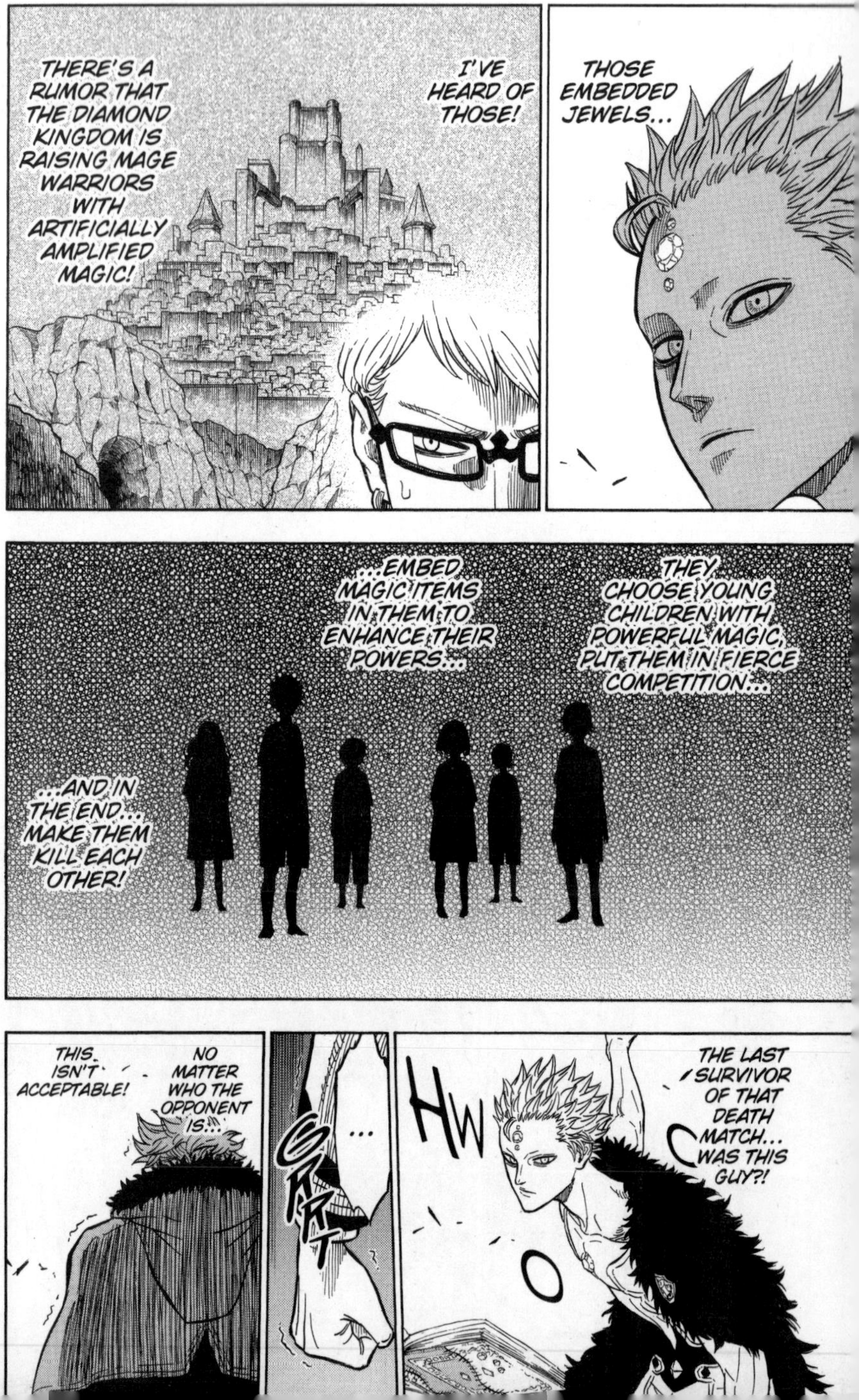
THOSE EMBEDDED JEWELS...
I'VE HEARD OF THOSE!
THERE'S A RUMOR THAT THE DIAMOND KINGDOM IS RAISING MAGE WARRIORS WITH ARTIFICIALLY AMPLIFIED MAGIC!
THEY CHOOSE YOUNG CHILDREN WITH POWERFUL MAGIC, PUT THEM IN FIERCE COMPETITION...
...EMBED MAGIC ITEMS IN THEM TO ENHANCE THEIR POWERS...
...AND IN THE END... MAKE THEM KILL EACH OTHER!
THE LAST SURVIVOR OF THAT DEATH MATCH... WAS THIS GUY?!
...
NO MATTER WHO THE OPPONENT IS...!!
THIS ISN'T ACCEPTABLE!

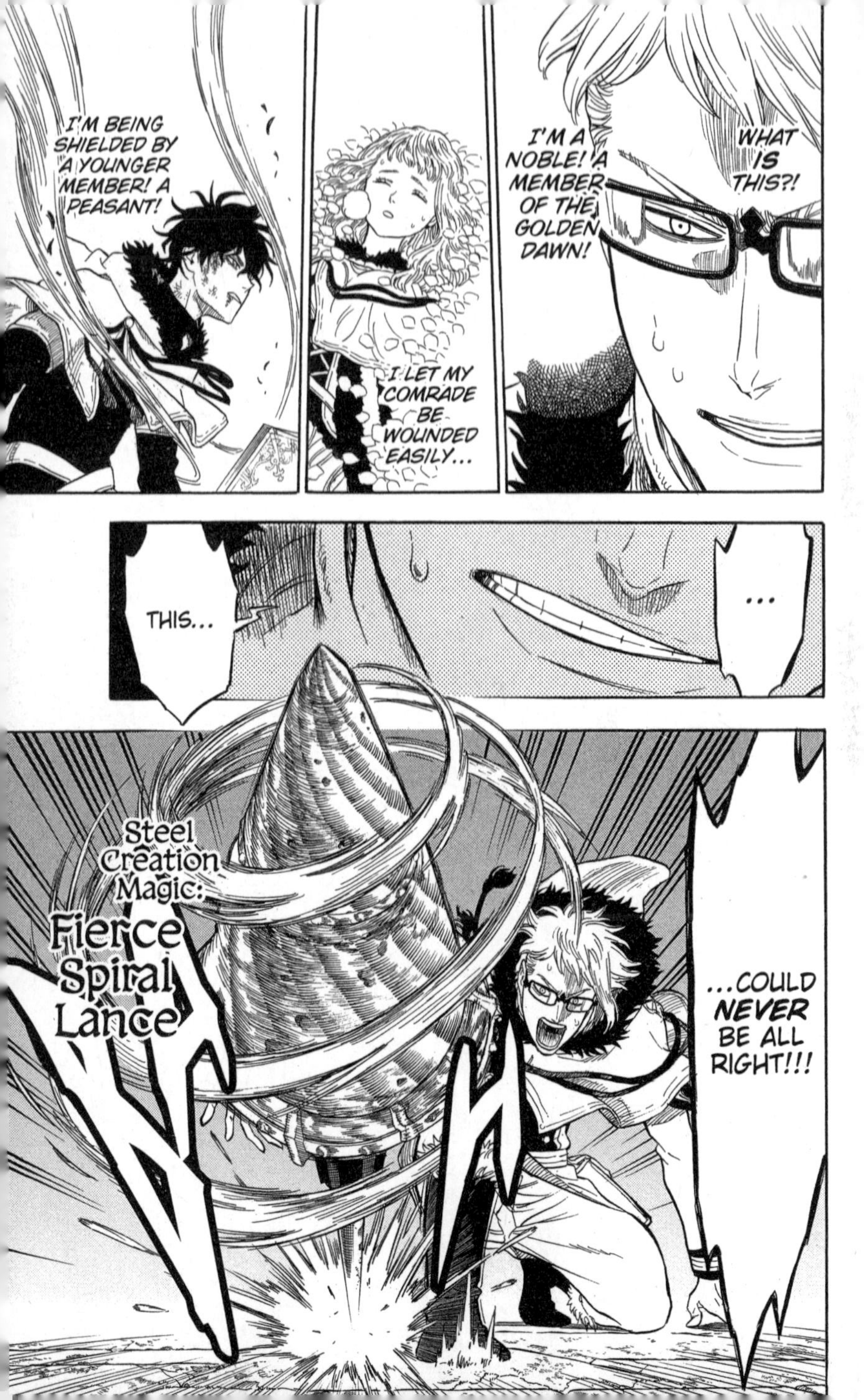
WHAT IS THIS?!
I'M A NOBLE! A MEMBER OF THE GOLDEN DAWN!
I LET MY COMRADE BE WOUNDED EASILY...
I'M BEING SHIELDED BY A YOUNGER MEMBER! A PEASANT!
...
THIS...
...COULD NEVER BE ALL RIGHT!!!
Steel Creation Magic:
Fierce Spiral Lance

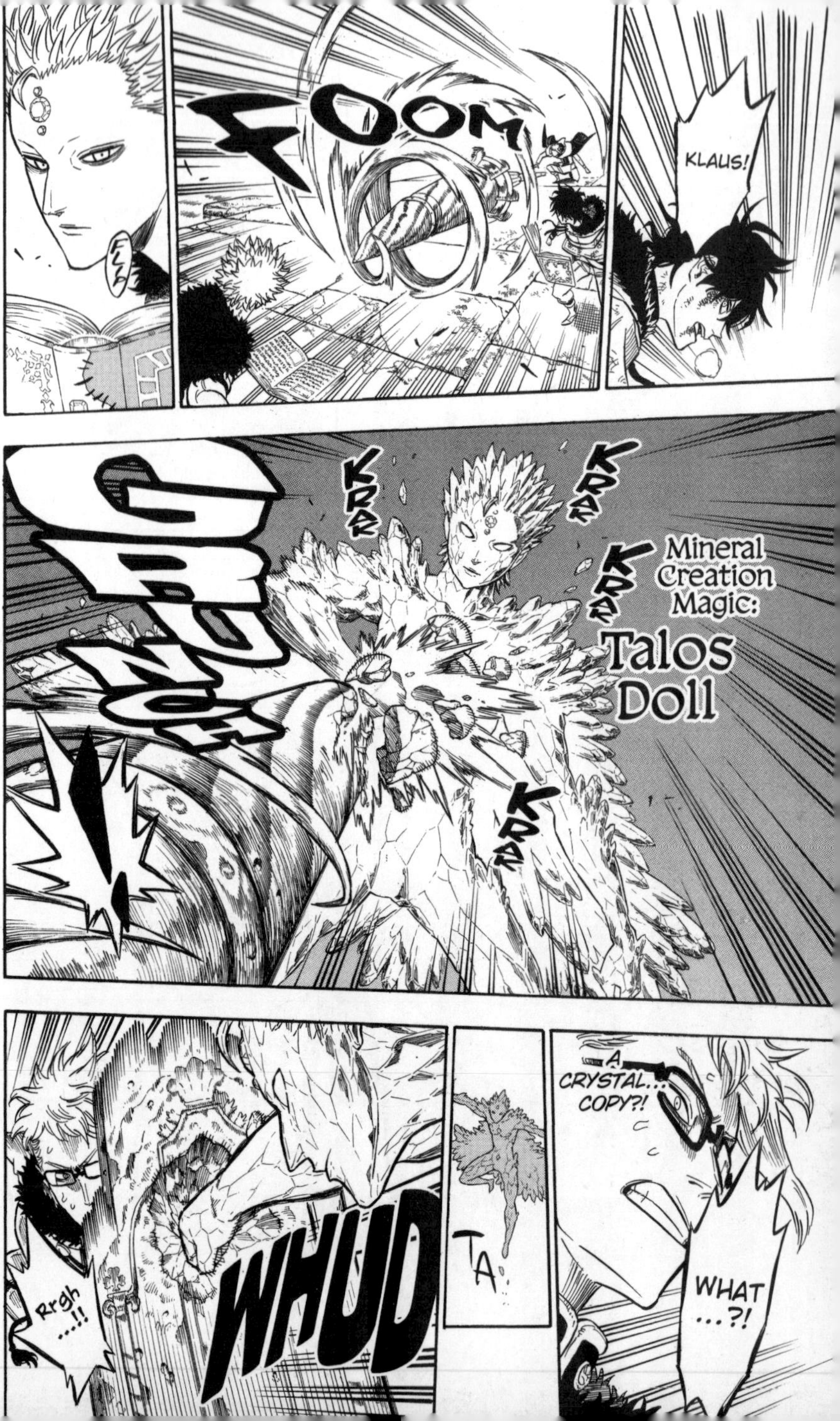
KLAUS!
FOOM
KRRR
KRRR
Mineral Creation Magic: Talos Doll
KRRR
KRRR
A CRYSTAL... COPY?!
WHAT...?!
TA
WHUD
Rrgh ...!!

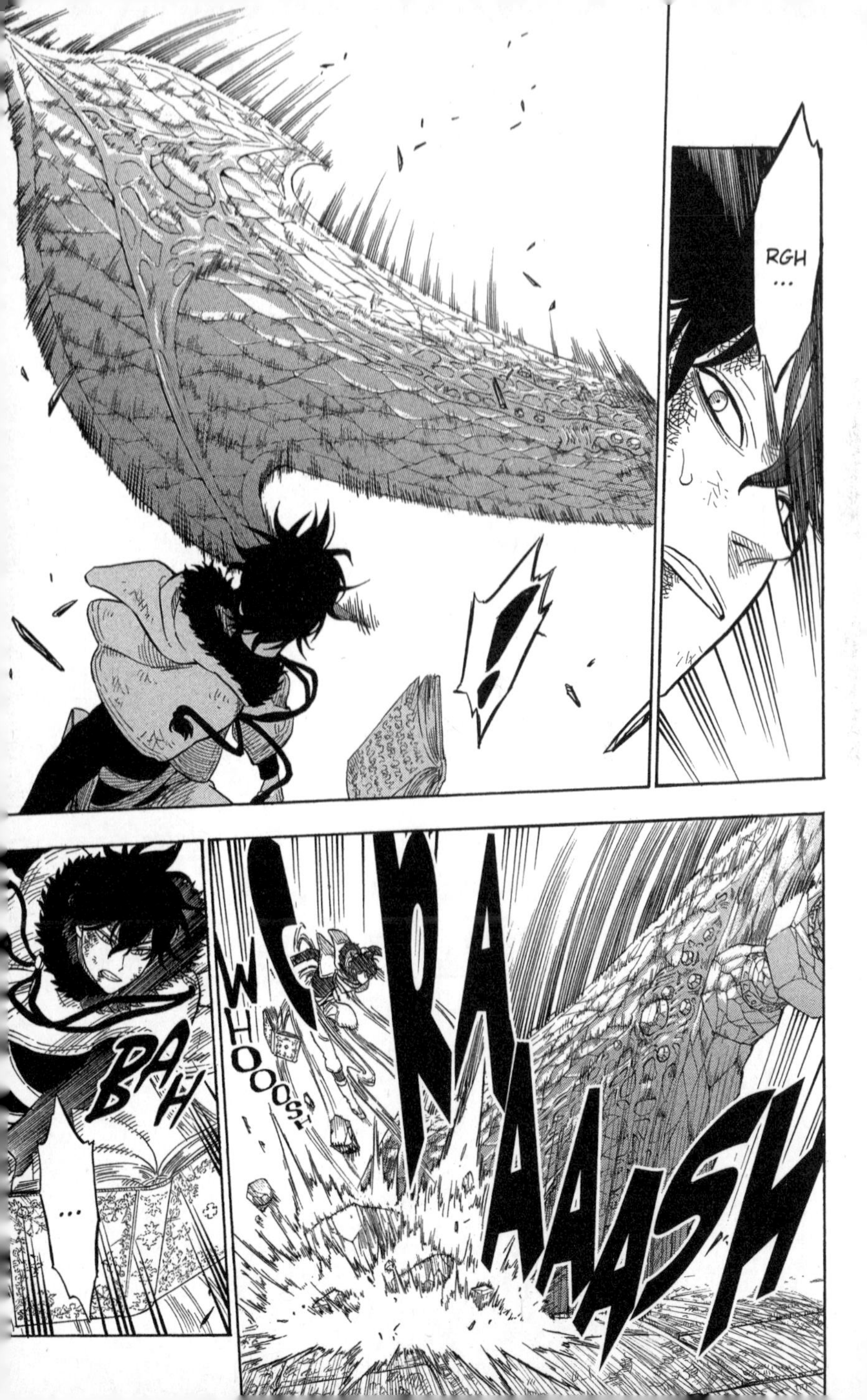
RGH ...
!
CRAAAASH
WHOOOSH!
BAH
...

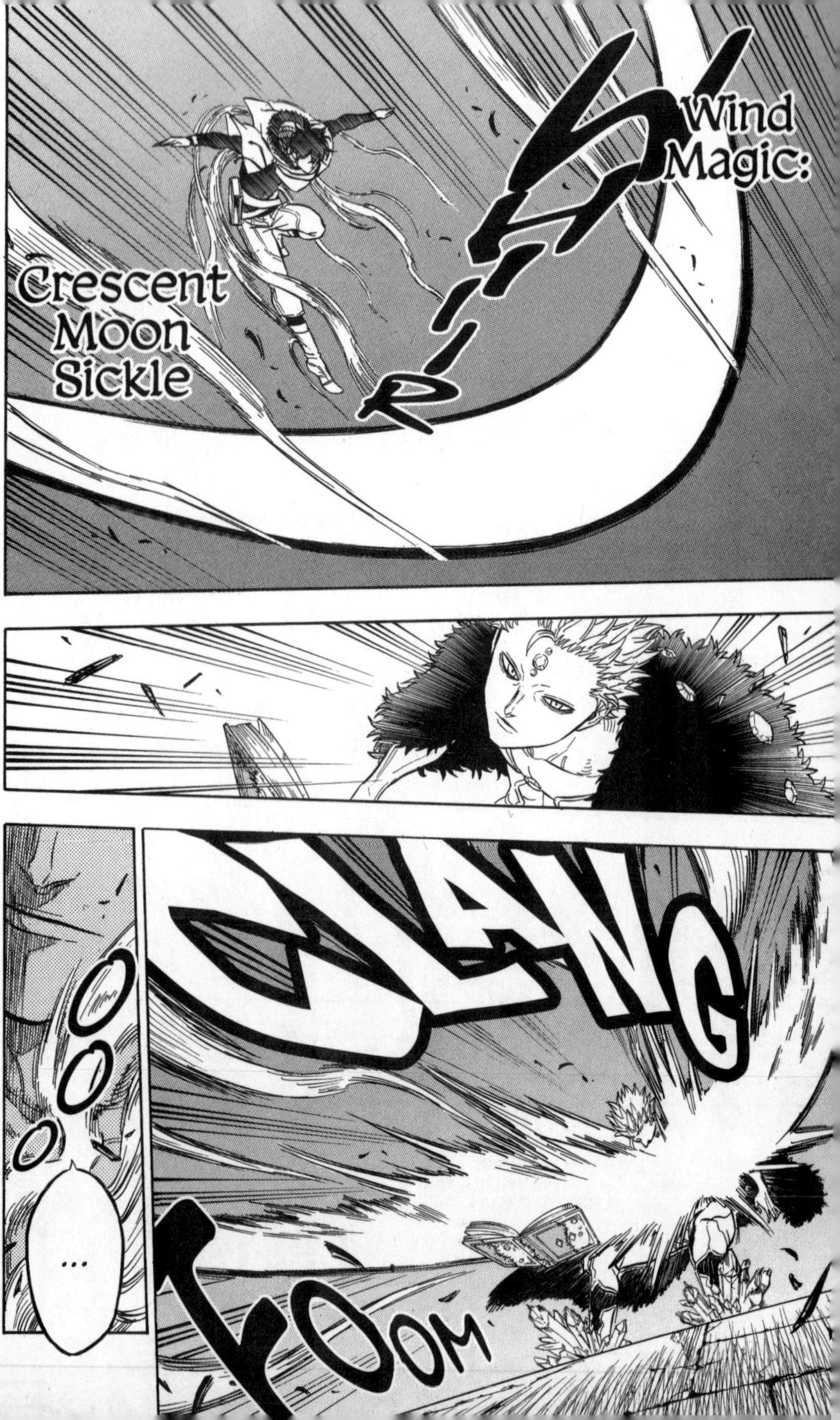
Wind Magic:
Crescent Moon Sickle
CLANG
OOOOO
...

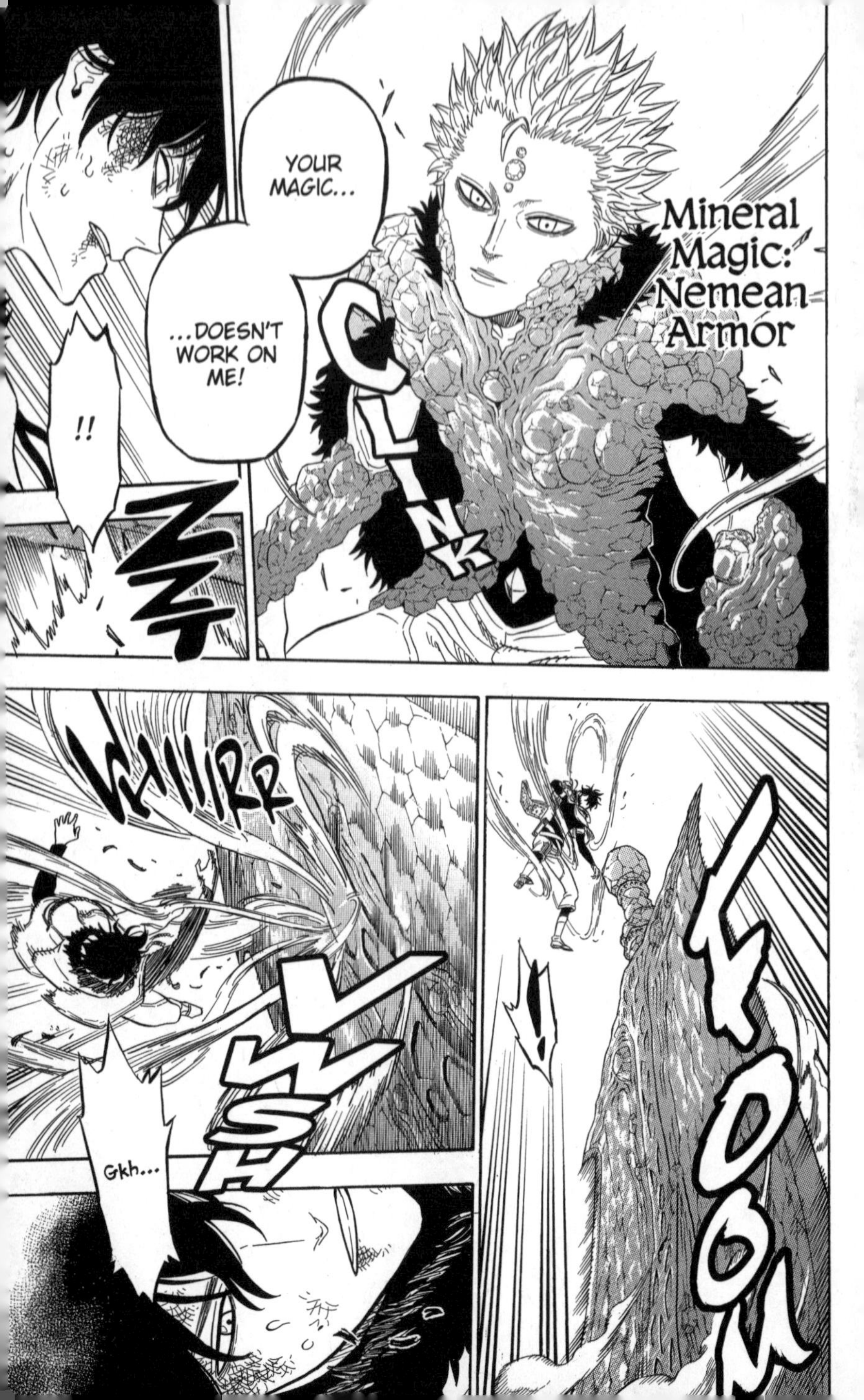
YOUR MAGIC...
...DOESN'T WORK ON ME!
CLINK
Mineral Magic: Nemean Armor
!!
!
WHIRR
Gkh...

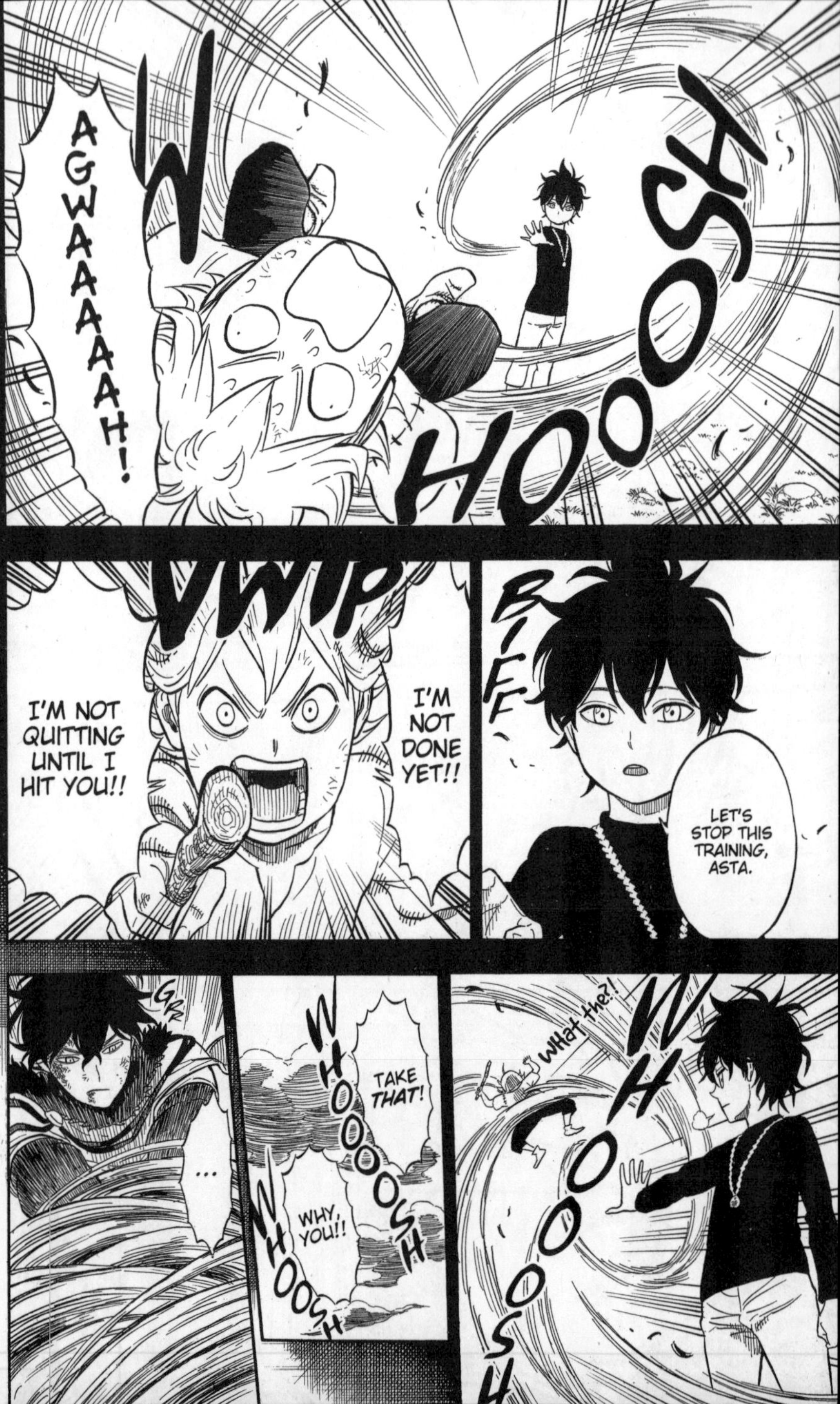
WHOOOOSH
W
AGWAAAAAAAH!
BRIFF
LET'S STOP THIS TRAINING, ASTA.
VWIP
I'M NOT DONE YET!!
I'M NOT QUITTING UNTIL I HIT YOU!!
WHOOOOSH
what the?!
WHOOOOOSH
TAKE THAT!
WHY, YOU!!
WHOOSH
GRR
...

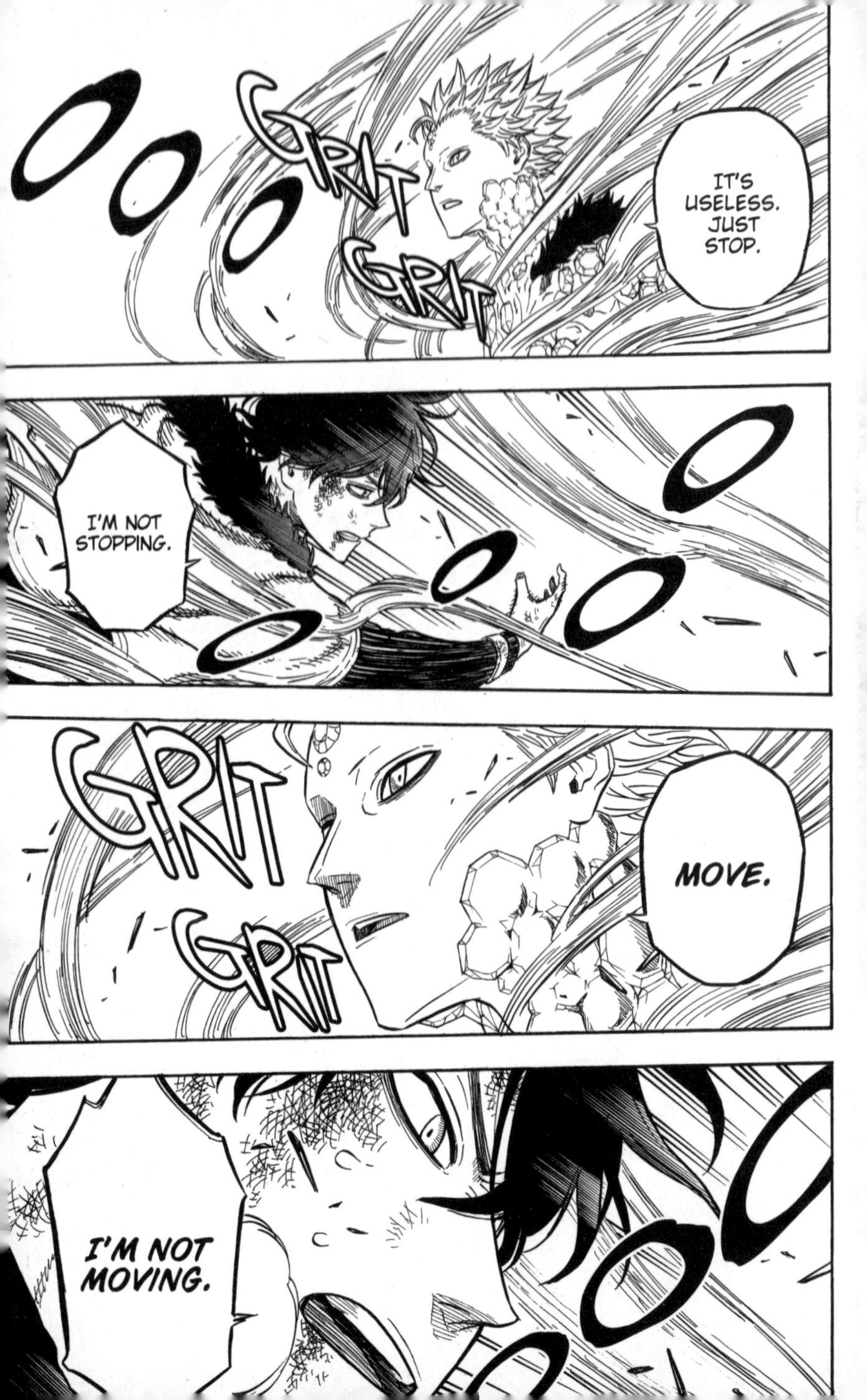
GRIT
GRIT
IT'S USELESS. JUST STOP.
I'M NOT STOPPING.
MOVE.
GRIT
GRIT
I'M NOT MOVING.

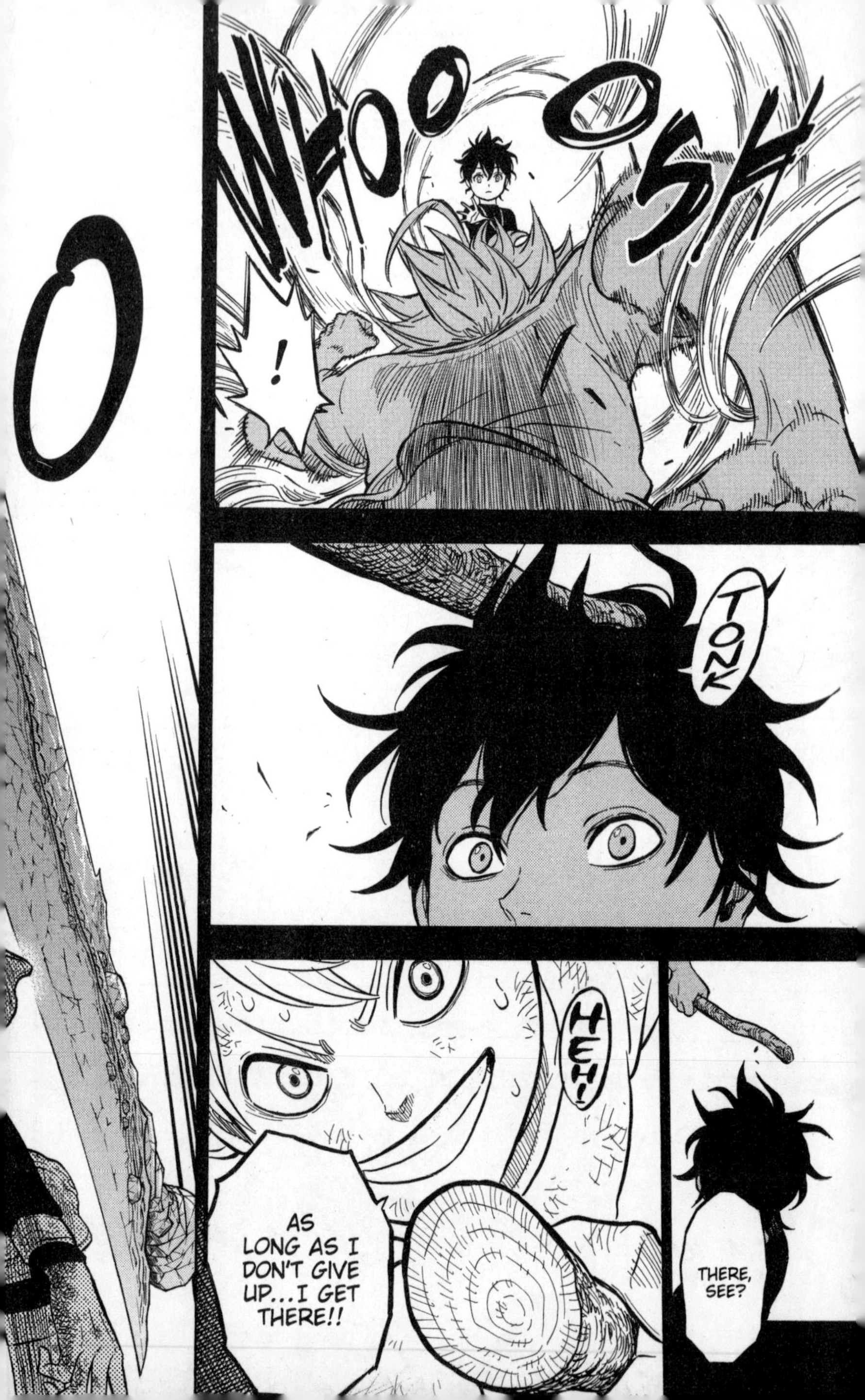

WHOOOSH
!
TONK
THERE, SEE?
HEH!
AS LONG AS I DON'T GIVE UP...I GET THERE!!
O

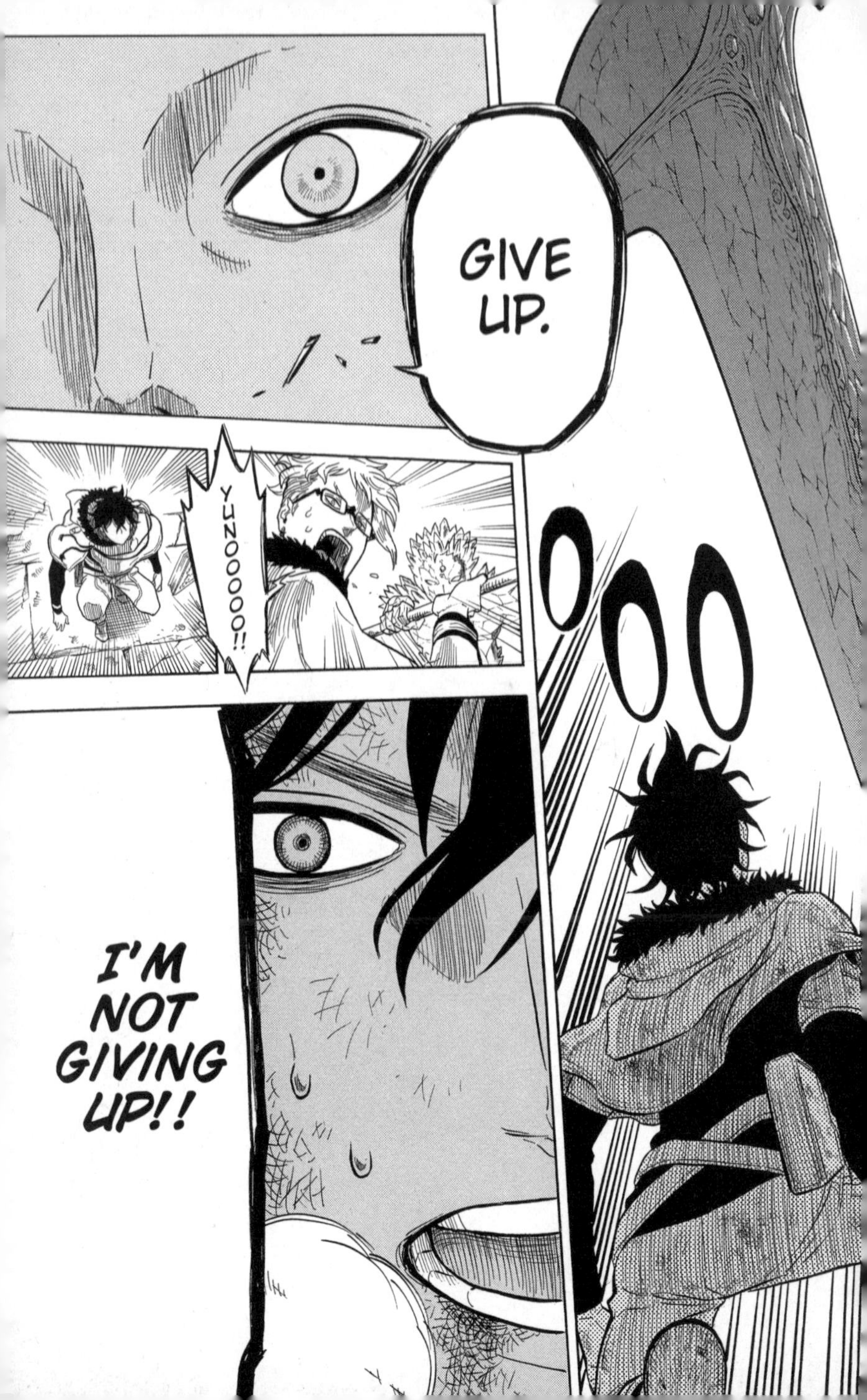
OOO
GIVE UP.
YUNOOOOOO!!
I'M NOT GIVING UP!!

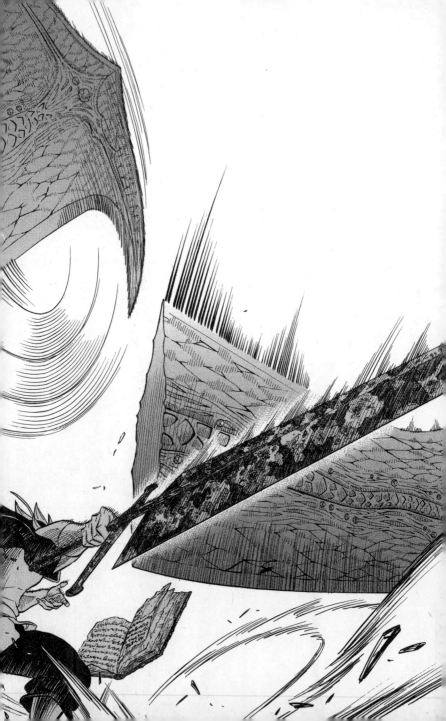

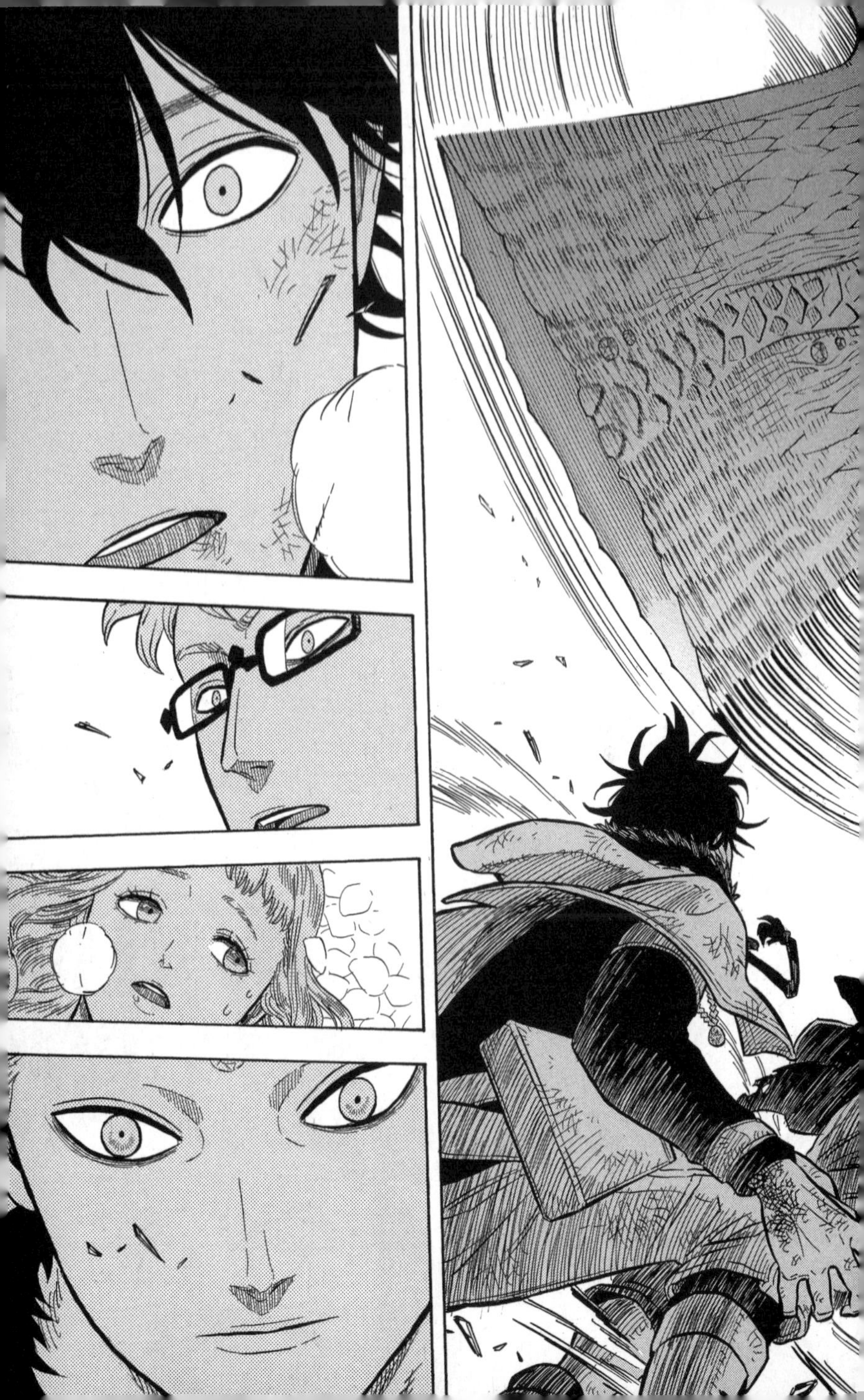

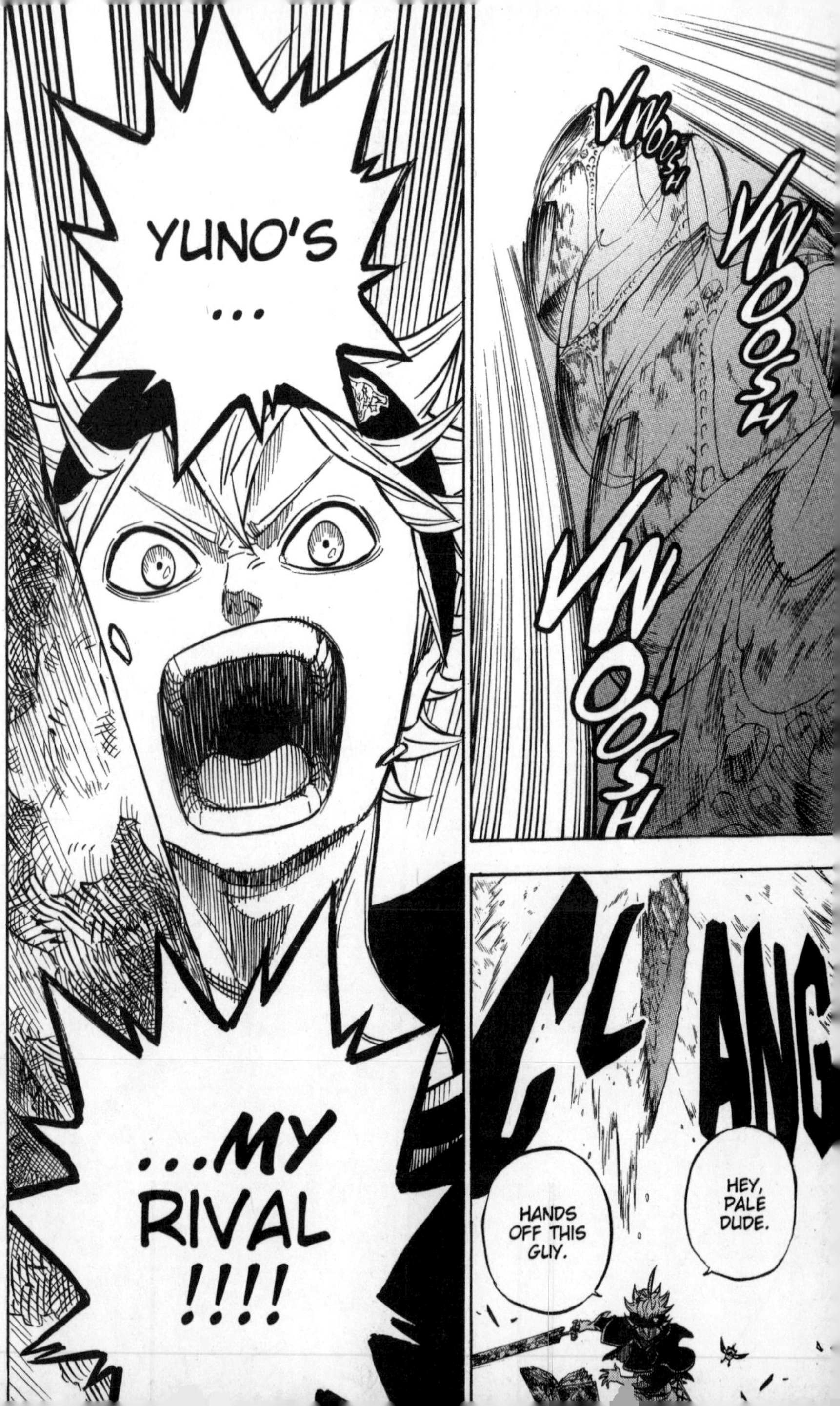
VWOOSH
VWOOOSH
VWOOOSH
CLANG
HEY, PALE DUDE.
HANDS OFF THIS GUY.
YUNO'S ...
...MY RIVAL !!!!

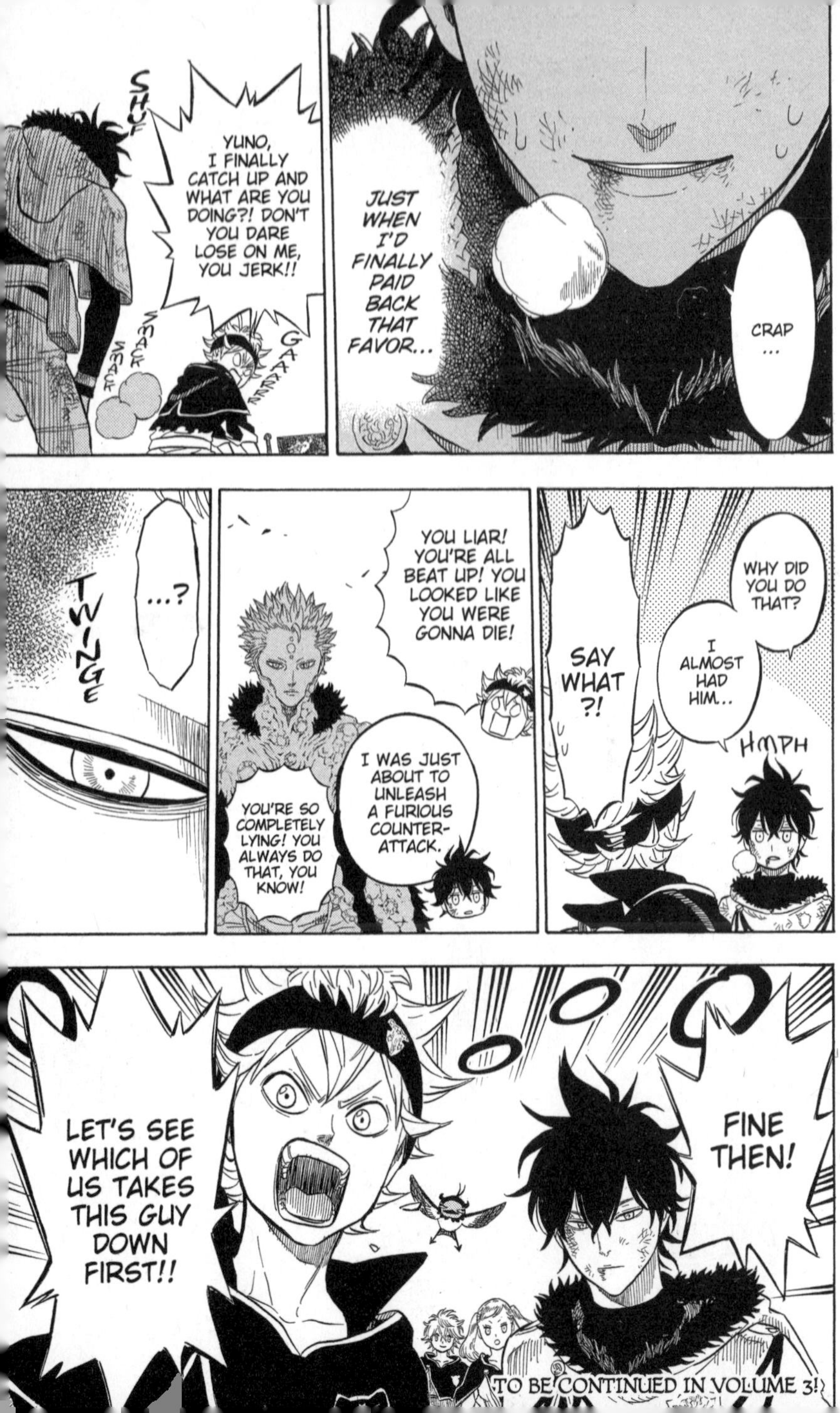
CRAP...
JUST WHEN I'D FINALLY PAID BACK THAT FAVOR...
SHUF
YUNO, I FINALLY CATCH UP AND WHAT ARE YOU DOING?! DON'T YOU DARE LOSE ON ME, YOU JERK!!
GAARRR
SMACK SMACK
WHY DID YOU DO THAT?
I ALMOST HAD HIM..
HMPH
SAY WHAT?!
YOU LIAR! YOU'RE ALL BEAT UP! YOU LOOKED LIKE YOU WERE GONNA DIE!
I WAS JUST ABOUT TO UNLEASH A FURIOUS COUNTER-ATTACK.
YOU'RE SO COMPLETELY LYING! YOU ALWAYS DO THAT, YOU KNOW!
...?
TWINGE
FINE THEN!
LET'S SEE WHICH OF US TAKES THIS GUY DOWN FIRST!!
TO BE CONTINUED IN VOLUME 3!

The Blank Page Brigade

This volume's topic: What type of girl do you like?

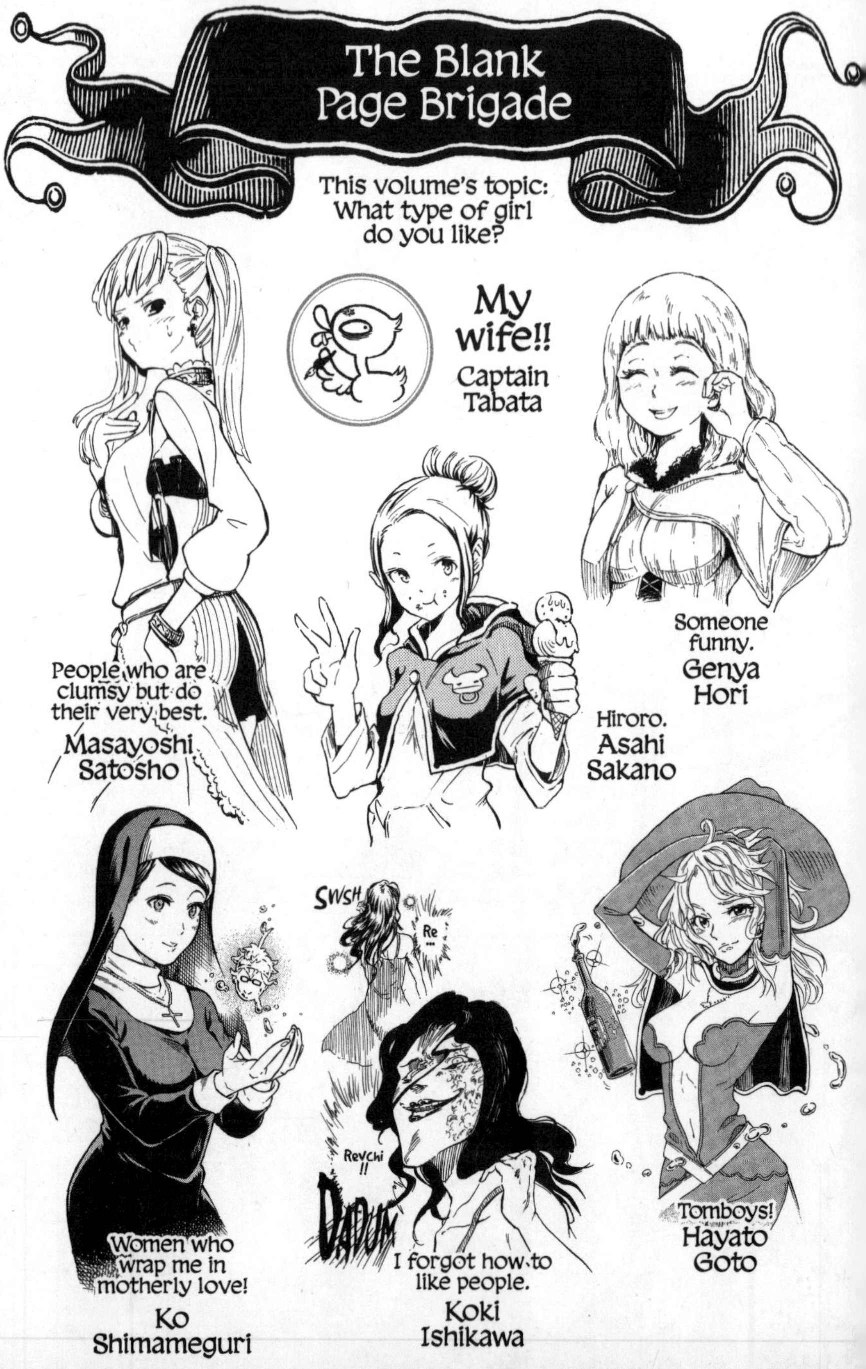
My wife!!
Captain Tabata
Someone funny.
Genya Hori
Hiroro.
Asahi Sakano
People who are clumsy but do their very best.
Masayoshi Satosho
Tomboys!
Hayato Goto
SWSH
Re...
Revchi!!
DADUM
I forgot how to like people.
Koki Ishikawa
Women who wrap me in motherly love!
Ko Shimameguri

Mage Lecture for Adults

Black Clover Bonus Manga 1

Never Use Your Grimoire Like This!!

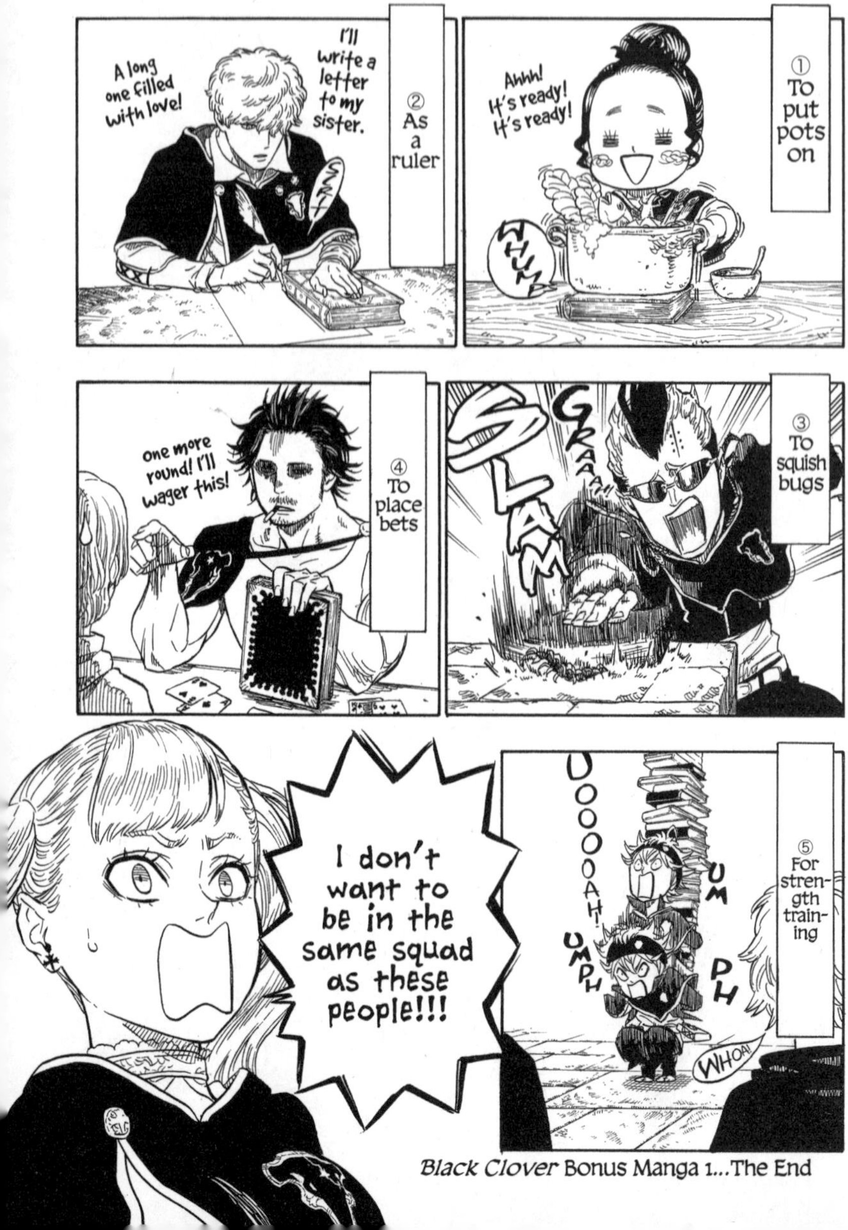

① To put pots on
Ahhh! It's ready! It's ready!
WHUM
② As a ruler
I'll write a letter to my sister.
A long one filled with love!
③ To squish bugs
GRAAAH!!
SLAM
④ To place bets
One more round! I'll wager this!
⑤ For stren-gth train-ing
UOOOOAH!
UMPH
UMPH
WHOA!
I don't want to be in the same squad as these people!!!

Black Clover Bonus Manga 1...The End

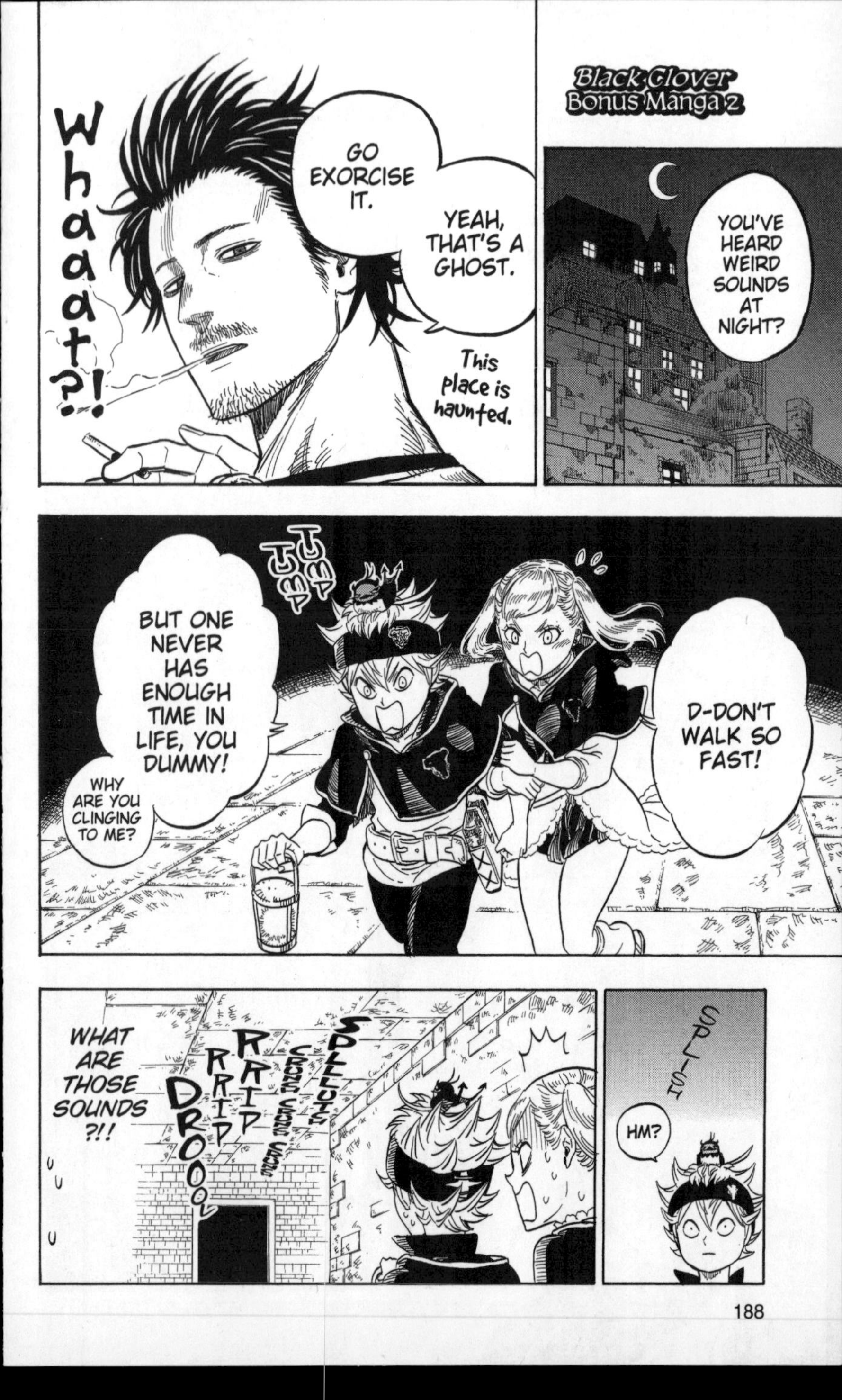
Black Clover
Bonus Manga 2
YOU'VE HEARD WEIRD SOUNDS AT NIGHT?
YEAH, THAT'S A GHOST.
This place is haunted.
GO EXORCISE IT.
Whaaaat?!
D-DON'T WALK SO FAST!
TUMP TUMP
BUT ONE NEVER HAS ENOUGH TIME IN LIFE, YOU DUMMY!
WHY ARE YOU CLINGING TO ME?
SPLISH
HM?
RRIP
RRIP
WHAT ARE THOSE SOUNDS?!!

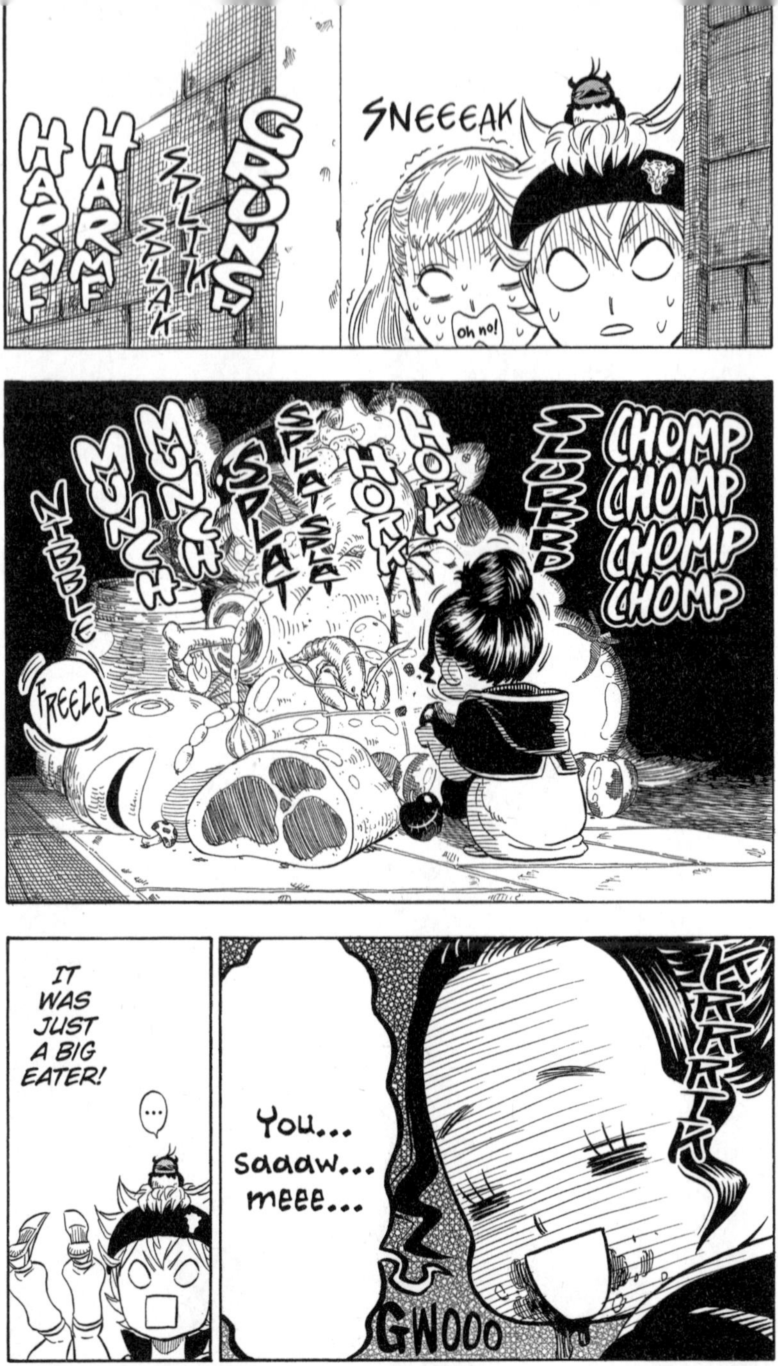
SNEEEAK
oh no!
GRUNSH
SPLINK
SPLAK
HARMF
HARMF
CHOMP CHOMP CHOMP CHOMP
SLURRRP
HORK
HORK
SPLAT
SPLAT
MUNCH
MUNCH
NIBBLE
FREEZE
You... saaaw... meee...
GWOOO
IT WAS JUST A BIG EATER!
...

Black Clover Bonus Manga 2...The End

Special Project Celebrating Volume 2!!

Special Support Manga from Ryuhei Tamura!!

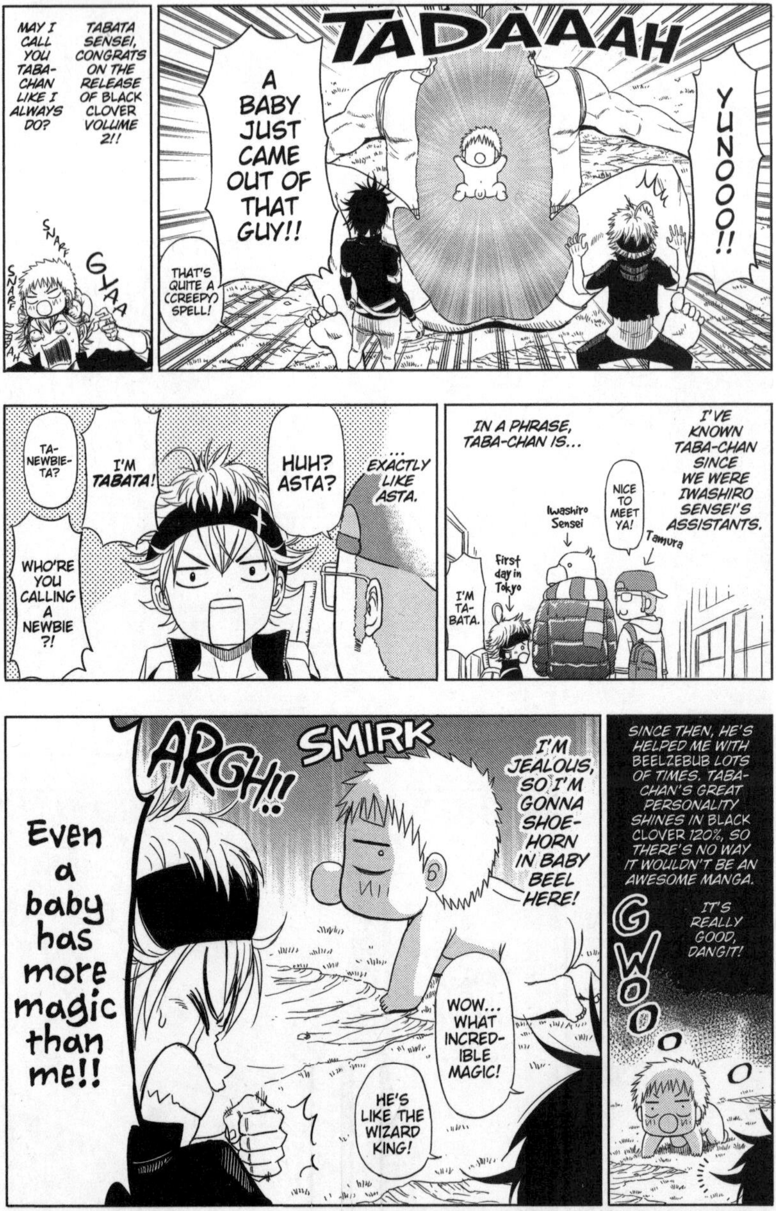

TADAAAH
A BABY JUST CAME OUT OF THAT GUY!!
YUNOOOO!!
THAT'S QUITE A (CREEPY) SPELL!
TABATA SENSEI, CONGRATS ON THE RELEASE OF BLACK CLOVER VOLUME 2!!
MAY I CALL YOU TABA-CHAN LIKE I ALWAYS DO?
SNARF
SNARF
GYAA
I'VE KNOWN TABA-CHAN SINCE WE WERE IWASHIRO SENSEI'S ASSISTANTS.
IN A PHRASE, TABA-CHAN IS...
NICE TO MEET YA!
Iwashiro Sensei
Tamura
First day in Tokyo
I'M TABATA.
...EXACTLY LIKE ASTA.
HUH? ASTA?
I'M TABATA!
TA-NEWBIE-TA?
WHO'RE YOU CALLING A NEWBIE?!
SINCE THEN, HE'S HELPED ME WITH BEELZEBUB LOTS OF TIMES. TABA-CHAN'S GREAT PERSONALITY SHINES IN BLACK CLOVER 120%, SO THERE'S NO WAY IT WOULDN'T BE AN AWESOME MANGA.
IT'S REALLY GOOD, DANGIT!
GWOOOO
I'M JEALOUS, SO I'M GONNA SHOE-HORN IN BABY BEEL HERE!
SMIRK
ARGH!!
Even a baby has more magic than me!!
WOW... WHAT INCREDIBLE MAGIC!
HE'S LIKE THE WIZARD KING!

The End

↑ All 28 volumes of *Beelzebub* (featuring Baby Beel) are on sale in Japan!! Check 'em out!!

AFTERWORD

✳

Thank you for reading *Black Clover*, volume 2!

This is Tabata, who hasn't put any of his regrets regarding volume 1 to good use and is in even worse shape than he was for volume 1!

This time around, I was lucky enough to have Tamura Sensei~who was already working under my mentor when I joined up~create a manga for me!

After we met, as illustrated by the manga on the right, I was such a newbie that I couldn't even use a pen right, and Tamura taught me everything, starting with how to draw tapering lines with a dip pen. But upon hearing this, Tamura says, "I did?!"

After that, he showed me a success story with *Beelzebub*.

So thanks, Tamuraaa!!
Who you callin' a newbie?!

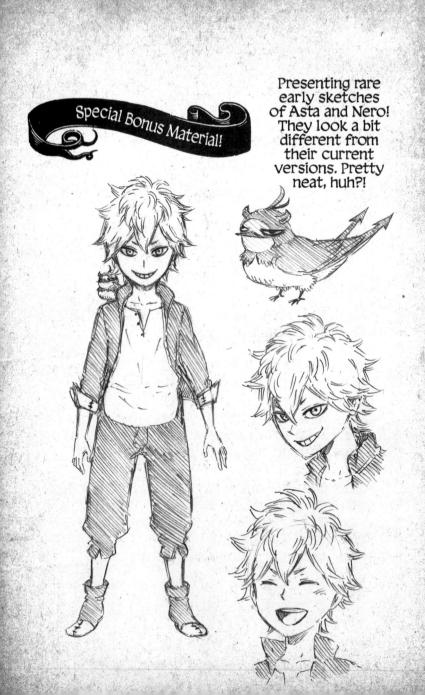

Special Bonus Material!

Presenting rare early sketches of Asta and Nero! They look a bit different from their current versions. Pretty neat, huh?!

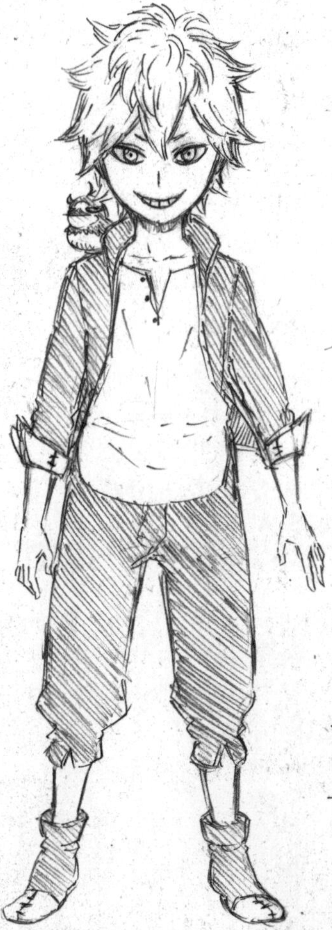

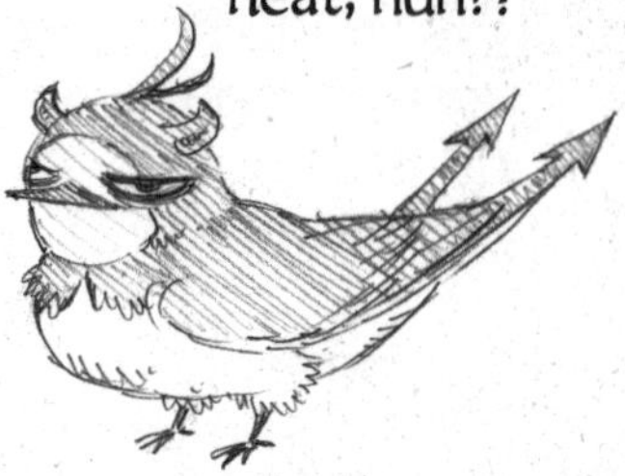

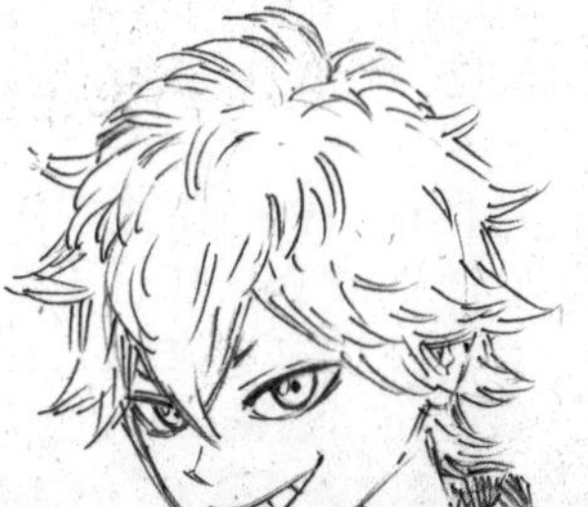

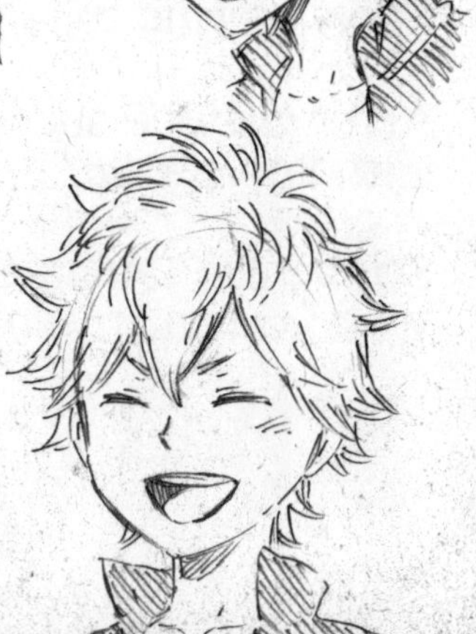

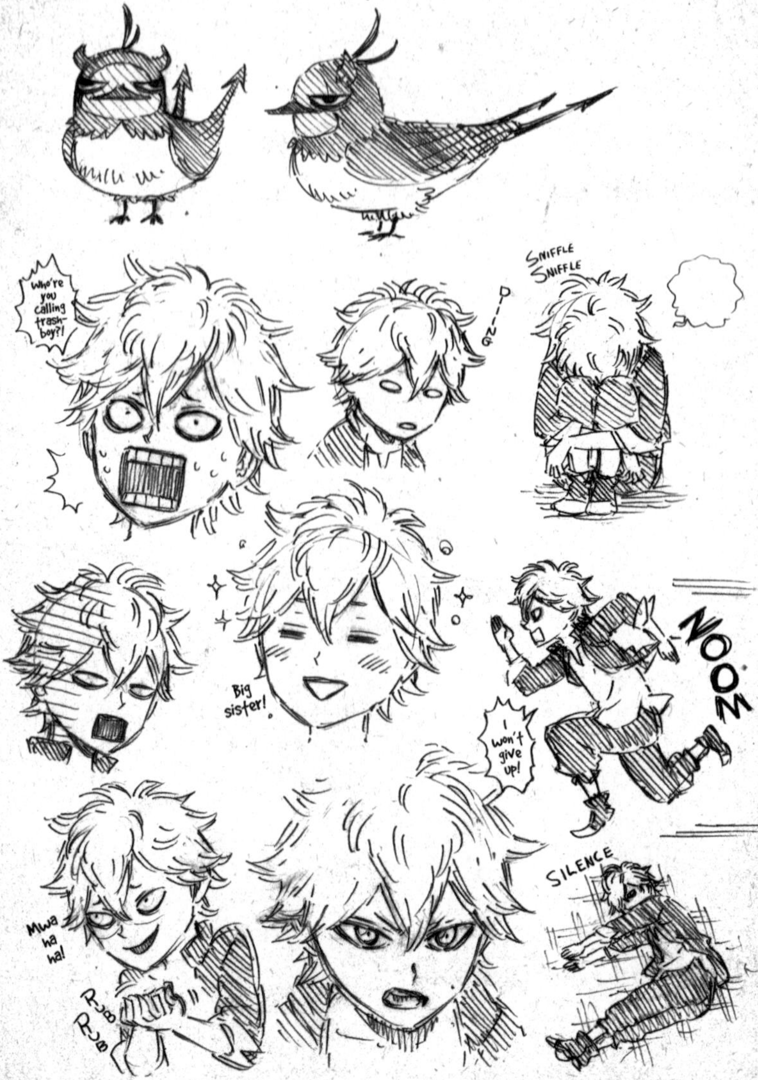

SNIFFLE SNIFFLE
D-I-N-G
Who're you calling trash-boy?!
ZOOM
I won't give up!
Big sister!
SILENCE
Mwa ha ha!
RUB RUB

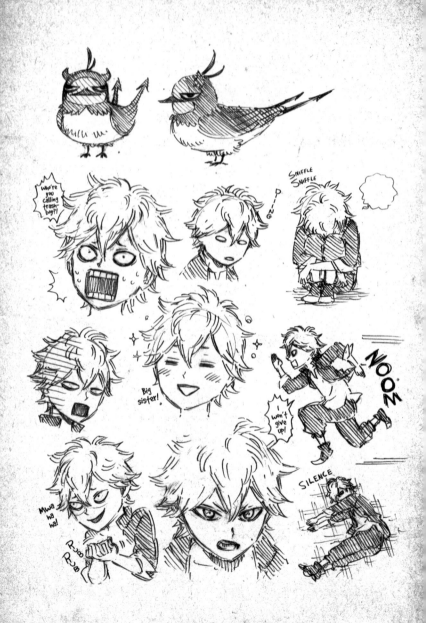

A KILLER COMEDY FROM *WEEKLY SHONEN JUMP*

A S S A S S I N A T I O N
CLASSROOM

STORY AND ART BY
YUSEI MATSUI

Ever caught yourself screaming, "I could just kill that teacher"?
What would it take to justify such antisocial behavior
and weeks of detention? Especially if he's the best
teacher you've ever had? Giving you an "F" on a quiz?
Mispronouncing your name during roll call...*again*? How about
blowing up the moon and threatening to do the same to
Mother Earth—unless you take him out first?! Plus a reward
of a cool 100 million from the Ministry of Defense!

Okay, now that you're committed... How are you going to
pull this off? What does your pathetic class of misfits have
in their arsenal to combat Teach's alien technology, bizarre
powers and...*tentacles*?!

ASSASSINATION
CLASSROOM

STORY AND ART BY
YUSEI MATSUI

1

SHONEN JUMP ADVANCED

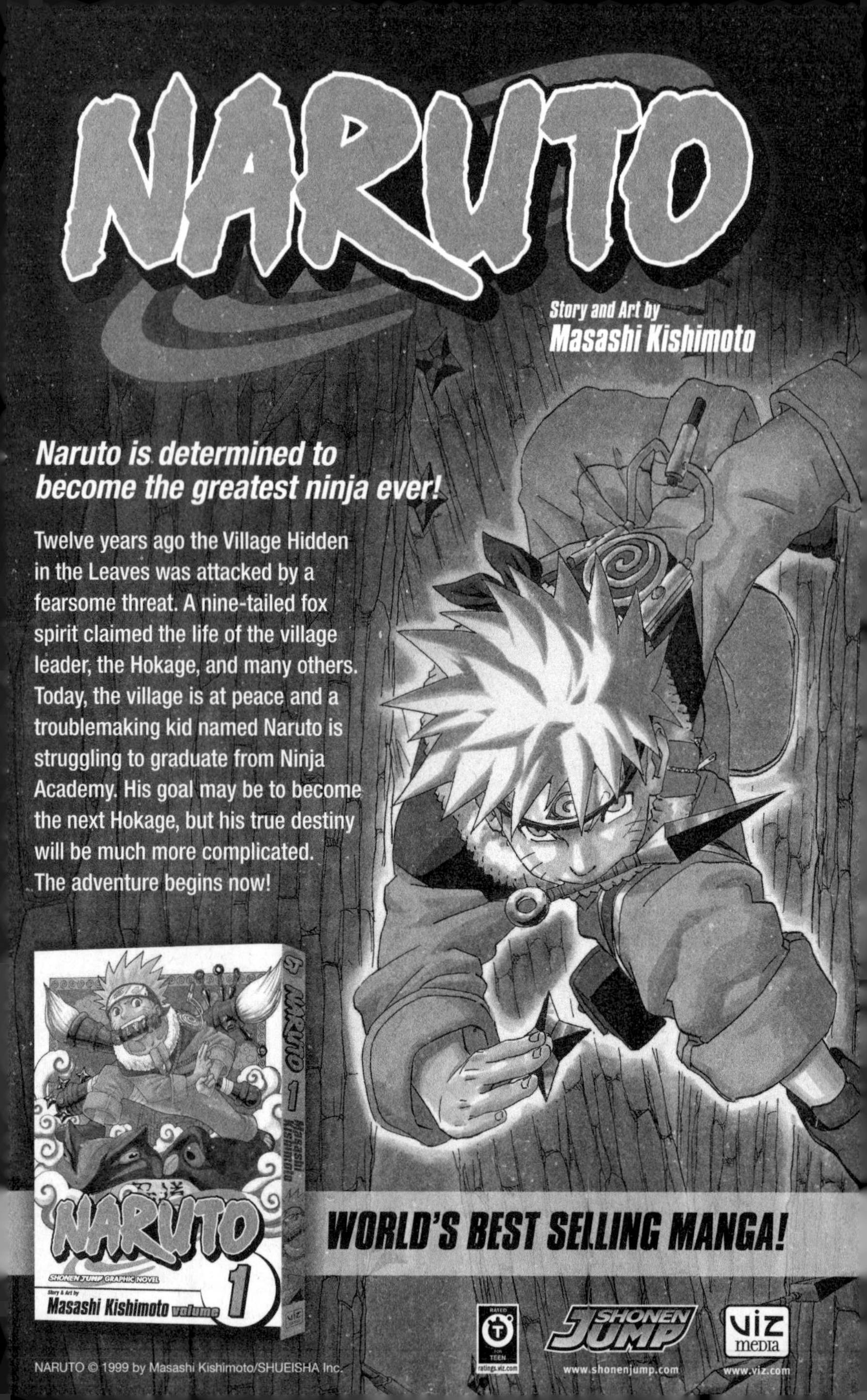
NARUTO
Story and Art by
Masashi Kishimoto
Naruto is determined to become the greatest ninja ever!
Twelve years ago the Village Hidden in the Leaves was attacked by a fearsome threat. A nine-tailed fox spirit claimed the life of the village leader, the Hokage, and many others. Today, the village is at peace and a troublemaking kid named Naruto is struggling to graduate from Ninja Academy. His goal may be to become the next Hokage, but his true destiny will be much more complicated. The adventure begins now!
NARUTO
SHONEN JUMP GRAPHIC NOVEL
Story & Art by
Masashi Kishimoto volume 1
WORLD'S BEST SELLING MANGA!
RATED T FOR TEEN
ratings.viz.com
SHONEN JUMP
www.shonenjump.com
VIZ MEDIA
www.viz.com
NARUTO © 1999 by Masashi Kishimoto/SHUEISHA Inc.

Stop

YOU'RE READING
THE WRONG WAY!

BLACK CLOVER

reads from right to left, starting
in the upper-right corner. Japanese
is read from right to left, meaning
that action, sound effects, and
word-balloon order are completely
reversed from English order.